DATE DUE

FRENCH FEMINIST CRITICISM

GARLAND BIBLIOGRAPHIES OF
MODERN CRITICS AND CRITICAL SCHOOLS
(General Editor: William E. Cain)
Vol. 9

GARLAND REFERENCE LIBRARY
OF THE HUMANITIES
Vol. 351

Garland Bibliographies of Modern Critics and Critical Schools

GENERAL EDITOR:
William E. Cain (Wellesley College)

FRENCH FEMINIST CRITICISM: WOMEN, LANGUAGE, AND LITERATURE
An Annotated Bibliography

Elissa D. Gelfand
Virginia Thorndike Hules

GARLAND PUBLISHING INC. • NEW YORK & LONDON
1985

Library of Congress Cataloging in Publication Data

Gelfand, Elissa D., 1949–
  French feminist criticism.

  (Garland bibliographies of modern critics and critical
schools ; vol. 9) (Garland reference library of the
humanities ; vol. 351)
  Includes indexes.
  1. Feminism and literature—France—History and
criticism. 2. Feminism—France—Abstracts. 3. Feminism
and literature—France—Indexes. 4. Feminism—France—
Abstracts. 5. Feminism—Belgium—Abstracts.
6. Feminism—Québec (Province)—Abstracts. I. Hules,
Virginia T. II. Title. III. Series: Garland
bibliographies of modern critics and critical schools ;
v. 9. IV. Series: Garland reference library of the
humanities ; v. 351.
HQ1386.G44 1985   305.4′2′0944   82-48275
ISBN 0-8240-9252-X (alk. paper)

Cover design by Mary Ann Smith

Printed on acid-free, 250-year-life paper
Manufactured in the United States of America

GENERAL EDITOR'S INTRODUCTION

The Garland Bibliographies of Modern Critics and Critical Schools series is intended to provide bibliographic treatment of major critics and critical schools of the twentieth century. Each volume includes an introduction that surveys the critic's life, career, influence, and achievement, or, in the case of the volumes devoted to a critical school, presents an account of its central figures, origins, relation to other critical movements and trends, and the like.

Each volume is fully annotated and contains listings for both primary and secondary materials. The annotations are meant to be ample and detailed, in order to explain clearly, especially for a reader coming to a critic or critical school for the first time, the point and purpose of a book or essay. In this sense, the bibliographies are also designed to be critical guides. We hope that the volumes will inform and stimulate the reader even as they give basic information about what material exists and where it may be located.

We have tried to include as many of the most important critics and critical schools in this series as possible, but some have been omitted. Some critics and critical schools have already received (or are in the process of receiving) adequate treatment, and we see no need to duplicate the efforts of others.

WILLIAM E. CAIN
Wellesley College

CONTENTS

PREFACE

PURPOSE, AUDIENCE, AND SCOPE

The subject of this bibliography is women, language, writing, and their interrelationship, as they have been conceived and articulated by French feminist thinkers. This volume also includes works of Quebecois and Belgian feminists, who substantially share their French counterparts' preoccupations and approaches. Our purpose has been to make this area of French feminist theory more accessible to a broad American and American-based audience: students and scholars, specialists of French feminism and French literary theory, American critics seeking to understand French feminist perspectives, and instructors in international women's studies. The bibliography lists not only the work of the most well-known and prolific theorists (Hélène Cixous, Catherine Clément, Luce Irigaray, Sarah Kofman, Julia Kristeva) but all books, essays, and articles from the period 1970-1982 that concentrate on women and language, including work by feminist scholars in the United States who are participating in the elucidation of French feminist theory. It does not include brief reviews or dissertations. We have not knowingly omitted materials that conform to the criteria outlined in this preface, with the exception of a small number of texts that were unavailable for consultation.

"Feminist Criticism": Further Clarifications of Our Definitions.

The focus of this bibliography is the textuality/sexuality of women, as formulated by women theorists giving voice to their understanding of female experience. Texts were considered "feminist" and were included if they give evidence of a re-evaluation or critique of traditional paradigms about women, language, writing, and their interrelationships, or document such efforts by others. Also included were texts that provide new analytic frameworks for further exploration of women and language. Among the areas of inquiry that offer the freshest analyses and have the most potentially radical implications are: the relation of language to the feminine unconscious, the inscription of the feminine in texts, cultural influences on women's language, and the existence and nature of a specifically feminine language and writing ("l'écriture féminine"). Many of the women engaged in this rethinking of

gender and language would refuse the label "feminist." Our
own approach has been an inclusive, non-partisan one. Our
goal is to bring the full spectrum of perspectives to the
users of this bibliography, who, ultimately, will categorize
them according to their own criteria.

The term "criticism" is used in the sense of "critique,"
not textual exegesis. The only instances of applied
literary criticism in this volume are those that devote
substantial space to the establishment of a theoretical
apparatus.

The decision to focus on theory has led us to exclude
texts that we deemed to be primarily fiction. We are well
aware that maintaining the customary distinction between
theory and fiction when treating French feminist writing can
be seen as paradoxical. Many women writers resist, indeed
seek to destroy, the boundaries between "theory" and
fiction." Our decision has a practical rationale--to keep
the project to a manageable size--and does not reflect an
intellectual hierarchy. In the case of "textes-limites,"
where the delineation between fiction and theory is
especially problematic, we have opted for those works that
do formulate some ideas about sexuality and language.

The Time Frame 1970-1982.

These were the first twelve years of the "new wave" of
French feminist theory that emerged in the wake of the
"events of May ´68." It was also a period of cultural
renaissance in Quebec, spearheaded in large part by women
writers. The only exceptions to this chronological scope
are Simone de Beauvoir´s Le deuxième sexe, to which we pay
tribute as the forerunner of contemporary French feminism,
and a handful of earlier texts reprinted during the period
1970-82. Of course, important feminist texts have been
published since 1983. Therefore, it is essential that
others continue to document this work.

Major Feminist Theorists in Context.

This bibliography does include texts by and about important
thinkers in which women and the feminine are not central,
for example Irigaray´s Le langage des déments, or Philip
Lewis´s review essay of Kristeva´s La révolution du langage
poétique. Our purpose in this is to illuminate the
evolution of their inquiry and to situate their feminist
writings in relation to the full scope of their production.
This contextualization also provides valuable information
about the Western intellectual tradition and current trends

that have shaped much of French feminist theory:
existential philosophy, structuralist linguistics and
anthropology, Freudian and Lacanian psychoanalysis, the
modernism of Derrida. However, we do not provide
comprehensive bibliographies of these women.

GENERAL ORGANIZATION

    This bibliography contains the following general
divisions and sub-headings:

I. A Topography of Difference. This introductory essay
provides the coordinates necessary to orient the
non-specialist: the roots of French feminist theory, the
contributions of its major figures, the similarities and
differences among their models and methods, and comparison
with American approaches and preoccupations.

II. The General Problematics of a Feminist Criticism.
Essential framing texts are grouped at the beginning of the
volume to highlight them for its users. These pieces,
chosen for their breadth of perspective, serve one or both
of the following functions: (1) they describe the
approaches French feminist theorists have employed to define
and explore the relationship between sexuality and
textuality (2) they review and interrogate the nature,
purposes, and methodologies of feminist criticism. Entries
are listed alphabetically by author.

III. French and Francophone Voices. The main body of the
bibliography is organized alphabetically by author and
contains the following sub-headings. (A) Books and
Collections of Essays. The tables of contents for all
books are given. In cases where book chapters can stand as
separate essays, they are listed separately under "Essays
and Articles" and their item number follows their listing in
the book's table of contents. When book chapters cannot
stand alone, they are annotated within the general book
entry and do not receive a separate item number. (B) Books
Edited. The tables of contents are provided. Annotated
essays from these books are found under "Essays and
Articles." Their item numbers follow their titles in the
tables of contents. (C) Essays and Articles.
(D) Interviews With. This heading includes interviews,
conversations, discussions, and debates, listed
alphabetically by interviewer. Listings are not meant to be
comprehensive but rather representative of major authors'
ideas about writing and gender. (E) Books About and

(F) **Essays and Articles About.** These are secondary
sources listed alphabetically by author.

   IV. <u>Special Issues Appendix</u>. A listing of the tables
of contents of entire issues or special dossiers (in which
case the dossier title appears on the line below the journal
name and date) of journals and literary magazines devoted to
women. Most, but not all, entries focus on language and
writing. Those articles annotated in the bibliography are
followed by their item number.

   V. <u>Indexes</u>. These include an alphabetical listing by
title and a subject index.

FORMAT DETAILS

   <u>Entry Order</u>. All texts by the same author are listed
alphabetically by title within the appropriate sub-heading.
When the number of entries for a single author is five or
more, the sub-headings indicated above appear in bold-face.
When there are fewer than five, these sub-headings do not
appear in print but are implicit in the order of the
entries. When no author is given, a text is alphabetized by
title. The title appears first in the entry; no space is
left blank.

   <u>Cross-Referencing</u>. Jointly authored texts appear as a
main entry (including the annotation) under the name of the
first person listed on the source and as asterisked
abbreviated entries (including only the bibliographic
citation) under the name(s) of the other author(s).
Within the annotations themselves, the indication (See XXX)
refers the user to other annotated texts that deal centrally
with the one in question. At the end of the annotations,
the indication "See XXX" refers the reader to other
annotated texts that address the same issue.

   <u>Translation and Reprinting</u>. These references are
provided at the end of the annotation.

   <u>Bibliographic Citation</u>. Whenever possible, the
information cited refers to the first publication of the
essay, article, or interview. On the rare occasions when
this information was incomplete, we cite the complete
reprint information. Although we have worked diligently to
avoid incomplete citations, there are instances where the
pages are missing because the original source was
unavailable.

Annotations. It has been our purpose to be informative,
clear, and honest. Therefore, annotations frequently end
with an editorial opinion about the usefulness or
accessibility of the work. However, we did not attempt to
express our purpose through a particularly standardized
format or style. There is, then, personal variation. For
example, differences in the length of annotations should not
necessarily be taken as an editorial judgment on the
importance of the text.

SOURCES

Sources consulted were the Klapp, PMLA, and French 20
bibliographies and the Catalogue des livres disponibles from
1970 to 1982; all issues and indexes of the Bulletin de
recherches et d´études féministes francophones (BREFF); all
issues of Sorcières and Les Cahiers du GRIF; specialized
bibliographies such as Current Sources on Women and
Literature (compiled by Whitney Walton, Cathy Loeb, and
Esther Stineman, Women´s Studies, University of Wisconsin,
1977) and "Sélection bibliographique" (compiled by Françoise
van Rossum-Guyon in La Revue des sciences humaines, 168,
October-December, 1977, 625-632); overview books and
articles that provided extensive bibliographic information
such as New French Feminisms (edited by Elaine Marks and
Isabelle de Courtivron, University of Massachusetts Press,
1980); special issues of such journals as Yale French
Studies, Signs, and Feminist Studies; and colleagues
specialized in various aspects of the field. Much of our
work required the careful examination of texts-in-hand for
further references. We also combed the card catalogs of the
Bibliothèque Nationale and the Bibliothèque Féministe
Marguerite Durand as well as the shelves of feminist
bookstores in Paris.

ACKNOWLEDGMENTS

The research required for this bibliography would have
been impossible without the generous financial support of
our home institutions, Wellesley College and Mount Holyoke
College. The Mount Holyoke Project on Gender in Context,
the recipient of a grant from the William H. Donner
Foundation, also provided invaluable financial assistance
and moral sustenance. In addition we are indebted to the
Interlibrary Loan Office of the Wellesley College library

for processing innumerable requests. We thank Wendy Bowis,
Tamah Terry, and Wendy Lieber, who shared some of the burden
of locating sources; Michel Grimaud, for his thoughtful
feedback; Alice Jardine and Hélène Wenzel for sharing
bibliographic information; and Robert Thorndike for helping
proofread the manuscript. We are grateful for the continued
patience of our editor at Garland, Julia Johnson, and
we thank Bill Cain of Wellesley College for his guidance
from the outset. Finally, we dedicate this book to Jim
Glickman and Ken Hules, in appreciation for their loving
support.

INTRODUCTION

A TOPOGRAPHY OF DIFFERENCE

Virginia Thorndike Hules

> There must be another place I told myself. And
> everyone knows that to go to other realms there
> are passages, signposts, "maps"--for an explor-
> ation, a voyage. These are books. Everyone
> knows that there is a place that is economically
> and politically free from all baseness and
> compromise. That is not forced to reproduce the
> system. And it is writing. If there exists
> another realm that can escape infernal
> repetition, it is over there where id writes,
> where id dreams, where id invents new worlds.
> (Hélène Cixous) (1)

In France during the 1970´s a significant number of
intellectuals in the social sciences and humanities became
engaged in a twofold re-evaluation: of women´s historical
and material reality and of the "feminine" as a metaphor for
the otherness that fascinates and perplexes the modern
imagination. Broadly speaking, this ongoing inquiry has
centered around the notion of sexual difference or
specificity: Does it exist? If so, what are its sources
and distinctive features? How does it function? What are
its philosophical, psychological, and political
implications? Much of this work has focused on the
inscription of difference in language and texts. Theorists
have been exploring the relation of sexual difference and
writing and debating the existence and characteristics of an
"écriture féminine."

This investigation, carried out to a great extent but
not exclusively by women (academics, creative writers,
psychoanalysts), has been shaped by trends in contemporary
French thought, particularly by structuralism,
psychoanalysis, and dialectical materialism.

The first section of this essay ("The ´Fatherland´ of
French Feminist Theory") will discuss the contributions of
the modern "maîtres à penser" who have had the greatest impact

upon this feminist re-evaluation: the linguist Ferdinand de
Saussure, the philosopher Jacques Derrida, and the
psychoanalyst Jacques Lacan. This section will compare the
ways in which these three theorists defined and used the
concept of difference. It will emphasize Derrida´s readings
of Saussure and Lacan, for in these critiques of
logocentrism and phallogocentrism, Derrida forged the
conceptual tools of a new generation of French feminist
theorists.

The purpose of the second section of this topography
("Feminist Theory and Difference") is to survey French (2)
feminist theory, elucidating the reference points necessary
for an understanding of the important trends and problematic
issues in the field. These reference points will illuminate
the connections and disconnections between feminists and
their intellectual fathers and will map significant areas of
conflict and commonality within feminist inquiry itself.

These reference points have been organized into four
sets of oppositions:

1. the affirmation of sexual specificity and the
exploration and rehabilitation of female attributes versus a
focus on bisexuality that places difference within each
individual.

2. the use of oppositional models that maintain man and
woman, masculine and feminine as binary categories and first
principles (although reversing them) as opposed to a
Derridean double model that employs both difference between
(through the reversal of the opposition masculine/feminine)
and difference within (through the deconstruction of this
same opposition).

3. a Marxist perspective that attributes primacy to
cultural factors in the constitution of sexual difference
versus a psychoanalytic perspective in which biological
factors predominate.

4. the use of a literal frame of reference in which
sexual markers ("feminine," "masculine," "Woman") refer to
men and women in their biological and/or socio-political
difference versus a figurative frame of reference in which
these same markers function metaphorically.

To begin establishing and illustrating these reference
points, I examine three of the first texts that brought the
new-fledged feminist theories to the attention of the French
public. (3) To extend and enrich the survey, I then analyze
the work of Luce Irigaray and Hélène Cixous, the two
theorists most associated with feminine specificity, and
representative materialist and lesbian materialist
feminists.

The third and last section of this essay ("Sexual

Difference: A Franco-American Comparison") shifts to a
cross-cultural perspective, stressing those aspects of
French inquiry most unfamiliar to Americans and examining
contributions American-based interpreters of French feminist
theory have made to transatlantic dialogue.

The "Fatherland" of French Feminist Theory

Ferdinand de Saussure, Jacques Lacan, and Jacques
Derrida are the founding fathers of much of contemporary
French thought. Specifically, feminist theorizing found its
major points of departure in Saussure's linguistic
principles, in Lacan's reformulations of Freud, and in
Derrida's critique of the basic presuppositions of
linguistic and psychoanalytic research.

Saussure, Structuralism, and Post-Structuralism.

The concept of difference played a fundamental role in
French structuralism's construction of reality. To sketch
this role, it is necessary to touch upon the work of
linguist Ferdinand de Saussure, whose Cours de linguistique
générale, published posthumously by his students in 1916,
established structuralism's conceptual framework. Saussure
postulated that meaning resides not in discrete entities, as
was traditionally thought, but in a combinatory system of
differential oppositions. That is, meaning is generated by
the relations among linguistic units (phonemes, morphemes,
words), by their differences from one another. Language
became a dynamic system of differences (minimal pairs,
semantic fields), the fundamental laws of which were not
readily apparent.
    Other social scientists, notably anthropologist Claude
Lévi-Strauss, (4) adapted the relational and differential
linguistic model to the description of other signifying
systems: kinship structures and myths.
    The structuralist paradigm, in which elements do not
signify in isolation, implied an ontology of absence. It
contrasted with the phenomenological perspective,
particularly powerful in France from the 1930's to the
1960's, with its emphasis on presence, that is, its
grounding in representationality, the existence of the
Absolute, the primacy and unity of the subject.
Structuralist thinkers, on the contrary, construed the self
as a centre de fonctionnement, a complex set of
relationships whose being and intelligibility are determined
by the interacting systems that constitute it. More than

one French intellectual denounced this dehumanization and
worried that after the death of God, the death of Man was
imminent.

Although for the most part structuralists retained the
belief that the world is coherent and intelligible, their
work also encompassed an epistemological re-evaluation.
Structuralism held that the laws organizing phenomena are
hidden from surface observation. They can be abstracted
from reality but are not in a one-to-one correspondence with
it. In addition, structuralism's shift in focus to the
relational nature of meaning fostered an increasing
attention to the conditionality of all knowledge. Observer
objectivity and autonomy were considered to be a fallacy.
The realization that the researcher is affected by the
parameters of his or her own subjectivity and method, that
language itself is not neutral, eventually led to a split
among structuralists. Those thinkers, such as Derrida,
Deleuze, Foucault, and Lyotard, (5) whose work centered on
the interrogation of epistemology came to be labelled
"post-structuralist." (6) During the late 1960's and 1970's
they elaborated a critique of the structuralist project that
revolved around the concept of difference.

Post-structuralism has been, in its widest sense, a
meditation on and a critique of traditional Western
philosophy. Following in the footsteps of Nietzsche, it has
rejected the notions of a "true science" and a "true
morality." In this light, Western metaphysics appears
conservative and reductionist for it has always proposed a
dialectical model in which difference functions only in
hierarchical relationship to a privileged a priori
principle. Difference in this classical model is false, for
it exists exclusively in the service of identity, to confirm
some Absolute. For post-structuralists this totalizing,
univocal paradigm has informed every aspect of our
experience. It is not surprising, then, that they see in
structuralism's (7) formal, rule-governed reality--one in
which difference is that which creates comparisons and
combinations and in which binary oppositions are the
components of intelligible systems--the latest manifestation
of a traditional humanism. Structuralism shares with
phenomenology the belief in an a priori principle: not
experience, but fundamental signifying structures.
Post-structuralists conceptualize difference
differently--less as a source of structures than that which
exceeds systematization.

For this reason post-structuralists have concentrated
their attention on the elaboration of a problematics of
alterity, exploring the difficult question of how one

theorizes and demonstrates non-contradictory, non-dialec-
tical difference, and how one speaks and writes about
Otherness. They have moved beyond considerations of
difference between apparently separate terms--the
dialectical model of Self/Other, Culture/Nature, Presence/
Absence, and so on--toward a focus on the difference within
entities previously conceived of as unitary--the divided
self, the double text, schizo-analysis. In this recon-
figuration they have interwoven structuralist, philosophical, and psychoanalytical discourses.

Derrida´s Differantial Model.

In terms of feminist theory, the most influential
post-structuralist philosopher of difference has been
Jacques Derrida, who early turned his attention to the
theory of language and the critique of philosophical
discourse. (8) Derrida coined the term logocentrism to
characterize Western philosophy´s preoccupation with first
principles and he devised strategies to show that its
cornerstones are not as they seem, unitary and unambiguous,
but rather heterogeneous. For example, Derrida contended
that a phenomenology of history is impossible. He argued
that Husserl´s paradigmatic "principle of principles," which
posits the coincidence of self and meaning (the ability of
any individual to intuit the truth about historical events
and artifacts), is a fallacy. This coincidence is assured
by postulating that the present contains an immutable
essence. But Derrida countered that the present is not a
static, unified principle. Its unity is dynamic, always
under construction. The present exists only by virtue of
its relationship to the past and the future. Thus, the
present is an impossible composite--no temporal
superposition uniting the three can ever occur. The
relation of present self to past meaning, as that of the
present to itself, is one of irremediable "differance," a
term by which Derrida designates not only the notion of the
inherent multiplicity underlying all "unity," but also
temporal displacement, a continual deferring of unity
implying that absence is an intrinsic property of
presence. (9) As Gayatri Spivak succinctly puts it: "The
law of differance is that any law is constituted by
postponement and self-difference."(10)
       Derrida´s extensive reflections on language and
writing (11) further illustrate his logic of differance. In
Of Grammatology, for instance, he argued that Saussure´s
theory of meaning both subverts and maintains logocentrism.

By defining the sign as differential opposition and meaning
as a product of differences, Saussure countered the
traditional essentialism that perceived words as positive
entities. By privileging speech over writing as the only
object of linguistic analysis, however, he retained a
long-standing hierarchy analogous to the centrality
attributed to the present in philosophical models. Derrida
pointed out that Saussure himself deconstructed his own
argument, both by stressing the dangers of attending to
writing (thus presenting as problematic an element of
supposedly secondary importance) and by using letters to
illustrate the concept of differential units that is the
core of his linguistic theory (thus reintroducing the very
objectionable element he postulates as inessential).
Saussure's text, like all texts, is a double text, divided
within itself.

Derrida examined other philosophical texts to show that
writing, which he defined here not only as literally
tangible meaning but also as all reproducible and
transferrable meaning, typifies all signs, including
speech. But by operating a reversal that subordinates
speech to writing Derrida sought not to proclaim a new
hierarchy but to dislodge the old one. His goal was to
prove that seemingly fixed oppositions exist in a state of
reversibility; they are always displaceable. Differançe is
the principle of non-principles.

In his various investigations Derrida does not deny or
categorically oppose the concepts he undermines. Truth,
Presence, Phenomenology, Metaphysics, the Dialectic exist,
although they are infinitely postponed, and they must be
taken into account. Through Derrida's deconstructionist
grid of differance, reality includes the set of all
possibilities. Elements of any opposition are like the
"inside" and "outside" of the apparently paradoxical Möbius
strip: they are at once different and indistinguishable,
separate and inseparable, the same and other.

Derrida's work on alterity encompasses the issue of
sexual difference and includes an influential critique of
the Freudian model that has guided much twentieth-century
thinking about masculinity and femininity.(12)

In rereading Freud, Derrida recognized, as he had with
Saussure, the originality of his pioneering formulations.
In many areas Freud reversed fundamental hierarchical
oppositions, positing, for example, that the unconscious is
the field in which the conscious is elaborated, the
pathological the key to understanding the normal, and the
death instinct the backdrop of life's dramas. The
philosopher also found in the complex relationships between

opposites and the irreducible otherness of the psyche a
decided affinity with his logic of differance.

Derrida noted, however, that Freud's treatment of sexual
difference appeared essentialist, reproducing the age-old
hierarchy: male-originary-superior/female-tributary-in-
ferior. With penis envy defining normal female
psycho-sexual development, man is constituted as central,
woman as supplementary.

To characterize the double philosophical and Freudian
paradigm that posits the male and his sexuality as the norm
and the female and her sexuality as a variation, Derrida
coined the popular neologism of the 1970's,
phallogocentrism.

Lacan's Pychoanalytic Model.

Derrida's critique of Freud brings us to a crucial feature
of the analysis of difference carried out in the 1960's and
1970's: the primacy of the psychoanalytic framework. The
unconscious evoked so powerfully the alien within the
familiar that otherness could not be thought of without
reference to the psychoanalytic model nor could language,
meaning, or writing. The focus of the intellectual arena
became highly sexualized: one could not inquire into the
ontology of difference without asking whether sexual
difference was the paradigm for all conceptualizations of
difference. One could not explore the nature of writing
without reference to sexuality: how the body is inscribed
in texts and whether sexual difference generates writing or
whether language structures sexual difference. The work of
Jacques Lacan, the disciple-turned-master, played a key role
in these developments.(13)

Excluded from the psychoanalytic establishment in the
1950's, Lacan continued to confound and delight the Parisian
intelligentsia in the 60's and 70's with his unfathomable
and controversial weekly seminars. Lacan's originality was
to develop the structuralist insights of Freud's theories
using the model provided by Saussurean linguistics. Lacan
postulated that the symbolic material in the unconscious
functions according to the rules that govern language. For
example, two of the most important psychic processes--
repression and displacement--correspond to the rhetorical
tropes of metaphor and metonymy.

In Lacan's theory, difference is foundational. Not only
does the unconscious, like language, signify by means of
binary oppositions, but difference in the guise of the Other
orchestrates the dynamics of the mind. The Other is the

object of desire and that which relates the subject to the
unconscious. Lacan´s Other is a composite, including
philosophical as well as psychoanalytic referents. Lacan
was influenced by Hegel´s Master-Slave dialectic,(14) which
posited self-awareness to be a function of the desire and
acknowledgement of the Other. But most importantly, the
Other and desire are sexualized.

For Lacan desire operates in relation to lack, to
absence. It is constituted during the Oedipal stage through
the agency of the castration complex for boys and penis envy
for girls. The subject becomes subject by incorporating the
Law-of-the-Father (le Nom-[non] du-père), which forbids
union with the pre-Oedipal, phallic mother. The Phallus,
not to be confused with the real penis or clitoris, is the
primary signifier of desire. It symbolizes the separation
from the complete, powerful mother and the absence through
which the subject is constituted.

Uniting linguistic and psychoanalytic theories, Lacan
posited that the internalization of the Law-of-the-Father is
the source of meaning. Creating the Other, it permits the
subject´s entry into the realm of the symbolic and into
language. In girls the acceptance of castration establishes
the relation of the subject to the signifier and thus to
desire. Lacan, then, sexualized two basic linguistic
axioms: that word and referent are not fused and that
language is not a system of presences but a play of
absences.

Like Freud´s, Lacan´s reflections on female specificity
are not extensive, (15) but they have elicited much
commentary. Lacan distinguished between desire, which is
masculine, and jouissance, which is feminine. Desire, born
of separation, is satisfaction ever deferred. It is also
integration into linguistic structuration, the laws of
grammar and syntax. Jouissance is a primal, contiguous
sexuality that seeks "to realize itself in rivalry with the
desire that castration liberates in the male." (16) It
exists outside of linguistic norms in the realm of the
poetic. In the linguistic register Lacan seems to posit a
kind of bisexuality, as he indicates that both sexes have
access to normative and poetic discourse. However, in the
metaphysical register, specificity is retained; woman and
the feminine operate as metaphors for alterity. They are
that which exceeds and defines the (masculine) Self: the
unnameable, the unrepresentable, the unconscious, the
divine.

Derrida's Critique of Lacan.

According to Derrida, Lacan has maintained the Freudian
opposition that effectively negates difference by subsuming
the female to the male. The transcendental phallus is the
principle of principles, the essentializing fetish. Both
the male and the female subject's relation to language is
structured by the Oedipal drama. By sexualizing differance,
Derrida proposes an alternative to this phallocentric model
for the creation of meaning. He chooses the terms
"dissemination" and the "hymen" to convey this decentered,
paradoxical vision.(17)
    Dissemination, in contrast to insemination, implies that
the male power to generate is short-circuited, for
penetration does not occur. Without penetration there is no
mastery of the feminine and no imprisoning of masculinity
within familiar (phallic) boundaries. At the same time,
generation through scattering plurality, non-phallic
multiplicity, is confirmed. The hymen, too, symbolizes
irreducibility for it connotes both sexual intercourse
(marriage) and the obstacle to penetration. In Derrida's
work, the terms "dissemination" and "the hymen" play a
double role: they mark the sexual categories of masculine
and feminine, thus evoking oppositional difference; but they
also function as synonyms of differance and of each other.
    By dislodging phallic privilege, Derrida reintroduces
sexual difference, thus reversing the neutralizing effects
of phallocentric logic. Concurrently he attempts to blur
and defer the distinctions between these revivified
differences. In a recent interview (18) Derrida reasserted
that words such as hymen and invagination do not serve only
to inject femininity or the female body into his texts.
Appearing as they do in contexts that carefully undermine
traditional reference points of sexual opposition, they
exceed these categories. Within the paradoxical space of
differance they convey both the familiar and the unknown,
sameness and otherness. And ultimately the hypothesis he
entertains, the dread he dreams is that we can approach

> the area of a relationship to the other where the
> code of sexual marks would no longer be discrimi-
> nating. The relationship would not be asexual, far
> from it, but would be sexual otherwise: beyond the
> binary difference that governs the decorum of all
> codes, beyond the opposition feminine/masculine,
> beyond bisexuality as well, beyond homosexuality and
> heterosexuality which come to the same thing.(19)

Feminist Theory and Difference

In the preceding section I sketched the important features of the French structuralist and post-structuralist investigation of difference. In this section, I will explore how French feminists have adapted these intellectual frameworks to their analyses of the oppression of women and the repression of the feminine.

The example of American feminists, coupled with the May 1968 insurgence against Gaullism and tradition, provided catalysts for a renewal of French feminism in the 1970´s. It gradually became apparent that this "new French feminism" indeed encompassed a departure from the past. In addition to the resurgence of a Beauvoirian perspective that conceptualized sexual difference as an exclusively cultural construct, one that could and should be eliminated, there emerged a new affirmation of feminine specificity, not only in France, but also in Belgium and in Quebec, where the affirmation of Quebecois identity went hand in hand with a feminist awakening.

1974: First Flowerings.

I will begin with an examination of three of the earliest texts to reach the general public: Annie Leclerc´s Parole de femme, the Quinzaine Littéraire´s "L´Ecriture a-t-elle un sexe?" and Tel Quel´s "Lutte de femmes," all published in 1974.

Observers on both sides of the Atlantic cite Parole de femme (20) as the text that inaugurated woman´s claim to and praise of sexual difference. In this widely read book Annie Leclerc exalts feminine values and attacks masculine ones. She declares the source of these values to be the body. The intermittent nature of erection threatens male sexual identity and leads to the creation of a compensatory panoply of virtues that bolster virility: action, appropriation, duty, force, heroism. Women´s sexual identity, on the other hand, is a rhythmic continuum assured by the menstrual cycle. Leclerc equates desire, masculinity, and death, opposing them to sexual fulfillment (jouissance), (21) femininity, and life. In the process she criticizes Georges Bataille´s formulation--desire = life, jouissance = death (22) - as typically masculine.

Leclerc, then, reverses the terms of the traditional dialectic model, thus granting superiority to women. Women,

in harmony with life forces, are the carriers of Truth,
Beauty, and Goodness:

> We have discovered within us a little light that is
> ours alone, and it is this light only
> that we will follow.... We will invent the world
> because we will speak at last of what we, silent
> women, know. And we know, I am sure of it, what is
> beautiful and good. (23)

Difference in Parole de femme is difference between the
sexes. Sexual categories are maintained, albeit reversed;
they do not appear to be blurred or undermined as in the
Derridean double movement. As a result, alterity is not
equivocal and problematic. In addition, the terms
"masculine" and "feminine" refer literally to men and women,
not to attributes of a bisexual mind.

Opponents of "écriture féminine," who accuse it of
biologism and fetishism, usually point to Parole de femme as
emblematic of all theories of specificity. As we proceed,
we will see to what extent this is, in fact, the case.

Leclerc affirms the potential for a specifically
feminine speech that flows from the female body--womb,
breasts, vagina--and whose origin ("terre originelle") is
the experience of childbirth. However, she does not
theorize as to the nature of this language nor does she
probe the implications of her assertions. As a consequence
it was not in Parole de femme that readers found the
question of "l'écriture féminine" developed, but in the
leftist intellectual journal Tel Quel and the moderate
literary magazine La Quinzaine Littéraire.(24)

In La Quinzaine Littéraire the question of sexual
specificity and its impact on writing was treated by
eighteen writers responding to a questionnaire that
succinctly evoked the complexities of this important area of
feminist inquiry. (25) These well-known women and men, few
of whom could be considered feminist themselves, were
overwhelmingly skeptical of the idea that the sex of a
writer marks her or his text. Many acknowledged that
biological and sociological factors could affect the
conditions of production of a work and, at most, its
thematics, but they distinguished a "deeper level," the
level of "écriture," where the sex of the author is
indiscernible. Six respondents posited that the writer is
bi- or "inter"-sexual, that creation flows from an
unconscious or a "sensitivity" encompassing both the
masculine and the feminine.

Two respondents contested both the paradigm of

oppositional specificity and the paradigm of bisexuality.
Pascal Lainé contended that, in the final analysis, "there
are as many sexes as there are writers." Viviane Forrester
voiced the avant-garde stance (26) that "écriture" is
precisely that operation which explodes all categories,
including sexual ones; the text is an irreducible play of
ambiguities, non-coincidences, and polysemy.

While the questionnaire results display the tendency to
reject specificity and to propose a bisexual model of
writing, they are punctuated by a tentativeness that attests
to the newness and complexity of the issues under debate.
If in 1974 French intellectuals in general approached the
problematics of sexual difference with some hesitation (as
evidenced by the Quinzaine Littéraire poll), feminist
theorists themselves had already elaborated the essential
lines of their inquiry. (27) These are briefly presented in
Tel Quel's "Lutte de femmes" dossier, an unequivocally
feminist document.

The first section of the dossier affirms that the
socio-economic oppression of women and the repression of a
specifically feminine "jouissance" are inextricably linked.
This "jouissance" constitutes a potentially revolutionary
otherness. By exploring and promoting it the French Women's
Liberation Movement (MLF) is putting into question the
rationalist, capitalist order that has ruled the West for
centuries. (28)

In the first of her two pieces, Xavière Gauthier (29)
evokes Lacan's phallic model to conclude that women are
profoundly alienated from "conventional [linear and
grammatical] language." She speculates that perhaps their
otherness can be inscribed in the white spaces, the holes,
the margins, the silences of discourse.

Marguerite Duras's (30) conversation with Gauthier
corroborates the preceding analyses. Duras associates her
own writing with empty spaces, fear, desire, madness, and
the rejection of syntax. She retains the model of
hierarchical opposition, reversing it to attribute
superiority to the writing of women: "One can say that only
women write fully."

Although, with the exception of Duras, the contributors
to "Lutte de femmes" do not reverse patriarchal hierarchy
with the elan of Leclerc, the dossier resembles Parole de
femme in that it presents sexual difference primarily in
terms of a binary opposition: difference between the
sexes. It is only in the brief interview with Julia
Kristeva (31) that bisexuality features prominently. While
maintaining the Marxist and psychoanalytic frames of the
dossier, Kristeva presents the dissenting view that "all

speaking subjects have within themselves a certain
bisexuality which is precisely the possibility to explore
all the sources of signification, that which posits a
meaning as well as that which multiplies, pulverizes
[destroys] and finally revives it." (32) "Jouissance,"
marginality, and the potential to disturb are not the
exclusive attributes of women or women´s writing.
  For Kristeva the difference between the sexes is
culturally imposed and politically motivated. Therefore,
when she uses the terms "feminine" and "masculine" it is not
to designate two categories of human beings, but as
metaphors for the attributes or attitudes of any subject.
She also uses sexual markers more impersonally, to describe
a dialectical modeling of socio-historical processes. Thus,
it is perfectly possible for her to call "feminine" "the
moment of rupture and negativity which conditions and
underlies the novelty of any praxis." (33)
  Kristeva, then, conceives of sexual difference as
difference within, both on the literal level--the ongoing
dynamics of differentiation within the psyche--and on the
figurative level--the dialectical model in which any status
quo (political, social, intellectual) contains the elements
that will contest and modify it. Her conceptualization of
sexual difference, which posits bisexuality and includes
metaphoricity, adds important aspects of feminist theory to
the Tel Quel dossier.
  An examination of Parole de femme, the Quinzaine
Littéraire´s "L´écriture a-t-elle un sexe?", and Tel Quel´s
"Lutte de femmes" provides an overview of most of the
principal issues that surround the French feminist
interrogation of difference. Reviewing the reference points
established at the beginning of this essay, we note:
  1. Leclerc, Gauthier, and Duras affirm sexual
specificity. Their views contrast with those of Kristeva,
who theorizes difference in terms of bisexuality, as do the
majority of the writers responding to the Quinzaine´s
questionnaire.
  2. Leclerc, Gauthier, and Duras perceive of difference
as difference between the sexes. They reverse the
hierarchical opposition of masculine and feminine but fail
to undermine this reversal. In these three texts there is
no Derridean sexualizing of differance, no deconstructionist
reversal and displacement of categories.
  3. The psychoanalytic perspective predominates in
Parole de femme. Leclerc contends that sexuality is primal,
that the signifying structures of Western culture reproduce
the paradigm of male genital sexuality. Accordingly, social
transformation will begin with a sexual revolution. The

psychoanalytic and Marxist perspectives coexist in the
Quinzaine Littéraire and in Tel Quel, where this double
framing is made explicit: "all [of the contributors] allude
to Freudianism and Marxism which are the only possible bases
for a materialist analysis of libidinal and political
economies [processes]." (34)   In the three texts examined,
there is no spokesperson for Marxist or materialist feminist
perspectives, which reject psychoanalysis and posit sexual
difference as culturally created and economically
motivated. (35)

     4. Leclerc, Gauthier, and Duras operate within a
literal framework with respect to sexual markers. Kristeva
(36) and the Quinzane Littéraire writers who also postulate
bisexuality use terms such as "masculine" and "feminine"
metaphorically.

     The lacunae these texts leave in the oppositional
framework of French feminism can be filled by an analysis of
the theories of Luce Irigaray, Hélène Cixous, the two most
prominent deconstructionist feminists, (37) and those of
Marxist, materialist, and lesbian feminists.

Luce Irigaray: Deconstructing Difference.

My discussion of Irigaray will describe how she defines
feminine specificity and how she employs Derrida's strategy
of reversal and displacement to deconstruct her own
essentially psychoanalytic model.   It will then proceed to
examine why Irigaray's deconstructionist approach has
brought her into conflict with both materialist feminists
and other psychoanalytically based theorists.

     In her work psychoanalyst Luce Irigaray (38) has
criticized the phallogocentric, "homo"sexual premises of
Freud and Lacan's theories: Woman is a plane mirror that
ensures the identity of Man; she exists not as difference
but as reflection.   Both this analysis and her
deconstructive readings--uncovering the ambiguities and
contradictions in her forefathers' theories of
femininity--bespeak the influence of Derrida.   Like Derrida,
she sees the strategic necessity of affirming specificity as
an antidote to the reign of the male status quo: "It is
sexual difference that I am trying to put back into
circulation, without the subordination of the other to the
one." (39)   How then does Irigaray construe feminine
difference?

     Like Leclerc, Irigaray situates difference in the female
body, in woman's capacity for decentered, multiple
sexuality: "She experiences pleasure pretty much
everywhere." (40)   In describing this model Irigaray tends

to focus on the genitals as emblematic. The two labia
contrast with the unitary penis. This duality permits
uninterrupted autoeroticism, a plenitude and
self-sufficiency that contrast with the mediated pleasure of
men, who require some sort of instrument to touch
themselves. This continual diffuse "jouissance" generates a
different mode of libidinal functioning and a different mode
of expression. "L´ecriture de la femme" is characterized by
fluidity and simultaneity:

> this rubbing of the two infinitely close neighbors
> which creates a dynamic state. Her ´style´ resists
> and explodes all solidly established forms, figures,
> ideas, and concepts. Which is not to say that her
> style doesn´t exist, as a discursiveness that cannot
> conceive of it allows one to believe. But her ´style´
> cannot be held as a thesis, cannot be taken as the
> basis of a position. (41)

Irigaray is aware of the difficulty that
post-structuralist theorists of difference face—how to
speak and write about difference when language itself is
identified as logocentric. To define the feminine is to
reify it and to reaffirm the phallic order. Still, she does
define it and in so doing operates a reversal of the
hierarchical opposition of masculine and feminine. But
reversal is accompanied by various strategies to displace
the opposition. In "Ce sexe qui n´en est pas un" (42) we
see this Derridean "double science" at work.
The feminine is brought forth, its specificity
proclaimed. However, unlike Leclerc, Irigaray evokes it in
such a way as to ever defer a full recognition of its
identity. Whereas Derrida deconstructs sexual opposition by
blurring the two terms, Irigaray does so by exploding her
principle of principles, by transforming it into a principle
of nonprinciples. Irigaray´s "feminine" can neither mirror
the masculine as it has traditionally, nor be mirrored by
it, for it escapes representation: "a kind of expanding
universe whose limits could never be fixed." (43) If we
return briefly to Irigaray´s description of the genitals,
which exemplify feminine difference although they are not
its locus, we note that they illustrate perfectly the
dynamics of difference: "ce sexe qui n´en est pas un" is
both different from the penis and within itself—it exists
as neither one nor two, in irreducible noncoincidence.
Irigaray´s project, in both theory and praxis, is
Derridean: "Never posit anything that is not reversed, and
also transposed into that which exceeds this reversal." (44)

However, the ambiguity concerning the literal or
metaphorical use of terms of sexual difference that can
occur in Derrida is much reduced in Irigaray. Despite her
often abstract and philosophical contexts the reader
interprets "woman," "she," "the feminine" as referring to
real women. The literality of Irigaray's specificity
invites reflection upon the way in which she articulates
biological and cultural factors in the constitution of
difference.

     In her theoretical expositions Irigaray repeatedly
affirms the interaction of the social and the sexual.
However, she does not expound upon their articulation. In
"Le marché des femmes" (45) the social mediation of
sexuality is central. Analyzing the exploitation of women,
Irigaray examines the exchange economy that Claude
Lévi-Strauss described as the very foundation of culture and
she shows that it manipulates the relations between and
within the sexes. She addresses the issue of causality
directly but refrains from positing either the primacy of
sexuality in the constitution of society or the opposite.
Instead, she asks <u>both</u> questions:

> <u>Which needs-desires of (so-called) masculine
> sexuality have determined a certain social order,</u>
> from its primitive form, private property, to its
> developed form, capital? But also: <u>to what extent
> are these needs-desires the effect of a social
> mechanism,</u> that has become partly autonomous, and
> produces them as they are? (46)

Here, then, no hierarchical opposition is created;
psychoanalytic and Marxist perspectives balance one
another. But at other times in her work sexuality is more
easily construed as primal. The repression of feminine
"jouissance" is fundamental to Irigaray's vision. Now, the
very notion of repression implies the existence of a
feminine sexuality that is separate from the culturally
fashioned one, a "jouissance" that is not a new construct to
be created but an essence to be discovered. The logic of
repression would appear to contradict the model expressed
through the balanced questions.

Irigaray and Her Critics.

Interpreters of Irigaray who are sympathetic to
deconstruction would argue that in her work hierarchical
oppositions--sexual versus socio-economic as well as
feminine versus masculine--are undermined. Her texts do not

establish a position and therefore remain irreducible in a
way consonant with her vision of the feminine. (47) But
materialist feminist readers have inveighed against her
"determinism." Monique Plaza, whose "Pouvoir
´phallomorphique´ et psychologie de la ´Femme´" appeared in
the first issue of Questions féministes, (48) is
a case in point.

Plaza´s arguments illustrate clearly that feminist
theorists have inherited and adapted the long-standing feud
that is one of the most salient features of the French
intellectual landscape: the rift between Marxism and
psychoanalysis. Like many twentieth-century thinkers, (49)
women such as Julia Kristeva and the group first called
"psychanalyse et politique" and then "politique et
psychanalyse" have sought to bridge this gap, to develop
synthetic models that would integrate sexuality and economic
theory, the individual and society. The Tel Quel dossier,
to which Kristeva and "psych et po" contributed, is an
example of this double framing. However, many feminist
theorists advocate or stress only one perspective. This
polarization has created conflict and misunderstanding.

In her article, Plaza contends that Irigaray´s
neo-Freudianism hinders her ability to effectively critique
the limitations of the psychoanalytic model, the crucial one
being its emphasis on genital sexuality. She considers
Irigaray´s awareness and inclusion of socio-economic factors
inadequate and characterizes her analyses as simplistic and
reductionist. Yet it is not her unidimensionality per se
with which she finds fault but her choice of the wrong
dimension. What Plaza seems to require of Irigaray is that
she reject the Lacanian psychoanalytical model (which Plaza
calls "phallomorphic," that is, based on male anatomy) and
espouse the Marxist one (which she calls "phallocentric,"
that is based on man´s appropriation of woman´s
reproductivity)--not that she nuance and enrich a synthetic
or deconstructionist approach.

Since Plaza´s theoretical model is founded upon a first
principle (the primacy of economic forces), she interprets
Irigaray in terms of a mistaken first principle. Plaza´s
distance from a Derridean model, in which first principles
themselves are placed "under erasure," is evinced in her
conceptualization of difference. Sexual difference is
evoked exclusively in terms of the difference between the
sexes: "a hierarchy in which women are differentiated and,
at the same time, evaluated negatively in relation to the
referent." (50) Biological difference exists, but it is a
"faux problème": "It is not the idea of the specificity of
each sex that is problematic, but the differential logic

according to which woman can only describe herself in
reference to her ´inferiority to man,´ and to her
´nature.´" (51)
    Plaza´s analytic framework is essentially the one
developed by Simone de Beauvoir in the Second Sex (1949).
Her critique of Irigaray illustrates the opposition between
Marxist and psychoanalytic models that remains an important
feature of contemporary French feminist theory. In
addition, it exemplifies a newer opposition: the one
between feminists who continue to theorize sexual difference
in terms of binary categories and first principles
(difference between) and those who use Derrida´s
differential model (difference within) and double strategy
(reversal and displacement).
    This more recent opposition can also be illustrated by
the quarrel between Irigaray and psychoanalyst Eugénie
Lemoine-Luccioni, (52) for it is not exclusively materialist
feminists who work within paradigms that posit first
principles. To Irigaray, Lemoine-Luccioni´s work contains
the same flaws as the Lacanian orthodoxy it perpetuates:
dependency on a first principle (the phallus as
transcendental signifier) and, therefore, an ideology of
mastery. Lemoine-Luccioni deems Irigaray´s undermining of
the universality of the phallus to be an inappropriate
politicizing of psychoanalytic theory, for she correctly
sees that by equating the phallus and the penis, Irigaray
affirms that the psychoanalytic model is a socially mediated
one, the product of male ideology.
    Neither an orthodox Marxist nor a true Lacanian,
Irigaray receives criticism from both sides--for opposite
reasons: from Plaza for her complicity with Freudian
essentialism and from Lemoine-Luccioni for her assertions
that psychoanalytic theory is a cultural construct.

Hélène Cixous: Differance and Bisexuality.

In the previous section I analyzed Irigaray´s application of
Derrida´s theories to a critique of the psychoanalytical
model of sexual difference and I examined the factors that
have influenced the response of her Marxist and
psychoanalytic critics. Now I will further develop this
topography of difference by situating Hélène Cixous´s
contributions.
    Like Irigaray, Cixous´s approach to sexual difference is
Derridean. It both reverses and displaces traditional
categories. Cixous, too, exalts feminine specificity and
locates it in the body--in a libidinal economy based on
generosity ("dépense"), not appropriation, (53) and on a

closer relationship with the "maternal," that is the
pre-symbolic fusion of self and other, the pre-linguistic
drives. Both theorists evoke feminine writing similarly
also, as an extension of feminine sexuality: dizzying
multiplicity, endless movement, profusion and complexity
that defy definition:

> now to write is to work; to be worked upon; (in) the
> in between space, to question, (to allow oneself to be
> questioned) the process of the same and the other
> without which no one is alive; to undo the work of
> death, by wishing the whole of the one-with-the other,
> infinitely energized by an incessant exchange from the
> one through the other knowing itself and renewing
> itself only from that which is farthest away--from
> oneself, from the other, from the other in me. A
> multiplying journey of thousands of transforma-
> tions. (54)

Both Cixous and Irigaray express an awareness of the dangers
of essentialism and of the inadequacy of a strategy of
simple reversal. Both displace the new hierarchy they
create by "exploding" their first principle. By configuring
the feminine as irreducible, cosmic, and ever-moving, they
transform this traditional category into a nonprinciple, a
synonym of differance. The sexual markers "feminine" and
"femininity" are double in their texts as they are in those
of Derrida: they simultaneously evoke and confound
conventional conceptions of sexual difference.
      Unlike Irigaray, Cixous uses the term "bisexuality,"
redefining it to create another signifier of differance. In
the important theoretical texts "The Laugh of the Medusa"
and "Sorties," this "other bisexuality" is set in opposition
to traditional usage, which, Cixous says, proposes a
neutrality resulting from the fusion of opposites, a
wholeness assured by the phallocentric subordination of the
other to the one. For Cixous, bisexuality "nourishes, seeks
out, and compounds differences." (55) It represents:

> each one's location in self ("repérage en soi") of the
> presence--variously manifest and insistent according
> to each person, male or female--of both sexes,
> non-exclusion either of the difference or of one sex,
> and, from this "self-permission," multiplication of
> the effects of the inscription of desire, over all
> parts of my body and the other body. (56)

Bisexuality, then, is the simultaneous nonhierarchical
presence of the feminine and the masculine, the self and the

other. It is associated with the blurring of categories,
with "being ´neither out nor in,´ being ´beyond the
outside/inside opposition.´" (57)
     Including bisexuality in her formulations of sexual
difference and textual dynamics, Cixous joins Kristeva and
many of the respondents to the <u>Quinzaine Littéraire</u>
questionnaire, for whom difference is difference within. In
her numerous textual exegeses, Cixous, like Kristeva, has
focused on male writers who subvert unitary meaning: Joyce,
Shakespeare, Kleist, Poe. In this context, sexual markers
function metaphorically. Feminine writing need not imply
writing by women but writing that inscribes the other. In
"Sorties" Cixous makes this figurative dimension explicit:

> I am careful here to use the <u>qualifiers</u> of sexual
> difference, so as to avoid the confusion man/mascu-
> line, woman/feminine: for there are men who do not
> repress their femininity, women who inscribe more or
> less strongly their masculinity. Difference is not
> distributed, of course, according to the socially
> determined "sexes." (58)

     However, in much of Cixous´s work this distinction is
effectively blurred. In those texts where the figurative
and the literal coexist, those texts that speak to the
oppression and liberation of women, there is slippage. Even
in "Sorties," which, as we have seen, articulates clearly
the two registers, ambiguity can develop. The assertion
that, for historico-cultural reasons, women are closer to
femininity and bisexuality than men paves the way for a
lengthy passage in which "woman" is described as virtually
synonymous with "the feminine." Moreover, the frequent use
of the pronoun "elle," which can replace the substantives
"woman," "femininity," and "feminine writing," contributes
to the possible confusion of literal and figurative
meanings. In a text like "The Laugh of the Medusa"--which
is not framed by both explicit cautions and passionate
readings of Kleist and Shakespeare, men who "pass woman
through" their texts (59)--the distinction between women and
"the feminine" is problematic.
     When isolated from the body of her theoretical and
interpretive work, a number of Cixous´s "feminist" texts can
supply material for the criticism that Cixous merely inverts
the sexual hierarchy and thus, in the last analysis, she is
an essentialist. (60) Taken as a whole, however, her work,
perhaps even more than Irigaray´s, encompasses ambiguities
that are consistent with a deconstructive perspective.
     The same irreducibility surfaces when one seeks to
ascertain Cixous´s position on another of our topographical

reference points: the origin of sexual difference. Cixous
repeatedly asserts the importance of culture in molding
gender identity from infantile bisexuality. And yet, as
with Irigaray, the reader cannot establish a clear-cut claim
of cultural primacy. There is too much variability in
Cixous´s formulations and too much ambiguity built into the
psychoanalytic model.
      It is true that in "Sorties" Cixous rejects the notion
that difference is in any way grounded in anatomy and warns
that the very question of the origin of difference is a
phallocentric trap. She affirms that:

> men and women are caught in a network of age-old
> cultural determinations of a practically unanalyzable
> complexity: one can´t speak of "woman" any more than
> of "man" without being caught inside an ideological
> theater where the multiplication of representations,
> images, reflections, myths, and identifications
> transforms, deforms, ceaselessly alters everyone´s
> imaginary and invalidates beforehand all
> conceptualization. (61)

She then proposes that radical social, political, and
economic changes could produce undreamed-of effects on the
libidinal economy.
      In "Sorties" Cixous posits the primacy of culture. The
libidinal economy, locus of sexual difference, is a cultural
construct. However, in "Castration or Decapitation," after
affirming that the unconscious itself is cultural, Cixous
adds that it is also shaped "by what is strange, what is
outside culture ... a savage tongue." (62) Likewise, in an
interview published by the American journal Sub-Stance,
having stated that anatomical difference is always mediated
by culture, she remarks that "this does not prevent the
libidinal economy of woman from functioning in a specific
manner which modifies her rapport with reality. (63) In
another interview, she distinguishes "the body-space where
writing shapes itself, from the stage-space, the space of
social performance where all discourse is elaborated," (64)
thus implying that the body possesses a certain autonomy.
These examples, which adumbrate extra-cultural influences,
illustrate the tendency of Cixous´s formulations to escape
categorization. This excess, like the ambiguous sex
markers, is consistent with a Derridean approach, which
considers unitary meaning and the mastery that it assumes to
be philosophically simplistic and politically reactionary.
      As with Irigaray, it is ultimately Cixous´s
unwillingness to posit a cultural first principle

consistently that brings charges of biologism. Such
critiques testify to the polarization that marks French
feminist theory and highlights the difficulty of obtaining
"objective" maps of this field of inquiry. The centrality
of the psychoanalytic model in Irigaray's and Cixous's
formulations and the accompanying emphasis on the body, the
unconscious, and repression make these theorists highly
suspect to those who work primarily within a Marxist or
Marxist-derived paradigm. In dealing with theorists of
feminine specificity, materialist feminists and Marxist
feminists do not distinguish deconstructionists--who attempt
to displace the primacy of the feminine over the masculine
and the sexual over the social--from those who appear to
maintain this primacy, such as Leclerc, Gauthier, Duras,
Claudine Herrmann, and Chantal Chawaf. All are grouped
together as Neo-Freudians, that is, reactionary
anti-feminists.

The power of the Marxist paradigm in French discussions
of difference can be illustrated by Catherine Clément's
categorically negative reaction to sexual specificity. In
her article "La femme dans l'idéologie," Clément labels all
theorists of sexual specificity "fanatics of difference." (65) While some are politically to the Left, they
are nonetheless misguided: guilty of mysticism, utopianism,
and idealism. They believe, she says, that speaking and
writing are directly liberating. They propose a total
refusal of culture on the grounds that it is
"phallogocentric," "phallocratic," and thus they effectively
marginalize and disempower themselves. Moreover, they lack
a well-articulated theory of oppression (one not based on
sex) and a commitment to political action that will change
women's relations to production.

Although Irigaray and Cixous are not named here, they
are certainly implicated in this sweeping generalization.
It is not ignorance of their work or of the subtleties of
post-structuralist thought that explains this inclusion.
Clément is a fellow academic, well versed in the
philosophical and psychoanalytic culture of the French
literary elite. While editor of the avant-garde journal
L'Arc she contributed short but appreciative pieces to the
issue on Derrida. She is well informed about and
participated in the re-evaluation of epistemology that gave
rise to deconstructionist feminism. Even so, for Clément
the ultimate test of any concept or theory has been its
compatibility with Marxism. In this light, Irigaray's and
Cixous's deconstructionist strategies--reversal and
displacement of first principles--do not differentiate them
from other proponents of difference.

Although one can argue that the polarization of French feminist inquiry has significantly impeded mutual understanding, it would surely be false to attribute all the generalizations and misinterpretations that occur to partisan loyalties. Another factor is important. The texts of theorists like Irigaray and Cixous present inherent interpretive problems, for the undermining of sexual categories that is crucial to identifying a Derridean perspective is necessarily subtle. Their texts are more evocative than discursive and, as Christie McDonald aptly notes: "In the economy of a movement of writing that is always elusive, one can never decide properly whether the particular term implies complicity with or a break from existent ideology." (66)

Monique Wittig: Lesbianism, Post-Structuralism, and Materialism.

In the preceding section I expanded this overview of deconstructionist, Marxist, and materialist feminist theory by examining Hélène Cixous, comparing her perspective with that of Irigaray, and exploring further the criticisms leveled against theorists of difference. It now remains to situate lesbian materialist feminism in relation to the framework of oppositional reference points guiding this topography, so as to extend our understanding of areas of commonality and difference.

Lesbian feminists, of whom Monique Wittig has been the most prominent spokesperson, add another dimension to the debate over sexual difference in France. For them neither feminine specificity nor bisexuality are fruitful concepts. For Irigaray and Cixous, phallocentric culture is only heterosexual in appearance. In reality, it is monosexual, based on a false symmetry, a reductionist Dialectic. It is imperative, then, to unveil and disturb this "homo"sexual "Empire of the Proper" by affirming sexual difference. For Wittig, phallocentric culture is indeed heterosexual. Rather than affirming the feminine in opposition to the masculine, she affirms homosexuality (particularly lesbianism) over heterosexuality. In so doing, she displaces the focus of difference, but she does not eliminate it. Homosexuality is her "specificity." We note, then, that Wittig's strategy, like those of theorists of the feminine, is grounded in the destabilizing reversal of a binary opposition. By asserting the primacy of homosexuality, she undermines heterosexuality's tacit claim to be a first principle, an arbiter of Truth.

Does Wittig deconstruct the first principle of her new hierarchized pair in a Derridean double movement, or does

she maintain the supremacy of homosexuality/lesbianism? The
post-structuralist theorists who have most influenced Wittig
are Deleuze and Guattari (<u>Anti-Oedipus</u>, 1973), not Derrida.
However, the theoretical projects of these three men share
important similarities. Deleuze and Guattari also voice a
critique of phallogocentrism and psychoanalysis and engage
in an exploration of difference. Like Derrida, they seek to
evoke new models of sexuality freed from specular Oedipal
desire and associated with multiplicity and fluidity. It is
not surprising, then, that in addition to more standard
definitions of homosexuality--desire for one's own sex,
resistance to the norm--Wittig also conceptualizes
homosexuality as "the desire for something else that is not
connoted" (67) and as an expanded, inclusive polysexuality:
"For us there are, it seems, not one or two sexes but many
(cf. Guattari/Deleuze), as many sexes as there are
individuals." (68) Wittig's formulation of homosexuality as
excess, as that which goes beyond cultural constraints into
the unknown and unnamed, and the association with
multiplicity and dissymmetry, rejoin the paradigm of
deconstructionist theorists of the feminine. One can argue
that, like Irigaray and Cixous, Wittig "explodes" her first
principle, transforming it into a principle of non-
principles. In her work, homosexuality/lesbianism is the
equivalent of differance.

We have seen that Wittig's lesbian feminist theory is
similar to as well as different from theories of the
feminine. Although she rejects the concepts of feminine
specificity and bisexuality, Wittig does operate the same
reversal of sexually marked terms. Moreover, certain of her
definitions reflect the influence of post-structuralist
philosophers of difference and are reminiscent of those of
Irigaray and Cixous. In France, these parallels have gone
largely unnoticed, submerged by an emphasis on the split
between psychoanalytic and materialist models.

Wittig condemns all psychoanalytic theory as another
example of heterosexual reductionism. She asserts
unreservedly the primacy of culture in the constitution of
difference:

> The category of sex is the one that rules as "natural"
> the relation that is at the base of (heterosexual)
> society and through which half of the population,
> women, are ʿheterosexualizedʾ (the making of women is
> like the making of eunuchs, the breeding of slaves, of
> animals) and submitted to a heterosexual
> economy....The compulsory reproduction of the
> ʿspeciesʾ by women is the system of exploitation on

which heterosexuality is economically based. (69)

Wittig does share this cultural first principle with
Marxist and materialist feminists. Nonetheless, her focus
on homosexuality sets her apart. Wittig´s theoretical
remarks emphasize sexuality more than those of her Marxist
and materialist sisters. Sexuality, broadly defined as "an
exercise of subjectivity that involves the search for
pleasure and the creation of a unique being, irreplaceable,
self-sufficient," (70) is the foundation of the pluralistic
alternative culture that lesbianism represents for her. As
Wittig defines it, lesbianism can operate as a metaphor for
alterity, for nondifferential desire, thus serving a
function similar to that of the repressed feminine for
theorists of difference. Wittig, then, pays greater
attention to difference--whose locus is the body--than do
other Marxist-inspired theorists. Like Deleuze and
Guattari, she conceives difference not as difference
between--between two opposing sexes--or difference
within--welcoming the other in the self--but as difference
among individuals. Rather than split humankind in half or
decenter the self, she disperses difference among the many.
In the preceding pages I have shown that Wittig´s
lesbian feminism shares common ground with both
post-structuralist theorists of the feminine and with
Marxist and materialist feminists. Like Irigaray and
Cixous, who can be situated between opposing reference
points (Marxists versus psychoanalytic orthodoxies), Wittig,
too, can be interpreted as bridging oppositions. On the one
hand, the reversal and displacement of a traditional binary
opposition marking sexual difference are central to Wittig´s
theoretical formulations, as is the case with Irigaray and
Cixous. On the other hand, her lesbian feminism
incorporates a Marxist first principle: the undisputed
primacy of cultural, specifically economic, factors in the
constitution of difference.

Conclusion

Wittig´s lesbian materialism represents yet another
combination of reference points in this topography of
difference, which is now as complete as space will permit.
I have illustrated the four sets of oppositional reference
points established to map the important directions and
problematic issues in French feminist approaches to
difference. Examinations of the theoretical formulations of
Luce Irigaray, Hélène Cixous, Monique Wittig, and

several Marxist and materialist feminists have supplemented
this topographical sketch.

The most salient opposition one finds in the French
feminist debate over sexual difference is that between
psychoanalytic and Marxist perspectives. We have seen this
opposition demonstrated in Catherine Clément's "La femme
dans l'idéologie," in Monique Plaza's criticisms of
Irigaray, and even in fellow analyst Lemoine-Luccioni's
disagreement with Irigaray. Yet another example is
Christine Delphy's thorough and impassioned critique of
Parole de femme's "reactionary naturalism and
biologism." (71)

The split between psychoanalytic and Marxist
perspectives coincides often, but not always, with the
split between post-structuralist and more traditional
theoretical approaches. Feminist deconstructionists such
as Irigaray, Cixous, and Kofman, who first reverse
traditional hierarchized concepts and then undermine the
new hierarchy, do work within a predominantly
psychoanalytic framework. Marxist and materialist
feminists, who reverse the biology/culture hierarchy and
then maintain intact the primacy of culture as creator of
sexual difference, do not seek to decenter first principles
per se. The substantial coincidence of these two sets of
oppositional reference points serves to sustain within
French feminism the theoretical polarization that has long
split French intellectuals into followers of Freud or
followers of Marx.

However, we have seen that all feminist theorists who
rely primarily on the psychoanalytic model are not
post-structuralists. Leclerc, Duras, Gauthier, Chawaf,
Lemoine-Luccioni establish and preserve a (feminine) first
principle. In this they join Marxist and materialist
feminists. Annie Leclerc and Christine Delphy are a case
in point. In Parole de femme, Leclerc posits the primacy
of the feminine over the masculine. In her critique of
Leclerc, Delphy attributes primacy to the economic paradigm
over the sexual one. Despite this much-noted difference,
both women share a dependency upon first principles, a
dependency that sets them apart from deconstructionist
feminists.

Likewise, a Marxist perspective may not preclude the
existence of deconstructionist strategies. Wittig's
treatment of the heterosexual/homosexual opposition
illustrates this. She both reverses the normative
hierarchy and displaces the primacy of homosexuality by
conceptualizing it as difference. Moreover, when compared
with the formulations of Delphy, Plaza, or Colette

Guillaumin, Wittig´s theoretical statements place sufficient
emphasis on alternative modes of sexuality to decenter
economic primacy.

Highlighting areas where these two powerful sets of
oppositional reference points do not coincide is important.
Examples of such divergence tend to go unnoticed in the
partisan atmosphere of French feminist theory. Yet, they
are valuable components of a topography of difference, for
they reconstitute complexity and testify to commonalities,
bridges, and alternatives that bear exploring. As we shall
see, American-based scholarly observers, benefitting from
their critical distance, have begun this task.

Sexual Difference: A Franco-American Comparison

The final section of this introduction compares French
approaches and preoccupations with those of American
feminist theorists and scholars of difference. It reviews
those aspects of French inquiry most unfamiliar to
Americans: (1) the centrality of the modernist perspective
in which language and writing ("écriture") are the locus of
sexual difference; (2) the overriding importance of the
psychoanalytic model in defining specificity and tracing its
effects in writing; (3) the differences between American and
French interpretations of Freud; (4) the metaphorical and
metaphysical dimensions of woman and the feminine that are
part of this approach, and (5) the prominence of a Marxist
critical tradition that politicizes and polarizes the
theoretical arena. Lastly, I sketch the contributions
American-based interpreters of French feminist theory are
making to both their American and their French colleagues.

As we have seen repeatedly, the structuralist and
post-structuralist movements have significantly shaped the
development of French feminist theory. The investigation of
difference has marked linguistic and semiotic,
philosophical, and psychoanalytic inquiry in France for over
twenty years. The elaboration of a problematics of alterity
has been a central concern for influential literary
theorists like Derrida and Kristeva who, sparked by Lacan´s
rereading of Freud, conceptualize writing in psychoanalytic
as well as philosophical terms. "Ecriture" inscribes known
and unknown, self and other, masculine and feminine. It is
a dynamic double process that flows "through" a speaking
subject, not an individual and identifiable author. Other
fundamental concepts of literary theory, such as mimesis or
representation, have also been called into question. In
this more abstract universe, "woman" and "the feminine" are
often metaphors for dissidence, negativity, and irreducible

otherness.

This epistemological interrogation, which revitalized
the examination of sexual difference in France, did not
occur in the United States and has but recently been
imported. Whereas, in France, deconstructionist strategies
that seek to reveal the plurality and ambiguity of language
and literature have been applied to illuminating sexual
difference, American feminists, unfamiliar with (or wary of)
this intellectual questioning have continued to approach
literature from a dialectical perspective, stressing woman
as historico-cultural construct and opposing her to man as
did Beauvoir in The Second Sex. Their model has been one
that posits difference between and oppression rather than
difference within and repression. They have proceeded more
empirically, analyzing both canonical and little-known
literary works to document the impact of cultural
constraints on the female imagination and to reconstruct
women's literary history.

In France, particularly after 1968, psychoanalysis
loomed large in intellectual debate and theoretical
renewal. Lacan and others stressed the subversive,
disturbing implications of the unconscious. Thus, many
feminists were able to incorporate psychoanalytic concepts
into their theoretical apparatuses. American feminists have
not had the same access to psychoanalytic models as critical
tools. American practitioners and theorists have
traditionally placed emphasis on realizing the curative
(normative) possibilities of psychoanalysis, a tendency that
Lacan, after Freud, strongly criticized. In an American
cultural context, where the unconscious did not dethrone the
(male) ego and was not explicitly linked to disruptive
literary practices, psychoanalysis had little to offer
feminist theorists and literary critics.

The politicization of French feminist inquiry is an
attribute that may surprise Americans, little accustomed to
channeling political energies into their scholarly work. In
France, most feminists share in the strong tradition of the
Left and espouse, in varying degrees, the principles and
goals of Marxism. Paradoxically, this common ideological
ground gives rise to a polarization whose intensity has
hindered productive exchange. We have noted several
instances of Marxist and materialist feminist attacks on
theorists of difference. Their psychoanalytic framework is
condemned as reactionary and antifeminist. Their
affirmation of writing as a subversive activity is seen to
be misguided utopianism. Thinkers such as Cixous, Irigaray,
Kristeva, and Kofman are also critical of their critics, for
they are convinced that unless the Marxist model is revised

in the light of post-structuralist theory feminism will
simply reproduce, in inverted form, the existing social and
political structures. What's more, they consider the
theoretical and creative work of individuals to be at least
as important as collective action in furthering cultural
transformation. Still, despite factional disagreements,
French feminist theory is characterized by the common
preoccupation with correctly (re)conceptualizing and
implementing a radical Marxist legacy that is foreign to
American scholars.

The enormous influence of post-structuralism and Marxism
has represented a very real barrier to American feminists
seeking to internationalize their understanding of
difference, a barrier that greater access to quality
translations will not dismantle. It is a question not only
of different theoretical traditions, but of a different
relationship to theory. French intellectuals have a
proclivity for abstraction and theoretical systems. In
comparison, Americans appear empirical. American feminism
has been correspondingly less theoretical and more focused
on validating the authority of women's experience than its
French counterpart. This said, the approaches and
preoccupations of Marxist and materialist feminists are less
foreign to Americans than those of Irigaray, Cixous, or
Kristeva. Not surprisingly, there has been a commensurately
greater effort made to explain post-structuralism and to
analyze the theories and textual experiments of its feminist
practitioners. The anthology New French Feminisms, Jane
Gallop's The Daughter's Seduction, the second chapter of The
Future of Difference, the special issues of Yale French
Studies, Diacritics, Signs, Sub-Stance, Feminist Studies, as
well as articles in such journals as Enclitic and Critical
Inquiry testify to these efforts. (72) This cross-cultural
bridging is most welcome, for post-structuralism has given
French feminism its newest dimension and it can surely serve
to enrich feminist inquiry into women, language and
literature in the United States as well.

In addition to making French feminist theory more
accessible to Americans, its American-based interpreters
offer French colleagues viewpoints that are both familiar
and different, work that is both well-informed and less
politicized, less polarized, less abstract. American-based
scholars have produced most of the feminist studies of
French men and women writers. They have contributed
valuable post-structuralist insights and interpretations,
such as those by Shoshana Felman and Naomi Schor. (73) And,
viewing the French intellectual landscape through a
different lens, American-based feminists have pointed out

features less noted in France, such as the multiplicity of
Irigaray's and Cixous's thought, which escapes polarizing
generalizations, and the possibility that Kristeva's
semanalytic approach may reconcile Marxism and
psychoanalysis within a feminist literary hermeneutics. (74)
The potential of cultural cross-fertilization is just
beginning to be realized. There is every reason to expect
that Franco-American dialogue will give rise to a richer
topography of difference.

NOTES

1. Editor's translation from La jeune née (Paris: Union
Générale d'Editions, 1975), pp. 131-132: Il doit y avoir un
ailleurs me dis-je. Et tout le monde sait que pour aller
ailleurs il y a des passages, des indications, des
"cartes"--pour une exploration, une navigation. Ce sont les
livres. Tout le monde sait qu'il existe un lieu qui n'est
pas obligé économiquement, politiquement, à toutes les
bassesses et tous les compromis. Qui n'est pas obligé de
reproduire le système. Et c'est l'écriture. S'il y a un
ailleurs qui peut échapper a la répétition infernale, c'est
par là, où ça s'écrit, ou ça rêve, où ça invente les
nouveaux mondes. (Subsequent translations are the editor's
unless indicated otherwise.)

2. The feminist theory produced in both Belgium and
Quebec shares the traditional underpinnings as well as the
current concerns and approaches of French feminist theory.
It is by virtue of these striking similarities that Belgian
and Quebecois women have been incorporated in a volume
focusing on France. The historical and cultural factors
that do contribute a unique tonality to these other
Francophone voices, then, will not be examined in this
essay. Evidence of a transnational partnership can be found
in many publications, for example La Venue à l'écriture (a
collaboration by Hélène Cixous, Annie Leclerc, and Quebecois
Madeleine Gagnon that was published in France), Le
corps-à-corps avec la mère (a lecture and interviews given
in Montreal by noted French theorist Luce Irigaray and
published there), and Les Cahiers du GRIF (a Belgian
feminist journal in which articles by Cixous and Julia
Kristeva appeared).

3. These are Parole de femme, a lyrical essay by Annie
Leclerc, and two dossiers "Lutte de femmes" and "L'Ecriture
a-t-elle un sexe?" published in Tel Quel and La Quinzaine

Littéraire in 1974.

4. Les Structures élémentaires de la parenté (1949);
Mythologiques 1-4 (1964-71).

5. Gilles Deleuze has engaged in a critique of
Metaphysics and the Dialectic (Nietzsche et la philosophie,
1962; Logique du sens, 1969), and more recently of
psychoanalysis (Capitalisme et schizophrénie. Anti-Oedipe,
1973, with Félix Guattari). Michel Foucault´s work, an
archeology of Western culture, examines discontinuity and
otherness (Histoire de la folie, 1961, trans. as Madness and
Civilization; La Volonté de savoir, 1976). Jean-François
Lyotard has posited that the power of the status quo is so
great that it will inevitably neutralize otherness and he
has expressed an antitheoretical perspective (La Condition
post-moderne, 1979).

6. Both Philip Lewis ("The Post-Structuralist
Condition," Diacritics, 12, Spring 1982, pp. 2-24) and
Jonathan Culler (On Deconstruction [Ithaca: Cornell
University Press, 1982]) ably argue the problematic status
of the distinction between structuralism and
post-structuralism. It is with this caveat that I use the
term.

7. Formalist structuralists include Lévi-Strauss,
linguist Roman Jakobson, and poeticians Roland Barthes,
Gérard Genette, and Tzvetan Todorov.

8. L´Ecriture et la différence (Paris: Seuil, 1967).
English trans. Writing and Difference (Chicago: University
of Chicago Press, 1978); De la grammatologie (Paris:
Minuit, 1967). English trans. Of Grammatology (Baltimore:
Johns Hopkins University Press, 1974).

9. "Differance" evokes not only the noun "différence"
but also the verb "différer": to differ, vary, postpone,
defer. The present participle contains an "a" (différant).

10. "Translator´s Preface," Of Grammatology, p. lvii.

11. It is important to remember that in Derrida´s
formulations "writing" and "textuality" can take on broad,
metaphysical connotations. As Freud used the metaphor of
writing to describe the complex workings of the psyche,
Derrida uses it to designate the state of differance in
which we invariably exist. The literal text is but one

illustration of this metaphysical "writing."

12. "La Double Séance" in La Dissémination. Paris:
Seuil, 1972. English trans. Dissemination. Chicago:
University of Chicago Press, 1982; "Le Facteur de la
vérité." Poétique 21, 1975; Eperons: Les Styles de
Nietzsche. Venice: Corbo & Fiore, 1976. Paris:
Flammarion, 1978. English trans. Spurs. Chicago:
University of Chicago Press, 1979.

13. (1900-1981) His major works include the collection
Ecrits (Paris: Seuil, 1966) and the seminars he delivered
that were prepared for publication by J.-A. Miller:
Séminaires Livre XI (1973), Livre XX (1975), Livre I (1975),
Livre II (1978).

14. As elaborated in the Phenomenology of the Mind.

15. Two essays written in 1958 and 1960 and published in
Ecrits: "La Signification du phallus," and "Propos
directifs pour un Congrès sur la sexualité féminine; and the
1972-3 seminar "What Does Woman Want?" published in Livre
XX, Encore, 1975.

16. Lacan, Ecrits, p. 735.

17. He adds the expression "double invagination" in
"Living On: Border Lines" in Bloom et al. Deconstruction and
Criticism. New York: Seabury Press, 1979 (French version
unpublished).

18. "Choreographies," interview with Christie V.
McDonald in Diacritics 12, 1982, pp. 66-76.

19. "Choreographies," p. 76.

20. Paris: Grasset, 1974.

21. "Jouissance" denotes not only sexual pleasure but
also enjoyment and fulfillment in general.

22. In L´érotisme (Paris: Editions de Minuit, 1957).

23. Parole de femme (Livre de poche, p. 13): Nous avons
découvert en nous une petite lumière qui nous est propre, et
c´est elle seule que nous suivrons.... Nous inventerons le
monde car nous parlerons enfin de ce que nous savons,
silencieuses. Et nous savons, j´en suis sûre, ce qui est

bel et bon.

24. "Lutte de femmes," _Tel Quel_ 58, Summer, 1974, pp.
93-103; "L'Ecriture a-t-elle un sexe?" _La Quinzaine_
Littéraire 192, August, 1974, pp. 25-30. Xavière Gauthier,
Marguerite Duras, and Julia Kristeva contributed to "Lutte
de femmes." Their texts were originally to be published in
Le Monde des livres in 1973, but the project was cancelled
by the editor. The dossier includes a critique of this
refusal and an analysis of the significance of the MLF.

25. (1) In the project and the practice of writing does
the fact of being a woman or a man engage the text in a
certain direction? Is the writer writing aware of being a
woman or a man? (2) Does the fact of being a woman or a man
reveal itself in the text? (3) If there is a difference is
it absorbed, suppressed, pushed aside or on the contrary
accentuated, used, exploited in the act of writing? Elaine
Marks's translation in "Women and Literature in France,"
Signs, Summer, 1978, pp. 837-8.

26. _Tel Quel_, under the editorship of Philippe Sollers,
was influential in promoting this view of writing, one
shared, as we have seen, by Derrida.

27. Subsequent years would bring a deepening of their
inquiry and also a hardening of positions.

28. The group "psychanalyse et politique" is mentioned
here. The group's brief statement of its research program
and announcement of the opening of the publishing house "des
femmes" end the dossier. The publishing collective has
caused much controversy, and been accused of partisan
politics and intellectual terrorism.

29. Xavière Gauthier: editor of the feminist journal
Sorcières and author of _Surréalisme et sexualité_ (1971) and
Dire nos sexualités. Contre la sexologie (1976).

30. Marguerite Duras: writer and film maker whose texts
are seen by many feminist critics to be the epitome of
"l'écriture féminine." Opposed to theorizing, she has
nonetheless expressed her views in interviews, including _Les_
Parleuses (1974) with Gauthier.

31. Julia Kristeva: semiotician and psychoanalyst whose
work focuses on theories of avant-garde writing. Her
Recherches pour une sémanalyse (1969) is a synthesis of

semiotics and psychoanalysis. Texts that study women and
the feminine include Des Chinoises (1974), trans. as About
Chinese Women, and "La Femme ce n´est jamais ça" (Tel Quel,
Autumn, 1974).

32. Tout sujet parlant porte en lui une bisexualite qui
est précisément la possibilité d´explorer toutes les
ressources de la signification, aussi bien ce qui pose un
sens que ce qui le multiplie, le pulvérise et le rénove.
Trans. in New French Feminisms. Elaine Marks and Isabelle
de Courtivron, eds. (Amherst: University of Massachusetts
Press, 1980).

33. New French Feminisms, p. 167.

34. Trans. in New French Feminisms.

35. Orthodox feminists such as Catherine Clément (her
principal texts on women are "La Coupable," in La jeune neé
and L´Opéra ou la défaite des femmes. Paris: Grasset, 1979)
and materialist feminists such as those grouped around
Simone de Beauvoir and Questions féministes all reject the
notion of sexual difference. A purely cultural artifact, it
is of little interest. For them, the pressing issues are
the analysis of oppression and the integration of women into
productive work. Sharing the "concrete" context of
historical materialism, they attribute primacy to economic
factors and use sex markers literally. For materialist
feminists, however, there is a specificity of women´s
oppression--the appropriation of their reproductivity--that
traditional Marxism does not adequately theorize.

36. Kristeva´s consistently metaphorical frame and, more
importantly, her acknowledged focus on dissidence and
negativity rather than on women keep her at some distance
from feminist debate and set her apart from the more
women-centered figures of this topography.

37. Three other women have much in common with Irigaray
and Cixous: Sarah Kofman (L´Enigme de la femme: La Femme
dans les textes de Freud. Paris: Galilée, 1980); and
Quebecois thinkers and writers Nicole Brossard (Un livre.
Montreal: Editions du Jour, 1970; numerous articles in La
Barre du jour) and Madeleine Gagnon (Pour les femmes et tous
les autres. Montreal: Editions de l´Aurore, 1974; "Mon
corps dans l´écriture," in La Venue à l´écriture. Paris:
U.G.E., 10/18, pp. 63-116).

38. Irigaray's Speculum de l'autre femme (Paris: Minuit) was also published in 1974. The lengthy essay "La Tache aveugle d'un vieux rêve de symétrie" is a critical reading of Freud's "Femininity." In the remainder of the work she criticizes Plato and Western philosophy in general. Ce sexe qui n'en est pas un (Paris: Minuit, 1977) a collection of essays, repeats, clarifies and develops her arguments. Irigaray's complex relationship to Freud and Lacan is treated in Jane Gallop's The Daughter's Seduction: Feminism and Psychoanalysis (Ithaca: Cornell University Press, 1982).

39. Ce sexe qui· n'en est pas un, p. 143: c'est la différence des sexes que j'essaie de remettre en jeu, sans subordination de l'autre à l'un.

40. Ce sexe, p. 28.

41. Ce sexe, p. 76: Ces frottements entre deux infiniment voisins qui font dynamique. Son 'style' résiste à, et fait exploser, toute forme, figure, idée, concept, solidement établis. Ce qui n'est pas dire que son style n'est rien, comme le laisse croire une discursivité qui ne peut le penser. Mais son 'style' ne peut se soutenir comme thèse, ne peut faire l'objet d'une position.

42. First published in Cahiers du GRIF 5, 1975.

43. Ce sexe, pp. 30 and 28: sorte d'univers en expansion auquel nulles limites ne pourraient être fixées... 'elle' est indéfiniment autre en elle-même.

44. Ce sexe, p. 77: Rien n'être jamais posé qui ne soit renversé, et renvoye aussi à l'en-plus de ce renversement.

45. First published in Sessualità e politica, ed. Feltrinelli, 1976. Reprinted in Ce sexe qui n'en est pas un.

46. Quels besoins-désirs de la sexualité (dite) masculine ont déterminé un certain ordre social, de sa forme primitive, la propriété privée, à sa forme développée, le capital? Mais aussi: dans quelle mesure sont-ils l'effet d'un fonctionnement social, pour une part autonome, qui les produit tel quels? p. 179.

47. See, for example, Carolyn Burke. "Irigaray Through the Looking Glass," Feminist Studies 7, No. 2 (Summer 1981) pp. 288-306.

48. November, 1977, pp. 91-119. The journal, which was under the editorship of Simone de Beauvoir, described its perspective as radical feminist. Although Plaza´s primary target here is Irigaray, she also aims at all feminist theorists who rely in a substantial way upon the psychoanalytic paradigm for their analyses of difference (Annie Leclerc, Hélène Cixous, Claudine Herrmann). Her views are consonant with those of other materialist feminists (such as Christine Delphy, Colette Guillaumin, and Andrée Michel), many of whom published in Questions féministes.

49. Jean-Paul Sartre´s Critique de la raison dialectique (1960); also Gilles Deleuze and Félix Guattari´s Anti-Oedipe which combines Marxist and psychoanalytic perspectives through the formulation of a political analysis of desire.

50. "Pouvoir ´phallomorphique´"... p. 99: une hiérarchie où les femmes sont différenciées et, dans le même mouvement, évaluées négativement par rapport au référent.

51. "Pouvoir ´phallomorphique;´"... p. 101: Ce n´est pas l´idée de la spécificité de chaque sexe qui est problématique, mais le questionnement différentiel par où la femme ne peut se décrire que par l´´en moins que l´homme´, et par sa ´nature.´"

52. See Lemoine-Luccioni´s Partage des femmes (Paris: Editions du Seuil, 1976) and Irigaray´s "La Misère de la psychanalyse," Critique 365 (October 1977).

53. Cixous´s conceptualization of feminine sexuality combines psychoanalytic and anthropological frames. The latter is most evident in her notion of generosity/expenditure, which derives from exchange theory as developed by Marcel Mauss (Essai sur le don, 1925) and Lévi-Strauss (Elementary Structures of Kinship, 1949).

54. "Sorties" in La jeune née. Catherine Clément and Hélène Cixous. (Paris: Union Générale d´Editions 1975), p. 159: Or écrire c´est travailler; être travaillé; (dans) l´entre, interroger, (se laisser interroger) le procès du même et de l´autre sans lequel nul n´est vivant; défaire le travail de la mort, en voulant l´ensemble de l´un-avec-l´autre, dynamisé à l´infini par un incessant échange de l´un entre l´autre ne se connaissant et se recommençant qu´ à partir du plus lointain--de soi, de

l´autre, de l´autre en moi. Parcours multiplicateur à milliers de transformations.

55. "Sorties," p. 156.

56. "The Laugh of the Medusa," New French Feminisms. Elaine Marks and Isabelle de Courtivron, eds. (Amherst: University of Massachusetts Press, 1980), p. 254. Trans. of "Le rire de la méduse," L´Arc 61, 1975, p. 46. This passage also appears in "Sorties."

57. "Castration or Decapitation," Signs 7, No. 1 (1981), pp. 54-5. Trans. of "Le Sexe ou la tête," Les Cahiers du GRIF 13 (1976).

58. "Sorties," p. 148: J´ai soin ici d´employer les qualificatifs de la différence sexuelle, afin d´éviter la confusion homme/masculin, femme/féminin: car il y a des hommes qui ne refoulent pas leur féminité, des femmes qui inscrivent plus ou moins fortement leur masculinité. La différence ne se distribue pas, bien sûr, à partir des "sexes" déterminés socialement.

59. "Sorties," p. 182.

60. This is most true for "The Laugh of the Medusa."

61. "Sorties," p. 152: hommes et femmes sont pris dans un réseau de déterminations culturelles millénaires d´une complexité pratiquement inanalysable: on ne peut pas plus parler de "la femme", que de "l´homme" sans être pris à l´intérieur d´un théâtre idéologique où la multiplication des représentations, images, reflets, mythes, identifications transforme, déforme, altère sans cesse l´imaginaire de chacun et rend d´avance caduque toute conceptualisation.

62. "Castration or Decapitation," p. 52.

63. "Interview with Hélène Cixous," Sub-Stance No. 13, 1976, p. 28.

64. "Entretien avec Françoise van Rossum-Guyon," Revue des Sciences Humaines No. 168 (1977), p. 480.

65. "La femme dans l´idéologie," La Nouvelle critique 82 (March 1975), p. 45.

66. "Choreographies," an interview with Jacques Derrida

in Diacritics 12, 1982, p. 71.

    67. "Paradigm," in Homosexualities and French
Literature. George Stambolian and Elaine Marks, eds.
(Ithaca: Cornell University Press, 1979), p. 114.

    68. "Paradigm," p. 119.

    69. "The Category of Sex," Feminist Issues 2, No. 2
(Fall 1982), pp. 66-7.

    70. "Paradigm," p. 119.

    71. "Proto-féminisme et anti-féminisme," Les Temps
modernes 346 (May 1975), pp. 1469-1500.

    72. New French Feminisms. Elaine Marks and Isabelle de
Courtivron, eds. (Amherst: University of Massachusetts
Press, 1980); The Daughter's Seduction. Jane Gallop.
(Ithaca: Cornell University Press, 1982); The Future of
Difference. Hester Eisenstein and Alice Jardine, eds.
(Boston: G. K. Hall & Co., 1980); Yale French Studies 62
(1981); Diacritics 5, No. 4 (Winter 1975) and 12, No. 2
(Summer 1982); Signs 7, No. 1 (Autumn 1981); Sub-Stance No.
32 (1981); Feminist Studies 6, No. 2 (Summer 1980) and 7,
No. 2 (Summer 1981); "Theories of the Feminine," Alice
Jardine. Enclitic 4, No. 2 (Fall 1980), pp. 5-15; "Feminist
Criticism in the Wilderness," Elaine Showalter. Critical
Inquiry 8, No. 2 (Winter 1981), pp. 179-205.

    73. Felman: "Women and Madness: The Critical
Phallacy," Diacritics 5, No. 4 (Winter 1975), pp. 2-10;
"Rereading Femininity," Yale French Studies No. 62 (1981),
pp. 19-44. Schor: "Female Paranoia: The Case for
Psychoanalytic Feminist Criticism," Yale French Studies No.
62 (1981), pp. 204-19.

    74. "Irigaray Through the Looking Glass," Carolyn
Burke. Feminist Studies 7, No. 2 (Summer 1981), pp.
288-306; "Theories of the Feminine," Alice Jardine.
Enclitic 4, No. 2 (Fall 1980), pp. 5-15.

PART I

THE GENERAL PROBLEMATICS OF A FEMINIST CRITICISM

1   **Beauvoir, Simone de.** Le Deuxième sexe. 2 vols. Paris:
     Gallimard, 1949.

     Volume 1: Introduction; Part I--"Destin": Ch. I, "Les
     données de la biologie"; Ch. II, "Le point de vue
     psychanalytique"; Ch. III, "Le point de vue du
     matérialisme historique." Part II--"Histoire": Ch. I;
     Ch. II; Ch. III; Ch. IV. Part III--"Mythes": Ch. I.
     Part IV--"Formation": Ch. I, "L'enfance"; Ch. II,
     "La jeune fille"; Ch. III, "L'initiation sexuelle"; Ch.
     IV, "La lesbienne."
        Volume 2: Part I--"Situation": Ch. I, "La femme
     mariée"; Ch. II, "La mère"; Ch. III, "La vie de société";
     Ch. IV, "Prostituées et hétaïres"; Ch. V, "De la maturité
     à la vieillesse"; Ch. VI, "Situation et caractère de la
     femme." Part II--"Justifications": Ch. I, "La
     narcissiste"; Ch. II, "L'amoureuse"; Ch. III, "La
     mystique." Part III--"Vers la libération": Ch. I, "La
     femme indépendante." Conclusion.

        The essential text for an appreciation of the
     intellectual heritage of contemporary French feminism.
     Represents the first written treatment of the question,
     "How does a woman become a woman?" thereby insisting on a
     process common to all women's lives rather than an
     isolated event or issue. From its premise, "One is not
     born a woman: one becomes a woman," examines with
     extraordinary documentation and detail, first, the range
     of forces (historical, social, economic, biological,
     psychological, sexual, artistic) that have shaped women's
     concrete situation in the world, then the implications
     and possible responses to that situation. Is marked by
     both the existential concepts of "self" and "other" and
     the socialist politics in which Beauvoir was immersed at
     the time; as a result, the terminology is somewhat
     specialized and the author's bias not centrally
     feminist. Although the entire book influenced all
     subsequent feminist thought, some descriptive portions
     are now outdated for France and the United States.
     Annotated below are those sections which have most
     directly served contemporary feminist theory.
        Volume I: Introduction--presents the concept of
     "otherness" that underlies social oppression in general.
     The particular conformation of woman's relationship to
     man--she being the "immanent other," he being the active,
     "transcendent self"--has been reexamined in Cixous's
     writings on sexual analogy and the structure of thought
     (104). The introduction also establishes the spectrum of

domains in which women's subordination has been
institutionalized (law, religion, philosophy,
literature), thus foreshadowing the transdisciplinary
nature of current feminist investigation.

Part I--"Destin"--"Le point de vue psychanalytique":
refutes, in what is now accepted feminist critique, many
of Freud's assumptions about women. An example of the
sort of preliminary, "classic" analysis upon which
contemporary feminists such as Irigaray (314) and Clément
(148) have built refined, psychoanalytic-oriented
strategies.

Part II--"Histoire"--traces the condition of women
throughout the traditional periods of Western European
history, from the earliest pre-agricultural society to
1949. Asserts that the "general mediocrity" of women's
condition--their lack of education and their material
dependence--explains the absence of important collective
(versus individual) contributions by women to history.
There were "exemplary figures" (Joan of Arc, queens) and,
beginning with the Renaissance, a privileged literary and
artistic elite of women. But because of the obstacles
they faced (Beauvoir's account of the material and social
barriers confronting women writers has now become
standard), these women could not reach "the heights of a
Dante or a Shakespeare."

Part III--"Mythes"--Perhaps the most important section
of the entire book. Explains "how the female reality
took hold," that is, the "economic, ontological and
moral" reasons for the development of myths concerning
women. Created from the male imaginary to fill certain
individual needs, an array of contradictory images (Eve,
the Earth-Mother, the Virgin, the Witch, the
Woman-Object, the sacrosanct Mother, the Prostitute,
others) was appropriated and institutionalized by society
in general. Grounded in fear of female sexuality, early
myths were assumed, neutralized and reshaped by
Christianity in ways that further entrenched women's
inferiority. Beauvoir's ideas about the existential
wellsprings of myths (woman as man's "other," as Death,
as external "eye") were crucial for the theories of
Cixous (104) and for the writings of other feminists.

Volume II: Part I--"Situation"--"La femme mariée":
distinguishes men's and women's expectations and
experiences of marriage. Supporting examples are drawn
from literature.

Part I--"Situation"--"Situation et caractère de la
femme": summarizes previous sections on women's economic,
social and cultural conditioning as a means to explain

character traits traditionally thought inherent to
women. Beauvoir states that there is truth in these
negative characterizations (women as passive,
conservative, unambitious, contradictory). Though she
attributes these traits to women's powerlessness and
sense of limited possibilities, Beauvoir seems to
reproach women (particularly upper-class) for not
aspiring to "universal" thought and action. Many of
Beauvoir's negative characterizations have been picked up
by contemporary feminists, but have been turned into
positive attributes (particularly women's discomfort with
"masculine logic"). The latter, which only serves to
"mystify" and to impose a false order on multiplicity, is
the focal point of current feminist theory on masculine
discourse.

Part II--"Justifications"--explains the false solutions
some women choose to react to their oppression. All
based on a flight from woman's concrete situation, the
choices of narcissism, all-consuming love, and mysticism
represent ineffective responses. The differences
described between men's and women's experiences of love
are currently being explored by French feminists
(Irigaray, 309 and Cixous, 104).

Part III--"Vers la libération"--propounds the
importance of socialism and of economic independence for
women's progress. Repeats earlier assertions of women's
"defeatism" and limited ambition, though from a
psychological rather than a materialist point of view:
women suffer from trying to reconcile work with love;
they also cannot achieve sufficient "unawareness of
self." Most important in this section is the discussion
of women and writing: because of their "marginality,"
women see the world from a "singular" (versus
"universal") vision. Beauvoir maintains the
stereotypical characterizations of feminine writing but,
unlike some contemporary feminists who exalt this
specificity, Beauvoir blames women for not taking writing
and art seriously enough as craft and as effort.
However, recalling Virginia Woolf, she justifies women
writers' inability to "transcend" the simple attainment
of lucidity--that is, to conquer new and original
dimensions--since they must expend their energy "freeing
themselves from external constraints." Beauvoir's
compelling call for women's "transcendence" in
self-expression is undergoing a strong revival today.

1a   Trans. as The Second Sex. New York: Knopf, 1952.
   "Introduction" reprinted in (19).

2   **Braidotti, Rosy.** "Qui sait calculer les effets des
     idées?" Pénélope No. 3 (Fall 1980), 5-11.

     A cogent overview of the intentions of the feminist
     theoretical enterprise in France. Summarizes the
     feminist reevaluation of traditional rational discourse
     launched by The Second Sex (1), one that has exposed that
     discourse as based on the exercise of power, a certain
     (masculine) economy, and false "universality." Says
     feminists have sought a non-hierarchical and non-hegemonic
     rationality, even while many have resisted theory as an
     approach to new conceptualizations. Sees the emergence
     of a multiplicity of feminist "mobile strategies" or
     "angles of reflection," and not closed, immobile systems
     of thought. Praises feminist reflections as "an open
     path that is in continuous displacement."

3   **Burke, Carolyn Greenstein.** "Report from Paris: Women's
     Writing and the Women's Movement." Signs 3, No. 4
     (Summer 1978), 843-855.

     A brief, informative introduction to French feminism.
     Provides an overview of the fortunes of the women's
     movement since its inception in the aftermath of May '68,
     with particular emphasis on the ideological split between
     the "revolutionary" publishing collective Editions des
     femmes and the other "feminist" MLF groups. Also
     outlines the contributions of the three influential
     figures Julia Kristeva, Hélène Cixous, and Luce
     Irigaray. Concludes with a summary of the state of
     women's studies in the French university.

4   **Cesbron, Georges.** "Ecritures au féminin. Propositions
     de lecture pour quatre livres de femmes." Degré second
     4 (July 1980), 95-119.

     Says the question of a "feminine literature" can be
     approached in two ways, which it calls "cultural" and
     "natural" viewpoints: a sociological, "objective"
     consideration of the reality visible in women's texts, or
     a "subjective" look at the "differences" in women's
     literature that arise specifically from their being
     women. Says the second view argues for a "feminine
     discourse" and writing that, until now, masculine
     discourse has repressed. Then, examines four books by
     women in which a "vision of society, a language and a
     writing are put forth," in an effort to reconcile these

nature/culture ideas about women: Leclerc's Parole de
femme (469), Groult's Ainsi soit-elle, Cardinal's
Autrement dit (74), and Chawaf's Rougeâtre. Finds the
following similarities: all posit women's social
inferiority and the role of the different "phallocratic
discourses" in devalorizing women; all regret the
violence, failure, poison and hate existent male/female
roles have given rise to (failure of the couple, of
language); and all urge action for change, including
through writing ("writing means inscribing an unexpressed
desire, an unheard of wish"). Analyzes selected passages
from the four books to illustrate the importance of
language for women's progress, the need to both "master"
the discourse in place and "invent" new words for a
better world. Sees Chawaf as most strongly writing the
immediate, affective, and "incoherent" "linguistic flesh"
("chair linguistique") repressed by centuries of
rationalism. Concludes that what is new in these women's
works is their insistence on "homologies between the
structuring of writing and unconscious structuring," and
therefore on new systems of meaning. Very useful.

*   **Courtivron, Isabelle de** and Elaine Marks, eds. New
    French Feminisms: An Anthology. Amherst: University of
    Massachusetts Press, 1980.

    (See 19).

*   ———— and Elaine Marks. "Introduction I: Discourses
    of Anti-Feminism and Feminism." New French Feminisms:
    An Anthology. Amherst: University of Massachusetts
    Press, 1980, 3-9.

    (See 20).

*   ———— and Elaine Marks. "Introduction III: Contexts of
    the New French Feminisms." New French Feminisms: An
    Anthology. Amherst: University of Massachusetts Press,
    1980, 28-38.

    (See 21).

5   ————. "Women in Movement(s): 1968-1978." French
    Literature Series. University of South Carolina, 1979.

    Situates, clearly and concisely, current French
feminism in France's "heritage of a traditionally

politicized intelligentsia" even while it explains how
many feminists, since 1968, have broken with that
tradition. Though trained as specialists, they have
"subverted" their acquired "master's discourse" by using
the very analytical tools of their training. Considering
language the prime instrument of oppression, some of
these women have also explored new areas of a
specifically "feminine language." The essay focuses on
Wittig and Cixous to show creative and theoretical
aspects of a "feminine writing" and, despite their
differences, these authors' shared refusal of a codified,
immobilized "feminism."

6   **Didier, Béatrice.** "Préambule." L'écriture-femme.
     Paris: Presses Universitaires de France, 1981, 5-40.

     An introduction to her study of French women authors.
After interrogating the whole question of a "women's
writing," pointing to the traditionally negative
implications of the concept (ghettoization, reduction of
women to their anatomy), goes on to argue that careful
comparative reading of women's works does reveal
similarities of theme and effect: the presentation of the
practical situation of the woman writer encountering
social obstacles and marginalization; a preoccupation
with their identity through presentation of self, other
women, and surroundings; and a sense of another reality,
evoked through formal characteristics such as fluidity,
cyclicalness, ruptures, or discontinuities. Says that,
though male models of writing alone have marked culture,
women should not dismiss that writing as they develop
their own newly-discovered kinds of expression.

7   **Eisenstein, Hester** and Alice Jardine, eds. The Future
     of Difference. Boston: G. K. Hall & Co., 1980.

     Hester Eisenstein, "Introduction"; Alice Jardine,
"Prelude: The Future of Difference."
     Part I--Differentiation and the Sexual Politics of
Gender. Nancy Chodorow, "Gender, Relation, and
Difference in Psychoanalytic Perspective"; Jane Flax,
"Mother-Daughter Relationships: Psychodynamics, Politics,
and Philosophy"; Jessica Benjamin, "The Bonds of Love:
Rational Violence and Erotic Domination."
     Part II--Contemporary Feminist Thought in France:
Translating Difference. Domna C. Stanton, "Language and
Revolution: The Franco-American Dis-Connection" (28);

Josette Féral, "The Powers of Difference" (8); Christiane
Makward, "To Be or Not to Be...A Feminist Speaker" (18);
Jane Gallop and Carolyn G. Burke, "Psychoanalysis and
Feminism in France" (270 and 72).

Part III--The Language of Difference: Female and Male
in Speech and Literary Production. Audre Lorde, "Poetry
Is Not a Luxury"; Rachel Blau DuPlessis and Members of
Workshop 9, "For the Etruscans: Sexual Difference and
Artistic Production-The Debate Over a Female Aesthetic";
Sally McConnell-Ginet, "Difference and Language: A
Linguist's Perspective"; Naomi Schor, "For a Restricted
Thematics: Writing, Speech, and Difference in Madame
Bovary"; Clare Coss, Sondra Segal, and Roberta Sklar,
"Separation and Survival: Mothers, Daughters, Sisters:-
The Women's Experimental Theater."

Part IV--The Naming of Difference: Morality, Power, and
Social Change. Quandra Prettyman Stadler, "Visibility
and Difference: Black Women in History and Literature-
Pieces of a Paper and Some Ruminations"; Barbara Omolade,
Black Women and Feminism"; Carolyn Heilbrun, "Androgyny
and the Psychology of Sex Differences"; Pamella Farley,
"Lesbianism and the Social Function of Taboo"; Carol
Gilligan, "In a Different Voice: Women's Conception of
Self and of Morality"; Ruth Messinger, "Women in Power
and Politics"; Elizabeth Janeway, "Women and the Uses of
Power."

A collection of essays resulting from Barnard College
Women's Center's 1979 conference "The Scholar and the
Feminist." Includes a variety of disciplines and
theoretical approaches and makes available to its readers
a view of feminist inquiry that is both panoramic and
richly articulated. The pieces in Part II--Contemporary
Feminist Thought in France--constitute a truly excellent
introduction to the problematics of French feminist
theory. Careful attention is paid to comparing French
and Anglo-American perspectives. An invaluable resource.

8   **Féral, Josette.** "The Powers of Difference." The
    Future of Difference. Ed. Hester Eisenstein and Alice
    Jardine. Boston: G. K. Hall, 1980, 88-94.

Refutes women's "difference" as traditionally defined
for male needs, difference based on a repression of
feminine existence and authenticity that validates
masculine identity and superiority. Argues this
definition of woman reduces her to a "plane mirror" or

"mere reflection" of what is in fact man's other (and
unacknowledged) side. Claims that what has most
threatened the male order and been most silenced is the
female unconscious—a specific and woman-identified
unconscious. Says that for some French thinkers
recognizing the female unconscious means recognizing a
female discourse and calls this theory the point of
divergence between French and American feminists.
Explains "difference," as reconceived by contemporary
French theoreticians, as being outside of the existent
binary structures of masculine thought and the French
view of American feminist approaches as remaining within
and perpetuating the existing order. Quotes Cixous,
Leclerc, and Kristeva to evoke women's positive
marginality and "heterogeneity" and to suggest the
multiplicity of "differences" sought.

9   **Granjon, Marie-Christine.** "Les femmes, le langage et
     'l'écriture.'" Raison présente No. 39 (July-September
     1976), 25-32.

     Examines the premises underlying the French feminist
viewpoint that writing ("l'écriture") is an "essential
and primordial instrument of women's struggle."
Summarizes the political and sexual role of language for
Cixous, Gauthier, Duras and others who see writing as a
revolutionary act for women. Points out the weaknesses
of this view of language by presenting Kristeva's ideas
(see 436), criticizing in particular the notion of a
one-to-one correspondence between language and the social
order and between writing and revolution. Sees
Kristeva's understanding of the relation between
"semiotic modification" and changes in social practice as
a more sophisticated and fruitful one, even while
criticizing the obscurity of her writing.

10   **"Introduction."** Yale French Studies: Feminist Readings:
     French Texts/American Contexts No. 62 (1981), 2-18.

     Introduces this special issue on French and American
feminist criticism by discussing the method, purpose, and
contents of the volume—all of which are themselves
emblematic of feminism's challenge to established
scholarly procedures and forms of analysis. Sees the
collective approach undertaken by seven Dartmouth College
faculty to prepare this issue as, inherently, a challenge
to "the institution of literary criticism." Presents the

overall purpose of the volume as the "questioning of
pre-established modes of relating" (between reader,
character and author; between male and female; between
mother and daughter) on the psychological, social and
textual levels. Finally, explores, in the form of a
transcribed conversation among several American scholars,
the interaction between French and American feminist
modes of inquiry. Illuminates the following points of
connection and "dis-connection" between the two cultures:
(1) the importance of French feminist texts for American
critics, and yet the obstacles critics face in reading
them (the paucity of translations and the inaccessibility
of the writing itself); (2) the urgent need for
psychoanalytic interpretations in criticism, and yet the
potentially dangerous implications of some of those
interpretations (e.g., neo-essentialism); and (3) the
immense usefulness of French critical theory, and yet its
sometimes questionable applicability to literature (an
apparent theoretical/empirical split). Argues that the
disjunctures between the two cultures are less profound
than they appear, and are often extremely fruitful. A
fresh and engaging "essay" that opens to further
investigations.

* **Jardine, Alice** and Hester Eisenstein, eds. <u>The Future
  of Difference</u>. Boston: G. K. Hall & Co., 1980.

  (See 7).

11   ————. "Gynesis." <u>Diacritics</u> 12 (Summer 1982), 54-65.

     Examines the crucial place of "woman" and "the
feminine" in contemporary French formulations of
modernity. Characterizes French theory of the past
twenty years as eliminating the unitary self or speaking
subject, focusing on the process that results in
fictional representation rather than on the product
itself, and requestioning the status of truth. Notes
that "woman" has been and continues to be that which
escapes control in male-elaborated reality. Coins the
neologism "gynesis" to designate "the putting into
discourse of 'woman' as that process beyond the Cartesian
Subject, the Dialectics of Representation, or Man's
Truth." Stresses the non-coincidence of this
philosophical abstraction and "woman" as the historically
and socially grounded entity that interests French and
American feminists and is integral to Anglo-American

feminist literary theory. Explores briefly what feminist
literary criticism can gain from an understanding of this
perspective. Reviews the impact of male theorists
(especially Lacan) on women, speaking at greatest length
of Lemoine-Luccioni and Montrelay. The former asserts
that women incarnate "woman" and, as such, maintain the
symbolic order and the social contract. Women can only
claim their difference-as-not-all. Montrelay does not
equate "woman" and women. Rather, "woman" is "the locus
of a 'primary imaginary' dedicated to 'feminine
jouissance'" and is available to both men and women. An
extremely valuable overview.

12   **Jones, Ann Rosalind.** "Writing the Body: Toward An
     Understanding of 'L'écriture féminine.'" Feminist
     Studies 7, No. 2 (Summer 1981), 247-63.

A fine overview of current French feminist theoretical
positions that articulates, first, the shared tenet of
feminist inquiry—that Western "phallogocentric" thought
has systematically repressed women's experience—and then
delineates the different responses to that repression.
After positing that the principal French women agree on
the importance of feminine "jouissance" or the "direct
re-experience of the physical pleasures of infancy and of
later sexuality," distinguishes among the strategies put
forth by Kristeva, Irigaray, Cixous and Wittig.
Summarizes Kristeva's stress on the "maternal" (see 416,
443 and 410) and her idea that women should keep
challenging existing discourse, rather than formulate a
new one. Describes Irigaray's contrasting belief in a
feminine specificity arising from women's bodies and in
a feminine language that would express their sexuality
(see 309). Explains Cixous's conviction that women's
unconscious—"totally different from men's"—and the
physical drives that mark it can create new female
discourses (see 104 and 102). Then, evokes the problems
that adhere to the concepts of a "feminine" specificity
and writing, in particular the dangers of
neo-essentialism and of isolating sexuality from social
experience; also presents and defends the materialist
feminist critique of "neo-femininity" as bound up in the
very oppositional ideology feminists seek to destroy (see
541 and 186). Discusses Wittig in light of this last
critique, describing her focus as "social relationships
among women-identified women." Criticizes, in addition,
"neo-femininity"'s "flattening out" of lived differences

among women. States that both theory (such as that
elaborated by proponents of specificity) and material
practice together should be developed. A first-rate
introduction to central issues.

13   **Kamuf, Peggy.** "Replacing Feminist Criticism."
     Diacritics
     12, No. 2 (Summer 1982), 42-47.

     Criticizes American feminist literary theory for
     limiting itself to "cosmetic modifications on the face of
     humanism." Asserts that both American tendencies--to end
     the exclusion of women by expanding academic disciplines
     and to abandon phallocratic institutions in favor of
     gynocentric models--rest upon totalizing, essentialist
     assumptions and maintain existing power structures. Uses
     the work of Michel Foucault to support her critique of
     feminism as humanism and to adumbrate an alternative
     approach that would be based on "eccentricity" and
     undecidability. Avoids labeling this perspective, which
     readers will recognize as deconstructionist.

14   **Ketchum, Anne Duhamel.** "Vers une Ecriture féminine?"
     La Revue du Pacifique 3, No. 1 (Spring 1977), 24-31.

     Claims that women possess no literary tradition that
     can attest to their specificity because most women
     writers accepted total submission to masculine values.
     Harshly criticizes current women writers who wallow in
     their misery, citing Benoîte Groult (Ainsi soit-elle) and
     Françoise Lefèvre (La Première habitude) as examples.
     Identifies three groups of women writers who are
     innovating: those associated with Simone de Beauvoir, of
     whom she mentions Christiane Rochefort, those in the
     publishing collective "des femmes," and the lesbian
     "gouines rouges." Approves the "negative function"
     Kristeva proposes for women--refusal of the status quo.
     Calls for the expression in writing of the "unconscious
     cry," the "feminine unconscious." Short and schematic.

15   **Makward, Christiane Perrin.** "La Critique féministe,
     éléments d'une problématique." Revue des sciences
     humaines (December 1977), 619-24.

     An essential, provocative discussion of the goals of a
     feminist literary criticism and of feminist criticism in
     general. Compares, in the first part, American and
     French perspectives on and approaches to a literary

criticism that "imposes women's point of view" (cites C.
Herrmann, les Voleuses de langue, 293) in order, finally,
to arouse awareness of the need for social change. Says
the differences between the two countries are both
material and intellectual: conditions in America, versus
France, foster the development of women's studies. And
methods have been almost antithetical: Americans first
amassed textual exegeses and then drew theories from that
material, while French feminists sought before textual
analysis to articulate the theoretical problems of
feminist thought. Sees the French approach as further
complicated by the "crisis of conscience" French literary
criticism in general is now experiencing and by splits
among various feminist strategies. In the second part,
exhorts French feminists to "unite (their reflective)
energies" and to "borrow (the specialized) tools" of
contemporary French thought in order to "bring the myth
of femininity to the collective (literary) conscience."
For written texts, suggests a variety of techniques
(stylistic, psychoanalytic, semiotic, sociological) for
exposing the mythical structures about sexuality which
all cultural discourse, including literature, transmits.
Also presents dangers and potential strengths of the
present search for a specifically "feminine writing."
Concludes by postulating that the current "explosion" of
the relationship between language and domination, when
utilized to show and contest the position of women in all
cultural and social domains, will ultimately render
"feminist criticism" obsolete.

16 ———— and Sylvie Weil. "Directions in French Women's
    Studies." Women in Print I: Opportunities for Women's
    Studies Research in Language and Literature. New York:
    MLA, 1982, 173-86.

Gives an overall picture of the status of French
women's studies by clarifying what work has been done
and, more particularly, remains to be done. Presents,
first, a few important library and publishing resources.
Then, traces the essential areas of the entire French
feminist critical enterprise, mentioning studies that
exist and those that are needed. The issues and areas
described are: (1) re-readings of the French literary
canon from the "gynocentric" point of view of "images of
women" and feminine archetypes; (2) a re-evaluation of
the French tradition of the "woman question"--the

"Querelle des femmes"--to recover and reassess lost or
under-appreciated women authors; (3) locating and making
available French women's correspondence, journals,
biographies and autobiographies, and other personal
documents; (4) a comprehensive assessment of French
feminist theoretical work to date and of literary
movements concerned with "writing in the feminine"; (5) a
breaking with certain of the "traditional values in
research and publication" (in France and the U.S.) that
have hampered efforts in women's studies and a developing
of "better communication strategies"; and (6) development
of useful and available pedagogical tools--e.g., cheap
monographs--to alleviate the current paucity and
inaccessibility of teaching materials for French women's
studies. Also highlights the major figures in French
feminism and the essence of their contributions to
literature and theory. Describes the current feminist
"literary front" in France as one of "sustained
creativity and theoretical quiet." A very helpful
overview.

17   ————. "Nouveau regard sur la critique féministe en
France." Revue de l'Université d'Ottawa/University of
Ottawa Quarterly 50, No. 1 (January-March 1980), 47-54.

Compares current French and American feminist
scholarship and approaches. Distinguishes between the
paucity of feminist literary exegeses in France and their
profusion in the U. S. Describes feminist criticism in
France as sociological, philosophical and psychoanalytical
"reflections," rather than applied studies. Contrasts
the American "behaviorist" approach to studying women's
linguistic comportment with the French exploration of
"internal" sexual differences. Goes on to explain the
French feminist concern with theorizing a "feminine writing" postulated on "the difference between a masculine
and feminine (not men's and women's) relationship to
writing" and on "psychic bisexuality." Says this theoretical inquiry into a "feminine language" has evolved
from first viewing it as "silence," as an "a-symbolic"
and "a-phallic" act of the body, to seeing it as a
positive, expressive "marking" or "inscription" of
femininity. Evokes the French discomfort with the term
"feminism" itself (versus America) as merely reformist
and modeled on "phallocratic" power definitions.
Elaborates on the "loving" exploration of the "feminine
principle" in writing being undertaken in France, one

that illuminates and valorizes the "lacks" ("manques")
and "incoherences" visible in women's texts (e.g., Duras,
Chawaf, Cixous). Says this exploration views "woman's
style" as one that rejects correct and "well-constructed"
forms in favor of "simultaneity" and "fluidity." Makes
the essential distinction between the conventional
biological use of the terms "masculine" and "feminine"
and their renewed sense in French feminist theory as
internalized "differences" affecting the imagination,
discursive practice, and writing. Advocates the dismantling of the entire univocal "theoretical machinery" in
place in our culture, rather than an insistence on and
fetishization of sexual difference per se. Predicts the
result would be a pluralization and a "liberation" of
languages. Also points up the wide divergence in France
and America in terms of university environments and
academic receptivity to women's studies, the U. S. being
much more open. Calls for continued and intensified
feminist research of all kinds. An excellent
introduction to current French feminist inquiry.

18   ————. "To Be or Not to Be...A Feminist Speaker." The
        Future of Difference. Ed. Hester Eisenstein and Alice
        Jardine. Boston: G. K. Hall, 1980, 95-105.

Describes current French feminist thought as a
"passionate vindication of difference" occurring through
the articulation of theory and the writing of literature
in the feminine. Sees this writing as a "celebration of
a feminine principle." Seeks in particular to point up
the contradictions within French theories of femininity
and practices of feminine writing: the danger of those
theories' reaffirming traditional essentialist views of
women; the difficult distinguishability between women's
and men's writing; and the problematics of a feminist
criticism, particularly the implications of the
discourses it uses. Pursues this last issue by
considering the split between two conceptions of women's
relation to language: women's speech ("parole de femmes")
and feminine writing ("écriture-au-féminin"). Says the
question of women's expression is now at an impasse
caused by the impossibility of its "saying itself"
outside masculine discourse, the same "impasse of
silence" at which psychoanalysis has arrived. Concludes
that such conflicts are "debates of pure form" and that
change will be accomplished more through understanding
"objective, factual differences due to sex" and affirming
the necessary coexistence of differences.

19   **Marks, Elaine** and Isabelle de Courtivron, eds. <u>New</u>
      <u>French Feminisms: An Anthology</u>. Amherst: University of
      Massachusetts Press, 1980.

      Introductions: 1. "Discourses of Anti-Feminism and
      Feminism" (20); 2. "Histories of France and of Feminism
      in France"; 3. "Contexts of the New French Feminisms"
      (21). "Beginnings": Simone de Beauvoir, "Introduction to
      <u>The Second Sex</u>" (1); "Demystifications": Françoise
      Parturier, "An Open Letter to Men"; Françoise d'Eaubonne,
      "Feminism or Death"; Benoîte Groult, "Night Porters";
      Dominique Poggi, "A Defense of the Master-Slave Relation-
      ship"; Annie Leclerc, "Woman's Word" (469); Claudine
      Herrmann, "The Virile System" (300); Hélène Cixous,
      "Sorties" (104); Luce Irigaray, "This Sex Which Is Not
      One" (316); Luce Irigaray, "When the Goods Get Together"
      (320); Marguerite Duras, "Smothered Creativity" (195);
      "Warnings": Antoinette Fouque, "Quoted in 'The MLF is
      you, is me'"; Denise le Dantec, "From an Interview";
      Maria-Antoinetta Macciocchi, "Feminine Sexuality in
      Fascist Ideology"; Arlette Laguiller, "From an Interview";
      Madeleine Vincent, "A Basic Fact of Our Time"; Catherine
      Clément, "Enslaved Enclave" (150); Julia Kristeva, "Woman
      Can Never Be Defined" (449); Simone de Beauvoir, "From an
      Interview" (39); "From an Interview" (38); Evelyne
      Sullerot, "The Feminine (Matter of) Fact"; "Creations":
      Xavière Gauthier, "Is There Such a Thing as Women's
      Writing?" (284); Julia Kristeva, "Oscillation between
      Power and Denial" (452); Claudine Herrmann, "Women in
      Space and Time" (295); Marguerite Duras, "From an
      Interview" (196); Chantal Chawaf, "Linguistic Flesh"
      (78); Madeleine Gagnon, "Body I" (256); Viviane Forrester,
      "What Women's Eyes See" (244); Christiane Rochefort, "Are
      Women Writers Still Monsters?" (517); "Manifestoes-
      Actions": "Women Arise/Debout les femmes!"; Manifesto of
      the 343"; Simone de Beauvoir, "Introduction to 'Les
      femmes s'entêtent'"; "Editions des femmes"; "Rape Is an
      Abuse of Power"; "The Women Prostitutes of Lyon Speak to
      the Population"; C. D., "For a Materialist Feminism"
      (186); Xavière Gauthier, "Why Witches?" (286); Nathalie
      Roncier and Claudie Landy, "After 48 Hours of Women's
      Films in La Rochelle"; "'Defense of Violette C.'"; Gisèle
      Halimi, "The Common Program for Women"; "Research on
      Women"; "Variations on Common Themes" (541); "Utopias":
      Simone de Beauvoir, "Liberation: The Independent Woman";
      Françoise Parturier, "An Open Letter to Men"; Françoise
      d'Eaubonne, "Feminism or Death"; Annie Leclerc, "The Love
      Letter" (472); Marguerite Duras, "From an Interview"

(196); Maria-Antonietta Macciocchi, "Feminine Sexuality
in Fascist Ideology"; Julia Kristeva, "Chinese Women
against the Tide" (406); Julia Kristeva, "About Chinese
Women" (372); Monique Wittig, "Les guérillères"; Suzanne
Horer and Jeanne Socquet, "Smothered Creativity" (302);
Hélène Cixous, "The Laugh of the Medusa" (102); Bio/
Bibliographies; Selected Bibliography of New French
Feminisms.

Probably the single most important publication for
English-speaking feminists who seek access to current
French feminist thought. Contains several excellent
introductions that trace the feminine and feminist
traditions in France and establish the contexts of current
French feminist inquiry. Comprises translations--whole
or partial--of the essential French texts representing
the various tendencies within contemporary feminist
activity in France.

20 _____ and Isabelle de Courtivron. "Introduction I:
Discourses of Anti-Feminism and Feminism." New French
Feminisms: An Anthology. Amherst: The University of
Massachusetts Press, 1980, 3-9.

Traces the principal historical shifts in the terms of
the feminist/anti-feminist debate in France from the
Middle Ages to The Second Sex (1949, 1). Posits
"discourse" ("the relation between language and the
object [social reality] to which it apparently refers")
as the key to understanding, critically, how women have
been written about. Says that while true "feminisms"--
those combining self-conscious written inquiry with
activist politics--appeared only after 1789, isolated
feminist writers, benefiting from the prestige historically accorded "the spoken and written word" in France,
had occasionally surfaced earlier. Claims, however, all
feminist texts prior to Beauvoir's The Second Sex have in
common a "defensive" stance: they all respond to the
anti-feminist views of their time in the same terms and
within the same ideological systems used by the original
misogynist text. Argues that Beauvoir was the first to
engage in an "analysis of process" whereby the ongoing,
structural relationship of women to all domains of life
could be illuminated.

21 _____ and Isabelle de Courtivron. "Introduction III:
Contexts of the New French Feminisms." New French

<u>Feminisms: An Anthology</u>. Amherst: The University of
Massachusetts Press, 1980, 28-38.

Characterizes French feminisms since <u>The Second Sex</u>
(1), beginning with a brief historical description of the
"reformist" efforts (through 1968), which sought and won
certain concrete goals for women, and then focusing at
length on the post-1968 "New French Feminisms." Says
that, rather than a continuation of earlier movements,
the new "radical" feminisms are rooted in both the
general social unrest and the analytical "structuralist
vision" that emerged in the 1960's in France. Also
outlines the important and varied radical feminist
tendencies, from the highly intellectual "politique et
psychanalyse," to the separatist "Féministes révolutionnaires," to Beauvoir's watchdog "Ligue du droit des
femmes"; also describes important feminist publications.
Claims the essential difference between French and
American feminists is that the French are "more convinced
than their American counterparts of the difference
between male and female; they are more imbued with
notions of sexual specificity." As a result, French
feminist critiques are more pointed and profound. Says
that, plus the general prestige of "the French word in
French culture," suggests these critiques will have
far-reaching repercussions.

22   _____. "Women and Literature in France." <u>Signs</u> 3,
No. 4 (Summer, 1978), 832-842.

Summarizes in eminently readable form the theoretical
perspectives that inform avant-garde feminist inquiry in
France: "linguistic and structuralist theory, Marxian
culture, psychoanalytic theory, and deconstruction
strategies." Situates major writers and theoreticians,
compares French and American critical modes, and provides
a wealth of information on important women and texts in
numerous footnotes. An excellent article.

23 **Miller, Nancy K.** "The Text's Heroine: A Feminist Critic
and Her Fictions." <u>Diacritics</u> 12, No. 2 (Summer 1982),
48-53.

A response to Peggy Kamuf's "Replacing Feminist
Criticism" (13) that, without denying the value of
French-inspired deconstructionist strategies, defends
"American" feminist critics' concern with the sexual

identity of authors on ethical and political grounds.
Contends that indifference to gender "is one of the
masks...behind which phallocentrism hides its fictions,"
for only men can discount sexual identity without
"reauthorizing their oblivion." Asserts that feminist
criticism focused on women as speaking subjects does
"concretely challenge the confidence of humanistic
discourse as universality." Finally, calls for a
"decentered vision but a centered action."

24   **Schwartz, Danielle.** "Les Femmes et l'écriture."
      La Nouvelle Critique 116 (August-September 1978), 18-23.

An interrogation of the relation of women to writing
using French feminist inquiry to frame her reflections.
Focuses on the relation of language and the (sexually
specific) body. Aims to identify as many contradictions
and raise as many questions as possible. Does provide a
large repertory. Somewhat schematic.

25   **Showalter, Elaine.** "Feminist Criticism in the Wilder-
      ness." Critical Inquiry 8, No. 2 (Winter 1981),
      179-206.

An overview of the state of feminist criticism that
distinguishes between theoretical and antitheoretical
modes and between approaches that address the feminist
reader ("feminist critique") and those that focus on the
woman writer ("gynocritics"). Argues for a feminist
criticism based on its own subjects and voice--including
investigations of women's writing and definitions of the
feminine. Credits European feminist thought, and
specifically French inquiry into "l'écriture féminine,"
with stressing sexual difference and with reasserting
positively (rather than justifying negatively) the
feminine. Goes on to explore four models of sexual
difference--biological, linguistic, psychoanalytic and
cultural--to show their advantages and limitations for
defining women's writing. Refers to the centrality of
language in particular for French feminist theory. Sees
a culturally-based theory of women's specificity as the
most comprehensive, incorporating the other three
models. Ends with the claim that women writing are
"inside two traditions simultaneously" (the female and
the male) and that the specificity of feminine writing
will emerge from a dual analysis of women's relationship
to both these traditions.

25a   Reprinted in <u>Writing and Sexual Difference</u>. Ed.
        Elizabeth Abel. Chicago: The University of Chicago
        Press, 1980-82, 9-35.

26   **Slama, Béatrice.** "De la 'littérature féminine' à
        'l'écrire-femme.'" <u>Littérature</u> 11, No. 44 (December
        1981), 51-71.

        A discussion of "l'écriture féminine": its history,
        characteristics, pitfalls, and potential. Begins by
        situating "écriture féminine" in relation to the
        tradition of women's literature, particularly as
        manifested in the first half of the twentieth century.
        Criticizes current proponents of "écriture féminine" for
        lacking an appreciation of their predecessors' invaluable
        contributions. Points out the strong influence of many
        male theorists of modernity in the shaping of feminist
        perspectives on writing and warns against the danger of
        conformity. Sees "écriture féminine" as both a "romantic
        illusion" and the herald of profound changes in the
        condition of women. Views the focus on difference as
        ghettoizing and finds the fight for equality more
        subversive. Cautions that the mass media's interest and
        the proliferation of special "collections femmes" are
        operating to disempower women's writing by absorbing it
        into the literary establishment. Clear and informative.

27   **Spivak, Gayatri Chakravorty.** "French Feminism in an
        International Frame." <u>Yale French Studies</u> No. 62
        (1981), 154-84.

        Examines the benefits and limitations of all forms of
        feminist activity, theoretical and political (academic
        and material), from a trans-cultural perspective
        comprising "First-World" and "Third-World" women.
        Connects that multiple viewpoint to Spivak's own
        multi-cultural background. Meanders through personal and
        societal issues about women, outlining the strengths and
        highlighting the weaknesses of various approaches to
        understanding and solving them. Is framed brilliantly by
        the problem of clitoridectomy, presented, first, as the
        literal mutilation many Third-World women suffer and
        opened, at the end, to its metaphorical implications as a
        "metonym" for the cultural "excision" of women and female
        sexuality. Uses this framework to pose the many
        epistemological questions feminists face--questions it
        elaborates on at length--in trying to change social,
        linguistic, political and economic structures. Raises

questions about "what the constituency of an international feminism" is; how the academic feminist can "speak
to" and "listen to" non-privileged women of other
cultures and classes; who the researcher ("subject") is;
who the "object" (woman) of her study is; and how, if
possible, the scholar/feminist can acknowledge and
perhaps use the "East"/"West" dialectic that inevitably
informs our very way of thinking. Goes on to address
these questions by looking at the ways specific French
feminist theoreticians have viewed women and articulated
the feminine: first, reads and critiques Kristeva's Des
Chinoises (372) as "obsessively self-centered" and as
displaying a "colonialist benevolence" in its method of
exploring the East; then, examines the search for a
feminine discourse undertaken by Cixous (102 and 104) as
potentially more useful for approaching an international
feminism. Backs up to situate the problematics of a
feminine discourse within the post-1968 "anti-humanist"
trend in French philosophy (Derrida, Lyotard) and within
the French psychoanalytic reevaluation of Freud (Lacan,
Irigaray, Kofman--see 314 and 352). Evokes the
"anti-feminist" strains in all contemporary feminist
theories. Advocates a two-pronged struggle for women:
"against sexism, where women unite as a biologically
oppressed caste; and for feminism, where human beings
train to prepare for a transformation of consciousness."
Recommends this struggle, in the academic arena, take the
form of politicized and critical "symptomatic readings"
of texts, readings that continually raise questions--
however unanswerable--rather than answer them. Concludes
with the clitoridectomy issue, now expanded and deepened
by a consideration of female sexuality and pleasure: says
feminism must acknowledge and deal with not just the
objectification of woman-as-reproducer (as a socially
essential "uterus"), but also woman-as-agent (as asserter
of her heretofore denied "clitoral" pleasure). Favors
this "heterogeneous sex-analysis" as one that would
"disclose...the repression of the clitoris in the general
or the narrow sense...by both patriarchy and family." An
extremely convoluted, complex and rich essay that weaves
in and out of layers of context, but that also digresses
a good deal.

28   **Stanton, Domna C.** "Language and Revolution: The Franco-
      American Dis-Connection." The Future of Difference.
      Ed. Hester Eisenstein and Alice Jardine. Boston: G. K.
      Hall, 1980, 73-87.

A fine overview of the various French feminist
perspectives on sexual difference that also shows the
points of contrast and connection between American and
French views. Posits that all the French thinkers
believe women's critique must focus on the "Logos," or
the entire system of language, thought and meaning that
is the foundation of our world. Summarizes the particular projects of the major French women: Irigaray's
shattering of the "old dream of symmetry" that has
repressed the feminine and her exploration of the new
"wonderland" of female sexuality and expression;
Kristeva's "deconstruction" of the Western concept of the
subject as having a unified identity and her advocating
the assertion of "negativity" (dissidence from all
quarters) to challenge the Logos; Cixous's insistence on
the revolutionary power of "l'écriture féminine," claiming
women's writing their sexuality will reshape the world.
Explains the shared attention paid by French thinkers to
the unconscious as locus of sexual difference. Examines
the problematic relationship between French and American
feminist scholars, criticizing the latter for resisting
the vital contributions of the former and urging them to
"tap into" French inquiry into language and the
unconscious. Also says, however, that French thinkers
should listen to the criticisms of American women. Ends
with a call for fruitful transatlantic exchange that will
point up the fundamental similarity between the two
sides: the common belief in the "connections between
language and revolution." Very helpful.

29   ———. "Parole et écriture: Women's Studies, USA." Tel
        Quel 71/73 (Fall 1977), 119-35.

Gives a sobering account of the nature and practice of
academic Women's Studies in the U. S., from the point of
view of one woman assuming her "voice," as feminists in
general are doing. Evokes the deeper obstacles American
Women's Studies faces, despite apparently encouraging
statistics for programs and courses: marginalization,
cooptation and lack of influence on the traditional
curriculum; trivialization or neutralization; student
fear; and scholarly dismissal. Also describes the
project of feminist criticism in the U. S., its creation
of a considerable written corpus, its quest for new
methodologies, and its transgression of disciplinary
boundaries. Evokes the dilemma of the feminist critic in
the face of either rejecting or perpetuating the
discourse and instruments of traditional (masculine)

criticism. Looks at American and French feminist views
of Freud, particularly in regard to sexual difference and
bisexuality. Stanton herself opts for pursuing the
concept of bisexuality, or what she calls "gyandry," in
order to recognize a positive female principle. Ends
with a brief comparison of French versus American
feminist critiques of language--the American being more
empirical, the French more theoretical--and a call to
women to write their own words.

* **Weil, Sylvie** and Christiane P. Makward. "Directions in
   French Women's Studies." Women in Print I:
   Opportunities for Women's Studies Research in Language
   and Literature. New York: MLA, 1982, 173-86.

   (See 16).

PART II

FRENCH AND FRANCOPHONE VOICES

30   **Allen, Suzanne.** L'espace d'un livre. Paris: Gallimard,
      1971.

An allegorical novel and meditation on writing told by
a woman writing about a woman who is writing about a
woman. Conveys an eroticization of the act of writing in
which spatial parallels are made between the body and the
written word. Also brings up love as primary theme both
to distinguish men's and women's experiences of love and
to connect love with writing. Evokes pleasure as the
principal source of imaginative activity. Concludes, "In
the same way that in love language stirs up refinements
of desire, so, in the fatal text ("le texte mortel"),
every word plays with its lack ("joue de son manque"),
and all otherness slips away from writing (that is) never
satisfied...fatal passion." Hard to enter into.

31   ————. "Plus oultre." Revue des sciences humaines No.
      168 (1977), 503-515.

Analyzes the discourse of sex--specifically, of women's
sexual pleasure--in our culture to show how it incorrectly
and inadequately expresses women's experience. Takes as
its approach the connection between body and symbolization, or between women's anatomy and the language that
purports to evoke it and its responses. Starts with a
critique of modern studies that describe women's orgasm,
saying they reduce the complexity, variety and individual-
ity of that experience (e.g., they ignore responses in
the uterus and the pelvis and insist on the vagina only).
Makes parallels with the etymological history of the word
"uterus" as one in which the word's multiplicity of
meanings has been reduced and rendered uniform--as have
notions of women's sexual pleasure. Demonstrates how all
reference to the autonomy, activity and "elasticity" of
female erogenous sites has been lost and absorbed into
monolithic, phallus-centered definitions springing from
the masculine imagination (e.g., women's organs described
as serving only to "envelope" or "take in" the penis).
Explains the binary or oppositional structure of masculine
logic and language and the consequent reduction of
feminine sexuality in the symbolic domain to "mutism" and
negativity. Calls on women to discover their own
"signifiers/bodies," in all their "fantasmic" diversity.
Dense but highly suggestive.

32   **Alphant, Marianne.** "Ranger, déranger." Sorcières 12
      (1978), 46-47.

Says women, "strangers" to the transcendent contemplation that is theory, have on occasion turned to writing--
not the kind that fills blank spaces, but rather that
maintains them. Calls this a vital "space of uncertainty"
from which a different kind of theory--non-generalizing,
non-"totalizing"--can emerge.

33   **Aubenas, Jacqueline.** "Abécédaire quotidien et tout en
     désordre." Les Cahiers du GRIF 12 (June 1976), 14-17.

     A brief catalogue of the language of women's daily
     lives. Lists words and expressions from their
     sociological reality to show their linguistic place in
     the world.

34   **Baliteau, Catherine.** "La fin d'une parade misogyne:
     la psychanalyse lacanienne." Les Temps modernes (July
     1975), 1933-1953.

     Critiques psychoanalysis on the grounds that, despite
     its theoretical intention to subvert traditional Western
     metaphysics, it is in fact rooted in the same moral
     criteria that underlie metaphysics. Puts this
     contradiction another way: within psychoanalysis coexist
     both "the refusal of a moralizing psychology and a search
     for responsible parties." Pushes this critique further
     to say that the guilty party analysis locates is usually
     female. Summarizes Lacanian theory of child development
     to show its privileging of "the phallic referent," of
     "the intervention of the (symbolic) Father," in the
     "normal" growth process and its blaming of the Mother
     only for psychotic development. Uses the works of
     Françoise Dolto and Maud Mannoni to illustrate this
     imbalance. Says psychoanalysis's privileging of the
     Father is based on the Lacanian conception of the
     structure of the unconscious and of language: the
     "paternal signifier" is the transcendent norm, the
     "foundation of meaning," and thus a "theology" or
     patriarchal "moralizing viewpoint" is introduced.
     Concludes that Lacanian psychoanalysis serves ultimately
     to reinforce sexist ideology through a regressive
     exculpation of the Father and condemnation of the
     Mother. Lucid and persuasive.

35   **Bartkowski, Frances.** "Feminism and deconstruction: 'a
     union forever deferred.'" Enclitic 4, No. 2 (Fall
     1980), 70-77.

Advises feminist critics attracted to deconstruction to
be wary of its latent essentialism. Suggests that
Irigaray and Cixous have avoided theorizing and thus
fixing the other, but that Derrida has not. In his work
("La Double séance" and Spurs) the feminine as metaphor
for the unnameable, the undecidable, still serves
phallocentric mastery.

Beauvoir, Simone de:

BOOKS AND COLLECTIONS OF ESSAYS

*   ────. Le Deuxième sexe. 2 vols. Paris: Gallimard,
        1949.

(See 1).

INTERVIEWS WITH

36   Jardine, Alice. "Interview with Simone de Beauvoir."
        Signs 5, No. 2 (Winter 1979), 224-36

Presents Beauvoir's position on several controversial
feminist issues, including the importance of psychoanalysis, the existence of a "feminine writing," and the
question of human subjectivity. First, rejects Freud and
Lacan as anti-feminists. Then, criticizes attempts at
"feminine writing" (e.g., Cixous) for being inaccessible
and false. Advocates women's use of language as a
"universal" weapon against male domination but not as a
means of reasserting a specifically feminine "nature."
Finally, agrees that women's writing is marked by their
"sensibility," since gender is part of the writer's
subjectivity.

37   Patterson, Yolanda. "Entretien avec Simone de Beauvoir."
        The French Review 52, No. 5 (April 1979), 745-54.

Beauvoir compares autobiography with fiction, expressing
a preference for the former, but acknowledging that the
latter allows one to address issues beyond one's own
life. Recounts and assesses women's political struggle
in France.

38   Schwarzer, Alice. "Entretien avec Simone de Beauvoir."
        Marie-Claire (October 1976).

Repeats a few essential ideas from The Second Sex (1):
that there is no "eternal feminine," that "woman" is a
social construct, and that sexuality as it has been
ascribed to women is a "trap" that makes them dependent
on men.

38a   Partially trans. in (19).

39   ———. "Interview with Simone de Beauvoir." Ms. (July
        1972).

Traces the course of Beauvoir's feminist engagement,
beginning with her involvement with the MLF (Mouvement
pour la libération des femmes), Soviet women, and women
in socialist societies. Describes her loss of faith in
the "revolution" of 1968 and in the possibility of a
complete revolution in general.

39a   Partially reprinted in (19).

40   **Bédard, Nicole.** "L'Oscillé(e)." La Barre du jour
      No. 50 (Winter 1975), 105-122.

A reading of Hélène Cixous's story, "Un vrai jardin,"
that also points to Cixous's text as an example of "the
feminine of writing." This writing is the "bringing into
play of a body that is writing itself...the refusal of
all in writing which is finite, definite, fixed and
immobile." Uses a vocabulary of female sexuality to
evoke women's writing as "an affirmation of the bisexual"
and of "orgasm/pleasure" ("jouissance").

41   **Bloch, Michelle.** "La Femme et la Création." Pénélope
      No. 3 (Fall 1980), 51-53.

Recounts the obstacles women writers encounter during
the entire writing process, from doubt and difficulty in
"seizing" words, to uncertainty about the viability of
their work, to a hostile critical reception.

42   **Boucher, Denise** and Madeleine Gagnon. Retailles: Com-
      plaintes politiques. Montreal: l'Etincelle, 1977.

Reproduces the "subjective fictions" written by a
Quebecois women's collective in order not only to fight
women's silence, but also to present an example of texts

which, by their being "passionate" and uncensored "risks,"
will ultimately transform politics as well as writing.
This transformation, in which women will cease being
"object" and become "the subject of a new history/story
of sharing between men and women," will signal the end of
traditional power relationships. The collective's own
unfortunate internal evolution from a concern with
"affective affinities" to a reproduction of the very
power configurations it had condemned--this evolution
marks the texts themselves--gives authenticity to its
call for poetic and political change. Reveals Boucher's
and Gagnon's somewhat angry heterosexist bias at the
time.

43   **Boucquey, Eliane.** "Choisir ou créer." Les Cahiers du
      GRIF 7 (June 1975), 10-21.

      Examines the role of women as a group in our culture as
      one of the base "supports" (c.f., oppressed races and
      classes) of the male-dominated social hierarchy. Desig-
      nates as the organizing principles of our culture (1)
      "choice" of one term or group at the expense or "death"
      of the other; (2) "hierarchy" or a pyramidal power
      structure in which the ruling authority offers "balms" to
      calm and appease its "victims"; and (3) "sub-cultures" or
      means of adaptation to the superior order adopted by the
      subordinated groups. Elaborates on women's "sub-culture,"
      the domestic world to which they are relegated and which
      they need to uphold, at the cost of self-contempt.
      Describes the options women have chosen until now as
      either quiet acceptance or identification with and
      aspiration toward the so-called "neutral" dominant
      caste. Says there is a third choice: "refuse to be
      confined to one or the other of these camps" and opt for
      "lucidity."

44   **Boukobza-Hajlblum, Claude.** "Retrait." Sorcières 7
      (1977), 47-48.

      Evokes the act of writing in terms of the child's
      psycho-sexual drama. Calls the maternal body the "womb
      of writing" with which females and males have different
      relations--the woman's being a constant movement between
      "cutting" or separation and identification. Says this
      experience marks women's writing. Difficult.

Brossard, Nicole:

BOOKS AND COLLECTIONS OF ESSAYS

45   ————. <u>Un livre</u>. Montreal: Editions du Jour, 1970.

   Is representative of Brossard's early critique of
   conventional fictional forms as insufficient to express
   human experience. Self-consciously describes its own
   writing process as its story unfolds. Suggests that the
   variability and vitality of life--which includes women's
   realities--are more closely (though still frustratingly)
   rendered by textual spaces and discontinuities.

   45a   Trans. as <u>A Book</u>. Toronto: The Coach House Press,
          1976.

ESSAYS AND ARTICLES

46   ————. "Allocution d'ouverture." <u>Liberté</u> Nos. 106-107
      (July-October 1976), 10-13.

   Introductory remarks for the "Rencontre québécoise
   internationale des écrivains." States that the essential
   question regarding women and writing is that of "difference," but not as defined in the old "phallocentric"
   way. What has been different for women and men is the
   right to "make their bodies speak": women's bodies,
   always "censored" and "suffocating beneath the law,
   order, and hierarchy," must free themselves and express
   "that which is effeminate," the non-linear "disordering
   of linguistic conventions." Claims the question of the
   nature of feminine writing is premature and essentially
   false. For now, it is important that women write and
   speak their as yet "unedited literature"; later, they
   will "infiltrate and sabotage language" through their
   fictions.

47   ————. "Ça fait jaser." <u>Sorcières</u> 14 (1978), 23-24.

   Gives definitions of the word "jaser" (to talk or to
   blab) in the sense of its having special importance for
   women and for the Quebecois in particular. The word is
   "typical" rather than "universal" and means for Quebecois
   women: "to sustain one another," "to nourish one another,"
   "to keep one another alive." Women's "yacking" will
   "make the world <u>around them</u> yack."

48 ————. "Champ d'action pour figures inédites." Masculin
grammaticale in Mécanique jongleuse, suivi de Masculin
grammaticale. Ottawa: l'Hexagone, 1974, 73-85.

Evokes, in telegraphic form, women's relationship to
language or the "codes" in place, saying women must
"exorcise" their memories in order to communicate their
"new perceptions" and knowledge. Says women's memory
will generate a new code marked by their sexual
difference and that this new writing will expand the
boundaries of signification and redefine "imagination."

49 ————. "Le Cortex exubérant." La Barre du jour
No. 44 (Spring 1974), 20-22.

Unreadable in the conventional logical and continuous
way, evokes the issue of writing and women in a
thoroughly mimetic and self-conscious text. Demonstrates,
rather than defines or explains, the new and unspoken
languages of "invisible humanity" that must be expressed.
Uses associational movement, elliptical sentences, puns,
visual devices, and surprising images in a text that is
itself emblematic of what the phallocentric writing and
language of Western culture do not tolerate: the exploding
and enlarging of the limits of discourse; the multiplication of meaning and of symbolic relationships; the non-
literal; the playful; and the questioning of received
logical and psychological "truths." Uses, cites and
undermines some of the psychoanalytic and philosophical
theories prevalent in French critical thought. Continuously evokes the writing it itself is doing in images--
some of which, individually, are stunning--suggesting
women's bodies and intimacy with the self. The title's
image--that of the body's "unfolding" itself, of the
"cortex"'s releasing itself "without constraint"--
describes this new and uncensored relationship to writing
and discourse. Also, keeps undermining its own statements
and purposes by questioning what has preceded: "Do not
become an historical anecdote," that is, do not become
the fixed and dead writing it (the text) is trying to
subvert. Ends with an acknowledgment of the ultimate
contradiction inherent in writing a piece such as this
even while critiquing such texts. Though completely
resistant and virtually inaccessible, succeeds in
disrupting and disturbing traditional reader expectations
and, at its best, shows an unshakable intellectual and
creative integrity.

50   ————. "E muet mutant." La Barre du jour No. 50
        (Winter 1975), 10-27.

Describes and at the same time demonstrates women's
writing that will "assume itself" as an autonomous act in
which "woman becomes subject." Uses sexual metaphors in
its three-part evocation of what women's texts will be:
first, calls women's writing a "Transgression" which puts
the "master"'s thought and reason into question and which
"traces the censored (female) body"; second, argues for
undoing the false and reductive opposition between
fiction and reality; finally, asks women to embark on a
practice of writing that "opens the lesion" and frees
female desire, thus transcending writing as an act of
possession and power. Elliptical and fragmented, but
mimetically suggestive.

51   ————. "L'épreuve de la modernité ou/et les preuves
        de la modernité." La Nouvelle barre du jour Nos. 90-91
        (May 1980), 55-63.

Meditates on writing and modernity, specifically the
"intolerable" situation of the modern author whose need
to write encounters existential obstacles. Interrogates
the problem of cooptation or neutralization of poetic
writing by convention, ideology, and literary theory.
Includes the "feminine" among the disruptive textual
"effects" manifested in modern literature. Difficult.

52   ————. "Extrait." Journal of Canadian Fiction 25-26
        (1979), 26-30.

A poetic meditation on writing, which Brossard alludes
to as an "enigma," a puzzling passage from "prose to
anecdote" and from "the holes of memory" to narrative
"certainty." Evokes her female characters, whose lives
she renders imaginatively. Describes women's writings as
moving in a spiral, in repeated rhythms of "births and
rebirths" that open to the "totally new" ("l'inédit").

53   ————. "Mais voici venir la fiction ou l'épreuve au
        féminin." La Nouvelle barre du jour Nos. 90-91 (May
        1980), 64-68.

Claims women are now writing with the awareness that
they are women—in body, memory and anecdote. Questions
how women can write, given that the symbolic "place" is

occupied by men: says women will write outside of the
masculine discourse that has "neutralized" them. Calls
this new feminine imagination a "sixth sense," one of
"deviation" ("dérive") from patriarchal notions of
reality and meaning.

54   ——————. "Naissance et dispersion du désir." Liberté
        14 (1972), 20-23.

Describes, self-consciously, Brossard's sense of her
own writing: a playful "wandering" that is, ultimately,
an "intervention into the collective language." Uses
Derridean concepts of writing as a dynamic, continuously
generating and generated process, one that also often
"detours" and "transgresses" appropriate syntax and
vocabulary. Also defines literature in spatial terms, as
a "terrain" in and upon which the writer's verbal
"intervention" brings about change and redefinition of
the "geography." Suggestive but a bit hard to follow.

55   ——————. and France Théoret. "Préface." La Nef des
        sorcières. Montreal: Quinze, 1976, 7-13.

Introduces this feminist fiction-manifesto, originally
a play composed of six monologues and performed in
Montreal in 1976. Stresses that these "women's words"
allow the maternal language--the private murmurings that
mediate between physical bodies and between private and
public--to take form. Notes that not all of the six
pieces written by different women are new at the level of
"écriture," but that their content and coexistence in one
work are new.

56   ——————. "Préliminaires." La Barre du jour No. 50
        (Winter 1975), 6-9.

Poses questions that introduce this special issue on
Quebecois women's relationship to language and literature.
Outlines areas in women's writing that must be explored:
feminine desire, feminine space, and feminine writing
strategies that use and explode the "phallocentric
language" that works against women. Addresses the
situation of Canadian women, but also of women in general.

57   ——————. "Séance inaugurale." Revue de l'Université
        d'Ottawa/University of Ottawa Quarterly 50, No. 1
        (January-March 1980), 7-8.

Introduces the Conference of Women Writers in America
by predicting that an array of approaches to feminine
reading and writing would be put forth during the
meeting, all of which would nonetheless be part of a
shared uncovering of woman's identity. Says women's
writing permits them to identify with one another,
through the circulation of words and energy.

58   ———. "Si je jouis." Sorcières 7 (1977), 46.

Describes how she writes as "with a woman's gaze
resting on me." Calls women "illiterates of desire" who,
when they "know how to read on the body of other
(women)," can experience the pleasure of writing. Hard
but suggestive.

59   ———, France Théoret, Madeleine Gagnon, et al. "Tables
rondes." Revue de l'Université d'Ottawa/University of
Ottawa Quarterly 50, No. 1 (January–March 1980), 9–29.

Proceedings from the Conférence des femmes–écrivains en
Amérique: I. "Existe-t-il une voix féminine en
littérature?" II. "Femmes écrivains et société"; III.
"Les femmes et la tradition théâtrale"; IV. "La poésie en
tant que moyen de communication dans les oeuvres des
femmes poètes"; V. "Tradition féminine en littérature."
A discussion among various Quebecois women writers,
playwrights, and poets that addresses issues about women
and literature. Specific questions and respondents are
as follows:
"Existe-t-il une voix féminine en littérature?" In "De
nos fictions," Nicole Brossard speaks of her "fiction"––a
combination of "the body, thought, imagination, and
history"––as the expression of a new and disturbing
reality. Says all women's fictions are "political" in
that they shake up "the masculine (notion) of neutral"
literature. In "Y a-t-il une voix spécifiquement
féminine en littérature?" France Théoret expresses
suspicion about a "women's writing" as a new mythifica-
tion and "ossification" of thought. Describes the dual
nature of writing––as true and false, ideological and
real––for any author, though subscribes to the belief
that the unconscious, and therefore one's relation to
language, is "sexualized."
"Femmes écrivains et société." In "Femmes écrivains et
société," Janou Saint-Denis contests all cultural
constraints on creative energy, the primacy of rational

discourse, the power of the publishing establishment, and myths of women.

"Les femmes et la tradition théâtrale." In "La femme et la tradition théâtrale," Monique Bosco urges women to "invent," to "liberate" theater through new forms and expressions of their "desire." Explains that the absence of women playwrights in the past was due to theater's being "the site of their (women's) desire," and thus denied them. Then, France Théoret recounts her own participation in the production of a play and lists Quebecois women playwrights. Says, "Women are always on show" ("en représentation").

"La poésie en tant que moyen de communication dans les oeuvres des femmes poètes." Denise Boucher evokes her own coming to poetry and the traditional political importance of the poet. Suzanne Paradis explains her search "for a poetry," for a "clearer and more complete knowledge of reality" and calls poetry itself a "magic space" in which sexual difference diminishes.

"Tradition féminine en littérature." Louky Bersianik, while tracing the masculine traditions with which she had been raised, talks of her inability to assume a masculine "procreativity" when writing. Says that there is no feminine heritage in literature, but that at the same time there is the "terrible" feminine tradition of self-denial, the one from which she had to break free. Ends with a critique of current literary criticism that "flattens" and kills works and a call for a new criticism which would "let (the text's) light pass through." Madeleine Gagnon states firmly that "there is no feminine tradition in literature" because historically there has been no ongoing feminine relation to discourse, but rather a "non-tradition" of silence. Decries the "exclusion"-- external and self-imposed--of women's words and the price women who did write often paid: madness and loneliness. Calls for a new language from "the space of (women's) corporal movements," the recovering of French and Quebecois literary foremothers, and the "de-construction" of masculine projections of the feminine.

60 ⸻. "La Tête qu'elle fait." La Barre du jour, Nos. 56-57 (May-August 1977), 83-92.

Expresses, explicitly, the desire to "see women's (written and spoken) form organize itself," to see women "politically ready" to affirm themselves through writing.

Uses images of the body to describe this task, in
particular achieving "the look on her (woman's) face"
("la tête qu'elle fait") that will mean she/woman has
realized new imaginative expression--the "body put into
words." Fragmented but very effective in parts.

61   ——. "Tiret." La Barre du jour No. 31 (Winter 1972),
        No. 2-4.

Introduces a special issue on the Quebecois militant
journal, Parti Pris, which had just ceased publication.
Attempts to assess the situation of Quebecois intellectuals in light of the socio-political role that journal
had played: says they are in a period of wait between
years of extensive theoretical elaboration of Quebecois
"alienation" and the urgent need for action to create an
autonomous Quebecois society.

62   ——. "Vaseline." La Barre du jour No. 42 (Fall 1973),
        11-17.

Justifies and exemplifies writing that is a "transgression" of the mechanical and stultifying forms of
expression that are in place. Says transgressing
stretches one's knowledge, brings pleasure, and ultimately
performs a moral act of opposition to social control.
Describes the playfulness and movement of this gesture
that embraces contradiction and produces sensory
impressions.

63   ——. "La Vie privée est politique." Les Têtes de
        pioche 2 (April 1976), 1-2.

Counters the traditional division between "private vs.
public," "personal vs. political" relationships which is
based solely on the male/virile model of the role of the
body. That male model is responsible for the dominant
symbolic values called "power" and "love," which in fact
correspond to masculine "hardening" (brings both pleasure
and destruction) and "repression" (implies that only
masculine forms of release are acceptable). Women must
express the "scandal" of their lives publicly. The
"history of the body"--so-called "private life"--is
precisely that "unwritten" history which women have
maintained (through birth, health care and sex) and
which, for women, has always functioned in the "outside
world" as well. It is time to put an end to the "virile

machination of power" which makes men and women into
marionnettes.

INTERVIEWS WITH

64   Bayard, Caroline.   "Entrevue."   Les Lettres québécoises 4
     (November 1976), 34-37.

     Raises some of Brossard's general ideas about the
     process and function of writing.   Says that fiction
     always manifests "a dissatisfaction with those relations
     we engage in with patriarchal, hyperproductive society"
     and that social change is possible only through effective
     modification of expressive forms.   Says women must impose
     themselves as the referent and not write in reaction to
     dominant masculine forms.

65   Fisette, Jean and Michel van Schendel.   "Un livre à venir:
     Rencontre (et Entrevue) avec Brossard."   Voix et Images
     3 (1977-78), 3-18.

     Traces Brossard's works, saying she has come to
     understand that "one can speak of pleasure only if one
     experiences pleasure in writing."   Evokes Brossard's
     works as highly self-conscious: her analytic self is
     always watching her "narrative" self write or, put
     another way, there is a dialectic between the pleasure of
     writing and the force of social conditioning that
     intervenes.   Refuses the traditional distinction between
     "poetry" and "fiction."   Also elaborates on the associa-
     tion between body and text for Brossard: "I am a being
     with desires, and therefore a being of words."   Shows
     Brossard's ideas on "l'écriture féminine": she believes
     that men, by social conditioning, are more able than
     women to "affirm themselves as subject" but refuses the
     idea that women possess a sex-specific relationship to
     pleasure ("jouissance") when writing.

66   Roy, André.   "La Fiction vive: Entretien avec Nicole
     Brossard sur sa prose."   Journal of Canadian Fiction
     25-26 (1979), 31-40.

     A discussion of Brossard's prose works, which she
     describes as attempts to "undo conditioned ways of
     writing and reading," as contestations of bourgeois
     novelistic conventions.   Talks about "women's writing" as
     having two dimensions: that of the interpenetration of

fiction with reality, and that of a certain "angle of
vision" that gives rise to a specifically feminine
content and form. Speaks of her own experience of
"writing her body" as an expenditure of "energy."
Expresses her preference for American feminist approaches
over French "psychoanalyzing" ones.

* Schendel, Michel van and Jean Fisette. "Un livre à venir:
  Rencontre (et Entrevue) avec Brossard." Voix et Images
  3 (1977-78), 3-18.

  (See 65).

ESSAYS AND ARTICLES ABOUT

67 Bayard, Caroline. "Nicole Brossard et l'utopie du
    langage." Revue de l'Université d'Ottawa/University of
    Ottawa Quarterly 50, No. 1 (January-March 1980), 82-88.

    Examines Nicole Brossard's work to see if and how it
    represents a "utopia of language," as per Roland
    Barthes's definition of a writing that breaks with
    linguistic moulds to produce a new discourse. Sees
    chronologically in Brossard's work, first, a rupture with
    previous models, then the "coming" of a new language.
    Traces the evidence of "subversion" in her earlier novels
    and poems, whose common premise is that fiction precedes
    and permits reality, not vice-versa. Says these
    "unsubordinated" texts point to a new writing to come,
    one more collective in scope and socio-historical in
    reference.

68 Duranleau, Irène. "Le texte moderne et Nicole Brossard."
    Etudes littéraires 14, No. 1 (April 1981), 105-21.

    Situates Nicole Brossard's work in the contexts of the
    evolution of fiction in general and the evolution of the
    Quebecois novel in particular. Summarizes, in the first
    section, the changes the French novel has undergone in
    moving from the Balzacian classical narrative to the new
    novel's "discursive" experiments with voice and order to
    contemporary avant-garde "textual" constructions. Says
    Quebecois fiction, though still primarily classical,
    evinces some works that displace traditional narrative
    concerns, including those of Brossard. Using the
    theories of Jean Ricardou, describes how each of
    Brossard's novels "translates its own textuality," that

is, affirms a theory of writing at the same time as it
generates itself. Says her works display "intersections"
of different processes of signification, thus allowing
multiple readings. Studies Un livre (45), Sold-Out,
French Kiss, and L'amer as "games" of "the subversion of
meaning" that function on the level of textuality, that
demystify reading, and that contest the dominant
ideology. Good overview.

69   Kravetz, Marc. "Nicole Brossard: Une revue, des livres,
      un journal." Magazine littéraire No. 134 (March 1978),
      98-99.

      A very brief account of Brossard's involvement with
      several Quebecois journals. Describes the origin and
      project of the feminist journal, La Barre du jour, as
      that of being a place for the practice of writing and
      creative thought. Hypothesizes that women are relatively
      more visible as writers in Quebecois literature than in
      other literatures because Quebecois men have historically
      been politically and economically powerless (thus giving
      women room to speak) and because the women there have
      generally been more educated than men.

70   Moisan, Clément. "Ecriture et errance dans les poésies
      de Gwendolyn MacEwen et Nicole Brossard." Canadian
      Review of Comparative Literature/Revue canadienne de
      littérature comparée 1 (Winter 1975), 72-92.

      Summarizes Brossard's poetics through references to her
      poetry and essays and through a stylistic comparison with
      an English-Canadian poet, MacEwen. Says Brossard is
      engaged in a theoretical search for a "decoded poetic
      language," an "unmasking" of the dissimulating powers of
      words. Claims she seeks this "purity" by "breaking"
      language to arrive at its source and its potential for
      truth. Analyzes several poems in detail to show
      Brossard's belief in the possibilities for individual and
      collective freedom offered by language and form, rather
      than content or theme. A good introduction to Brossard's
      general poetic concerns, though it does not discuss the
      feminist implications of her ideas.

71   Vasseur, François. "J'écris." La Nouvelle barre du jour
      No. 99 (February 1981), 65-71.

Reviews Brossard's Le sens apparent and Duras's
collected pieces, Navire night, Césarée, Les mains
négatives, and Aurélia Steiner, in an impressionistic and
highly self-conscious form imitative of the authors it
discusses. Says both women "write themselves" in texts
that "fill the gap," "rip them (the authors) from death,"
"permit the joining of their desire with the body."
Contrasts the feminine "reading body" engaged by these
works with the reviewer's own intractable "masculine
self." Hard to follow.

* **Bruno, Pierre,** Catherine Clément, and Lucien Sève.
  Pour une critique marxiste de la théorie psychanalytique. Paris: Editions Sociales, 1973.

  (See 141).

72 **Burke, Carolyn.** "Rethinking the Maternal." The Future
    of Difference. Ed. Hester Eisenstein and Alice
    Jardine. Boston: G. K. Hall, 1980, 107-14.

    Advocates the use of "a certain psychoanalysis" in
    feminist theory, one that values woman positively,
    despite the general American feminist rejection of
    psychoanalysis. Takes as central experiences for a
    theory of female difference those of being mothered and
    mothering--not necessarily in the literal biological
    sense. Examines the concepts critical to French feminism
    (difference, identity, the female, the maternal) in light
    of the enormous differences between French and American
    readings of Freud. Summarizes French (Lacanian)
    Freudianism's focus on the fluid unconscious--in contrast
    to American concern with a stable ego--and its stress on
    parallels between language and the unconscious. Claims
    French psychoanalysis offers feminists a potentially
    revolutionary tool: a return to the subversive power of
    the unconscious that exposes the maternal and female
    forces. Explains Kristeva's adoption of psychoanalytic
    theory to introduce sexual difference and plurality into
    the creation of meaning and to propound disruption of the
    paternal Logos by maternal discourse. Favors our calling
    upon the work of both American and French feminists
    dealing with the maternal (Rich, Chodorow, Dinnerstein,
    Kristeva, Irigaray) to "reclaim" the significance of the
    mother-daughter relationship. Highly useful.

73   **Canto, Monique.** "La théorie immobile." <u>Sorcières</u> 12
     (1978), 33-36.

     Treats women's "discomfort" with theory, linking it to
     Freud's ideas on girls' and boys' differing initial
     sexual discoveries and relationships to self and
     knowledge. Sees women's relation to knowledge, on the
     "fantasmic" level, as one of ambivalence and men's as a
     desire for research for its own sake.

74   **Cardinal, Marie.** <u>Autrement dit</u>. Paris: Grasset, 1977.

     Touches on a variety of topics--psychoanalysis, life in
     Algeria, the texture of women's lives, the reading and
     writing of women's texts, rape, sexuality, and
     woman-as-mother--in a free-flowing alternation between
     personal testimony by Cardinal and recorded dialogue
     between Cardinal and Annie Leclerc. Cardinal describes
     the writing process in physical terms ("jouissance" or
     pleasure, physical struggle, and birth). In the most
     provocative passage, a conversation about how women's
     works are written and read, Cardinal refutes the idea of
     a feminine writing, but claims that women's texts are
     read differently from men's: women's relationship to
     accepted language is different from men's, and women's
     texts are therefore generally "mis-read." Cardinal asks
     women to "feminize" language by speaking plainly "at the
     level of their bodies" ("au ras le corps"). A "spoken"
     text, immediate and moving, that seeks to share a life
     experience rather than develop an argument or analysis.

75   ————. "Témoignage." Suzanne Horer and Jeanne Socquet.
     <u>La Création étouffée</u>. Paris: Pierre Horay, 1973,
     153-63.

     A testimony that recounts frankly her relationships to
     the men in her life. Evokes her earlier years of
     psychological and personal crisis, then her positive
     experience of psychoanalysis. Tells how writing opened
     "the door to (her) life" and her femininity that
     bourgeois codes of female behavior had closed. Describes
     writing as a "liberation," as her "combat" with the "old,
     traditional culture."

* Cesbron, Georges. "Ecritures au féminin. Propositions
  de lecture pour quatre livres de femmes." Degré second
  4 (July 1980), 95-119.

  (See 4).

76 **Cassin, Barbara.** "Code code code codé." Sorcières 12
    (1978), 6-7.

    A nearly opaque essay that calls on women to do "what
    can't be said": "make theory as women." Welcomes the
    profusion of research on sexual difference in all fields
    and urges women to transcend the "double impasse" of
    either theorizing "like a man" or not writing at all,
    "like a woman."

77 **Cauwenberghe, Geneviève van.** "'Comment dire?'" Les
    Cahiers du GRIF 23-24 (December 1978), 138-39.

    Views the forms of expression that women tend to use
    and that the media emphasize at present as "testimonies,
    accounts of lived experience." Criticizes this mode as
    perpetuating the "phallocentric" narrative values of
    logic, linearity, and mastery and also as emptying the
    problems they discuss of any analysis. Calls for an
    outcry against the stereotyped images of women presented
    in the media. Proposes instead "transitory"
    "fragmentations," or unclosed and heterogeneous
    narratives.

Chawaf, Chantal:

ESSAYS AND ARTICLES

78 ———. "La Chair linguistique." Les Nouvelles
    littéraires No. 2534 (May 26 1976) 18.

    A brief passage postulating that the goal of writing is
    to "pronounce the body," "liberate our unconscious" and
    regenerate us. Affirms that this can be achieved by
    "disintellectualizing language," by returning to "the
    ancient physical language (la vieille langue matérielle)."

    78a   Trans. in (19).

79 ———. "L'Ecriture." Chair chaude. Paris: Mercure de France, 1976, 71-83.

A poetic evocation of writing as a magical path to reunion with the physical and spiritual source of life ("le commencement"), and a reconciliation of culturally created opposites. Presents writing in the feminine as "writing corporally," and also as a linguistic displacement of woman's traditional domestic work, especially cooking, weaving, and nurturing, a displacement that allows woman "to speak herself." Stresses the power of individual words, which are the "pre-civilization," the pre-symbolic of sentences. Densely metaphorical.

80 ———. "Un piège sordide." Les Nouvelles littéraires. No. 2683 (April 19-26, 1979), 21.

Criticizes the public taste for erotic literature on the grounds that the "refined cruelty" of the latter is at base a denial of love and an espousal of death. Says this literature "censors" full human sensual experience.

INTERVIEWS WITH

81 Accad, Evelyne. "Interview avec Chantal Chawaf." Présence francophone 17 (Autumn 1978), 151-61.

Describes her personal relationship to her writing and the role of her writing in male-dominated society. Speaks of the "tenderness" she feels toward language—her search to express what the culture of war, neurosis, violence and oppression has destroyed—and of writing as a physical and spiritual act of love. Says society has literally squelched women's lives but that each woman possesses and must express the life force that is in her.

82 Bonnefoy, Claude. "Chantal Chawaf: Ecrire quand les enfants dorment." Les Nouvelles littéraires No. 2684 (April 26-May 3, 1979), 10.

Discusses Chawaf's book Maternité (Stock, 1979), saying her writing is "at one with her body" and that it follows the exact shape of her body's "pulsions." Recounts some of Chawaf's literary biography. Says all love contains the "maternal" element, in the sense of a "profound bond with the species." Connects the act of writing with life forces, with love, and with pleasure.

83   Clédat, Françoise T. "Livres: Interview with Chantal
      Chawaf." Sorcières 12 (1978), 48-52.

      A conversation around two of Chawaf's works, Le soleil
      et la terre and Rougeâtre. Asks what revolutionary power
      writing has to change social structures, to which Chawaf
      answers that writing from "the place of desire," of
      "love," contributes to redefining women's and men's
      relationships. Uses the mother-child relation as
      metaphor for the uncovering of the repressed "feminine"
      in men--a force of life and creativity that women can,
      for example, transmit to their sons or bring to their own
      political activity. Says "recognizing the mother" is an
      opening to the "infinite." Questions feminist responses
      of violence to counter violence and argues for life over
      death. Describes Chawaf's writing as a "flow" that
      "brings one back to something that is in the past,
      something that predates structures." Calls language one
      of the body's "organs" and the "search for continuity"
      with the "other." Designates three possible languages:
      poetry, theoretical language, and the "language of
      impossibility" or "direct expression of the body."

ESSAYS AND ARTICLES ABOUT

  *   Cesbron, Georges. "Ecritures au féminin. Propositions
      de lecture pour quatre livres de femmes." Degré second
      4 (July 1980), 95-119.

      (See 4).

84   Cortanze, Gérard de. "L'infini plaisir des sens."
      Magazine littéraire No. 180 (January 1982), 22.

      A brief discussion of Chawaf's "written art" that
      centers on its "infinite pleasure of the senses," its
      speaking to what is "deepest" and "most intimate."

85   Jean, Raymond. "Pour Chantal Chawaf." Pratique de la
      littérature. Paris: Seuil, 1978, 120-22.

      A very brief overview of Chawaf's texts Retable,
      Rêverie, and Cercoeur, which it describes as evincing a
      new writing "plucked live from a woman's body." Praises
      the "biological elan" that Chawaf's language so intensely
      transmits. Also finds, amid the life force in her
      writing, a certain inexplicable "despair" in Cercoeur.

Cixous, Hélène:

BOOKS AND COLLECTIONS OF ESSAYS

* ———— and Catherine Clément. La jeune née. Paris:
UGE, 10/18, 1975.

  (See 138).

86 ————. Prénoms de personne. Paris: Seuil, 1974.

"Prédit"; "Du côté de l'autre": 1. "La fiction et ses
fantômes, Une lecture de l'Unheimliche de Freud" (94); 2.
"Les noms du pire, Lecture de l'Homme au sable" (99); 3.
"L'incertitude intellectuelle, La proposition de Jentsch;
4. "Les comptes d'Hoffmann"; 5. "Les Marionnettes,
Lecture de Kleist, Le dernier chapitre de l'histoire du
monde" (97); "Ensemble Poe": 1. "Une poétique du revenir"
(108); 2. "Paradoxe du jamais plus, Le nom de Morella"
(100); 3. "L'autre analyste, Introduction à Double
Assassinat dans la rue Morgue" (90); "Ensemble Joyce": 1.
"Texte du hors" (105); 2. "Les hérésistances du sujet"
(96); 3. "La crucifiction, Figures de l'anti-exil" (92);
4. "Trait portrait de l'Artiste en son autre j'aimot."

A collection of essays that evokes, describes and gives
examples of "the poetics of creative doubt," of the ways
certain 19th and early 20th century texts subverted the
psychic, cultural, economic and sexual constraints on
free creative expression. Essays are interconnected by a
common theme--the struggle against "conservative
narcissism" or "the enslavement of the self"--and a clear
internal progression--from more covert to more openly
defiant texts. Is representative of Cixous's early work
in two ways: (1) is an example of her early literary/
philosophical practice or textual exegesis, versus later
theorizing; (2) uses deconstructive techniques to discuss
existing "subversive" texts from the past, versus her
later preoccupations with future, still uninscribed
"feminine writing." The introduction ("Prédit") presents
Cixous's theoretical framework for analyzing the authors
that follow: based on a parallel between writing and
"desire," her approach looks for fiction that stems from
true desire (desire that is a life-affirming "gift,"
"action," "movement" and not logocentric and phallocentric
"possession," "appropriation," and "death"). Such

fiction liberates "la Personne" (the self or subject)
from all limits so it can enjoy a freedom analogous to
the multiple French meanings of the word "personne"
itself: absence ("no one") and unlimited individualities
("some one"). The "personne" (author and reader), thus
freed, will be like a "prénom": not restricted by the
destructive and reifying effects of an attached (sur)name
(e.g., the creative restrictions imposed on "names" in
the literary establishment, like monolithic life
experience of a fixed identity); and also, like the
pre-conscious self before socialization, not restricted
by the institutionalized primacy of logic. Then, in
succeeding chapters, examines works by Freud, Hoffmann,
Kleist, Poe and Joyce. Chooses non-French texts since
the French, claims Cixous, have "enslaved doubt" since
Descartes. Says all are texts that "deconstruct," that
"undo" the very story they are in the process of
organizing in the course of their own unfolding. Each
textual analysis borrows imagery and vocabulary from a
different discourse (psychoanalysis, economics, art,
music, dance, mathematics, philosophy, politics) in an
effort to question and multiply the relationships between
"fiction" and "reality." An extremely difficult book,
but one that both uncovers the literary heritage of
current Marxist and Freudian "deconstructive" efforts and
also points to the "surprising," "strange," and explosive
nature of possible future fictions. (See 126 and 132).

87   ———, Madeleine Gagnon, and Annie Leclerc. La Venue
        à l'écriture. Paris: UGE, 10/18, 1977.

Hélène Cixous, "La venue à l'écriture" (109); Madeleine
Gagnon, "Mon corps dans l'écriture" (256); Annie Leclerc,
"La lettre d'amour" (472).

Contains three personal testimonies about these authors'
coming to writing, each of which is also a compelling
call to all women to write. All the essays posit that
the feminine has been repressed by our culture and that
it survives in women's "desire," which must now be
expressed. All outline strategies for women's understanding the nature and dangers of the repressive systems
in place and for their moving toward autonomous self-
expression. And all are written in forms and styles that
are themselves examples of possible new female fictions.
Essential.

ESSAYS AND ARTICLES

88   ———. "L'Affiche décolle." Cahiers Renaud-Barrault
        83 (1973), 27-37.

Looks at and analyzes visually several of Aubrey
Beardsley's illustrations (for Tristram and Ysoud and
Salomé) from the viewpoint that each catches a moment of
psycho-sexual "theater." Evokes the human, animal and
vegetal elements of the drawings as being in a state of
transformation that corresponds to the (bi)-sexual dramas
(specifically, castration) taking place. Situates the
effects of the illustrations both in Belle Epoque
preoccupations with "spectacle" and "sexual activity" and
in Beardsley's own chronology—his imminent death. A
telegraphic and suggestive text.

89   ———. "L'Approche de Clarice Lispector." Poétique
        (November 1979), 408-19.

Reviews admiringly the texts of the Brazilian author
Clarice Lispector as calling upon new ways of reading and
thinking. In a text itself mimetic of the qualities
found in Lispector's works—slow-motion, respectful, and
non-appropriative or reductive—Cixous evokes the latter
in "economic" terms of their "exchange" with the reader
and with the reality they present. Lispector's texts
"offer themselves to live" ("se donnent à vivre"): unlike
most contemporary "mass-mediatized" works, hers restore
strangeness, multiplicity and life force to the things
they look at. Difficult by its style and philosophical
references, Cixous's piece nonetheless makes rich
comparisons between women—long appropriated, reduced and
ignored—and the things (especially flowers) Lispector's
vision restores to life.

90   ———. "L'autre analyste." Prénoms de personne. Paris:
        Seuil, 1974, 215-29.

Looks at Edgar Poe's "The Murders in the Rue Morgue" in
light of the author's combining science with eroticism,
mathematics with poetry, the rational with the irrational,
the certain with the uncertain. Says the result is a
"textual economy" of "excess" and virtuality, best
typified by the story's "games" of all kinds.

91   ───── "The Character of 'Character.'" New Literary
           History 5, No. 2 (1974), 383-402.

    Begins by analyzing the traditional function of
    characterization: to repress subjectivity, restrict the
    imaginary, reappropriate meaning, and maintain identifi-
    cation with the reader, thus inserting literature in the
    "social machine." Asserts that "The ideology underlying
    this fetishization of 'character' is that of an 'I' who
    is a whole subject...conscious, knowable..." whereas in
    fact "'the subject' is an effect of the unconscious...it
    never stops producing the unconscious--which is unanalyz-
    able, uncharacterizable... 'I' must become a 'fabulous
    opera' and not the arena of the known."
        In the remainder of the article examines Hoffmann's
    Kreisleriana, "a sort of fantastical musical notebook...
    that gathers together diverse thoughts, dispersed
    portraits, disconnected people," in order to show how
    these texts "bring [the subject] back to its
    divisibility," to its irreducibility.

92   ─────. "La crucifiction, figures de l'anti-exil."
           Prénoms de personne. Paris: Seuil, 1974, 287-331.

    Evokes Joyce's "staging" of the "comedy of castration"--
    of this act of a particular psychic "economy"--even while
    he subverts that play. Traces Joyce's blow to this
    orthodox psychic drama in several of his works, saying it
    undoes all of Judeo-Christian history by putting into
    question the notions of logocentric mastery, traditional
    sexual relationships, phallocentric possession, and
    economic exchange. Says Joyce moves toward mixing and
    multiplying all forms of desire, in a kind of "wandering
    grace" (Finnegan's Wake). Ends with brief extracts, in
    French, from various texts by Joyce.

93   ─────. "L'Essort de Plusje." L'Arc 54 (1973), 46-54.

    A fable evoking the dynamics of Derrida's principle of
    non-principles: difference. Presents various versions of
    the flight/fate of "Plusje" (child, thief, flyer, excess)
    in conflict with his uncle(s), the guardian(s) of order.
    A blend of fiction and theory, this is a nervous text,
    both disconcerting and humorous in its constant word
    play. A virtuoso performance that is an excellent
    example of Cixous's poetic investigations and her affinity
    with Derrida.

94   ———. "La fiction et ses fantômes, Une lecture de
        l'Unheimliche de Freud." Poétique 10 (1972), 199-216.

        Shows how Freud's text, through persistent hesitation,
        inverts the scientific demonstration it sets out to make
        and ends up as a "novel."

        94a   Reprinted in (86).

95   ———. "Grâce à la différence." Les Nouvelles
        littéraires No. 2534 (May 26 1976), 18-19.

        Outlines the major attributes of the feminine text—it
        is open, unpredictable, generous; through it flows the
        long repressed voice of the mother—and claims that the
        production of such uncensured texts is a political
        endeavor. An excellent summary of Cixous's vision.

96   ———. "Les hérésistances du sujet." Prénoms de
        personne. Paris: Seuil, 1974, 237-86.

        Discusses "subjectivity" in Joyce's Dubliners and
        Ulysses as a contestation of orthodox logocentric
        concepts of self and other. Says Joyce's search for a
        new "intersubjectivity" puts into question phallo-
        centrism, with its traditional sexual codes and power
        relations. Traces the "subversion" that takes place on
        the levels of the art of the text, the text's subject,
        and its language. Explicates specific passages. In a
        long appendix, examines Joyce's disruption of the concept
        of "identity" in several works, as well as the role of
        the "mother" as inexhaustible source of "textual energy"
        for him. Extremely detailed analysis.

        96a   A portion of the essay ("Le discrédit du sujet")
                previously published as "Joyce, la ruse de
                l'écriture" in Poétique 4 (1970), 419-32.

97   ———. "Les Marionnettes, Lecture de Kleist."
        Prénoms de personne. Paris: Seuil, 1974, 127-52.

        Examines Kleist's Les Marionnettes to show how it is
        like a "dancer" in a text of movement that "asks about
        the source of its own movement."

98   ———. "La Missexualité, où jouis-je?" Poétique 26
        (1976), 240-249.

An examination of the function of M in Joyce's
Finnegans Wake leads to conclusions about the nature of
the feminine in literature. "No story without M.
Without her--Without Marge no place for men's scene."
She is the outsider in relation to whom the male situates
himself. He tries to analyze, reduce, incorporate her
into his economy, but to no avail. She cannot be
controlled. So it is on the level of the text itself:
"the text as M, as that which cannot be structured. And
that is femininity. The femininity of the text of
Finnegans Wake, the text-enigma as femininity." Joycean
word play makes this piece difficult and fascinating.
(See 123).

99   ———. "Les noms du pire, Lecture de l'Homme au sable."
        Prénoms de personne. Paris: Seuil, 1974, 39-99.

Analyzes in great detail Hoffmann's Der Sandman. Says
it presents visual and musical "spectacles" which,
through constant de-centering games of reflections,
reverberations and illusions, end up as the "internal
vision" of the author, as a "great opera" of liberation.

100   ———. "Paradoxe du jamais plus." Prénoms de personne.
        Paris: Seuil, 1974, 183-214.

Analyzes Edgar Poe's story "Morella," showing how its
"impossible repetitions" take the reader to "where there
is no longer such a thing as difference" between life and
death, Eros and Thanatos, the possible and the
impossible. Claims understanding the story requires a
different kind of "poetic" "reason." Examines the
character Morella not as woman, but as representation of
another kind of knowledge--of desire and death.
Prefigures themes about women, eroticism and death
developed in Le Rire de la Méduse (102).

101   ———. Preface to Les Femmes et la folie. Phyllis
        Chesler. Paris: Payot, 1975, 7-8.

A passionate preface to the French edition of Women and
Madness. Praises Chesler's denunciation of "a crime as
old as history: the condemning of women to madness."
Reviews the reasons for this persecution. Sees the book
as illustrative of the contribution American feminism can
make to French women: a truly women-centered perspective,
a high degree of solidarity, the ability to place itself
outside the discourse of mastery.

102 ―――. "Le Rire de la Méduse." L'Arc 61 (1975), 39-54.

In this fundamental text, part manifesto, part essay,
part prose poem, Cixous puts forth her theories on
femininity and the inscription of difference in writing,
exposes the mechanisms of repression, and proposes a
means of liberation. Subverting psychoanalytic theory,
she affirms that women must free themselves from the
reign of the Phallus and recognize the true nature of
their sexuality: "dispersible, prodigious, stunning,
desirous and capable of others, of the other woman that
she will be, of the other woman she isn't, of him, of
you." Women, writing from their bodies, have the power
to transform the symbolic, to "bring about a mutation in
human relations, in thought, in all praxis."

102a Trans. as "The Laugh of the Medusa" in Signs 1,
      No. 4 (Summer 1976), 875-893. Trans. reprinted in
      (19).

103 ―――. "Le Sexe ou la tête." Les Cahiers du GRIF 13
        (October 1976), 5-15.

In a highly readable form, presents Cixous's basic
theories about the organization of culture and its
expressions (the various discourses) as well as the
potential and need for other languages and representations (See 138 and 102). Beginning with Western and
Eastern myths representing the relationship between the
masculine and the feminine, points up the masculine
psychic "economy" underlying prevailing monolithic
concepts of order and hierarchy, and the concomitant
"decapitation of the feminine economy," resulting in the
"silence" of the feminine. Shows the systems of
oppositions that organize culture and which spring from
the masculine imaginary, thereby excluding the feminine
and making it "other." Ends with a mimetic suggestion of
how women can, in their writing, affirm their "difference," "strangeness," "desire," "unlimitedness" by
liberating their "phantasies." (See 129).

103a Trans. as "Castration or Decapitation?" in Signs
      7, No. 1 (Autumn 1981) 41-55.

104 ―――. "Sorties." Catherine Clément and Hélène Cixous.
        La jeune née. Paris: UGE, 10/18, 1975, 114-246.

A comparison of masculinity, femininity and their
inscription in writing. Argues that for historico-
cultural reasons all symbolic systems are rooted in
hierarchized oppositions and that the perception of
difference in terms of superior/inferior is masculine.
Drawing upon Freudian theory and the Hegelian dialectic
of the subject ("L'Empire du propre"), describes
masculine desire as monosexual, governed by the primacy
of the phallus and the fear of castration; feminine
desire as bisexual and decentralized. Whereas the
masculine libidinal economy is one of self-preservation
through the appropriation of the Other, the feminine
libidinal economy is characterized by the ability to
"give away the self spontaneously" ("se dé-proprier sans
calcul"). Feminine writing is "never simple or linear or
'objectivized', generalized." It resonates with "the
Voice," the "song before the law" whose source is the
"mother," that is, the pre-symbolic "non-nom." Feminine
writing flows from the unconscious, making manifest what
history forbids and what the real excludes. It has, on
rare occasions, been practiced by men (Kleist,
Shakespeare). In the second half of "Sorties" Cixous
turns to literary exegesis, interpreting Aeschylus's
Oresteia--the transition from matriarchal to patriarchal
order, Kleist's Penthesilea--the defeat of "love-other"
("l'amour-autre") by the law, and the story of Anthony
and Cleopatra--the triumph of transcendent love.
Combines expository prose and incantatory poetry. An
important text. (See 123).

104a   Partially trans. in Diacritics 7, No. 2 (Summer
         1977), 64-69.

104b   Portions of "Sorties" also appear in 102.

105   ———. "Texte du hors." Prénoms de personne. Paris:
         Seuil, 1974, 231-36.

A brief preface to the essays on James Joyce that
follow. Praises the "invincible originality" of Joyce's
texts, their resistance to all efforts to "code,
interpret, or translate" them. Admires their
"progressive force," their "inexhaustible gifts of
multiple forms," and calls them "global contestation(s)
of property/proprietorship in all its forms."

106   ———. "Un Morceau de Dieu." Sorcières 1 (January
         1976), 14-17.

Difficult but playfully suggestive allegory about
women's desire. Uses metaphors from Christian ritual
(particularly communion) to portray a female saint's
"appetite" for her God ("unlimited," "unmeasured") and
the love her God gives back ("controlled" and "measured").
Also includes a dream within the story in which an
"ordinary" man, like her God, determines the saint's
desire: "Your rules tell you only to love according to my
law." Ends with Cixous's comparing herself to the saint:
they share the same "appetite" but have a different
"relationship to the symbolic, to idealization, to
mediation (or desire)."

107   ———. "Une passion: l'un peu moins que rien." Samuel
      Beckett. Ed. Tom Bishop and Raymond Federman. Paris:
      Edition de l'Herne, 1976, 326-35.

A three page tribute to Beckett followed by excerpts
from Cixous's text Le Paradire. Praises Beckett's
passion, courage, and Titanic battle against Nothingness. Affirms that "his works savagely deconstruct the
capitalist system of appropriation and consumption."
Attests to his abiding influence, most evident in Le
Paradire.

108   ———. "Une poétique du revenir." Prénoms de
      personne. Paris: Seuil, 1974, 155-82.

Examines several of Edgar Poe's stories from the point
of view of their repetition, their "art of encore," their
multiple internal reflections that "push to the limit"
and "break." Calls his stories writings of "death" that
"gnaw away at themselves" and ultimately undo all
difference between death and life, dream and reality.
Explains the interest of these stories for psychoanalytic
exploration, as they raise questions of identity,
knowledge, discourse, and desire. Typical of Cixous's
"deconstructive" method of textual analysis.

109   ———. "La Venue à l'écriture." Hélène Cixous,
      Madeleine Gagnon and Annie Leclerc. La Venue à
      l'écriture. Paris: UGE, 10/18, 1977, 9-62.

Traces, in a spiraling, impressionistic, non-linear and
non-expository text, Cixous's personal trajectory toward
writing, which is offered also as a call for all women to
come to writing. Uses various kinds of metaphors,
allegories and puns to evoke the passage from silence to

writing, from death to rebirth and life, from exile to
self-love and love--a passage seemingly marked by
critical points of "discovery" (verbs in the "passé
simple") in the past--even while it undercuts this
apparently linear movement with its own textual echoes,
repetitions, and superabundance. The poetic, overfull
and gyrating effect of the text also mirrors the ongoing
generative, life-producing and multiple experience Cixous
claims feminine living/loving/writing is. States at the
outset that Cixous's trajectory evolved in the realm of
"signs," signaling the multiple symbolic significance of
all the terms used.

Within the wealth of reference and imagery, certain
stages leading to and allowing for the "gesture" of
feminine writing are discernible: (1) understanding
women's estate and all the forces that constrain women
(and all of society) as responsible for the current
masculine, logocentric, univocal, exclusionary, death-
centered, capitalistic and proprietary nature of
"accepted" discourse and writing. Masculine discourse
posits a single subject, "Je," and dominates all
"others." The repression that has made for the cultural
inferiority of the feminine is suggested by geographic
("diaspora"), ethnic/religious ("Jewwoman"), economic
("market value"), medical ("illness"), and literary/
mythical ("Oedipus") analogies. Both reading and writing
have always been determined by the priorities of this
cultural repression of the feminine; (2) struggling
against and breaking with these imposed negative and
monolithic forces and definitions--in a sense, embracing
"death," "losing" old concepts of self and other, as a
prelude to freedom. This struggle is evoked as a
"psychic" drama (against imposed taboos defining "self"
and "madness"), "economic" expansion (against limited,
capitalistic "market" expectations), intellectual and
political battle (against "reason" and the language that
has codified it), and physical upheaval (against the
repressed body of gender assignation). These struggles
liberate the many "others" in the writer/reader; (3)
discovering and opening in oneself the way to "desire"
and to the "passion" for writing, which passion Cixous
calls a "fusion," a "practice of the greatest passivity"
in which we "know things by letting ourselves be known by
them." This "fusion," an unimpeded, pluralistic
"detachment" from monolithic identities and meanings,
occurs in the Unconscious and its metaphoric seat, the
body. The absolute inseparability for Cixous of writing
from love, of expression from "gift," of word from flesh,

opens to future writing that is "infinite, inexhaustible, eternal."

All the principal themes and key words from Cixous's works appear in this essay. Like all her texts, this one is a call to women to take risks, to free all the (other) women who are (within) them, to "give birth" to themselves and to others ("accoucher"/"s'accoucher"). A difficult, resistant, and extremely moving document of self and "manifesto" for others.

INTERVIEWS WITH

110 Cameron, Beatrice. "Letter to Hélène Cixous." Sub-
     Stance No. 17 (1977), 159-65.

     An intensely personal reflection on feminism and
     literature responding to Cixous's "Le Rire de la Méduse"
     (102) and her interview with Christiane Makward (114).
     Cameron argues for the establishment of a "network of I's
     that understand," a feminist "literature of direct
     dialogue," of dynamic interplay between reader and writer,
     that would exist outside of the capitalist publishing
     industry.

111 Casanova, Nicole. "Le quitte ou double de la pensée
     féminine." Les Nouvelles littéraires No. 2603
     (September 29, 1977), 8.

     Aligns herself with the group Psychoanalysis and
     Politics against feminists who seek "mirror reproductions"
     of masculine structures. Explains that the book Angst
     appears to precede La for it presents the dilemma of
     women condemned to death in the name of love, the dis-
     guise of the Law. Maintains that writing, like psycho-
     analysis or woman-centered love, is a means of combatting
     and exploding this censorship.

 *   Clément, Catherine. "Echange." Catherine Clément and
     Hélène Cixous. La jeune née. Paris: UGE, 10/18, 1975,
     247-96.

     (See 170).

112 Collin, Françoise. "Quelques questions à Hélène Cixous."
     Les Cahiers du GRIF 13 (October 1976), 16-20.

     Because of Collin's precise and probing questions,
     brings out Cixous's overall ideas about women's writing

in a highly accessible and personal form. Discusses,
first, the primacy for Cixous of writing over other
"languages" or "sign systems" (the spoken word, corporal
expression) on the grounds that only writing, by its
power to "name" and to leave "traces," can truly change
the oppressive dominant discourse of culture; then, the
psychic benefits of writing for women, that is, its being
a means to overcome external and internal taboos and to
arrive at healthy self-love; finally, the differences
between men's and women's writing, which arise from
Cixous's premise, "L'Ecriture, c'est du corps" ("Writing
is body, is of/from the body"): in substance, men's
writing is "reproduction" and women's "production," and
in the writer's relation to writing, men display
fetishistic "attachment," women, open "detachment." Also
describes Cixous's work with students at Vincennes.

113 Finas, Lucette. "L'Etrange traversée d'Hélène Cixous."
     Le Monde (May 13, 1977), 21.

     Begins a discussion of the "itinerary" that led to
Cixous's poetic fiction, Angst--which text Cixous calls a
"plan for emancipation," an "exit," a "rebirth" that
represents "the feminine gesture" par excellence--and
proceeds to evoke, in psychoanalytic terms, the struggle
with "angst" (anguish, fear) all women must embrace to
gain their political freedom. Describing women's current
state as a forced "exile" in the domain of the male
psychic drama only, as "death" and as "madness," both
Cixous and Finas urge women to reject the fatal trap of
masculine-defined love and to tell their own story; this
is the only way for women to "come out alive" and to
enjoy another kind of love, one that "does not need to
defend itself or to prohibit anything, for it takes place
beyond (the masculine drama of) castration."

114 Makward, Christiane. "Interview with Hélène Cixous."
     Sub-Stance No. 13 (1976), 19-37.

     Touches on a large number of topics, the most developed
being (1) Cixous's work at Vincennes, (2) her relation
to organized feminism, especially the Politics and
Psychoanalysis group--a mixture of support and
reservations about its contradictory problematics--(3)
her view on the most urgent task facing women--a
"re-appropriation of femininity, starting with a thorough
rethinking of the body, of sexuality"--and (4) her
reflections on the reading/writing process. Comments on

her own praxis centered on <u>Révolutions pour plus d'un Faust</u> and <u>Souffles</u>.

115   Rambures, Jean-Louis. "Lorsque je n'écris pas, c'est comme si j'étais morte." <u>Le Monde</u> (April 9, 1976).

After a brief announcement of the appearance of Cixous's novel, <u>La</u>, described as a celebration of "the arrival of woman in a world previously forbidden to her," this short interview provides a microcosm of Cixous's encounter with the literary and critical establishment. Within the particularly confrontational dynamics of this conversation, involving incompatibilities between Cixous's ideas and the interviewer's presuppositions about the writer and writing (e.g., a writer has a "method" and follows "rules"; a writer spaces the appearances of his texts; a writer can "teach" writing to university students), there are passages evoking Cixous's unorthodox and intense relationship to her own writing: it is an "erotic" experience of "making love with the text" through intimacy with her "unconscious." A swirling, anguishing "struggle" in which her life, body, dreams, history, and text blend within the "blood" of her "inner life," writing is, at the same time, what sustains her: "When I don't write, it's as if I were dead."

115a   Reprinted in Jean-Louis Rambures. <u>Comment travaillent les écrivains</u>. Paris: Flammarion, 1978, 56-63, with word changes and additions made by Cixous in 1977. She praises the Editions des femmes as women's only chance to write outside of the "sterile" establishment and to "elaborate new forms of thought..., to be a woman in desire and in reality," and to transform "all symbolic structures"; describes her work at Vincennes as both a critical reading of recognized and powerful texts of "authority" on the level of their "imaginary structures" and an analysis of the relationships between "writing, power, women, and politics"; refers to the "femininity" in Joyce's texts as arising from his transcribing the "'stream of consciousness' of his own life"; concludes by saying she looks in writing not to finish anything, but to keep beginning again.

116   "La Réponse de Hélène Cixous." <u>Les Lettres françaises</u> No. 1361 (November 25-December 1 1970), 4.

A response to the survey, "Crise de la littérature?"
Shows the formative "structuralist" stage of Cixous's
ideas on writing and reading as they evolved out of the
general post-1968 French malaise concerning literature
("une crise de la littérature"). Responding to a
questionnaire about this "crisis"--evident in the
declining popularity of traditional fiction and the
disaffection with avant-garde works--Cixous defends
continued literary experimentation on intellectual and
political grounds. "Reading, like writing, is at once a
pleasure and an effort," and both must constantly advance
and change. Some changes, she says, may disturb the
general public since they dislocate and "decenter" the
bastions of the "literary edifice": Meaning ("le Sens")
and the literary Subject or Self ("le Sujet"). Cixous's
view of texts not as inert representations, but rather as
transformative "systems," as dynamic "signifying
surfaces" that are always "working upon themselves" to
engender "sens" and "sujet," foreshadows her subsequent
reflections on the nature of writing. And her call for a
two-pronged "battle" in writing and reading, against both
social/ideological censorship and the traditional notion
of the "Subject," points toward her later concern with
"intersubjectivity" or redefinitions of self, other,
others, and desire.

117 "Rethinking Differences." Homosexualities and French
       Literature. Ed. George Stambolian and Elaine Marks.
       Ithaca: Cornell University Press, 1979, 70-86.

Homosexuality is the subject of much of this 1976
interview. Cixous distinguishes between lesbianism,
where "a woman...'counterfeits' ("contrefait") a man,"
and feminine homosexuality, where the "power relationship
is disassembled;" defines adult bisexuality as "being
with another, a woman with a man, in a state of dynamic
exchange;" and affirms that since masculine homosexual
discourse "omits the feminine totally," French feminists
and homosexuals have no common cause and engage in no
dialogue. She also discusses strategies for a
"dephallocentralization" of discourse ("metaphor breaks
free...I think that one must work on the metaphor"); and
comments briefly on works of Genet, Kleist, Michelet,
Shakespeare, Colette, Duras, Virginia Woolf and the
surrealists.

118   Rossum-Guyon, Françoise van. "Entretien avec Françoise
       van Rossum-Guyon." Revue des sciences humaines No. 168
       (1977), 479-93.

       A particularly rich interview centering on the
       essential problematics of French feminism--the relation
       of writing ("écriture"), femininity, feminism and power.
       While defining each of these terms, Cixous insists that
       women cannot begin to transform masculine discourse until
       they take into account the unconscious, the origin of
       difference. She also reiterates her criticisms of
       "feminists," who, unlike the radical group "Politique et
       psychanalyse," seek power and legitimacy within the
       existing system. In describing her own writing, Cixous
       discusses her use of old texts, which are stolen,
       displaced, turned upside down; and then speaks of the
       primacy she gives to the body, the unconscious: "language
       at the most archaic and at the same time most developed
       level." In response to the remark that such "phantas-
       matic" texts are difficult, Cixous comments that this
       difficulty is really the reader's resistance to the
       "naked unconscious." Angst, she admits, is so menacing
       as to be at the limit of readability.

119   Sudaka, Jaqueline. "Avec Hélène Cixous." Les Nouveaux
       cahiers 46 (Fall 1976), 92-5.

       Provides, first, the biographical facts of Cixous's
       relationship to her Jewish origins--the conscious and
       unconscious traces of her childhood experiences of
       antisemitism and of "otherness" ("mon étrangeté"), her
       attitude towards Jewish rituals, her judgment of the
       traditional role of Jewish women--then, suggests
       metaphorical extensions of that lived experience in her
       current thought and writing. Cixous claims her being a
       woman as the primary factor that has determined,
       absolutely, her sense of herself, but theorizes that
       elements from her Jewish background--the unconditional
       love offered by the women in her family, the oppressive
       power of the Law and of male figures in the Bible, the
       importance in the Jewish heritage of transmitting the
       written word, the ever-present threat of death--may also
       have informed her ideas and intellectual choices. While
       denying, somewhat contradictorily, that "the Jewish idea
       passes through [her]" when she writes, Cixous, at the

same time, calls the situation of the Jewish woman
"ideal" for writing: it allows her to "have no place"
("être sans place"), in the sense of being dislocated
from "normal" reference points, and thus to seek
unceasingly in her writing to establish "a relationship
with herself" ("un rapport à soi"). A look at Cixous and
her ideas about women and writing from a fresh,
interesting angle.

ESSAYS AND ARTICLES ABOUT

120 Andermatt, Verena. "Hélène Cixous and the Uncovery of
     a Feminine Language." Women and Literature 7, No. 1
     (Winter 1979), 38-48.

     An overview of the nature and premises of Cixous's call
     for women's writing and which is itself "Cixousian" by
     its ellipses, neologisms, puns and disconnectedness.
     Placing Cixous's preference for the "supple rhythm of the
     written word" over "the privilege of [spoken] voice"
     within Derrida's philosophical and psychoanalytic
     framework, looks at the multiple creative and political
     implications of the "feminine" writing Cixous espouses.
     Uses and explains implicitly the sexual, economic and
     artistic metaphors with which Cixous evokes the future
     female written production that will "assure the promotion
     of a woman's cause in the drama of life."

121 Backès-Clément, Catherine. "La Déroute du sujet, ou le
     voyage imaginaire de Dora." Littérature 3 (1971),
     79-85.

     Prefaces an excerpt from Cixous's Portrait du soleil
     that presents Dora, Freud, and Madame K in a dream
     sequence. Sketches the essentials of Dora's case and
     comments on the new relationship Cixous creates between
     literature and psychoanalysis: "This text makes one ill,
     it makes for disconcerting reading, between fiction and
     knowledge, playing the game of a Freudian mythology,
     which, for the first time, is the object of creative
     writing."

122 Bouraoui, H. A. "Le Vide enfin dépassé." Etudes
     françaises 7, No. 1 (February 1971), 79-84.

     An analysis of Hélène Cixous's Dedans (1969, prix
     Médicis). States that the book represents an important
     advance in novelistic technique for it extricates the new

novel from its "reducing diet ("cure d'amaigrissement")."
Praises the poetic richness of the text's "raw human
vision." Characterizes the work as Cixous's attempt to
present in novel form her theoretical meditations on
Joyce. In this "novel of encircling" the act of writing
fills the double void created by the ontological
emptiness of the narrator and the death of the father.
Bouraoui moves from a discussion of the thematics of
encircling to the narrative structure, proposing that the
two parts constitute two superimposed circles that echo
one another. Dedans, like Mallarmé's poetry, is a text
"suspended between life and death."

123   Conley, Verena. "Missexual Misstery." Diacritics 7,
      No. 2 (June 1977), 70-82.

A review essay in which "Sorties" (104) serves as the
point of departure for an overview of Cixous's textual
praxis. The essay also includes analyses of La, Partie,
and "La Missexualité" (See 98). Cixous's texts, written
"on the crease of alterity," are characterized by their
conotant displacement of meaning and their search for a
"discourse sufficient to the other." Assuming as it does
a familiarity with the work of Derrida (to whom Cixous is
repeatedly compared), this article is challenging,
perhaps even inscrutable, to the uninitiated reader.

124   Duren, Brian. "Cixous' Exorbitant Texts." Sub-Stance
      32 (1981), 39-51.

Characterizes Cixous's discourse as one of "excess," as
manifesting an "otherness" that puts into question
traditional structures of "property/propriety" ("le
propre"). Locates the source of this "exorbitance" in
feminine desire, conceived by Cixous as equivalent to the
Freudian/Lacanian "excessive" desire for death. Equates
text with body and writing with "pulsion" in Cixous's
works. Says she seeks "the discourse of the unconscious,"
whose "fantastic," unstructured form, by allowing for
multiple possible interpretations, subverts the dominant
discourse.

125   Evans, Martha Noel. "Portrait of Dora: Freud's Case
      History As Reviewed by Hélène Cixous." Sub-Stance 11,
      No. 36 (1982), 64-71.

A reading of the play that illustrates the alternative
logic of the hysteric, an important figure in Cixous's

re-evaluation of the feminine. Juxtaposes the paratactic, synthetic, multi-valent discourse of Dora and the hypotactic, hierarchical, unitary discourse of Freud. Points out the ambiguity that underlies even "sane" discourse. Uses the central image of the door to develop her comparison. For men, it is a metaphor for the sexual availability of women and as such exists in an either/or logic. For Dora, doors are double, "always in the process of being both opened and closed."

126   Forrester, Viviane. "Les relectures d'Hélène Cixous." La Quinzaine littéraire No. 202 (January 16 1975), 6.

Praises Cixous's "lyrical analysis" of the authors she studies in Prénoms de personne (86) for its "exploding" the various internal and external "authorities" that have traditionally constrained critics and their writing. Discusses, first, Cixous's renaming of the term "death": no longer signifying limitation, censorship, or the ultimate power, the word is opened, dislocated, and filled with new life and meaning. Then, describes Cixous's discovering in the texts she studies their destruction of "the empire of the 'I'" ("l'empire du 'je'"), or the stultifying, traditional monolithic concept of the "self." A dense and detailed review.

127   Jean, Raymond. "Le texte-amant d'Hélène Cixous." Pratique de la littérature. Paris: Seuil, 1978, 115-19.

Though principally a review of Cixous's novel Tombe (described as the presentation of an "imaginary ethnography" whose area of study is "the space of esoteric mythologies") and a comment on her novel Angst (called a "cry of anguish" whose source is the original break from the mother), this brief piece also evokes the "Cixous phenomenon" in general: the latter is the unrelenting, enveloping "presence" of an author whose irrepressible and superabundant writing, by its being an endlessly self-generating "producer of words that are torn away" ("productrice de parole déchirée"), is totally original.

128   Kattan, Naim. "Remplir le vide: Hélène Cixous, romancière." Synthèses 304-305 (October-November 1971), 80-2.

Summarizes Cixous's fiction as inextricable from biographical elements in her life, in particular her

father's early death as source of the dominant effort in
her texts to "reconquer the father." Sees her novels as
seeking refuge from "the real" in "the imaginary and the
mythic."

129 Kuhn, Annette. "Introduction to Hélène Cixous's
     'Castration or Decapitation?'" Signs 7, No. 1 (Autumn
     1981), 36-40.

     Situates Cixous's work--in particular, her "interroga-
     tion of [linguistic] meaning"--in the context of the
     French feminist exploration of women's relation to
     language. Summarizes the Lacanian psychoanalytic model
     on which much of this exploration is based and which many
     feminists, including Cixous, criticize for its "phallogo-
     centrism" and its ascription of "negativity" to the
     feminine. Describes Cixous's concern with a "writing
     that inscribes femininity," a "repressed feminine pleasure
     ('jouissance')." Encapsulates the overall evolution of
     Cixous's work. (See 103).

130 Makward, Christiane. "Structures du silence/du délire."
     Poétique No. 35 (September 1978), 314-24.

     A "partially formalist" approach to the poetics of
     Marguerite Duras and Hélène Cixous, this comparison
     points to the recent progress made by erotic feminine
     writing: "the inscription of the feminine has swung from
     'hysterical' regression to 'paranoiac' strength; from
     quasi-silence to pseudo-delirium; from imprisoned
     ('enlisée') woman to winged woman."
         In Duras's writing Eros becomes Echo. The nature of
     love is to be the "reflection of the desire/discourse of
     the other." "The reduction/regression of the subject to
     the echo of desire requires the silence of the subject...
     of the feminine ego." This silence, "horrible and
     fruitful," represents both the rejection of life as it is
     and the hope of another life, freed from Western
     monotheisms.
         To sketch the salient features of Cixous's "art
     poétique" Makward focuses on La, a voice of the "future
     feminine" in dialogue "with phallocentric discourse and
     psychoanalysis." By her playful use of language and her
     polymorphous style, "which escapes the cage of defini-
     tion," Cixous resembles Lacan's patient Aimée, treated
     for paranoiac psychosis.

131   Micha, René. "La Tête de Dora sous Cixous." <u>Critique</u> 33
         (Feburary 1977), 114-21.

         Briefly characterizes Cixous's fiction: it is a
      "transcription or recollection of...dreams...a mixture of
      scenes, poems, fables, images." The language is
      "proud/arrogant ('orgueilleux')." The succession of her
      works creates a labyrinth. Micha then touches on the
      individual texts, ending with <u>Portrait de Dora</u>. He
      includes also a longer summary of <u>La jeune née</u> (138).
      Finds in her work "an open, extravagant, magnificent
      subjectivity" and claims that she "seduces and irritates
      us with her excessive passion...with a certain
      disequilibrium."

132   Moreau, Jean A. "Question de personne." <u>Critique</u>
         31 (March 1975), 297-306.

         A review of <u>Prénoms de personne</u> (86) that speaks
      favorably of both the "pleasurable" effects of Cixous's
      book--its "seductive," "inviting" quality that imitates
      the very sexual origins of the analysis it puts forth--
      and its "meanings"--its debunking of the traditional
      notion of the "subject" in its general attack on all
      forms of "le propre" ("proprietorship"/"ownership").
      Praises Cixous's analysis for "caressing," rather than
      "penetrating" the texts it studies and for transmitting
      honestly the "resistances" (versus a false "transparency")
      the critic encountered when reading these texts.
      Finally, discusses the contradictions that arise from the
      coexistence of traditional and new readings of texts such
      as those Cixous examines, and criticizes Cixous, in spite
      of her intentions, for imposing a directed, linear
      structure on her book rather than allowing a freer
      "va-et-vient" ("oscillation"). This review is difficult
      to read because of its specialized vocabulary and its
      recondite critical references.

133   Richman, Michèle. "Sex and Signs: The Language of French
         Feminist Criticism." <u>Language and Style</u> 13, No. 4
         (Fall 1980), 62-80.

         Uses Hélène Cixous's and Catherine Clément's <u>La jeune
      née</u> (138) to structure her reflections on French feminist
      re-evaluations of the relation of women and writing.
      Focuses on Cixous's commentaries, which she also compares
      with Carolyn Heilbrun's thoughts on androgyny and Julia
      Kristeva's "pulsion machinique." In addition, situates

feminist inquiry vis-à-vis certain prominent twentieth
century male theorists (Mauss, Lévi-Strauss, Barthes,
Bataille, Lyotard, Foucault). Describes the essential of
Cixous's formulations: there exists a specifically
feminine libidinal economy—characterized by bisexuality,
"jouissance," and "dépense" (cosmic expenditure)—that
inscribes itself into texts. Evaluates this model,
finding positive its incisive critique of structuralism
as well as its vitality and intensity. Considers more
problematic, however, the contention that an original
bisexuality must be liberated and the absence of adequate
development of the role of cultural factors in the
creation of specificity.

134   Vuarnet, Jean-Noel. "Portraits du soleil." Lettres
      nouvelles 4 (September–October 1974), 175-87.

      As Cixous's "quasi-novels," "a magma of dreams and
delirium," are unsuited to "a real critical approach,"
this overview of her poetics is more evocative than
analytical. The perspective is Derridian. Hers is "a
writing of fantasy...of loss...of difference," embodying
the impossible quest for identity, for the origin. Her
work is irreducible: "Insidious resistance of difference
which defies reduction...Resistant difference of writing
that Meaning does not homogenize, that the Center does
not control."

135   Clédat, Françoise. "L'écriture du corps." Magazine
      littéraire No. 180 (January 1982), 20-2.

      Discusses one tendency within current women's
literature in France: the writing of the body, or the
immediate translation of women's physiological being.
Says this writing is a "double transgression" that
violates the censorship of both women's writing and
women's bodies. Looks at the different kinds of texts
that have appeared, theoretical and "immediate" or
"linear" ones, saying the former only have truly opened
to new formal conceptualization and experimentation.
Says such theoretical or "metaphorical" texts connect
women's interiority with the "real" world.

Clément, Catherine:

BOOKS AND COLLECTIONS OF ESSAYS

136 ——. <u>Bildoungue</u>. Paris: Christian Bourgois, 1978.

"Fantaisie" (Introduction); "Enfances"; "Jeunesses";
"En famille"; "En voyage"; "Séances"; "Agonies"; Sources.

A series of very short vignettes constituting a
fictionalized account of Freud's life: from vulnerable
child to self-centered adult, and, finally, fragile old
man. In her introduction, Clément acknowledges that the
text is personal and "phantasmatic" and was motivated by
"a latent and insidious revolt against Freud the man."
In dreamlike, sensual settings women figure centrally--
powerful, frightening, arousing. Illustrative of the
strong influence Freud (and Lacan) have exercised over
many feminist theorists, at once critical and fascinated.

137 ——. <u>Les Fils de Freud sont fatigués</u>. Paris:
Grasset, 1978.

I. "Les nouveaux riches de l'intelligentsia"; II. "Les
psychanalystes appliqués"; III. "Medicine-men"; IV. "Les
contrebandiers"; V. "Vouloir guérir, ou la mère de
Rimbaud"; VI. "Tombeau de Groddeck"; Avertissement.

Describes and criticizes the psychoanalytical practice
in France most closely descended from Freud and Lacan.
Traces its evolution, showing that the less fruitful
aspects of their theoretical formulations have been
institutionalized whereas their more "positive" contributions have been marginalized. Finds psychoanalysts
defaulting on their curative obligations. Contends that,
instead of a practical and ethical focus, theirs is a
narcissistic project: to join and maintain the
intelligentsia. In the wake of Lacan, psychoanalysts
have allied themselves with the literary elite. However,
lacking the master's talent and conceptual audacity, they
produce poorly constructed books that vampirize their
patients, transforming their discourse into mediocre
nineteenth century narratives. Claims that although
writers and analysts are centrally involved with
language, the nature of their work is fundamentally
different. Develops her reflections on the social
function of psychoanalysis by situating it in the
tradition of healers (shamanism, witchcraft...) of which

it is the most recent avatar. Also, stresses that
thinkers should articulate the personal and the social
when presenting their own work and that of others.
Uncovering the subjective roots of theory is both an
ethical and methodological necessity. Approaches Freud
from this perspective, concluding that his personal
history (fear, guilt, an obsession with death) robbed his
theory of the vitality and compassion of a Winnicott or
Groddeck. Ranges from the coolly explanatory to the
passionately indignant. Fleshes out the corpus of her
theoretical work.

138 ———— and Hélène Cixous. _La jeune née_. Paris: UGE,
        10/18, 1975.

Part I: Catherine B. Clément, "La Coupable" I. Sorcière
et hystérique," II. Séduction et culpabilité," Bibliographie (148); Part II: Hélène Cixous, "Sorties" (104); Part
III: "Echange," a discussion between Clément and Cixous
(170).

One of the most often cited works in the field, and
rightly so. Clément and Cixous both analyze the nature
and function of Western representations of woman. Cixous
also describes feminine libido and writing. The third
section offers readers the relatively rare opportunity to
witness a direct dialogue between prominent theorists who
disagree. (See 266)

139 ————. _Miroirs du sujet_. Paris: UGE, 10/18, 1975.

"Introduction: Miroirs du sujet" (157); "Le temps du
regard: roman, regard, régression" (167); "Mythe et
Sexualité" (161); "'Un miroir, c'est-à-dire un piège'"
(168); "L'incarnation fantasmatique" (155); "Les
charlatans" (146); "L'impossible réel, ou le leurre en
vente" (154); "La structure et le regard" (166); "Mythe
et Musique, ou l'opéra rêvé" (160); "L'opéra ou le
réalisme excessif" (162); Notice bibliographique.

A Marxist perspective informs this collection of
articles: studies of literary texts, painting, cinema,
and the opera. Pieces tend to engage a critical dialogue
with structural anthropology and psychoanalysis,
illustrating and evaluating their methodologies. Lacan
substantially escapes criticism for Clément finds his
formulation of the mirror stage and phantasy ("fantasme")
most compatible with historical materialialism. Does not

explain or develop this articulation. Rather repetitive.
Several essays do discuss women.

140 ———. L'Opéra ou la défaite des femmes. Paris:
     Grasset, 1979.

"Prélude." I. "Les cantatrices ou le cirque des
femmes"; II. "Mortes"; III. "Affaires de famille ou les
parents terribles"; IV. "Les jeunes filles et le saut
dans le vide"; V. "Les furies et les dieux ou les déclins
de la lune"; VI. "Les fous, les nègres, les bouffons ou
les héros de la déception"; VII. "Tétralogiques ou la
fille perdue"; "Eloge du paganisme"; Index. Indications
bibliographiques.

A study of the opera as a mirror of phallocratic and
gynophagic society. Dedicated to her son and to
anthropologist Lévi-Strauss, whose Introduction to a
Science of Mythology frames the work. Analyzes the
characters and plots of numerous operas (among them
Carmen, Madame Butterfly, Don Giovanni, Norma, La Bohème,
and the Ring cycle) to show the implacable repetition of
the same mortal logic: the unsuccessful revolt of women
(and "feminine" men) leads to madness and/or death.

141 ———, Pierre Bruno, and Lucien Sève. Pour une critique
     marxiste de la théorie psychanalytique. Paris: Editions
     Sociales, 1973.

Avertissement. Part I--"Le Sol freudien et les mutations de la psychanalyse" (164): I, "Le sol freudien";
II, "Développements et mutations de la psychanalyse."
Part II--"Psychanalyse et anthropologie. Problèmes d'une
théorie du sujet": I, "L'anthropologie explicite"; II,
"Du 'culturel' au 'structural'"; III, "L'anthropologie
marxiste et la psychanalyse." Part III--"Psychanalyse et
matérialisme historique." Annexes.

Purports to be "a more scientific" re-evaluation of the
possibilities of articulating psychoanalysis and Marxist
theory. The first part, by Catherine Clément, traces the
history of psychoanalysis from Freud to Lacan and
provides an overview and comparison of both theorists'
contributions. The second part, by Pierre Bruno,
compares anthropology and psychoanalysis to set forth
areas of compatibility and incompatibility. Asserts the
greater theoretical power of the anthropological model.

In the third part, Lucien Sève summarizes earlier
critiques of psychoanalysis made by Marxist thinkers and
formulates his own.

142 ────. Le Pouvoir des mots. Tours: Mame, 1973.

Avertissement. Part I--"Symbolique et idéologique": Ch.
I, "Le pouvoir des mots et les mauvais sujets" (163); Ch.
II, "Freud et Lacan: symbolique et production idéologique"
(153). Part II--"Fantasme et mythe": Ch. III, "Continuité
mythique et construction historique" (147); Ch. IV,
"L'événement: porté disparu" (151); Ch. V, "De la
méconnaissance: fantasme, texte, scène" (149). Part
III--"Services du langage": Ch. VI, "Lacan ou le 'porte-
parole'" (158); Ch. VII, "La stratégie du langage" (165).
Références bibliographiques.

A collection of seven essays, six previously published,
that describes and evaluates theoretical attempts to
formalize the relation between the subject and culture.
From an overtly Marxist perspective, reviews anthropology
(primarily Lévi-Strauss) and, most extensively, psychoanalysis (Freud and Lacan) to show the strengths and
weaknesses of such concepts as phantasy ("fantasme"), the
imaginary, the symbolic, the traumatic event, and
semanalysis. Rather repetitive. Requires familiarity
with Marxist and psychoanalytic theory. Useful and
thought provoking for these readers.

143 ────. Vies et légendes de Jacques Lacan. Paris:
Grasset, 1981.

"Ecoute bûcheron, arrête un peu le bras." I. "Plaisirs
d'amour"; II. "Le chemin des dames"; III. "La bouchère ne
voulait pas de caviar"; IV. "La marelle et les quatre
coins"; "L'oiseau de feu"; Notes; Bibliographie.

Provides an introduction to the "Lacan phenomenon" and
an accessible overview of his theoretical formulations.
Traces the development of his theory and explains
important components (the mirror stage, desire, the
Other...) and their articulation in increasingly
mathematical models. Encloses this chronological
approach within a mythic frame, interpreting Lacan as
both shaman and prophet, caught in the irreducible
contradiction of those two poles. Shaman--that is,
healer, analyst, madman, poet, mystic, outcast,
androgyne--and prophet--teacher, disseminator, master,

founder of an institution. Is critical at times of
Lacan's behavior, but not of his theory. Notes his
passion for women as inversion and describes how women
hysterics were the source of crucial discoveries: the
mirror stage and desire as desire of the Other. Contends
that although Lacan's behavior may support claims that he
was a misogynist his theory does not. Briefly reviews
quotes repeatedly used by feminist critics, showing that
they have been misinterpreted. A useful book, both
personal and penetrating.

143a   Trans. as The Lives and Legends of Jacques Lacan.
         New York: Columbia University Press, 1983.

ESSAYS AND ARTICLES

144   ————. "A l'écoute de Derrida." L'Arc 54 (1973), 16-19.

    An account of a conversation with philosopher Jacques
Derrida that touches on the nature, purpose, and impact
of his work. Stresses his linguistic audacity (the
example used is "Glas," published in this issue) and the
scope of his critique of Western civilization. Brief but
useful overview.

145   ————. "A-topie: Description d'un rituel." Littérature
         6, No. 21 (February 1976), 105-10.

    Presents the process of psychoanalysis as a myth and a
ritual of contemporary culture, using Lévi-Strauss's
anthropological model. Describes the rules governing
analysis, explaining how they create an a-topia where
language is invested with the power to effect change.
Mentions that although this process "doubles [literary]
creation," it is radically different, for language never
becomes text.

146   ————. "Les charlatans." Miroirs du sujet. Paris:
         UGE, 10/18, 1975, 181-205.

    A loosely articulated essay that uses psychoanalytic
categories to interpret the celebrated expressionist film
Dr. Caligari and that, to some extent, uses the film to
explore Freud and his theories. Develops parallels
between the film and the phantasies of hysterics and also
between expressionist cinema and psychoanalysis. Reflects
upon the role of the demoniac double in bourgeois society.

146a   Also appeared in the issue of Communications on
        "Psychanalyse et Cinéma."

147   ———. "Continuité mythique et construction historique."
        L'Arc 34, 1968. Reprinted in Le Pouvoir des mots (142).

        Examines Freud's notions of construction and
        deconstruction to explore two issues: (1) the relation
        between literary and artistic creation and a fundamental
        phantasy ("fantasme"); (2) the relation between myth and
        phantasy as expressed in the concept of archaic heritage.
        Describes and illustrates the methodology Freud used to
        develop his notion of phantasy and explores why his work
        inaugurated a new historical method—"substitut[ing] a
        constructed continuity for an imaginary continuity."

148   ———. "La Coupable." Catherine Clément and Hélène
        Cixous. La jeune née. Paris: UGE, 10/18, 1975, 10-113.

        Examines the role of "guilty party" that women have
        played in Western cultural mythology by focusing on two
        exemplary figures: the witch and the hysteric. Draws on
        the writings of Lévi-Strauss, Michelet and especially
        Freud to illustrate woman's dual function—"disruptive"
        and "conservative." The first part of the essay,
        "Sorcière et hystérique," develops the parallels between
        the witch, "metaphor of the people" and the hysteric,
        "metaphor of the lower middle class." Both serve as the
        repository of "the repressed past," the former represent-
        ing the paganism that preceded christianity, the latter
        embodying pre-conscious sexual trauma. Both play out
        their "crises" before a male public, and both constitute
        anomalies that simultaneously violate and confirm the
        cultural Order. The second part, "Séduction et
        culpabilité," describes Freud's evolving theory of
        hysteria, centering successively on "the perverse
        father," "the lying daughter" and the "guilty mother."
        Characterizes Freud's approach as the search for the
        guilty family member. Concludes that witches and
        hysterics have ceased to exist and that it is within the
        power of contemporary women to break out of the prison
        imposed upon their predecessors.

149   ———. "De la méconnaissance: fantasme, texte, scène."
        Langages (Autumn 1973).

        Describes the evolution toward a coherent formalization
        of the relation between the individual subject and the

historical, ideological situation of which she or he is
part. Focuses on the concept of phantasy ("fantasme").
Then comments on the new light Julia Kristeva's
"semanalysis" throws on the problem. Commends her for
formulating a theory of the production of texts.

149a   Reprinted in (142).

*   ————. "La Déroute du sujet, ou le voyage imaginaire de
    Dora." Littérature 3 (1971), 79-85.

    (See 121).

150   ————. "Enclave esclave." L'Arc 61 (1975), 13-17.

    Addresses the problem of the role of the intellectual
within the women's movement, using as a reference point
her personal experience during a public debate on
sexuality. Argues forcefully that women's cause can and
must be served by reasoned discourse. Warns that
feminist rejection of language and theory on the grounds
that these are masculine will only perpetuate the
marginality of women. Clément supports this assertion
with a brief analysis of the function of the hysteric.

151   ————. "L'événement: porté disparu." Communications
    18, 1972.

    Examines Freud's conceptualization of the "traumatic
event" to show that it leaves open the possibility of an
articulation between psychoanalysis and the Marxist
dialectic. By replacing the essentialist and static
notion of a unitary "real" event with that of a
constructed phantasy ("fantasme"), Freud created a
complex, dynamic model of an individual's history, unlike
Jung and Rank. Applying this model to the history of
humanity (Moses and Monotheism), Freud laid the
groundwork for a theory of history as "a succession of
repressions and displacements: and on the partial
re-emergence of the repressed, which continually produces
new fragments of the lost real, depends change in the
structure."

151a   Reprinted in (142).

152   ————. "La Femme dans l'idéologie." La Nouvelle
    critique 82 (March 1975), 41-6.

Presents a Communist analysis of femininity, the
oppression of women and the means to end it. Asserts
that the notion of feminine specificity is an ideological
trap and that only a socialist revolution in the
relations of workers to production will bring about the
cultural transformation necessary to eliminate the
exploitation of women. Women then will make a massive
entry into the public labor force and the family as an
economic unit will disappear. Stresses the importance of
the Communist party's efforts to assure women the right
to work. Points to the progress of women in Soviet
Asia. Deplores the emphasis placed on sexual difference
by both the Right and the Left on the grounds that both
exclude women from productive work--the Right by
relegating them to the home, the Left by encouraging
marginality, the refusal of male roles, values, and
language. Further criticizes leftist intellectual-
philosophical feminism for its idealism and its
overemphasis on language at the expense of large-scale
political struggle.

153 ——— (Baokèo Clément). "Freud et Lacan, Symbolique
et production idéologique." La Nouvelle critique 70
(April 1970), 202-07.

A philosophical articulation of the relations between
Marxism and psychoanalysis that finds interplay between
them in the conceptual areas of: the (false) individual/
collective dichotomy; individual therapeutic and general
ideological change; and language and creativity. Posits
that the "symbolic moment (event) forms the framework in
which material production inscribes itself." Reviews
Freud's and Lacan's "styles" as entries into the
historical and ideological contexts from which their
"subjects" wrote. Also examines their differing
conceptions of the "subject" or the structure of the
self, and the way Lacan transforms Freud's id, superego
and ego trinity into his own real/symbolic/imaginary
categories. In each case finds political and social
homologies. Evokes the theoretical problems that remain
in joining psychoanalysis with historical materialism, in
particular the need for a "theory of the production of
the symbolic" that would also be a political project.
Rough going.

153a Reprinted in (142).

154 ———. "L'impossible réel, ou le leurre en vente."
Miroirs du sujet. Paris: UGE, 10/18, 1975, 206-11.

A brief assessment of hyperrealism in art. Suggests
that hyperrealism's close relation to phantasy
("fantasme")--fixity, fetishism, and excess ("le trop
plein du réel")--is the true source of its impact.

154a   Also appeared in L'Art vivant.

155 ———. "L'incarnation fantasmatique." Miroirs du sujet.
Paris: UGE, 10/18, 1975, 162-82.

Analyzes Pierre Klossovski's Bain de Diane, comparing
his decentering techniques (disjunction, contradiction,
anamorphosis) with the structures of phantasy ("fantasme")
posited by Freud and Lacan. Proposes that despite his
fragmentation of representation, Klossovski remains
within the unifying tradition of absolutes. Compares
Klossovski with the baroque to show how both, through
mobility, plurality, and disguise, "mark the place of an
absent God," and "move toward the one via the many."

155a   First appeared in the Klossovski issue of L'Arc.

156 ———. "Inconscient et langage dans la psychanalyse."
La Nouvelle critique 97 (October 1976), 12-16.

Traces Freud's and Lacan's theories on the language of
the Unconscious. Affirms that Freud's work on the body
language of hysterics, the analysis of dreams, and the
perturbations of "normal" speech provided solid groundwork
for Lacan's structuralist innovations. Contends that
both theorists elaborated models permitting the
articulation of the collective and the individual through
language, thereby making invaluable contributions to a
"science of the subject." A succinct overview.

157 ———. "Introduction: Miroirs du sujet." Miroirs
du sujet. Paris: UGE, 10/18, 1975, 9-27.

States that this collection of essays focuses on the
structures of the imaginary--myth and phantasy
("fantasme")--studied in their different settings--
textual, musical, cinematographic, and pictorial. Says
her goal is to elucidate further the dual function of
myth and phantasy to transmit the dominant ideology and

to permit innovations leading to cultural revolution.
Explains the title of the volume: the term mirror is used
in the Lacanian context to designate the relations among
the symbolic, the imaginary, and the real. Phantasy, a
screen ("écran") between the subject and the real, is
part of this specular structure that constitutes and
protects the subject. Explores the relation of myth and
phantasy, proposing (1) that the subject's phantasies
exist within the frame created by collective mythic
structures and (2) that myth plays for societies a role
analogous to phantasy for individual subjects. Asserts
that the expression "mirrors of the subject" describes
the limit between the infantile split body and the
"unified" adult subject that is part of the structure of
the subject. Affirms the value of this concept for the
analysis of artistic production, for it assures the
insertion of the subject in culture (history, ideology).
The most broadly theoretical of the essays in the volume.

158   ———. "Lacan ou le porte-parole." Critique 249, 1968.
       Reprinted in Le Pouvoir des mots (142).

A reading of Les Ecrits that focuses first on the
theory of the subject elaborated by Lacan and subsequently
on the question of ethics. Explains Lacan's decentered
subject; reviewing such important concepts as the
symbolic, the imaginary, the real, the mirror stage,
phantasy. Then considers the relation of the Ego to the
Other--a relation of structural inaccessibility for it is
governed by the unconscious--and the power of the analyst
in therapy.

159   ———. "Michelet et Freud: de la sorcière à l'hysté-
       rique." Europe 535-536 (November-December 1973),
       111-17.

Proposes that Michelet and Freud formulated analogous
romantic myths based on a belief in original cause and
the autonomy of language. The witch and the hysteric
serve as epistemological keys for the historian and the
scientist. It is the repressed feminine that reveals, by
inversion, the Symbolic Order. Develops this premise in
(148).

159a   Also appeared in (142).

160   ———. "Mythe et Musique, ou l'opéra rêvé." Miroirs
       du sujet. Paris: UGE, 10/18, 1975, 255-90.

Explores the seductive power of the opera, focusing on the songs (arias) of female singers and using anthropological and psychoanalytical frames of reference. Examines first the function of laughter (in the stories of Demeter, Dracula, and Parsifal), which Lévi-Strauss associates with music. Proposes that laughter is a reaction to the transitional object, Lacan's object of desire. Claims that the operatic aria, also, is the language of the pre-linguistic, dismembered body, the realm of pulsional discharge within a cultural code. Comments on the double role of woman—witch/transgressor and "mother of the seasons"—and on her martyrdom in the opera. Intriguing and quite diffuse.

160a   First appeared as "Le rire de Déméter" in Critique.

161   ————. "Mythe et sexualité." Miroirs du sujet. Paris: UGE, 10/18, 1975, 62-103.

A critique of the methodology of myth analysis, followed by a detailed examination of the myth of the hermaphrodite whose purpose is to illustrate the traps and misreadings theorists fall into, in particular, idealist simplification. Returns repeatedly to the work of Marie Delcourt, deemed exemplary of this regressive essentialism. Begins by reviewing the evolution of the theory of myth from Jung, Bachelard, and Delcourt to more complex scientific approaches that integrate the individual and the collective, the imaginary and the real, and are more compatible with dialectical materialism (Lévi-Strauss, Freud, and, especially, Lacan). Passes to a lengthy description of versions of the myth of the phoenix, commenting on interpretations by Delcourt, Lévi-Strauss, Freud, and Lacan. Asserts that stories of the phoenix-hermaphrodite-androgyne, like all myths, "contain the very signifier of myth: indifference," by which she means the unified subject. Proposed that Freud's and Lacan's interpretations reveal the myth of the phoenix as the attempt to hide the schism, the rupture through which the subject and sexual difference are constituted. Concludes that there is still much work to be done before Freudian and Marxist principles are articulated into a single approach. Slow going but interesting and useful.

161a   Also appeared as "Le mythe indifférent" in Critique's special issue on Marie Delcourt.

162   ———. "L'opéra, ou le réalisme excessif." Miroirs
       du sujet. Paris: UGE, 10/18, 1975, 291-314.

       Loosely articulated reflections on the opera informed
       by a Marxist perspective. Calls the opera a "spectacle à
       jouissance" and locates its seductive power in the song,
       which evokes the "voice of God." Situates Brecht and
       numerous philosophers in relation to the opera. Asserts
       that both traditional and Marxist operas are political as
       well as affective. Constructs a comparison between the
       Russian Bolshoi and the Bayreuth Festivals to illustrate
       this. Examines the spectrum of operatic structures—from
       the aria (the individual) to the chorus (the collective)
       to show that the opera possesses the means to represent
       social reality.

       162a   First appeared in La Nouvelle critique.

163   ———. "Le pouvoir des mots et les mauvais sujets."
       Le Pouvoir des mots. Tours: Mame, 1973, 11-45.

       Studies the theoretical models of ethnology (Lévi-
       Strauss) and psychoanalysis (Freud and Lacan) focusing on
       mechanisms for the articulation of superstructure (the
       collective) and infrastructure (the individual), most
       specifically language. Compares both models, presenting
       their strengths and weaknesses. Criticizes at length
       their humanism and essentialism. Asserts that, despite
       contributions to a more precise notion of the unconscious,
       ethnology and psychoanalysis remain grounded in tradi-
       tional hierarchical oppositions (civilized/savage, sane/
       insane, etc.) that serve to hide the economic and ideolog-
       ical reality of the class struggle and its political
       implications. Their focus on the dispossessed ("les
       marginaux") and their attribution of power ("efficacité
       symbolique") to the excluded and repressed elements of
       society—women, children, the mentally ill—are reversals
       that do not significantly alter the social dynamic within
       which the dispossessed have always assured equilibrium.
       Supports her argument by discussing the "romanticizing"
       of witches and hysterics by Michelet and Freud. Ulti-
       mately does commend Lacan for creating a concept that
       successfully articulates subjectivity and collectivity
       (the Symbolic) and for severely limiting the notion of
       "l'efficacité symbolique." By establishing limits to the
       therapeutic power of language, Lacan left open the space

in which to posit dialectical materialism as the theoretical key to understanding and effecting social change. A polemical piece. Very interesting, for it reveals the broader and highly politicized origins of the argument that in "La Coupable" (148) she applies specifically to women.

163a   The section "Sorcière et hystérique" (pp.35-40) also appeared as 159.

164   ————. "Le Sol freudien et les mutations de la psychanalyse." Catherine Clément, Pierre Bruno, and Lucien Sève. Pour une critique marxiste de la théorie psychanalytique. Paris: Editions Sociales, 1973, 11-138.

Describes Freud's major discoveries and the development of his thought--studies of hysterics, analyses of dreams, the relation of the individual and the historical. Situates Freud within his historical and ideological context to show the limitations of his work. Asserts that Freud shed much light on the workings of the psyche, but that he failed to create an adequate theory of culture. Then presents the many factions that developed as psychoanalysis spread, stressing the work of Rank and Ferenczi, Adler and Jung, Marcuse, Reich, Klein, Anna Freud, and, in most detail, Lacan. Claims that Lacan's formulations constitute significant progress toward a science of the unconscious compatible with dialectical materialism.

165   ————. "La stratégie du langage." Littérature 3 (October 1971).

Studies, from a Marxist perspective, the problematic relationship between psychoanalysis and literature. Focuses on two recent trends: the increasing tendency of psychoanalysts to write, about both analysis and literature, and the integration of psychoanalysis into the formulations of avant-garde literary theorists. Inquires into the similarities and differences of psychoanalysis and literature, the limits of each activity, and the conditions on which viable theoretical articulations of the two depend. Begins by addressing the question "Why do analysts write?" Cites Foucault and Starobinski to establish the narcissistic function of interpretation. Moves, then, to present at some length Lacan's notions of "style," "letter," and "literality,"

asserting that they formalize the possibility of
"revolutionary transformation through language." By
positing the divided subject and the subversion of
discourse through punctuation, Lacan "introduces into
psychoanalysis a movement very close to the dialectic."
Thus, the role of the analyst includes bearing witness to
the "holes" in language, knowledge, and power. The
primacy of "style" for Lacan brings together the analyst
and the writer ("écrivain"), both of whom have the same
single medium: language. Turns lastly to Kristeva's
theory of semanalysis. Finds Kristeva's formulations
particularly powerful because they inscribe psychoanalysis
within a larger model--a theory of the production of
texts. Moreover, her concept of geno-text situates
semanalysis within dialectical materialism. Her theoretical paradigm, then, is a complex and inclusive one,
articulating psychoanalysis, textuality, and history.
Informative and provocative.

165a   Reprinted in (142).

166   ————. "La structure et le regard." Miroirs du sujet.
       Paris: UGE, 10/18, 1975, 212-54.

A critique of structuralist methodology--specifically
Lévi-Strauss, Foucault, and Lacan--applied to non-verbal
representation. Asserts that although these thinkers
seem to develop the consequences of historical
materialism--questioning the transcendental subject, for
example--their conceptualizations are "amputated from
materialism and thus from real historical development."
Analyzes their approaches to painting: Lévi-Strauss on
body painting, Foucault on Velasquez's Las Meninas, and
Lacan's dialogue with Foucault and Velasquez. Attributes
to Lacan the most progressive analysis--one that "under-
lines the void" and accounts for "the structures of
vacuity essential to works of art." Affirms that Lacan
rightly sees the subject of the painting to be "the
object of desire."

166a   First appeared in Les sciences humaines et l'oeuvre
       d'art, Weber, 1969.

167   ————. "Le Temps du regard: roman, regard, régression."
       Miroirs du sujet. Paris: UGE, 10/18, 1975, 29-61.

Studies the romantic myth of "impossible unity" to show
the common (mythic) origin of philosophical and literary

discourse. Uses psychoanalytic theory (Freud and Lacan)
to analyze the "romantic phenomenon"--regression,
narcissism, aggressivity--and to explain its enduring
power. First examines the formulations of Hegel and
Kierkegaard, showing that both theorize time as a
relation with death, that is, a return to the origin, and
for both the relation between subjects is a specular one:
in its search for "impossible unity" the subject reduces
the Other to the Same. Then defines each of the three
terms describing the romantic myth-regression,
narcissism, and aggressivity--using the scientific
categories of psychoanalysis. Finally, explicates
Aragon's novel La Mise à mort, using the mythic and
psychoanalytic concepts discussed. Demonstrates the
presence of the romantic myth (here comments briefly on
woman as Other) and its simultaneous interrogation and
death through self-reflective narrative techniques.
Concludes that the romantic myth remains alive in Western
culture, but that the novel is no longer its favored
arena.

167a   Earlier versions appeared in Romantisme 1 and as
        "L'Ame pupilline" in L'Arc 53 (1973), 43-8.

168   ————. "'Un miroir, c'est-à-dire un piège'." Miroirs
       du sujet. Paris: UGE, 10/18, 1975, 104-61.

An analysis of writer Roger Laporte's work, originally
published in two separate articles: "Histoire d'un
sourire" and "Le shamanisme de l'écriture." Begins the
first text with some reflections on literary theory,
describing briefly the different but complementary
"affective" and "empirical" approaches. Situates herself
here among those who, like Freud, practice "hedonistic
criticism." Moves to Laporte's writing, which she
characterizes as telling "of the impossibility of a
coming into being ("avènement") that is happening."
Develops a comparison with Jean Vauthier's play Le
personnage combattant--finding in both a search for
pleasure through language and an "opening without
object"--and Marguerite Duras's novel Le ravissement de
Lol V. Stein--whose main character is also looking for "a
past deliberately lost." Uses Lacan's conceptualization
of the real, the event, and phantasy ("le fantasme") to
inform her lengthy explication of Laporte's Une voix de
fin silence and Pourquoi? Says that these texts tell of
"pure events," the emblem of which is the smile. Quotes

extensively. A dense analysis. Asserts, in the second
text, that Laporte has created a "phantasmatic theory of
writing" that places him among the small number of
writers, philosophers, and thinkers in the forefront of
linguistic-cultural change. Calls him a shaman, or its
contemporary equivalent, an analyst. Presents his theory
developing her analogy of writer-shaman/analyst and
making comparisons with Freud, Lacan, and Lévi-Strauss.

168a   "Histoire d'un sourire" appeared in Critique.

168b   "Le shamanisme de l'écriture" first appeared in
        Sud 10 (1973), 68-77.

169   ———. "Un numéro." L'Arc 58 (1974), 1-3.

    Introduces this special issue on Lacan. Explains the
genesis of this study of Lacan by women only, as well as
its guiding "principle": to show the impact of the
Lacanian cultural "mutation" on women's writing.
Describes briefly Lacan's appearance on the intellectual
and academic scene and the ways he has changed language,
history and ideas.

INTERVIEWS WITH

170 Cixous, Hélène. "Echange." Catherine Clément and Hélène
        Cixous. La jeune née. Paris: UGE, 10/18, 1975, 247-96.

    A two-part dialogue. In "Une maîtresse femme" the
authors debate women's relationship to organized
expository discourse ("le discours de maîtrise"). They
agree that women can and should use such coherent
discourse, but disagree as to whether the transmission of
knowledge can ever occur outside of repressive power
structures. The lively exchange in "L'Intenable"
(literally, the unruly one) revolves around the hysteric--
her socio-historical and metaphoric roles. Evoking
Bataille, Cixous asserts that woman's "anti-establishment
force," epitomized in the repressed desire of the
hysteric, "smashes the family to pieces." Clément
rejects this conjunction of the psycho-sexual and the
political, retorting that the hysteric, even one such as
Flaubert, who enters into the production of the symbolic,
effects no true change in society.

* ———— and Luce Irigaray. "La femme, son sexe, et le
   langage." <u>La Nouvelle Critique</u> No. 82 (March 1975),
   36-9.

   See (337).

171 ———— and Bernard Pingaud. "Roman-Analyse." <u>Revue</u>
    <u>française de psychanalyse</u> 38, No. 1 (January <u>1974</u>),
    5-16.

   Discusses with Pingaud the characteristics of the
   "analytical novel," the role of its author, the relation
   of psychoanalysis and "écriture," and the cultural
   function of both, using as a springboard his <u>La voix de</u>
   <u>son maître</u>. Proposes that the experience of analysis is
   crucial for it allows for the existence in the novel of a
   "relational voice," "the echo that occurs between two
   voices." Asserts that analysis is fundamentally
   novelistic and that the function of the analytical novel
   is to offer "in traditional form what psychoanalysis
   deals with in a new form." Points to the "fictional"
   component of theoretical works by psychoanalysts to
   support her claim that the process of analysis is
   analogous to that of writing.

Collin, Françoise:

ESSAYS AND ARTICLES

172 ————. "Conter n'est pas compter (Mais est-ce que ça
    compte?)." <u>Le Récit et sa représentation</u>. Proceedings
    from the Colloques de Saint-Hubert, May 1977. Paris:
    Payot, 1978, 125-31.

   Gives Collin's definition of a "writer," based on her
   own experience: one who accomplishes the task of giving
   form to the "unformulable," whose discipline and
   concentration remove her from "the prodigality of life"
   and point her toward organization, durability and death.
   Describes the narrative ("le récit") in economic terms as
   an "appropriation," and "exploitation" of the "capital"
   of words and images, whence the pun in the title: a
   "story" ("conte") is an "account" or "calculation"
   ("compte"). Asks if women's writing is not a contestation
   of this capitalist/patriarchal conception of the text.
   Examines the material conditions under which women
   write. Speaks of "feminine language" as arising from

"the resurrection of the woman and of the mother" by the
"daughter." Evokes this language as an "outflow of the
body" that rejects the categories of "literary paternity"
and effects a "deliverance" of language.

173 ─────. "Le corps v[i]olé." Les Cahiers du GRIF No. 3
(June 1974), 5-21.

Criticizes the way the female body is currently viewed
as one promoting violence, and thus "denaturing"
intersexual relations. The female body is perceived and
portrayed as a "producer" (of children, of work, of value
as merchandise); as an object that undergoes rape,
prostitution, reproduction, and the exigencies of fashion
and inaccessible images; as an invisible screen on which
masculine desire is projected; and as the repressed
figure of imposed morality and "proper education." The
way out is for women to assume and express their desire:
their desire for self-love, for the world, and for the
"other," without any power relationships. A lyrical
piece.

174 ─────. "D'une langue déplacée." Liberté 19 (July-
October 1977), 275-79.

Describes her relation to writing and identifies
herself first and foremost as a "woman who writes," and
not as the embodiment of her native Belgian national
culture, saying, "It is when I write that I am closest to
myself." Situates herself in relation to the French
language "that is assigned to her" and that always
"escapes her." Calls writing a "clearing away" of
repression and women's writing, by nature, a form of
political contestation. Criticizes so-called " national
literatures" as a form of domination that has "displaced"
the languages of the oppressed.

175 ─────. "Ecriture et matérialité." Critique 26 (1970),
747-58.

Discusses a collection of Maurice Blanchot's essays,
L'entretien infini (1969), describing how it "forces us
to come up against the ambiguity of writing." Elaborates
on Blanchot's "plural language" ("parole plurielle")
which, rather than any sort of traditional dialogue, is a
language that "escapes any point of view," a generous
discourse of "disappropriation" and "negativity" on the
part of the writing subject. Goes on to explain two key

ideas in the collection: the "deconstruction" by the text
itself of the terms it puts forth; and its joining of a
theory of writing with the revolutionary praxis of
communism. An example of an early study that sheds light
on both Collin's intellectual evolution and the roots of
feminist theory on the disappropriation of language.

176 ————. "Féminitude et féminisme." Les Cahiers du GRIF
No. 1 (November 1973), 5-22.

Proposes, "for reflection and discussion," some
"dominant themes" of feminism. First, defines "feminitude" as "the discrimination common to all women" and
traces the areas in which that discrimination is manifest:
work and professional training, love, and sexual proscrip-
tions. Then, introduces the issues of biological determinism, reproductive freedom, and ecology as essential
areas for change. Finally, calls feminism "the desire
for another society," one based not on the inversion of
the present power structure, but on changed economic and
social priorities. In order to achieve the two essential
conditions for this society--women's economic independence and their biological independence--women must regroup
collectively and work at once within and without the
present system. A very basic, somewhat outdated analysis,
but a good example of early 1970's feminist perspectives.

177 ————. "Polyglo(u)ssons." Les Cahiers du GRIF 12 (June
1976), 3-9.

A fragmentary introduction to this special issue that
develops several aspects of the problem of women and
language: (1) language as a "coding" of the body in which
sexual difference makes for linguistic variations.
Posits that the dominant "public language"--one of
mastery and appropriation--is "foreign" to women and is a
"rhetorical" self-representation of male power. Calls
the masculine language "manipulative" and says times of
revolution have been only brief sexually equalizing
moments; (2) the problematic notion of a language that
inscribes the body. Says it is not a single women's
language but the "freedom" to speak numerous "de-terri-
torialized" languages ("polyglotte"). Cautions against a
new "encoding" of another normative "feminine" rhetoric.

178 ————. "Le volet descend." Les Cahiers du GRIF 23-24
(December 1978), 60-2.

Reflects on her experience with GRIF, at this point of its ceasing publication. Describes her own evolution within feminism, then her confrontation with the problem of writing. Evokes her writing as "double," as the clear and "useful" writing demanded by Belgian cultural norms and also the subjective, "unreadable" one that is her own. Sees "surprising" and "use-less" new kinds of writing as the most radical acts, as a "relationship with the unknown" that should be a model for social change.

INTERVIEWS WITH

179 "Le langage pauvre." Les Cahiers du GRIF 13 (October 1976), 26-8.

A debate centered on women's use of "elaborate" (scholarly or specialized) language versus "poor" language. While some maintain women should "run free" among all languages--including that of theory--others insist language must be accessible to all women. Also, some see "poor" language as the "closest," most authentic one while others defend theoretical discourse as a possible source of "pleasure" for women.

180 ————, Michèle Montrelay, et al. "Débats." Le Récit et sa représentation. Proceedings from the Colloques de Saint-Hubert, May 1977. Paris: Payot, 1978, 133-39.

A heated discussion of "masculine" and "feminine" writing that is a response to Collins's talk, "Conter n'est pas compter" (172). Montrelay asks what the function of a book is for women if for men making a book "replaces" making a child. Collin repeats that her concern is women's relation to writing, and not the definition of a "feminine writing." Several male questioners nonetheless ask for characterizations of "feminine" and "masculine" writing. Ends with a reference to the importance of psychoanalysis for any discussion of the body.

181 Coquillat, Michelle. "Introduction." La Poétique du mâle. Paris: Gallimard, 1982, 23-34.

Introduces her book--a detailed study of the hierarchical opposition man-creator/woman-reproducer as it is demonstrated in the French literary canon from

Corneille to Sollers. Summarizes the logic by which men
have justified their monopolization of creativity and
probes the causes of this oppression. Reflects on the
power of literature, which directly addresses the
unconscious, to perpetuate debilitating stereotypes.
Calls literature a "trap" for women, endlessly reitera-
ting their contingency, their exclusion.

182 **Daguenet-Teissier, Maryvonne.** "Le concret c'est de
     l'abstrait rendu familier par l'usage." Sorcières 12
     (1978), 17-20.

     Examines the social reasons for women's absence from
     the creation and elaboration of theory. Defends her own
     desire for theory as enriching her encounters with the
     world and insists on the need for women to contribute
     their perceptions to the elaboration of thought.

183 **"Debate."** Liberté Nos. 106-107 (July-October 1976),
     26-64.

     Involves many participants at the "Rencontre québécoise
     internationale des écrivains" (including Nicole Brossard,
     France Théoret, Annie Leclerc, Christiane Rochefort,
     Dominique Desanti, and Anne Philippe). Jumps around in
     its discussion of the relationship of women to writing,
     focusing principally on the obstacles they have
     encountered. Brossard draws a distinction between the
     situation in France and Quebec, since, in colonized
     countries, the relationship of both women and men to
     writing is different from that in non-colonized
     countries. In Quebec, men assume a partly "passive" role
     as creators and writers, a sort of "feminine identity"
     not necessary in France. Brossard also describes the
     relationship of an individual to her or his body as
     differing for women and men. Rochefort raises the
     material obstacles to writing women have faced. Desanti
     points to women's historical relationship to writing.
     The central question is not always addressed in this
     debate.

184 **Delphy (Dupont), Christine.** "L'ennemi principal."
     Partisans Nos. 54-55 (July-October 1970), 157-72.

     Analyzes the feminist struggle in relation to Marxist
     theory of class struggle, in terms of the contradictions
     and conflicts between them. Attempts to reconcile the
     two struggles and to furnish the women's movement with

"bases for a materialist analysis of the oppression of women." Proceeds, first, with a study of women's relationship to systems of production, specifically their work in the home and with children, that views the family as a place of economic exploitation. Sees as causes of that exploitation the exclusiveness of women's responsibility for the home and the absence of remuneration for their work. Concludes that women's specific relation to production is one of "servitude." Establishes parallels between so-called "productive" (remunerated) and "nonproductive" (non-remunerated) activities in terms of benefits to the overall economy. Then, uses the framework of a class analysis to evaluate women's situation and states that if industrial production gives rise to capitalist exploitation, familial production (domestic services) gives rise to patriarchal exploitation. Concludes that women's providing free work in a marriage constitutes a relationship of "slavery." Finally, terms the patriarchal exploitation of women "common" (shared by all married women), "specific" (peculiar to women only), and "principal" (determinant of their class condition). Sets forth as goal of the women's movement "the total destruction of the patriarchal system of production and reproduction." Typical of the earliest post-1968 radical feminist/leftist analyses.

184a   Trans. as "The Main Enemy" in Women's Research and Resources Centre Pamphlet, 1970/77. Trans. reprinted in Feminist Issues I, No. 1, (1980).

185   ———. "A Materialist Feminism is Possible." Feminist Review 4 (February 1980), 79-105.

Responds, initially, to attacks on her earlier piece, "Pour un féminisme matérialiste (186), then goes on to clarify and defend "materialist feminism" as the best method for dealing with women's oppression. Claims that combining theory with practice—which only an extended application of Marxist principles permits—will reconcile the current anti-intellectual/intellectual split among feminists. Stresses "those things in Marx which are consistent with women's revolt"—not primarily Marx's analysis of capitalism, but rather his "materialist" theory of history as one of domination. Concludes by saying would-be feminist critiques that attack the individual rather than her/his ideas continue to exempt men from responsibility for the oppression of women.

*   ————. "Proto-féminisme et anti-féminisme." Les Temps
     modernes 346 (May 1975), 1469-500.

     (See 476).

186 ————, (C. D.). "Pour un féminisme matérialiste."
     L'Arc 61 (1975), 61-7.

     Argues in forceful though difficult Marxian terms that
     feminism is at once a revolution of society and a
     revolution of knowledge. After positing that the
     oppression of women is an "arbitrary" (vs. "natural"),
     changeable, "social" situation and that all social
     sciences, to be valid, must therefore take oppression as
     their premise; goes on to explain why "materialism" is
     the only approach to a truly feminist inquiry. A
     feminist materialist interpretation--one that treats
     "intellectual products as the result of social
     relationships and the latter as power relationships"--
     rejects existent categories of knowlege because these
     categories themselves are "weapons of the (ruling)
     ideology." The intellectual procedure of materialist
     feminism is not yet defined; but it is, fundamentally, a
     new way of "looking" which, unlike psychoanalysis,
     perceives "sexuality" in its true political sense.
     "Materialist feminism will not leave untouched any part
     of reality, any domain of knowledge, any aspect of the
     world."

     186a   Partially trans. as "For a Materialist Feminism"
            in (19).

187 Denis, Marie. "Pour parler je ne crains personne."
     Les Cahiers du GRIF 13 (October 1976), 21-5.

     A "devil's advocate" dialogue with herself in which
     Denis raises questions about women and language. Defends
     her belief in the individual language of her own body.
     Refuses to generalize or "essentialize" a "woman's
     language." Speculates that language is "the place where
     oppressed class and sex meet most clearly," since the
     dominant language is "linked to sex and money." Says
     women are too "polite" in accepting the language imposed
     on them and in not sufficiently expressing the authentic
     language of their experience. Somewhat ambiguous.

188 **Desanti, Dominique.** "Communication." <u>Liberté</u> Nos.
     106-107 (July-October 1976), 67-74.

     Advocates the "expression of their total self"--of
     their masculine and feminine components--in women's
     writing, claiming that, until now, women have internalized
     and followed the male model only.

189 **Dhavernas, Marie-Jo.** "Puisque ces mystères me dépassent,
     feignons d'en être l'organisateur." <u>La Revue d'en face</u>
     4 (November 1978), 24-9.

     Argues strongly against theories of a feminine
     specificity or specific "féminitude" on the grounds of
     their dogmatism: "the right to be different has more or
     less become the prohibition of diversity." Claims
     differences between the sexes are not "a-temporal," but
     "historico-social." It is untrue that, as the new
     "discourse" would have it, each woman is representative
     of all other women; rather, only the individual woman can
     judge her own "déchirement" (literally, internal
     "tearing").

190 **Dupré, Louise.** "L'écriture féminine dans <u>Les herbes
     rouges</u>." <u>Revue de l'Université d'Ottawa/University of
     Ottawa Quarterly</u> 50, No. 1 (January-March 1980), 89-94.

     A general description of the women's fiction that has
     been published recently in the Quebecois journal, <u>Les
     herbes rouges</u>. Presents the common themes of that
     fiction: the difficulty for women of speaking; the search
     for the body and autonomous sexuality; the connection
     between social and verbal power and powerlessness. Also
     mentions the particular preoccupations of such writers as
     Madeleine Gagnon, France Théoret, Yolande Villemaire, and
     others.

Duras, Marguerite:

BOOKS AND COLLECTIONS OF ESSAYS

191 ⎯⎯⎯⎯ and Michelle Porte. <u>Les Lieux de Marguerite
     Duras</u>. Paris: Editions de Minuit, 1977.

     A long conversation about Duras's motivation for
     writing and about the places she uses in her films,

spaces she says are women's not men's (forests, houses,
the sea). Describes this feminine space as one of
silence, reflective of the "natural intelligence" women
possess and also of the maternal womb. Compares visual
images with the written word, saying Duras "writes" both
from the "same place," a static, unchanging spot that is
the site of memory and of desire. Discusses Duras's
family background and gives interesting photos.

192 ————— and Xavière Gauthier. Les parleuses. Paris:
     Minuit, 1974.

A series of conversations between the two women that
illuminate Duras's work—its use of language, its
political intentions, its themes and figures. Addresses
principally Duras's refusal to "make sense" in her
writing, opposing woman's "organically" intelligent
discourse to masculine "theoretical" intelligence.
Points to the "white spaces" ("blancs") characteristic of
the Durassian text and their meaningfulness as sexual
subversions of traditional writing. Calls for a
"negative" political action by women, in the sense of
refusing the social order and its language. Also
discusses the use of the "double" in Duras's books and
films, as a form of verbal and visual displacement and
movement. An essential entry into the Durassian creative
universe.

ESSAYS AND ARTICLES

193 —————. "Seyrig-Hiss." Sorcières 2 (March 1976), 32.

Compares women's words to a "child": they are now an
intact, whole "provision" within women which, when used,
will take on life. And these words will be powerful.

INTERVIEWS WITH

194 Gauthier, Xavière. "Il y a comme des cris, mais silen-
     cieux." Tel Quel 58 (Summer 1974), 97-9.

Evokes Duras's experience of writing as one that begins
with space, image, and movement, followed by fragmented
words and "white spaces," or new broken syntactic
chains. Traces her writing history as beginning with
safe, male-oriented "imitations" and evolving toward
painful and uncharted feminine experiments. Describes

the "state" Duras is in when she writes--the same as that
her readers enter--as "inside" a space within herself.
Distinguishes this expression of feminine "displacement"
and rupture from the full linear, "theoretical" writing
of men.

195 Horer, Suzanne and Jeanne Socquet. "Marguerite Duras:
     Interview." La Création étouffée. Paris: Pierre
     Horay, 1973, 172-87.

     Responds to the book's theme of "stifled creation" by
     presenting dissuasive elements in Duras's own literary
     autobiography, incuding difficulties in her childhood,
     social obstacles facing the woman writer, and the
     problems of maternity. Calls men "theoretical cops" who
     cannot stop talking and who impede women's expression and
     says women need to transgress prohibitions in their
     writing.

     195a Partially trans. in (19).

196 Husserl-Kapit, Susan. "An Interview with Marguerite
     Duras." Signs 1, No. 2 (Winter 1975), 423-34.

     Affirms strongly Duras's belief in sexual specificity
     and difference, especially in the areas of ideas and
     feelings. Says Duras's own writing is a contestation of
     male domination whose free-flowing, rhythmic, unchronolog-
     ical style translates the "darkness" and silence women
     have been living. Privileges the feminine and infuses
     with positive meaning female madness and the female body:
     "The rhetoric of woman is anchored in the body." Useful.

     196a Partially reprinted in (19).

197 Porte, Michelle. "Entretien (avec Marguerite Duras)."
     Le Camion, suivi de: Entretien avec Michelle Porte.
     Paris: Minuit, 1977, 85-136.

     Uses Duras's film Le camion as a basis for discussion
     of language and women. Insists on the primacy of words
     for Duras, particularly words that "say nothing," that
     make no logical ties, that instead make "holes" in the
     text. Explains the film's image of the interior of a
     truck as representative of the dark, silent, closed space
     from which writing arises. Also interprets the woman in
     the truck as "everywoman," whose response to oppression

in the world is to invent, to "create herself" unceasingly. Identifies the "madness" visible in the film with
Duras's own--and all women's--fear of going mad in our
culture. An interesting viewpoint on the link between
personal and more general politics.

   *   Socquet, Jeanne and Suzanne Horer. "Marguerite Duras:
       Interview." La création étouffée. Paris: Pierre
       Horay, 1973, 172-87.

       (See 195).

BOOKS ABOUT

198 Marini, Marcelle. Territoires du féminin: Avec Margue-
     rite Duras. Paris: Minuit, 1977.

     "(S')écrire avec..."; "Le Vice-Consul: Territoires du
     féminin."

     The introductory essay, "(S')écrire avec," evokes the
presentation of women in Duras's novels, in a text that
itself reproduces the qualities of the Durassian
evocation of the feminine: describes women as "surviving
in a presence/absence that skirts life, history, without
touching them." Says that, according to Duras, the
feminine subject "disappears" in the dominant discourse,
is reduced to a "living dead," a "distracted obedience,"
a "silent body"; this "disappearance" is reflected in
both Duras's and Marini's language. Claims Duras sees
two options for women under the current order: either
they "perish" in masculine definitions of them, or they
rebel and are marginalized for being "mad." Describes
Duras's sense of women's relation to time as an
obstructed connection to memory, a lack of place in the
past, which makes women's construction of the self
difficult. Speaks of the "violent" events in Duras's
stories in which a woman is "ripped" from her dead
existence and gains access to language. Elaborates on
the fundamentally "tragic" vision of our world in Duras's
works, evident in her belief in irremediable sexual
difference and impossible union and in the inevitable
madness caused by the search for absolute love. Says
Duras seeks a way out of the stifling social order
through her writing, one that "opens the space for the
emergence of a true language about women's body and
desire." Claims her writing, which gives us access to

the unconscious, resists traditional analysis and categorizing. Looks at Duras's texts in light of Irigaray's theories about the inscription of sexual difference (see 314). Ends with a reflection on the "disorienting" effect of Duras's texts on her, Marini, whose writing in turn was transformed by the experience. Subsequent chapters examine in great detail one of Duras's novels, Le Vice-Consul.

ESSAYS AND ARTICLES ABOUT

* Cixous, Hélène and Michel Foucault. "A propos de Marguerite Duras." Cahiers Renaud-Barrault 89 (1975), 8-22.

(See 201).

199 Forrester, Viviane. "Territoires du cri." Marguerite Duras. Ed. François Barat and Joël Farges. Paris: Editions Albatros, 1975, 134-6.

Describes the qualities of Duras's films, in particular India Song, in terms of time and space: they seem to have "destroyed" the "distance" of memory in time and they take place in a "pure presence" of life reduced to its simplest "being." Says underlying all of Duras's work is the inexpressible: "the cry." Difficult but suggestive.

200 ———. "Voir. Etre vue." Magazine littéraire No. 158 (March 1980), 11-13.

Situates all of Duras's novels and films in relation to the ball scene in Le ravissement de Lol V. Stein, a scene of painful and passionate abandonment it likens to a Freudian "primitive moment" to which the rest of life refers. Says other key Durassian scenes use the same topos of seeing/being seen and discusses them in terms of their psychoanalytic content.

201 Foucault, Michel and Hélène Cixous. "A propos de Marguerite Duras." Cahiers Renaud-Barrault 89 (1975), 8-22.

A conversation between Foucault and Cixous that evokes the "Duras effect," a force in her work that is difficult to grasp. Cixous points to the ongoing "stripping away" ("dépouillement"), the "art of poverty" in Duras's texts, in which all is reduced to a "nothing" that is "love"

itself. Also raises the power of the "look" in Duras's
work, one comparable to the effect of "memory without
(specific) memories." Foucault distinguishes the flow in
her films from that in her novels, and Cixous picks up on
this to discuss the erotic in Duras. Also talks about
"voice" and the visual/tactile in both her films and her
novels and the unusual effect they create. Highly
abstract.

202 Gauthier, Xavière. "La danse, le désir." Cahiers
     Renaud-Barrault 89 (1975), 23-32.

     Uses the motif of the dance--its eroticism and its
     relation to death--to evoke the link between women's
     bodies and their creative expression.

203 ────. "Marguerite Duras et la lutte des femmes."
     Magazine littéraire No. 158 (March 1980), 16-19.

     Inquires into Duras's feminism, saying her vision of
     women is complex: sees both a "materialist" thread in
     Duras's view of women as an oppressed "class," as well as
     an abstract and problematic reaffirmation of female
     specificity rooted in her belief in the "organic intelli-
     gence" of women. Claims Duras calls upon women to refuse
     social structures by turning to their "interiority."

204 Lacan, Jacques. "Hommage fait à Marguerite Duras, du
     ravissement de Lol V. Stein." Cahiers Renaud-Barrault
     (December 1965). Reprinted in Marguerite Duras. Ed.
     François Barat and Joël Farges. Paris: Ed. Albatros,
     1975, 93-9.

     Primarily an analysis of the character Lol V. Stein in
     Duras's novel of the same name. Refers to the relation
     between the psychoanalyst and the artist, saying the
     latter "knows" things before the former does, and praises
     Duras on the grounds that in her works "the practice of
     the (written) letter converges with the use of the
     unconscious." For the initiated.

*   Makward, Christiane. "Structure du silence/du délire."
     Poétique No. 35 (September 1978), 314-24.

     (See 130).

205 Montrelay, Michèle. "Sur Le ravissement de Lol V. Stein."
     L'ombre et le nom: Sur la féminité. Paris: Minuit,
     1977, 7-23.

     A combination of a talk given in a seminar with Lacan
     in 1965 and several lessons on Duras taught at Vincennes
     in 1969. Analyzes Duras's novel, Le ravissement de Lol
     V. Stein, in a Lacanian perspective. Reinterprets the
     key "event" in the novel (the ball scene)--the fugitive
     and "lost" moment that nonetheless persists and "insists"
     for the protagonist--as setting off not an effort to
     remember, but rather, a movement toward further
     "forgetting." Describes the reader's experience of the
     novel as one of a similar "forgetting." Evokes the
     inscription in Duras's texts of the "pulsions," the
     spaces, the "holes" in language as the inscription of the
     unconscious. Discusses the "nothing" at the core of the
     novel, both in formal terms of the book's refusal of
     "realism" and in psychological terms of the dynamics of
     love. Speaks of Lol, a woman with a "void," an "absence"
     at her center, not only as a specific character, but also
     as representation of the feminine, of "the Shadow"
     ("l'Ombre"): "Lol is that part of us that stays on the
     side of things, that remains in the realm of pleasure
     ("jouissance"), in the Shadow...without it, the
     unconscious cannot exist." Difficult.

206 Rabant, Christiane. "La bête chanteuse." L'Arc 58
     (1974), 15-20.

     Likens the effect of reading Lacan's Séminaires with
     that of reading Duras's Le ravissement de Lol V. Stein,
     saying they produce a similar sense of "exteriority," of
     spatial "opening" ("béance") without limits. Says all
     senses, especially hearing, are engaged in this effect of
     "deafness." Evokes for both authors the Lacanian concept
     of femininity: "division." Is itself intentionally
     imitative of Lacan's style. Suggestive and metaphorical,
     but obscure.

207 Tytell, Pamela. "Lacan, Freud, et Duras." Magazine
     littéraire No. 158 (March 1980), 14-15.

     Examines the relationship between psychoanalysis and
     literature, beginning with Freud's search in imaginative
     texts for "proof" of his theories. Elaborates on Lacan's
     appreciation of Duras's novels, of the convergence of her

texts with the unconscious, specifically her understanding and use of "the look" ("le regard") and of the human
triangle.

* Vasseur, François. "J'écris." La Nouvelle barre du jour
   No. 99 (February 1981), 65-71.

   (See 71).

208 Eaubonne, Françoise d'. "De l'écriture, du corps et de
     la révolution." Les Cahiers du GRIF 20 (April 1978),
     9-10.

     After stating that "[her] relationship to [her] body is
     [her] relationship to writing and to revolution," d'Eau-
     bonne says the role of writers is to spread revolutionary
     erotic "flames" everywhere. Gives examples of different
     kinds of "body pride" women can possess, including her
     own.

209 "Editorial." La Revue d'en face: Revue de politique
     féministe 1 (May 1977), 3-6.

     Explains publication of this journal in terms that
     clearly reject the dichotomy of a women's versus a men's
     language. Refuses a "fetishism of languages," claiming
     that its own writing, while open to the "expression of
     everything that remains in darkness," will be primarily
     "functional." Sees the journal as a vehicle for
     expressing "the full extent of the (women's) movement,
     the latter being a totally autonomous struggle."

210 Fauré, Christine. "Le Crépuscule des déesses, ou La
     Crise intellectuelle en France en milieu féministe."
     Temps modernes 414 (January 1981), 1285-91.

     Analyzes and criticizes from a historian's perspective
     the current tendency within French feminism that is
     searching for a feminine sexual specificity, which it
     calls "a retreat into aesthetics" and a revival of "the
     old naturalistic ideal." Says that, though this response
     is understandable in light of the current anti-feminist
     backlash, it is a dangerous avatar of the "eternal
     feminine" debunked by Beauvoir (1). Likens such post-
     1968 "utopian" thought to that of the last century, in
     that political liberation movements brought women to

affirm positively precisely what had been previously
censored: their bodies and their sexuality. Mentions
specifically the work of Luce Irigaray (309 and 308) as
examples of this new "tribute to female nature" and of
the "reactionary" "devaluation of the temporal and
historical dimension of women," in favor of a celebration
of women's eternal "generative power." Lucid and
convincing.

210a   Trans. as "The Twilight of the Goddesses, or The
        Intellectual Crisis of French Feminism" in Signs 7,
        No. 1 (Autumn 1981), 81-6.

Felman, Shoshana:

ESSAYS AND ARTICLES

211   ——— . "La méprise et sa chance." L'Arc 58 (1974),
        40-8.

        Inquires into the point of psychoanalysis, saying it is
in essence contradictory: if psychoanalysis aspires to
"truth" or "meaning," it is also true that "meaning"
itself is always a "fiction." In order to make analysis
meaningful, calls not for the resolution of this
contradiction, but for the purposeful articulation of
it. Says this conception of psychoanalysis as "a
question" requires a fundamental change in discourse and
shows how Lacan has contributed to this. Goes on to
discuss how a change in the concept of language, one
incorporating the unconscious, implies a different
understanding of knowledge: the myth of a "knowing
(human) subject" is replaced by the fact of "unconscious
knowledge that knows itself"; the subject can grasp this
knowledge only through "scorn" ("méprise"), or the
"effects of non-sense." Says Lacan, in his theoretical
exposition, is always aware of the "untenability" of his
theoretical stance and evinces "scorn" in his writing.
Elaborates on "scorn" by using Lacanian models of grammar
and rhetoric for the language of the unconscious. Shows
how philosophers have misread and misunderstood Lacan, in
their search for a discourse of mastery in what is an
"unlocalizable" writing. Very hard.

211a   Reprinted in La Folie et la chose littéraire.
        Paris: Editions du Seuil, 1978.

212 ———. "Rereading Femininity." Yale French Studies
No. 62 (1981), 19-44.

Treats the problem of "reading" in several ways
connected to women: woman as reader and active interpreting subject (Felman herself); woman as reader of a male
text (in this case, Balzac's La fille aux yeux d'or);
woman as reader of femininity; and woman as reader of men
(here, Freud and Balzac) reading femininity. Addresses
the "riddle of femininity" in its importance for women by
reading a Balzac text that dramatizes this riddle in its
importance for men. Connects the subversion of sexual
polarization that ultimately occurs in Balzac's story—
which subversion it goes on to illuminate—with that in
Freud's essay on "Femininity." Describes, for Balzac's
text, its presentation of sexual difference and hierarchy
and its dramatic wellspring, a character's "misreading of
femininity." Also explains the story's exposition of a
"theory of rhetoric relating sexuality to language," one
characterized by "the interchangeability and the reversibility of masculine and feminine"—a fluidity portrayed
as ultimately threatening. Asserts the male character
comes to discover that "the feminine is not outside the
masculine, its reassuring canny opposite, it is inside
the masculine, its uncanny difference from itself."
Looks at the structures of psycho-sexual desire that
underlie the story's plot and that raise questions about
(literary) representation itself. Difficult.

213 ———. "Women and Madness: The Critical Phallacy."
Diacritics 5, No. 4 (Winter 1975), 2-10.

A discussion of three texts—Phyllis Chesler's Women
and Madness, Luce Irigaray's Speculum de l'autre femme
(314), and Balzac's story "Adieu"—that also elaborates
theoretically on the issue of women and madness. First,
summarizes Chesler's analysis of women's mental health as
a state defined by masculine norms and of women's madness
as "a manifestation both of cultural impotence and of
political castration." Then, contrasts Chesler's social
and empirical approach with Irigaray's interrogation of
Western male-centered theoretical discourse in general,
an inquiry undertaken through a critique of psychoanalysis and philosophy. Isolates Irigaray's central
argument as being against the philosophical "illusion of
duality" which masks a "logical principle of Identity" or
masculine sameness—a principle that subjugates and

defines negatively the other, woman. Questions from what
point, feminine silence or masculine discourse, Irigaray
herself is speaking and raises the danger of "speaking
for" women, a danger Chesler avoids by documenting
women's own voices. Also, asks a general question about
the current radical "deconstruction" of cultural codes of
which feminism is representative: "How can woman be
thought about outside of the Masculine/Feminine framework, other than as opposed to man, without being
subordinated to a primordial masculine model?" Raises
the same question of breaking away from "the logic of
polar oppositions" for an analysis of madness. Goes on
to examine all these interwoven problems by reading
Balzac's short story, "Adieu," a presentation of feminine
madness. Shows, first, the misogyny of traditional
criticism that has totally ignored the story's principal
plot, a woman's descent into madness, while focusing on
"realistic" male-centered concerns only. Then,
re-interprets the story through a feminist reading that
moves women and madness to the center. Reveals and
develops the story's premise that madness is "the absence
of womanhood" and that "cure" is the recognition of
masculine identity. Ends with a statement of the
challenge all women critics face: they must "'re-invent'
language" to "speak outside of the specular phallogocentric structure"--that is, they must "change the mind."
Dense and rich in implication.

213a   Trans. as "Les Femmes et la folie: histoire
        littéraire et idéologique" in La Folie et la chose
        littéraire. Paris: Editions du Seuil, 1978, 138-55.

INTERVIEWS WITH

214   ————, Viviane Forrester, et al. "Don Juan ou la pro-
       messe d'amour." Tel Quel 87 (Spring 1981), 16-36.

A discussion of the theme of Don Juan and love--based
on Felman's book, Le scandale du corps parlant--that
addresses seduction as a "relationship between the sexual
and the linguistic." Calls the discourse of seduction
one of "promises" made and broken, the breaks being
necessitated by the demands of the unconscious and human
mortality. Describes the women characters in the
different versions of Don Juan as well as differences
between masculine and feminine seduction.

215 Sollers, Philippe. "La chose littéraire: sa folie, son
     pouvoir." Tel Quel 80 (Summer 1979), 73-83.

     An interview with Shoshana Felman that centers on the
     purpose and genesis of her book La folie et la chose
     littéraire. Defines her project as studying "literary
     things" with common features but that manifest varying
     conceptions of "madness." Points to the source of her
     interest in the inscription of madness in texts as her
     thesis (and book) on madness in Stendhal. Summarizes the
     concept of madness in Flaubert, Nerval, Rimbaud, Balzac
     and Henry James, and the theoretical problematics of
     studying madness. Also discusses the use of the term
     "literary thing" in contrast to "literature." Refers
     occasionally to the link between madness and contestation
     of sex roles.

216 ———. "La chose littéraire: sa folie, son pouvoir."
     Tel Quel 81 (Fall 1979), 37-51.

     Continuation of previous interview with Felman.
     Discusses the relationship of psychoanalysis to
     literature and the transformations from 19th to 20th
     century texts as parallel to the shift from Freudian to
     Lacanian psychoanalysis. Distinguishes Freud's and
     Lacan's application of psychoanalysis to literature and,
     conversely, their use of literature for analysis. Also
     defines the relation of the philosopher to literature as
     like that of the analyst--one of "desire." Ends with a
     consideration of what makes for the power of a text.

217 Féral, Josette. "Du texte au sujet." Revue de
     l'Université d'Ottawa/University of Ottawa Quarterly
     50, No. 1 (January-March 1980), 39-46.

     Addresses the issue of a specifically feminine writing
     by applying psychoanalytic and semiotic approaches to
     texts. Questions whether there is a sex-specific
     discourse, saying it could exist only at the very deepest
     roots of language, and not in superficial textual
     characteristics. Finds the most probing and radical
     research into a feminine writing in the work of Luce
     Irigaray, whose critique of traditional psychoanalysis it
     summarizes and whose insistence on a new concept of
     "difference" it sees as crucial. Connects the denial of
     a true feminine sexual specificity in Freud and Lacan--

for whom female "difference" is merely "otherness" and
"non-maleness"—with the absence of a feminine linguistic
specificity. Claims women must think and write outside
of the established system that posits a unified subject
and discursive coherence. Suggests feminine linguistic
disruption would be characterized by simultaneity,
plurality, mobility, contiguity, change, and fluidity.
Also asserts there is no critical discourse capable of
addressing this multiple feminine discourse and explains
the limitations of current semiotic approaches (that
focus on the text) and of psychoanalytic theories (that
focus on the writing subject), all of which partake of
the dominant de-sexuated critical "metalanguage." Says
Irigaray poses rather than answers questions, since the
conceptual tools to define a feminine discourse are not
yet in place. Concludes, "The true critical discourse
about a feminine text would in fact be another feminine
discourse." Very useful.

218   ————. "Towards a Theory of Displacement." Sub-Stance
       32 (1981), 52-64.

Compares definitions of "woman" in the present,
constraining culture with new, reinvented identities
possible in a different social order. Says the current
society sees women as "marginal" and "delirious," since
they lack a phallus, and consequently lack power,
identity, and rational language. Also sees the present
order as unable to accept feminine specificity—as
conceiving the feminine only as an inverted image of the
masculine—with the result that woman is dispossessed of
her sexuality and rendered "absent." Views culture as
having separated and opposed "woman" and "mother."
Claims women have, however, retained a link with their
bodies through which they can reinvent themselves and
"inscribe" their "presence," and proposes that women do
this in order to disrupt phallocentric society.

Finas, Lucette:

BOOKS AND COLLECTIONS OF ESSAYS

219   ————. _Le Bruit d'Iris_. Paris: Flammarion, 1978.

"Question de _tempo_" (préface de Roland Barthes); "Le
choc de la baguette sur la peau du tambour" (222);
"L'Iris d'Horus" (225); "La charge" (221); "Salut"

(231); "La dissection" (223); "L'oeil artisan" (228);
"Hors corps" (224); "Des corps en eau trouble" (227);
"Parages" (229); "Le coup de D. e(s)t judas" (226); "Le
pourpre du Neutre" (230).

A collection of essays, each of which is an analysis of
a text by a French author and which, together, comprise a
theoretical work about the act of reading. Takes as its
overall concern the question of "l'excès," or the "modification of rhythm and tempo" (slowness, acceleration),
the varying "intensities" (insistence, holding back)
these texts transmit, and the meaning of this "excess" in
each case. The authors, studied chronologically, are
innovative and "poetic" writers of the 18th, 19th and
20th centuries; the method used is a very close
examination of the textual arrangements (semantic,
phonic, poetic, grammatical, stylistic) that create the
impression of modulation. Each essay uses imagery and
lexicon that synesthetically evoke sound and sight (c.f.,
the title, "le bruit d'Iris"), music, and theater.
Manifests an increasingly personal voice as the subject
goes from the critic "Nous" to the objectified reader
"Je" to the author/reader "je." Is prefaced by comments
by Roland Barthes that praise Finas's approach. Essays
vary in difficulty from barely comprehensible to highly
readable but all are lovely "poetic" texts in themselves.

220 ———, Sarah Kofman, et al. Ecarts: Quatre essais à
     propos de Jacques Derrida. Paris: Fayard, 1973.

Lucette Finas, "Le coup de D. e(s)t Judas": 1. "Le
meurtre de l'écolière" (226); 2. "Le théâtre de la
pièce" (232); 3. "La dissection" (223). Sarah Kofman,
"Un philosophe 'unheimlich'": 1. "L'opération de la
greffe" (362); 2. "Un philosophe inouï" (369); 3. "Le
simulacre" (367); 4. "Graphématique et psychanalyse"
(358). Roger Laporte, "Une double stratégie":
Avertissement; Avant-propos; 1. "La voix, la présence,
l'écriture humiliée"; 2. "Dé-construire la présence";
3. "La différance". Jean-Michel Rey, "Notes en marge
sur un texte en cours"; Annexes à l'essai de Lucette
Finas.

A collection of difficult essays on the philosopher/
author, Jacques Derrida, that traces the linguistic,
philosophical, and psychoanalytic underpinnings of his

work. Discusses Derrida's various textual strategies and
his ideas on literature and literary production.

ESSAYS AND ARTICLES

221 ————. "La charge." Le Bruit d'Iris. Paris:
      Flammarion, 1978, 77-91.

   Looks at Villiers de l'Isle Adam's short story, "Les
   brigands," which it calls a "game of catastrophe" that
   expends all its own forces. Says Villier's technique is
   the reinfusion and exploitation of clichés that create a
   movement of "echo," or of "amplification" and "repercus-
   sion."

222 ————. "Le choc de la baguette sur la peau du tambour."
      Obliques 12-13 (1977), 65-77.

   Examines Sade's Florville et Courval as an "impetuous"
   story that unfolds an enigma about identity. Presents
   the story's "vaudevillesque" elements, as well as the
   theatrical arrangements of its "troubled" exposition that
   lead, inevitably, toward incest.

   222a   Reprinted in (219).

223 ————. "La dissection." Ecarts: Quatre essais à propos
      de Jacques Derrida. Ed. Lucette Finas, Sarah Kofman,
      et al. Paris: Fayard, 1973, 57-105.

   Treats Mallarmé's poem "le Pitre châtié," which it says
   "echoes everywhere" within itself and in Mallarmé's whole
   poetic corpus. Traces in technical detail the text's
   aural and visual repetitions and interlacings. Also uses
   this discussion of Mallarmé to comment on two of Derrida's
   essays, "La dissémination" and "La double séance."
   References are quite difficult.

   223a   Reprinted in (219).

224 ————. "Hors corps." Le Bruit d'Iris. Paris:
      Flammarion, 1978, 223-33.

   Analyzes the "Introduction" to Georges Bataille's Le
   bleu du ciel. Sees it as a text whose "doublings" and
   "tremblings" give the effect of memory that is "adrift"

("à la dérive"). Also explores the progressive sensory
and corporal destruction of the book's protagonist.

225 ─────. "L'Iris d'Horus." Le Bruit d'Iris. Paris:
        Flammarion, 1978, 37-75.

        Analyzes Nerval's sonnet "Horus" (in Les filles du feu)
        as a "diffused diversion" of meaning. Describes the
        shifting references of the poem's title. Then both
        "listens to" and "looks at" the poem's "displacing"
        surface, via word by word analysis. Claims the entire
        sonnet "generates itself" out of its first line.
        Difficult.

226 ─────. "Le meurtre de l'écolière." Ecarts: Quatre
        essais à propos de Jacques Derrida. Ed. Lucette Finas,
        Sarah Kofman, et al. Paris: Fayard, 1973, 13-28.

        Examines several of Derrida's essays ("Coup de D," "La
        dissémination," "Hors livre") in an attempt to "stop [his]
        sentence" and uncover its machinations. Proposes a mode
        of "deciphering" Derrida's texts. Uses visual graphics
        and symbols as the best rendering of Derridean
        "machinery." Is almost unreadable.

227 ─────. "Nathalie Sarraute ou les métamorphoses du
        verbe." Tel Quel 20 (1965), 68-77.

        Analyzes five of Sarraute's novels in terms of the
        connection between character and language, tracing in
        them a movement from absent, "transparent" characters to
        material, "opaque" ones, and from pulsionistic words and
        silences to destructive, failed conversations. Specifi-
        cally, describes Tropismes as having "anonymous ghosts"
        whose clichéd words surge forth and give these "shadowy
        forms" their only "being"; Portrait d'un inconnu as
        presenting "figures" with a semblance of identity and
        more opaque, less revealing language; Martereau as
        showing a "family of shadows" into which a named stranger
        arrives, which stranger is made to "disintegrate" by the
        family's spoken suspicions; le Planétarium as having
        clearly identified, materialized, even "reified" charac-
        ters at the same time as it has increasingly "living"
        objects; and les Fruits d'or as presenting objects trans-
        formed into spiritual presences and "hyperconscious,"
        extremely opaque characters that reveal "the pitifulness

of conversation." In general, characters participate
increasingly in becoming "victims" of their own destruction, of their own words and silences that "gnaw away" at
them. A very readable discussion of the "ambiguities" in
Sarraute's fiction that make the reader feel both "inside"
and "outside" of her novels.

227a   Reprinted and revised as "Des Corps en eau
        trouble" in (219).

228   ⸺⸺. "L'oeil artisan." Le Bruit d'Iris. Paris:
        Flammarion, 1978, 181-221.

Studies Claudel's prose poem, "Décembre," claiming it
is a meditation that proceeds by a relaxation of tension.
Stems from Finas's own reaction to the text, a "perturbation" in the face of the poem's obstacles. Evokes in a
close reading the poem's sounds and rhythms.

229   ⸺⸺. "Parages." Reliefs. Paris: Ed. de l'Atelier,
        1975.

Examines Michel Deguy's Tombeau de Du Bellay as a work
that "disturbs" by its tentative, troubled and irreverent
relationship to its poetic ancestor. Says the modern
poet reads as "text" both du Bellay's poems and du
Bellay, the man, himself.

229a   Reprinted in (219).

230   ⸺⸺. "Le Pourpre du Neutre, artefact en trois actes
        et douze scènes." Critique 315 (October 1972), 876-91.

A very strong example of "criticism" that is a "text"
itself. Comments on Cixous's fiction, Neutre, in an
essay that is really a play. The "actors," who have
multiple identities, are "la Phénicienne" (representing
Cixous's writing and the "theatrical" relationship
between Cixous and her writing) and "Lui" or "Il"
(representing the reader, a sort of "voyeur"); the "set"
is composed of reflections and accumulations of things
and images; the "dialogue," replete with mythological and
psychoanalytic references, evokes images of porousness,
movement, multiplicity. A difficult but suggestive piece
that resembles Cixous's own and that shares with Neutre a
common dual purpose: to "assemble (verbal) debris" and
"waste" that will be "neutralized by and in writing"; and

to call on the reader to "scream," to write as well:
"Mais é-cri(v)ez-vous!"

230a   Reprinted in (219).

231   ———. "Salut." Esprit (December 1974), 871-901.

Begins with an important introduction that presents
Finas's changing relationship to her own previous works:
as she moved from fiction to theory, she, as writing
subject, went from a personal first-person "je" to an
objectified third-person "Je." Then, examines Mallarmé's
sonnet "Salut" as a text that "works on itself" until its
full meaning--"dénigrement" ("disparagement")--unfolds at
the end. Proceeds, very self-consciously, with an
elaborate discussion of the poem's title, followed by a
detailed line by line analysis, and finally appended
notes of commentary and self-evaluation.

231a   Reprinted in (219).

232   ———. "Le théâtre de la pièce." Ecarts: Quatre essais
à propos de Jacques Derrida. Ed. Lucette Finas, Sarah
Kofman et al. Paris: Fayard, 1973, 29-55.

Reads Derrida's play La pharmacie de Platon to understand its "inscriptions" even while it claims his text
discourages such an analysis. Says the "plot" of the
piece is the process of writing itself. Quite difficult.

INTERVIEWS WITH

233   Clerval, Alain. "Entretien avec Finas." Chroniques de
l'art vivant No. 35 (December 1972-January 1973), 26-7.

Refers primarily to Finas's La crue, a study of
Bataille, as representative of her perspective on
writing. Describes Finas's text as an "irreducible"
work, one that is an "excess" or an "overflowing" of
Bataille's work.

234   Coulange, Alain. "Entretien en marge de La crue."
Gramma 1 (Autumn 1974), 111-31.

Discusses Finas's work on Bataille, specifically on the
question of textual subversion, of the continued undermining of textual "excess" his works reveal. Analyzes at

length her way of "reading" Bataille, in regard to the
inevitability of the text-as-representation of something
(calls this representation "the text's excrement"). Says
her experience of his texts is a "gnawing insistance" or
constant effort toward "erasing" the conventions of
reading. Ends with mention of the political implications
of reading and writing that shatter the stability of the
signifying systems in place. Questions virtually
incomprehensible.

234a   Partially reprinted in (224).

ESSAYS AND ARTICLES ABOUT

235 Brée, Germaine. "Lucette Finas: An Introduction."
     Contemporary Literature 19, No. 1 (Winter 1978), 300-19.

     Introduces Finas's novels, critical essays and textual
     interpretations as texts that "tease the mind." Discusses
     in detail Finas's very original relationship to language
     and word play and the avant-garde "reading process" her
     work embraces. Examines the importance of theatricality
     in her writing, or the actors, roles, masks and
     encounters it "stages." Then, looks at each specific
     work for its narrative devices and experiments with
     language. A useful but difficult entry into an esoteric
     writer.

236 Cerquiglini, Bernard. "Figures d'histrion." Critique
     365 (October 1977), 949-54.

     A review of Finas's novel Donne that says she "disturbs"
     and "displaces" language and the reader, in a fiction that
     is nonetheless also "calculated." Claims her language
     critiques the notion of language's "transparency." Calls
     the novel a "painful," "anguished" and "obsessional"
     rendering of the "suffering of the world."

237 Jean, Raymond. "Donne de Lucette Finas." Pratique de la
     littérature. Paris: Seuil, 1978, 133-4.

     A very short review of Finas's novel Donne that evokes
     the strange corporal universe of the book. Describes the
     novel's unexpected and complicated linguistic "distur-
     bances," which it deems the result of its "metonymic"
     play with "the writing of the body."

Forrester, Viviane:

BOOKS AND COLLECTIONS OF ESSAYS

238 ———. _La violence du calme_. Paris: Seuil, 1980.

L'enfer est vide; L'épopée d'un troupeau; Mallarmé is a
machine gun; "Eccola!"; Le "rien" de Cordélia; "Je ne te
voyais pas si malheureux!"; Des habits sans le moine;
Albertine, Albertine, lama sabbachtani! M. Flaubert,
c'est moi; Le nom de la survivance; On est prié de fermer
un oeil.

A radical critique of History. Indicts the powers in
place--those who have made History--for imposing the
coercive false optimism and censorship that give our
culture the appearance of "calm," when in fact the human
"mass" is destined for and afraid of death. Says
"terror," "violence" and "death" are not allowed to
emerge and so remain within the individual. Claims the
violent coercive forces in our culture have become
imperceptible and invisible. Refers to the role of the
dominant discourse in repressing speaking and writing
"differences." Sees the body, if freed from violence, as
a sign of "life," but not life as defined by cultural
authorities. Asserts that certain artists and writers
have retained sufficient "memory of the present" to be
able to "ignore" the destructive powers in place but that
the vast majority of people have accepted, forgotten and
internalized the existing repression of difference and of
the present. Says this is the true "violence," the real
"scandal": that we acknowledge as scandal what is only an
exacerbated form of everyday violence and scandal. Also
shows how thought itself, represented here by knowledge
of certain great authors (Mallarmé, Sade, Artaud, Woolf,
Shakespeare, Proust, Flaubert, Freud), is used as an
instrument of power. Examines how creators must struggle
against the dominant "technological" discourse, especially
women, who are "excluded from the system of discourses."
Talks about the role of psychoanalysis in "exhuming" the
"un-said," including repressed sexuality. Highly imaged
and abstract but strong.

239 ———. _Virginia Woolf_. Paris: O.R.T.F. et _La Quinzaine
littéraire_, 1973.

1. "Des mots anciens dans un ordre nouveau"; 2. "La
Hogarth Press"; 3. "Virginia Woolf, précurseur du
Mouvement de Libération des Femmes"; 4. "Visages de
Virginia Woolf"; 5. "Combat contre les gouffres: la
folie"; 6. "Folie et Créativité. Les secrets du texte";
7. "'Jette un dernier regard...'"

The revised transcripts of seven programs at France
Culture that sketch a portrait of the British novelist.
Men and women who knew Virginia Woolf comment on her
literary and political views and explore the influence of
her recurrent madness. In section 3, Forrester is joined
by writers Ann Thomas and Monique Wittig. They focus on
the problems faced by women writers: the need to (re)dis-
cover their identity, the obstacles posed by an alien,
male language and culture, and the challenge to invent
new literary forms.

ESSAYS AND ARTICLES

240 ———. "L'autre corps." Trois guinées, Virginia Woolf.
      Paris. des femmes, 1977, 11-31.

A preface to Woolf's text that sees it through the
prism of the woman writer of 1938, specifically, of
Woolf's being denied access to "the world, to action, to
free movement, to independence, to a lucid relationship
with her own body." Describes Woolf as "knowing how to
read the world without passing through the translation of
language, discourse, syntax," and as denouncing "the
scandal that has reduced women to the status of a
minority." Speaks of the author's completely "organic"
universe, which in Three Guineas goes to the deepest
possible sensual level and "unmasks the horror of the
rational world." Concludes by saying Woolf epitomized in
her writing the shared "feminine destiny" of "not being,"
of being "incarcerated in a denatured society," and of
having to struggle in her mind and body to find the words
"that were inaccessible to her." Moving.

241 ———. "Féminin pluriel." Tel Quel 74 (Winter 1977),
      68-77.

Looks at women's relationship to language by focusing
on several Anglo-Saxon women authors, including Emily
Brontë, Gertrude Stein, Virginia Woolf, Emily Dickinson,
as well as the presentation of women in the works of
these and other writers (Poe, Flaubert). Posits that in

their stories, "there is no woman, woman is suppressed,"
as woman in general is in history and the masculine
imagination. Calls the language of women writers the
vital "silence" that has always been theirs. Sees women,
and all writers, as being in the same situation of
"absence" in relation to language: they are forced to use
a discourse that is inadequate to fully express reality,
that is, "their bodies, their destiny, their (sexual)
difference." Situates the "Absent" woman character in
part in the Anglo-Saxon tradition of the supernatural and
also in pre-Freudian familial "psychodramas." Reevaluates
the seeming "absence" in women's works as a different and
positive "presence," or the "letting in" of things
external to the dominant discourse—"the body, the senses,
the cerebral." States that there is such a thing as
"writing in the feminine" ("écriture au féminin") but
that there are no "feminine" or "masculine" texts.
Suggestive.

242   ⸻. "Je suis l'amour même." Cahiers Renaud-Barrault
        101 (1981), 31-6.

        Using mythological allegory and the contrasting figures
of Psyche and Venus, plays out traditional familial/
psychological dramas within which our culture has
assigned women contradictory roles: "mother" and "woman."
Sees psychoanalysis as perpetuating these myths, even
while it considers itself "anti-social." Requires
familiarity with mythology and psychoanalytic theory.

243   ⸻. "La Qualité de la voix." Sorcières 2 (March
        1976), 44.

        Proclaims women's voices, which have always been
silent, are those "of life itself." Poses the question
of whether it is the same language that "passes through
the voice and through writing" as it calls on women to
"hear" themselves speak.

244   ⸻. "Le Regard des femmes." Paroles...elles
        tournent! Ed. des femmes de Musidora. Paris: des
        femmes, 1976, 12-13.

        Says women's "look" or "gaze" ("regard") and what it
sees are unknown in our culture, which sees through
masculine eyes only. Considers the result of the absence
of women's perspective a partial and "deprived" view of
the world, one that is dangerously "lacking." Predicts

women--particularly in cinema--will "un-cover" these
fresh and un-seen visions.

244a   Trans. as "What Women's Eyes See!" in (19).

245   ――――   . "Le truc de l'histoire." Tel Quel 80 (Summer
        1979), 84-90.

A critique of history, as it has conventionally been
conceived, as the arbitrary and fraudulent imposition of
a particular mass of information. Attacks in particular
the false binarism underlying our notion of history
(e.g., "past" and "present," "man" and "woman"), a false
dualism that is in fact a monolithic, uniform movement
that suppresses all difference. Says our conception of
history has destroyed multiplicity and pluralism and has
"included" women only as "transvestites," as figures
"disguised" in masculine values. Asserts that history as
we know it is neither men's nor women's: its falsifica-
tions render it "the history of no one and nothing."
Finds what is lacking in the traditional view of history--
new life, immediacy, difference, pluralism, silence--in
literary and artistic "texts." Proposes in place of the
fraudulent and mythified "religiosity of History" a
"poetics of History" that would make accessible the
"cracks," the "unedited spaces" of thought. Claims the
reevaluation of history is part of the general reevaluation of language and rationality.

245a   Reprinted in (238).

INTERVIEWS WITH

*   ――――, Shoshana Felman, et al. "Don Juan ou la promesse
     d'amour." Tel Quel 87 (Spring 1981), 16-36.

     (See 214).

246 **Gagné, Sylvie.** "Mots d'elle." La Barre du jour Nos.
     56-57 (May-August 1977), 35-49.

Borrows heavily from other authors--including Lacan,
Blanchot, Irigaray and Cixous--to suggest what would be
"women's words" or language. Uses the Lacanian psychoanalytic model, in particular the idea of the "mirror
stage," to trace the notion of identity (fixed, single)
in patriarchal culture and the objectification of women

that results from that definition. Since language
translates that male-centered conception of self, argues
for women's "subverting the mirror (authority, unity,
identity of self)" by modifying language--such as this
essay itself does, with its shifting pronouns and word
plays.

Gagnon, Madeleine:

BOOKS AND COLLECTIONS OF ESSAYS

247 ⎯⎯⎯⎯. Pour les femmes et tous les autres. Montreal:
        Eds. de l'Aurore, 1974.

A collection of "revolutionary poetry" in which verse
and prose poems, in their form and substance, express
anger and a call for change. The free-flowing and
conversational poems--sometimes in Quebecois spoken
French, always unpunctuated and fragmented--convey
Marxist and feminist critiques of social, political and
sexual structures, in Quebec and in all cultures. Calls
women's experience "a suffocating parenthesis" like that
of all groups traditionally denied access to "high" forms
of expression. Uses marginal notes effectively (including
extensive quoting of the 1970 Marxist-feminist document,
Partisans, libération des femmes année zéro) to stress
the urgency of its message: "The awakening [of the
oppressed] must take place." Is representative of
Gagnon's earlier blending of feminist and leftist political concerns and of her ongoing use of disruptive and
innovative textual forms.

 *   ⎯⎯⎯⎯ and Denise Boucher. Retailles: complaintes
        politiques. Montreal: l'Etincelle, 1977.

        (See 42).

 *   ⎯⎯⎯⎯, Hélène Cixous, and Annie Leclerc.   La venue à
        l'écriture. Paris: UGE, 10/18, 1977.

        (See 87).

ESSAYS AND ARTICLES

248 ⎯⎯⎯⎯ (-Mahony), Madeleine. "'Angéline de Montbrun':
        le mensonge historique et la subversion de la métaphore
        blanche." Voix et images du pays V: Les Cahiers de
        l'Université du Québec No. 30 (1972), 57-68.

Studies the 19th century French Canadian novel, Laure
Conan's Angéline de Montbrun, through a "disalienating
reading," that is, one that rejects the "alienation" and
"historical lies" perpetuated by previous critical
readings. Previous readings focused on the novel's
poetic language and simply described or "translated" its
stylistic figures, thus making the text a static object
adorned with images. Gagnon's "disalienating reading"
posits that poetic language, in this novel and in
general, has a transformative power: metaphors and
metonymies are constantly engaging in the dynamic process
that is the production of the substance of the text. Her
analysis deciphers the "latent" and "manifest" chains of
signifiers which are continually producing meaning in the
novel. Gagnon's method combines concepts from Lacanian
"structural psychoanalysis" with some of Kristeva's
linguistic theories (Gagnon cites Kristeva's Sémiótiké:
Recherches pour une sémanalyse (377). The essay is
difficult, at times opaque, but it offers a fresh look at
a little-known author and also signals a marked departure
in Gagnon's work, from expository structuralist analysis
to more suggestive, poetic discourse.

249 _____. "Ce que je veux s'écrire ne peut pas m'écrire
autrement." Les Nouvelles littéraires No. 2534 (May
26, 1976), 19.

A short meditation on writing and the revolutionary
nature of women's texts.

250 _____. "Communication." Liberté Nos. 106-107 (July-
October 1976), 249-56.

Describes her writing and that of other women as one
that "releases from silence traces of desire." Because
of dominant logocentric preferences in discourse, her
writing is automatically "the word of otherness
('altérité')," the language of women's multiple voices.

251 _____. "Des mots plein la bouche." La Barre du jour
Nos. 56-57 (May-August 1977), 139-47.

Calls, poignantly, for the retrieval, by both women and
men, of their initial language--the stories arising from
the first maternal bond--that is repressed by the
dominant language of masculine culture. Uses a psychoanalytic framework to evoke this "pre-mirror" stage, this

time in women's lives that predates their alienation and
oppression as active subjects. Locates, at this moment
of alienation and break with the woman-to-woman continuity, the point of woman's exclusion from language.
Offers a plan of action in which women are urged to come
out of silence and "say what happened there" (in that
initial maternal place); to know, individually and
collectively, their poetic/political potential; and to
refuse any strategy of subversion that does not come from
women themselves. Suggests these un-heard words will
reflect a new relation to the world--one that is non-
antagonistic, non-appropriative--and previously unimagined
forms of love among women and men. A lovely piece that
is both poetic and theoretical.

252   ————. "Dire ces femmes d'où je viens." Magazine
           littéraire No. 134 (March 1978), 94-6.

A meditation on earlier Quebecois women writers that
expresses admiration for their courage in the face of
social obstacles and indebtedness for their literary
legacy. Says contemporary Canadian feminism can "read
itself" and its revolt in those earlier works. Evokes
the key authors and novels in Gagnon's own past: Laure
Conan's Angéline de Montburn; Anne Hébert; Gabrielle
Roy's Bonheur d'occasion; and Marie-Claire Blais's Une
saison dans la vie d'Emmanuel.

253   ————. "Ecriture, sorcellerie, féminité." Etudes
           littéraires (December 1979), 357-61.

Evokes women's writing by means of an allegorical
comparison with witchcraft. Suggests the way the
"scientist" has traditionally viewed sorcery--one that
serves his need to maintain "objectivity," certainty, and
definitions of comprehensibility and knowledge--is parallel to the way our culture has read women's writing--as
marginal, mad, incomprehensible. Traces the origins and
processes of witchcraft through an imaginary story in
which a sorcerer, asked by a peasant to interpret and
cure a series of physical ills he has endured, performs a
ritual of "words and gestures," of language. Sees the
same function of language--as mediator between "body" and
"meaning," between physical suffering and its metaphoriza-
tion--in women's writing. Says that, for both witchcraft
and women's writing, the "researcher"/reader must listen
to, not squelch or "violate" their authentic message.

Describes women's writing as a "conjuration" caused by
and conducive to "pleasure" in the writer and reader.
Difficult but provocative.

254 ————. "La Femme et le langage: sa fonction comme
parole en son manque." La Barre du jour No. 50 (Winter
1975), 45-57.

Urges an "ideological and political seizing of
language" by women, that is, a revolution by both word
and act. Presents Gagnon's premises and strategies in a
four-part discussion. First, eliminates from her analysis
both "the code" and "the anecdote," or the current
language of social convention and the individual instance,
respectively. Second, elucidates the Marxist and psychoanalytic underpinnings of her argument, claiming
specifically that (1) class and family institutions
predetermine an individual's relation to all systems of
representation, including one's sexual relation to those
systems; (2) men and women have different relationships
to the now-generalized Oedipal myth, thus invalidating
its universality, and (3) woman is "the other who rebels
in her body" and who exists "in absence." Third,
clarifies the long-standing psychoanalytic misinterpreta-
tion of difference between women and men as in fact
centered in power differentials and not anatomical ones.
Women must assume power, but through alliance, not
exploitation. Finally, calls for a dual "revolution
within a revolution," that is, both a feminist and a
class revolt. A strong and persuasive exhortation.

255 ———— and Mireille Lanctôt. "Femmes du Québec, un
mouvement et des écritures." Magazine littéraire No.
134 (March 1978), 97-9.

A very brief history of contemporary Quebecois feminism
since its origins in late 1960's political activism and
subsequent disenchantment with the Parti Québécois.
Situates current Quebecois feminist concern with writing
in this context of political and cultural movement.
Describes some of the principal feminist publishing
houses.

256 ————. "Mon Corps dans l'écriture," Hélène Cixous,
Madeleine Gagnon and Annie Leclerc. La Venue à
l'écriture. Paris: UGE, 10/18, 1977, 63-116.

Urges a revolutionary "reclaiming of [their] power" by

women through the expression of their "feminine" language
which has, historically, been excluded from the prevailing
discourse. Posits a psychic "bi-sexuality" in all
individuals of which the feminine term has been silenced.
Situates the origin of this domination of male over
female, present in all cultures, in the "inscription of
desire": masculine phallocentric desire not only
emphasizes "presence," "projection," "possession," and
"loss," it has also turned women into the object, rather
than the subject, of desire, denying them the existence
and expression of their own sense of love. Claiming
women's "polymorphous story/history" has survived within
their repressed desire ("la mémoire du corps femelle"),
Gagnon calls on them to revolt against the "master" and
to "reclaim their place as subject in history" by
liberating their imaginative and symbolic powers. The
necessary strategies, passionately and persuasively
argued, include: (1) understanding how and when the
mechanisms of ideological formation are "inserted" into
the human unconscious and working to change that process;
(2) understanding that the structures of sexuality are
mirrored in all social organizations and institutions,
including the divisions of knowledge and their various
discourses, and working against those systems; (3)
preserving the good, "polemical" elements of masculine
discourse in order to use them for women's own purposes;
(4) "letting [women's] story flow through their bodies"
so that their desires, dreams, and "phantasies" can bring
new, "surprising," "non-logocentric" representations and
fictions to discourse; (5) seeing that other forms of
domination (e.g., class inequalities, the oppression of
the Quebecois) have been grafted onto the initial
male/female struggle, in order then that both men and
women, and all oppressed groups, can engage together in
the solidarity of multiple combats.
  Is divided into four parts, each called "Corps"
("Body"), but in fact follows no specific plan other than
addressing the insights of the various literary and
political texts it quotes (especially les Nouvelles
lettres portugaises). An ardent, sometimes angry, often
lovely piece that is itself an example of the "newly-
imagined fiction" Gagnon espouses: its structure,
analogous to her woman's body, is non-linear, "circular,"
and changing; its style moves from lucid exposition to
pulsionistic poetry, its tone from anger to softness, its
language from "argot" to scientific abstraction; it
combines political analysis of "sexual materialism"
(feminism and communism), lyrical "unknown stories" of

Gagnon's mother and grandmother, a psychoanalytic
critique of the Oedipal myth, a philosophical analysis of
masculine and feminine attitudes towards death, and
direct associative transcriptions or "fictions." An
essential text for appreciating the interplay of creative
and political struggles.

256a   Partially trans. as "Body I" in (19).

257 ———— (-Mahoney), Madeleine. "Le Symbolisme litté-
        raire." Le Symbole, carrefour interdisciplinaire 1
        Montreal: Eds. Sainte-Marie, (1969), 9-27.

Representative of Gagnon's early studies on the nature
and forms of literary symbolism and of the emerging
general influence of structuralism in criticism, argues
for a "structural symbolism," that is, the presence in
each individual text of its "own private symbolism," and
against "conventional symbolism" based on standardized,
predetermined archetypes outside the text. First,
provides an overview of the major critics who, since the
19th century, have theorized about literary symbolism:
their ideas point up the looseness and confusion of terms
used synonymously with "symbol" ("myth," "allegory,"
"metaphor," "image"). Then, analyzes the process of
textual symbolization: it is, in each text, the "transformation of one reality into another reality" by means
of specific metaphorical, allegorical and mythical
techniques. That transformation is the movement from the
"subject-that-is-creating" to the "object-that-is-
created," a movement that the text effects and the reader
uncovers. While not specifically related to women, this
piece points toward Gagnon's later interest in women's
relationship to the symbolic: their relationship to the
unconscious and the conscious, to the subjective and the
objective. A clear, erudite and persuasive essay.

*   ————, Nicole Brossard, France Théoret, et al. "Tables
    rondes." Revue de l'Université d'Ottawa/University of
    Ottawa Quarterly 50, No. 1 (January-March 1980), 9-29.

    See (59).

258 ———— (-Mahony), Madeleine. "Un aspect du symbolisme
        structural des 'Cinq Grandes Odes.'" L'Oeuvre
        littéraire et ses significations, les Cahiers de
        l'Université du Québec No. 24 (1970), 91-123.

Analyzes the "rhetorical level" in Claudel's "Odes" to
establish the complexity of the poems' internal
structure, the coherence that joins the poems to one
another, and the textual causes for the "grandeur" they
convey. Defines "rhetoric" as internal (concerning the
relationship between speaker and addressee within each
poem) and external (concerning the author-reader
relationship), but shows ultimately how the internal and
external "fuse" together in the poems. Concludes by
designating "feminine" and "masculine" poles in the
"Odes," the former centering on the principal character,
the "Polyvalent Woman" (who is herself ambiguous, at once
the image of "wisdom" and of "Eros"), the latter on the
"virile" image of the poet's creative soul. Though a
literary exegesis, the essay prefigures Gagnon's
theoretical concern with textual "voices" that will
inform "Mon corps dans l'écriture" (256).

ESSAYS AND ARTICLES ABOUT

259 Lapierre, René. "Du meilleur et du pire: Autour de _Lueur_
     de Madeleine Gagnon." _Liberté_ No. 126 (November-
     December 1979), 128-34.

     Ostensibly a review of Gagnon's novel _Lueur_ that
     situates her fiction within recent redefinitions of
     "writing" as "a tracing of signs," a "hieroglyphics,"
     replacing the traditional sense of "literary composition."
     Says writing is now viewed as an "incantation of
     meaning," as in fact the pluralized practice of many
     different "writings" first conceived in the last century.
     Describes "feminist writing" in particular as a "frag-
     mented," "unstable" discourse that demands "deciphering."
     Goes on to criticize the "authority" it claims feminist
     literature, born of social and ideological struggle, has
     assumed for itself, on the grounds that (1) "feminist" is
     too limited a label for any important literary work, and
     (2) that label frequently gives value to texts that are
     only mediocre. After condemning a feminist writing
     which, it says, displays "a complicated game of useless
     metaphors" and therefore remains marginal, places
     Gagnon's text instead among "good" feminist works that
     "impose [their] own reality." Describes _Lueur_ as using a
     language that is not inscribed in the "habitual logic of
     'the discourse of order,'" but rather is "pulsional."

260 **Gagnon, Odette.** "Sans titre." <u>La Barre du jour</u> No. 50
     (Winter 1975), 62-4.

     Exhorts women to write, to "try to make [writing] into
     a drama that smashes everything in their attempt to write
     that drama in the feminine."

Gallop, Jane:

BOOKS AND COLLECTIONS OF ESSAYS

261 ————. <u>The Daughter's Seduction: Feminism and Psycho-
     analysis</u>. Ithaca: Cornell University Press, 1982.

     "Psychoanalysis and Feminism" (264a); "Of Phallic
     Proportions: Lacanian Conceit" (268); "The Ladies' Man"
     (267); "<u>Encore</u> Encore" (262); "The Father's Seduction"
     (263); "Impertinent Questions" (265); "Writing Erratic
     Desire" (271); "The Phallic Mother: Fraudian Analysis
     (269); "Keys to Dora" (266).

     A collection of essays that studies "the relation
     between contemporary feminist theory and the psychoanal-
     ysis of Jacques Lacan" and explores "problems of sexual
     difference, of desire, of reading, of writing, of power,
     of family, of phallocentrism and of language." Attempts
     to find points of contact between oppositional terms,
     e.g., between sexes, between feminism and psychoanalysis,
     and holds to the view that "any identity will be alien
     and constraining"--whence its search for ongoing dynamic
     exchange among points of view. Hopes to introduce
     mutual flexibility into and between psychoanalysis and
     feminism and loosen the hold "familial interpretations of
     power relations" have on both domains. Says, "It is not
     patriarchal culture, but the reduction of the Law of the
     Dead Father to the rule of the actual, living male that
     must be struggled against." Presents the ideas of some
     of the foremost French feminist theoreticians (Irigaray,
     Montrelay, Lemoine-Luccioni, Kristeva, Cixous, Clément)
     by having them "encounter" one another, and also the
     "patriarchs" (Freud and Lacan). Each chapter is self-
     aware and consistently self-evaluative. A refreshingly
     clear and often playful interpretation that will consider-
     ably enlighten American readers.

ESSAYS AND ARTICLES

262 ————. "<u>Encore</u> Encore." <u>The Daughter's Seduction:</u>

Feminism and Psychoanalysis. Ithaca: Cornell
University Press, 1982, 43-55.

"Opens up issues of men's relation to feminism" by
bringing in another British interpretation of Lacan
(besides Juliet Mitchell's), that of Stephen Heath, which
it calls "chivalrous devotion" to feminism. Chooses
Lacan's "macho aggression" over Heath's "chivalry" as a
necessary acknowledgment of the "glaring absence" of
relations between women and men. Elaborates on the
notion of "jouissance" in legal and economic terms and on
Heath's problematic use of it. Also expands on Lacan's
refusal to identify "woman"--a refusal to "possess"
her--and his dealing with "the impossibility of a female
identity, since identity passes through the 'Name-of-the-
Father.'

263   ———. "The Father's Seduction." The Daughter's
       Seduction: Feminism and Psychoanalysis. Ithaca:
       Cornell University Press, 1982, 56-79.

Is the central chapter of the book and explains the
central relation, that between daughter and father, and
the importance of "seduction" in it. Uses these roles
metaphorically to refer to Irigaray and Lacan, and also
to feminism and psychoanalysis. Describes Irigaray's
"encounter" with Freud as one in which she both "asks
questions" and "supplies associations" about occulted
female sexuality (314 and 309). Connects Irigaray's idea
of the "feminine" to the Lacanian notion of "literature"
(the "unthought," the "blind spot"). Praises Irigaray
for her "ceaseless questioning" rather than "wait[ing]
for an answer," in regard to both her position as
authority and her role as "student" of Freud. Raises the
questions of woman's acceptance of and complicity in her
own submission (to Freud as analyst, to Freudian theory,
and to psychoanalysis in general) and addresses them in
"familial" terms of the father-daughter relation.

264   ———. "The Ghost of Lacan, the Trace of Language."
       Diacritics 5, No. 4 (Winter 1975), 18-24.

Reviews Juliet Mitchell's Psychoanalysis and Feminism
as an anglophone-rooted reappraisal of Freud and a point
of departure for the study of Lacan. Praises Mitchell's
critique of the American feminist misunderstanding of
Freud and her urging of a rereading of the "true" Freud.
Criticizes Mitchell for not making clear her interpreta-

tion of and relation to Lacan nor the centrality of
language to Lacanian precepts. Summarizes Lacanian
theory of the "signifier," of language, desire and the
unconscious, to unmask the true front at which linguistics
and psychoanalysis should meet.

264a   Reprinted and revised as "Psychoanalysis and
        Feminism" in (261).

265   ———. "Impertinent Questions: Irigaray, Sade, Lacan."
       Sub-Stance No. 26 (1980) 57-67.

"Represents the struggle between Irigaray (309) and
Lacan," through the mediation of the Marquis de Sade.
Explores Irigaray's inquiry into the "ghosts" left out
during Lacan's mirror-stage formation of a fictional
total, cohesive, socialized identity. Then, looks at
Irigaray's treatment of (Sadian) pornography, her
breaking down of "phallic phantasies" and her identification of them as "homosexual" sciences of "sames, of
identities, excluding otherness." Says Irigaray sees as
the most subversive women in Sade the "pliant" prostitutes
who "give man all he wants without ever being broken" and
who do so for their own pleasure, not for money.

265a   Reprinted in (261).

266   ———. "Keys to Dora." The Daughter's Seduction:
       Feminism and Psychoanalysis. Ithaca: Cornell
       University Press, 1982, 132-50.

Looks at Hélène Cixous's and Catherine Clément's La
jeune née (138), along with Freud's and Cixous's versions
of the story of Dora. Discusses Cixous's relationship to
Dora (and to all women) and the role of the hysteric as
Clément and Cixous view it, that of victim and heroine,
respectively. Says both agree Dora is the "ultimate
seductress" who raises questions about woman's initiation
into "carnal knowledge" and the "universal fantasy of
seduction by the father." Ends with a re-evocation of
the connection between politics and psychoanalysis and
the need to stop opposing them and "accept the ambiguity," "pursue, love, and accept...both theory and flesh."

267   ———. "The Ladies' Man." Diacritics 6, No. 4 (Winter
       1976), 28-34.

Is a reading of Lacan's seminar on the question, "What

does Woman want?" and a consideration of his relation to
feminism. Describes his attempt to "get at the other"
(woman's) enjoyment, that which responds to the phallic,
the latter having failed because it is a "closed order."
Says any "conclusive answer" to the question of women's
desire closes off and "recuperates" the question--which
must continually be asked. Also addresses accusations
against Lacan for being "phallocentric" and introduces
Luce Irigaray's artful reading of Lacan into the dialogue
(328).

267a   Reprinted in (261).

268   ———. "Of Phallic Proportions: Lacanian Conceit." The
         Daughter's Seduction: Feminism and Psychoanalysis.
         Ithaca: Cornell University Press, 1982, 15-32.

Brings together Lacan and Ernest Jones over "the
question of phallocentrism" and articulates how Jones's
work intersects with Lacan's elaboration of sexual
difference. Cautions against seeing Jones as women's
champion, but rather as someone striving to deny the
existence of "symbolic phallocentrism" in favor of
revisionist "symmetry." Says Lacan, on the contrary,
"flaunts" phallic privilege--a necessary step, says
Gallop, toward understanding feminine sexuality.
Distinguishes "desire" from "sexuality" and, using the
interpretations of Michèle Montrelay (501), distinguishes
female from male sexuality.

269   ———. "The Phallic Mother: Fraudian Analysis." The
         Daughter's Seduction: Feminism and Psychoanalysis.
         Ithaca: Cornell University Press, 1982, 113-31.

Takes up the "question of the mother" as developed by
Julia Kristeva (372 and 374), by bringing Kristeva-as-
mother into contact with Irigaray-as-daughter (333 and
311). Discusses the problematic and unstable daughter-
mother relationship as evoked by Irigaray and as mediated
by language (the "paternal"), according to Kristeva.
Also looks at the inseparability of the mother-daughter
from the woman-woman relation. Elaborates on Kristeva's
curious "phallic mother" as a powerfully subversive
"dream." Speculates on how a dialogue springing from the
"contradictory relation" between Kristevan and Lacanian
theory "might mean a possibility of thinking the
impossible relation between the sexes." Ends with a
double or "split" exposition of two lines of thought:

Gallop's difficulty with the "privileg[ing] of heterosexuality" in French theory and the problem of the duality of expository versus poetic discourse.

270 ⸺⸺. "Psychoanalysis in France." Women and Literature 7, No. 1 (Winter 1979), 57-63.

Delineates, with impressive clarity and concision, the differences in the shapes post-Freudian psychoanalysis has assumed in America and France, then outlines the radical implications and usefulness of current French psychoanalytic investigations. Situates the difference between psychoanalysis in the two countries in "divergent readings of Freud": Americans have focused on "ego psychology" or the importance of "ego domination," based on a traditional, static and uncritical interpretation of Freud. Such a conservative reading maintains the original biological foundations of psychoanalysis and is therefore incompatible with feminism. Also, by perpetuating the unquestioned authority of Freudian dogma, American psychoanalysis, when applied to literature, has itself used an authoritative "grid" that has reduced and "abused" literature, instead of engaging in dialogue with it. The French, on the other hand, have kept returning to the source and have kept re-reading Freud dynamically and critically. Insisting on Freud's "bolder" tendencies—those "strong moments" in his texts when, instead of imposing a monolithic interpretation, psychoanalysis undercuts its own authority or contradicts itself—says radical French psychoanalysts, with the help of Lacan's rereading, have revealed the real potential power of psychoanalytic inquiry. Refusing the original biological grounding of Freud's ideas and focusing, instead, on the Unconscious as the arena of psychic activity, French interpretations open the way for radical feminist analyses of female sexuality and sexual difference, such as those of Irigaray (314). Other critics along with Irigaray, including Laplanche and Abraham (349) have also rejected the "masterful" and "phallocentric" thrust not only of Freud's, but of Lacan's studies as well. This phallocentric, monolithic and authoritative thrust of Freudian and Lacanian theory, when brought to bear on female sexuality or on literature, in both cases suppresses the "other" term and reduces its "plurality." Because, on the contrary, it maintains a constant questioning of authority and allows for a "different, non-masterful relation to literature" and to sexuality, the current French reading of psychoanalysis "may be

invaluable for a feminist rethinking of power" in all its
forms.

270a   Reprinted in (7).

271   ———. "Writing Erratic Desire." The Daughter's
       Seduction: Feminism and Psychoanalysis.   Ithaca:
       Cornell University Press, 1982, 92-112.

Introduces the ideas of the analyst Eugénie Lemoine-
Luccioni (479) in dialogue with and in conflict with
those of Luce Irigaray (314). Situates that dialogue in
terms of the "relation of psychoanalysis to politics as
it concerns women." Says Irigaray finds fault with
"orthodox Lacanians"--e.g., Lemoine-Luccioni--for their
having institutionalized "psychoanalytic dogma," thus
preventing true "listening" of the "specific subject"
(analysand). Shows the limitations of both women's
stances and the profound resemblances--"pursu[ing] a
practice, both of psychoanalysis and of writing"--between
them. Also examines the implications of the hyphen in
Lemoine-Luccioni's name and situates it in the context of
her career. Discusses the critical Lacanian distinction
between "phallus" and "penis" as one that is parallel to
and as uncertain as the one between psychoanalysis and
politics.

Garcia, Irma:

BOOKS AND COLLECTIONS OF ESSAYS

272   ———. Promenade femmilière: Recherches sur l'écriture
       féminine. 2 vols. Paris: des femmes, 1981.

Vol. 1: "Introduction" (278); "Une douloureuse
naissance": 1. "La femme et l'écriture" (277); 2. "La
femme dans l'écriture" (276); 3. "L'écriture dans la
femme" (273); "Temps et espaces": 1. "Temps" (280); 2.
"Espaces" (275).
Vol. 2: "Une chair linguistique": 1. "Ecriture: matière
à connotations" (274); 2. "La pâte de l'écriture" (279);
"Conclusion."

A massive, somewhat repetitive study of women's writing
whose approach is an intertextual examination of
recurring themes and forms in women's literature. Takes
as central premise that there is a relationship between
writing and the body. Quotes extensively from a variety

of authors, including George Sand, Colette, Katherine
Mansfield, Anais Nin, Virginia Woolf, Carson MacCullers,
Marguerite Duras, Hélène Cixous, Chantal Chawaf, and Luce
Irigaray. Principal sections are as follows: "Une
douloureuse naissance"--deals with how women come to
writing and looks at the source of their relation to that
writing. Says that for women, the act of writing springs
from an "opening" toward the body. Analyzes, first, the
woman writer's search for identity in the face of social
constraints, then, the way women writers approach and use
language, and finally, the literary structures that make
the female tradition incommensurable with established
genres; "Temps et espaces"--examines recurring themes in
women's texts through analysis of their unorthodox
treatment of space and time. Claims a consideration of
these two basic textual elements illuminates women's
general "sensibility and situation," even while revealing
each author's personal response to imposed "spatio-
temporal" structures. Sees a common fragmentation of
time and space in women's works that expresses a search
for a newly-organized universe; "Une chair linguistique"--
looks at the ways women writers are now working on the
language and sees as consequence of women's joining of
body and text the fusion/confusion of the literal and the
figurative. Elaborates on the specificity of feminine
writing as an "explosion" of language, in which the
latter is opened to "a multitude of connotations." Says
women are attempting to make language a new, living tool
that translates and traverses their bodies. Considers
both the process and the result, the "weaving" and the
"fabric" of women's writing.

ESSAYS AND ARTICLES

273   ————. "L'écriture dans la femme." Promenade femmi-
      lière: Recherches sur l'écriture féminine 1. Paris:
      des femmes, 1981, 132-96.

      Analyzes the forms chosen by women writers as most
hospitable to their creative expression. Says women have
refused rigid literary genres and turned to letters and
diaries, which it sees as more "open" forms that also
lend themselves to the feminine search for identity and
the motif of the "double." Describes women's writing as
"incomplete," "curved," "rounded," "split," as is the
woman's identity and the intimacy she establishes with
her reader. Also says short, "broken" forms such as
journals and letters, by their spaces and "holes," are

closer to the texture of women's lives, and analyzes
passages that reveal this textual "incompleteness."

274 ————. "Ecriture: Matière à connotations." Promenade
femmilière: Recherches sur l'écriture féminine 2.
Paris: des femmes, 1981, 13-114.

Examines the "proliferation" of connotations in women's
writing, particularly along the axes of "natural"
references such as food, drink, music, all of which are
tied to the body (calls these connotations "nourricri-
ture"). Says barriers between the self and the figurative
"fall away" in women's writing as metaphors become real
forms of nourishment and language the very material of
corporeal life (a living "batter" or "pâte"). Stresses
the importance of both visual and aural images in women's
texts.

275 ————. "Espaces." Promenade femmilière: Recherches sur
l'écriture féminine 1. Paris: des femmes, 1981, 292-
379.

Looks at the ways women writers observe the "shape of
the universe," saying their acute and scrupulous
attention focuses on both mental and material space.
Says women introduce in their writing a different
topology that embraces emptiness and that is outside of
traditional spatial "organization," which for women is an
"illusion." Finds movement in women's writing in which
interior and exterior spaces are juxtaposed. Describes
the spatial references common to women's texts: nature,
the body, and objects, all presented with a sense of
unity and feeling and therefore as markers of femininity.

276 ————. "La femme dans l'écriture." Promenade femmilière: Recherches sur l'écriture féminine 1. Paris:
des femmes, 1981, 84-131.

Examines how women are present in their writing by
positing that this writing self-consciously "watches
itself write," in the same way the woman "watches
herself." Gives examples of this self-reflexivity from
various women's texts. Discusses women's "apprenticeship"
of writing as the difficult approach to and apprehension
of an "unknown" language. Claims that once women come to
writing, they infuse it with the body--its biological
rhythms, its "respirations," its "explosions" of life.

277 ──────. "La femme et l'écriture." <u>Promenade femmilière:</u>
<u>Recherches sur l'écriture féminine</u> 1. Paris: des
femmes, 1981, 28-83.

Places the woman writer in the context of the obstacles
she faces: she is separated from "masculine" language;
her writing is often trivialized; she searches for
approval; and she has difficulty finding the words to
express herself. Traces the motivations for writing of
well-known female authors, claiming their texts all
express a sense of inadequacy or justification that
connects them intimately to these women's lives. Says
that, despite the obstacles, women still write but that
their writing evinces an "alienation" from language, a
"negativity" in relation to established discourse.
Claims, at the same time, that women draw pleasure from
writing, from its connection to the body. Sees in
women's works a common search for identity, one frequently
characterized by the motif of the "double," of mirrors,
of multiple facets of the female personality. Draws
examples from women's texts.

278 ──────. "Introduction." <u>Promenade femmilière:</u>
<u>Recherches sur l'écriture féminine</u> 1. Paris: des
femmes, 1981, 11-21.

Establishes the book's conception of women's writing as
a collective, and not just individual, phenomenon that
illuminates their shared history. Says women's writing
begins "in earnest" when they express awareness of and
denounce their position in society. Also presents the
method to be used in the study: an intertextual and
pluralistic examination of women's texts that nonetheless
searches for common threads of "solidarity." Provides
the invented term that will be used to signify particularities common to women's works: "féminie," or the specific
perceptions that women experience in the world and that
their writing evinces.

279 ──────. "La pâte de l'écriture." <u>Promenade femmilière:</u>
<u>Recherches sur l'écriture féminine</u> 2. Paris: des
femmes, 1981, 115-201.

Takes as starting point that women's writing is an
"artisanal" "kneading" or shaping of the linguistic
"batter" or "flesh" that possesses its own texture.

Identifies women's language with the body through an examination, first, of women's relationship to words--one of transgression, of suppleness, of breaking with masculine syntax and linearity--and then of the new forms that linguistic "explosion" gives rise to--word plays, neologisms, invention. Gives many examples , in particular Cixous. Concludes that it is impossible to "conclude," "close" or define women's writing.

280   ———. "Temps." Promenade femmilière: Recherches sur l'écriture féminine 1. Paris: des femmes, 1981, 202-91.

Analyzes how women writers use the three temporal dimensions of the literary text: the time of the "adventure," that of writing, and that of reading. Says women's works overall refuse and confuse traditional time divisions because theirs is an "affective time." Discusses, first, the hostile relationship of women and time, which accounts for its negative presentation in their writing. Argues that women "displace" time, amalgamating past, present and future to bring them closer to women's internal rhythms. Insists on the importance of the chronology of memory as a means by which women break the linearity of time. Also claims that short, intensely observed segments of daily life appear often in women's texts, as do their apparent opposite, intervals "outside of time" ("hors-temps") in which "nothing happens," a "nothing" grounded in women's internal temporality.

Gauthier, Xavière:

BOOKS AND COLLECTIONS OF ESSAYS

281   ———. Dire nos sexualités. Paris: Galilée, 1976.

Reproduces the voices of different people that Gauthier interviewed in an effort to give back to them their "word" ("parole"), the word that "speaks their bodies, their desires." Records these anonymous testimonies in a way that condemns the methods and purposes of sexologists. Introductory essay posits that sexologists have killed desire and pleasure by "purifying" and "correcting" them with scientific knowledge. Points out the paradox that the literature of sexology, generally considered reflective of sexual liberation, in fact imposes a single "truth," the "Law" of the "all-powerful Father." Criticizes sexological studies in detail for being reflective

of only one race, class, age group, sexual orientation
and sex--men. Examines the misogyny and total subjectivity of this literature. Presents the testimonies of a
great variety of interviewees.

*   ———— and Marguerite Duras. Les parleuses. Paris:
         Minuit, 1974.

         (See 192).

282   ————. Surréalisme et sexualité. Paris: Gallimard,
         1971.

         Préface; Part I--L'espoir surréaliste; Part II--L'oeuvre
         surréaliste: 1. Vers la femme; 2. La libido généralisée;
         Part III--Le fait surréaliste; Pour conclure.

         A consideration of the "failure" of surrealism to
         realize its "revolutionary" goals because it ultimately
         reconfirmed the existing ideology. Examines the
         contradictions inherent to the surrealist project--its
         exaltation of both the spiritual and the carnal--and sees
         the idealization of woman as an attempt to reconcile
         these incompatibilities. Locates the origin of this
         mystical/carnal dilemma in sexuality as viewed in the
         1920's and says the surrealists used eroticism as a force
         of subversion. Characterizes the representation of woman
         in surrealist art: she is both objectified and made
         sacred and her body receives the violence of the
         revolutionary anger. Also faults the surrealists for
         speaking incessantly about "woman" but never consulting
         women. Credits the surrealists with having "opened the
         unconscious" and appreciated the way the unconscious
         sexualizes language. Looks at their unsuccessful effort
         to join their revolt with that of the proletarian Left.
         Interesting.

ESSAYS AND ARTICLES

283   ————. "Autre écriture?" Magazine littéraire No. 180
         (January 1982), 17.

         Introduction to a special "dossier" that describes the
         general effect of the French women's movement on women's
         literature, pointing to 1974 as the year the issue of a
         "feminine specificity" in writing came to the forefront.
         Says the first texts on the question (Leclerc, Parole de

femme (469); Irigaray, Speculum (314); Duras, Les
parleuses (192)) opened the way for new theoretical and
fictional explorations of sexual difference.

*   ——— and Anne Rivière. "Des femmes et leurs oeuvres."
Magazine littéraire No. 180 (January 1982), 36-41.

(See 514).

284   ———. "Existe-t-il une écriture de femmes?" Tel Quel
58 (Summer 1974), 95-7.

Clarifies several responses to the idea of a "women's
writing," or views on how their writing connects to their
situation as women. Describes first two equally
"masculine" and dangerous positions: (1) the traditional
designation as "feminine" of such features as intuition,
nature, tenderness, and passivity, all male-determined
features; or (2) the denial of sexual difference in the
name of "neutral" literature, also a male-identified
stance. Then, describes women's place as alien to the
dominant ("phallic") linguistic system and women's
language as "silence," the "unsaid," the "holes in
discourse."

284a   Trans. as "Is There Such a Thing as Women's
Writing?" in (19).

285   ———. "Maman, j'ai faim." Sorcières 1 (January 1976),
32-5.

Presents the language of cooking—in particular,
"normal" words that also have a special culinary
meaning—as a kind of code passed on from mothers to
daughters.

286   ———. "Pourquoi Sorcières?" Sorcières 1 (January
1976), 2-5.

Announces publication and purpose of the journal by
explaining its title, "Witches." Because, historically,
witches were destroyed for fear of their knowledge and
their sexuality, this journal will exalt them for the
very reasons society and the Church condemned them:
"...because they dance,...because they sing,...because
they are alive,...because they feel (sexual) pleasure."
Calls on women to explore and express in new ways their

movement, language, and sexuality. The journal hopes to
bring together this "new women's history/story."

286a   Trans. as "Why Witches" in (19).

287   ——, et al. "Sorcières...nos traversées." Sorcières
       7 (1977), 3-10.

A series of personal comments by women writers about
their work and about the idea of a "woman's writing."
Gauthier favors "wild, true" texts that "work on writing-
as-matter" and that are part of a collective enterprise.
She says the "feminine" lies in the "margins," "between
the lines" and in the spaces of the dominant language.
Denies writing springs from pure spirit, saying sexual
"pulsional economies" make for multiple links between
body and text. Claude Boukobza-Hajlblum urges that each
woman speak her own language, so that the different
cultural images of women will be shattered. Anna Pillet
rejects defining a "woman's writing" and prefers works of
"reflection and discipline." Nancy Huston and Danièle
Carrer want vital, "invading" forceful texts that break
molds and transcend simple description. Yolande Igrecque
sees writing as a "gluttony," as women's "nourishment" as
they "convalesce" toward using language. Finally,
Françoise Clédat, in a mimetic passage, describes the
freeing of her "body-jouissance" when writing. Other
personal testimonies about the psychological and physical
practice of writing and the relation of self to text
constitute the rest of the issue. Also, poems, drawings
and quotes from well-known women writers. Readability
varies.

INTERVIEWS WITH

*   Irigaray, Luce, et al. "L'autre de la nature." Sorcières
    20 (1980), 14-25.

    (See 339).

288 Gelfand, Elissa. "Imprisoned Women: Toward a Socio-
     Literary Feminist Analysis." Yale French Studies No.
     62 (1981), 185-203.

     Offers one model of a trans-disciplinary feminist
     analysis that illuminates the interplay between the

structures of women's lives and those of their writing.
Examines a corpus of texts by imprisoned women to show
how these texts are informed by and respond to the social
and political forces under which they were written. Says
the cultural myths that surround criminal women and that
are represented in social and literary discourses are
emblematic of the normative codes under which all women
live.

289 **Gnesotto, Nicole.** "L'imaginaire féministe." _Esprit_
       9-10 (September-October 1979), 152-61.

Assesses the various discourses of feminism present in
1979 in what is generally a critique of certain tendencies within the movement. Attacks in particular as
utopian "myth" the feminist valorization of woman's body,
saying it reduces woman to the old "natural" "essence"
and separates her from mind and theory. Refuses any
return to biologically based difference, including
feminisms that glorify female goddesses and witches.
Says such attempts to reevaluate women's role in history
positively, while vital, bespeak a false and imaginary
nostalgia. Is not clear in the orientation for feminism
it favors.

290 **GRIF** (le). "Création, langage, culture." _Les Cahiers
       du GRIF_ 7 (June 1975), 5-9.

A collective statement by the editors that addresses
questions about women's creative production: have they
been less "creative" than men? If so, why? Is the
accepted definition of "creation" contestable and
contested by women's works? Do women have their own mode
of expression? Affirms the obstacles and neglect women
artists have faced and the existence of numerous unrecog-
nized art forms (weaving, decorating). Questions the
entire concept of "creation" that is valued in our
culture as one grounded in definitions of production,
consumption and economic good. Concludes that women have
tended to make different kinds of works and to work
differently, because of their different relationship to
culture.

  *   **Guedj, Evelyne** and Malka Weksler. _Quand les femmes se
       disent._ Paris: Seuil, 1975.

(See 544).

291 **Guillaumin, Collette.** "Question de différence."
     Questions féministes 6 (September 1979), 3-22.

     Refutes the current affirmation by some feminists of
     women's "difference" by saying it is ideologically and
     strategically dangerous. Claiming that any differences
     between women and men are "socio-mental" and "anatomo-
     physiological," goes on to explain that, for any group,
     assertion of "difference" is based on a "mythic belief in
     the independence" of that group from the dominating
     group. "Difference" is in fact a "relationship," one
     expressing the dominated group's defenselessness against
     the powerful, central "referent" group. For women, to
     lay (false) claim to an isolatable, group unity is to
     return to a "natural," passive definition of sex as a
     state of being. Women must instead use their awareness
     of their lack of unity and "self-unity" to develop a
     "class consciousness." With that, they can struggle
     against their externally-imposed "material obligations"
     towards the dominant group.

291a Trans. as "The Question of Difference" in Feminist
      Issues 2 No. 1 (Spring 1982), 33-52.

292 **Hamon, Marie-Christine.** "Le langage-femme existe-t-il?"
     Ornicar? 11 (1977), 37-50.

     First, criticizes the current preoccupation among some
     theoreticians with a "feminine language" as leading to
     eternal "impasses" and myths: those of women's "nature"
     or "essence." Says this feminist viewpoint reinforces
     old analogies between anatomy and discourse and also
     loses touch with the very linguistic and psychoanalytic
     theories it uses to reestablish the "feminine." Then,
     through a Lacanian prism, examines the works of three
     women psychoanalysts concerned with discovering
     femininity in language, all of whom do so by "listening"
     to the discourse of women's unconscious: Lemoine-
     Luccioni's Partage des femmes (479), which it criticizes
     as the most ideologically "assertive" and reductive and
     the one most marked by traditional sexual dichotomies.
     Says Lemoine-Luccioni's analysis destroys the specificity
     both of the language of the unconscious and of feminine
     expression; Irigaray's Speculum (314) and Ce sexe qui
     n'en est pas un (309), which it describes as more
     elaborate and ambitious efforts to rethink the "sexual
     economy of discourse." Claims Irigaray's enunciation of
     female "phantasies" merely reduplicates preexistent

categories of the masculine and feminine imagination,
without breaking with the traditional notion of a
coherent speaking subject. Criticizes Irigaray's
metaphors as presupposing the very analogies they seek to
make; and Montrelay's L'ombre et le nom (491), which it
says examines homologies between "the structure of
writing" and "the structure of the unconscious" and which
it blames for collapsing the difference between language
and the written text and for assimilating only feminine
discourse to the unconscious. Also sees danger of
"de-historicizing" women and language in Montrelay's
privileging of one kind of "feminine writing." Concludes
by saying the reflections on language and the unconscious
visible in these three texts do not take linguistic
theory sufficiently into account. Insists instead that
more attention should be paid to the relation between
signifier and signified in the discourse of the
unconscious, a discourse it labels "poetic." Difficult.

Herrmann, Claudine:

BOOKS AND COLLECTIONS OF ESSAYS

293 ————. Les Voleuses de langue. Paris: Editions des
      femmes, 1976.

      Introduction; Ch. I, Du propre et du figuré (297); Ch.
      II, Les Voleuses de langue (301); Ch. III, Le Système
      viril (300); Ch. IV, Amour et folie (294); Ch. V, Pour
      une critique féministe (298); Ch. VI, Les Coordonnées
      féminines: Espace et Temps (295); Conclusion.

      An analysis of the feminine dilemma illustrated with a
      wealth of examples taken from literature, history,
      psychoanalysis, and ethnology. An informed, insightful,
      and very personal critique of women's exclusion from
      culture and alienation from themselves.

ESSAYS AND ARTICLES

294 ————. "Amour et Folie." Les Voleuses de langue.
      Paris: Editions des femmes, 1976, 67-97.

      Characterizes both sexes by elaborating upon the
      traditional dichotomy woman/love versus man/intelligence.
      Likening society to a text, Herrmann associates woman
      with metaphor and absence, man with metonymy and
      presence; woman, "raised in ignorance of the syntax of

the world," occupies the paradigmatic axis; man,
"profoundly syntactical," occupies the syntagmatic axis.
Not only is woman forever frustrated in her search for
love as harmony, she is also punished for her difference:
"Male society produces hysterical women and labels those
who aren't delirious ('délirantes')." Considers the
hysteric in the light of Freud and Lacan and "la
délirante" as she is epitomized by Phèdre and Kleist's
Penthesilea.

295 ————. "Les Coordonnées féminines: Espace et Temps."
Les Voleuses de langue. Paris: Editions des femmes,
1976, 137-63.

Contrasts women's conceptions of space and time with
those of men. "Physical or mental, man's space is a
space of domination and hierarchy, a space of conquest
and expansion, a full space." Women, on the other hand,
"have learned to respect the space of others as well as
empty space." As they seek to abolish distance and
separation, they are frustrated by and uncomfortable in
man's space. Likewise "man lives within a temporal
perspective, one that is organized and marked by the
accomplishment of the goals he has fixed for himself"
whereas woman "lives in the present and doesn't project
herself into the future."

295a Partially trans. as "Women in Space and Time" in
(19).

296 ————. "Les difficultés du langage écrit." Sorcières 7
(1977), 37.

A very brief discussion of the "double difficulty"
women writers confront: harnessing previously un-expressed
feminine concepts and working at language so it will
convey these concepts. Says women must also be careful
not to either "be indifferent" to matters of form or
overdo attention to form, thereby creating hermetic texts.

297 ————. "Du propre et du figuré." Les Voleuses de
langue. Paris: Editions des femmes, 1976, 7-29.

Affirms that culture is a male construct in which women
are forced to be "the negative of men." The exclusion of
women from culture and language is exemplified by women's
constant inability to distinguish the literal from the
figurative. Herrmann supports her premise with examples

such as Zelda Fitzgerald, Molière's Agnès, Barbey
d'Aurevilly's duchesse de Sierra-Leone and Mme de
Lafayette's princesse de Clèves.

298   ———. "Pour une critique féministe." Les Voleuses de
   langue. Paris: Editions des femmes, 1976, 99-135.

   Feminist criticism applied to two different disciplines: literature and history. I. An analysis of Barbey
   d'Aurevilly's "A un Dîner d'athées" is meant to demonstrate that feminist criticism "involves stating woman's
   point of view--not by excluding other facts, which would
   give a distorted and necessarily biased result--but at
   every moment and in all occasions, so that this question
   not be erased but included among the elements that permit
   analysis to take place." A study of A la Recherche du
   temps perdu and La Princesse de Clèves supports the
   thesis that women are the victims of a "homosexual
   society," that is, a society in which male bonding is
   paramount and women's function is only "that of a message
   men send each other." II. The victimization of women is
   also the theme of Herrmann's study of Roman history from
   the rape of Lucretia to the Bacchantes' revolt.

299   ———. "Le sexe du langage." La Quinzaine littéraire
   No. 192 (August 1974), 25-7.

   Examines briefly the implications of women's absence
   from the elaboration of language in masculine culture.
   Uses Roland Barthes's equation of the unacknowledged and
   un-respected reader of a "bad text" with a mistreated
   woman, and of the bad text itself with a "frigid woman."
   Claims Barthes's parallel further reduces femininity to a
   "faceless," silent void. Says that in our culture "the
   good text is virile and therefore language naturally has
   a sex."

300   ———. "Le Système viril." Les Voleuses de langue.
   Paris: Editions des femmes, 1976, 49-65.

   States that male thought ("la pensée virile") is
   founded on abstraction (system and hierarchy) and
   destructive egotism, "the total inability to love
   anything but oneself or one's possessions." Develops her
   position through a critique of the judicial system and
   surrealist thought: an analysis of the formula nemo
   censetur ignorare legem shows the cardinal rule of the
   judicial system to be "destroy that which is outside it";

an interpretation of several of André Breton's texts
reveals the surrealist vision to be conformist and sexist.

300a   Partially trans. as "The Virile System" in (19).

301 ———. "Les Voleuses de langue." Les Voleuses de
langue. Paris: Editions des femmes, 1976, 31-48.

Discusses the difficult fate of the woman who seeks
education and self-expression. She is forced to "steal
culture...and if she wants to write, she must also
hide." Compares Mme de la Fayette and Dame Murasaki
whose carefully coded books "try to draw attention to the
suffering of women and to invent the man of the future."

302 **Horer, Suzanne** and Jeanne Socquet. La Création étouf-
fée. Paris: Pierre Horay, 1973.

"Introduction"; "Le Pouvoir créateur est subversif";
"Pourquoi?"; "Parce qu..."; "Le Lit de Procuste";
"Manipulationo deo différoncoo"; "Sottioier androcra-
tique"; "Alors?"; "Tables"; "Témoignages."

Outlines, in a lively and rhythmic text, "the why's,
the how's and the because's" of the exclusion of women
from creativity and creation, and summarizes the sources
of the disintegration of creative energy in general.
Takes as its thesis that creative power is pleasurable
and therefore subversive, and that various social
mechanisms (normalizing pressures, ill-digested psychoanalytic theories of "catharsis," hierarchic education,
the valorization of external over internal reality)
repress the spontaneous expression of desire. If the
book's analysis of women's absence from creative output
("belief in differences brought on the existence of these
differences") is not original, the call for autonomous
and multifaceted individual creation is compelling. Has
appendix with "testimonies" by women who have expressed
themselves in new, non-imitative ways (Marguerite Duras
[195], Marie Cardinal [75], others).

302a   Partially trans. in (19).

303 **Houdebine, Anne-Marie.** "Les Femmes et la langue." Tel
Quel 74 (Winter 1977), 84-95.

Treats the question of the effects of sexual difference

on a researcher's object of study, for the field of
linguistics in particular, claiming this analytic focus
on gender has never been considered or taken seriously by
linguists. Gives examples of different linguistic usage
for women and men in certain cultures to suggest that
access to elements of discourse is sex-specific and that
a "sexual coding" exists in our languages. Argues that
language not only reflects, but also reinforces sex
discrimination and that, while there is no specific
"feminine language," there is a "woman's-effect"
("effet-femme") in writing and in spoken language.
Highlights, in the Anglo-American empirical manner,
connections between ideology and language, between social
and linguistic asymmetries for feminine and masculine.
Advocates an analysis of language to transform, traverse,
and multiply it.

304   **Huston, Nancy.** "Le cercle de lumière." Sorcières 12
      (1978), 21-3.

Evokes her childhood pleasure of discovering mathematical and physical principles through her father's
explanations. Contrasts this experience of "complicity"
and shared understanding with the authoritative mastery
and appropriation of knowledge that has currency in our
culture. Says theory has traditionally functioned on a
dualism of the knower/the non-knower, certainty/
uncertainty, man/woman and that women must "wake up" and
break with these dichotomies.

305   ―――――. "Conjurations." Les Cahiers du GRIF 13 (October
      1976), 29-30.

A brief look at women and the language of insult and
obscenity, a language they are not supposed to use and
yet which is built on references to their bodies. Says
women are expected to hear curses, which are in fact
expressions of sexual aggression, as only "abstractions."

306   ―――――. "Mouvements et journaux de femmes." Magazine
      littéraire No. 180 (January 1982), 28-31.

A critical overview of the French feminist journals of
the past decade that categorizes them ("commercial" and
"militant") and also tries to explain their dwindling
number (internal divisions, public disaffection, choice
by the journal to move on). Useful reference piece.

307 ———. "S'en prendre à la lettre." <u>Les Cahiers du GRIF</u>
     12 (June 1976), 18-19.

     Evokes a child's acquisition of language as parallel
     phonic and psychological processes. Uses Lacanian
     references to connect sexual and linguistic development.
     Funny and biting.

Irigaray, Luce:

BOOKS AND COLLECTIONS OF ESSAYS

308 ———. <u>Amante marine de Friedrich Nietzsche</u>. Paris:
     Minuit, 1980.

     "Dire d'eaux immémoriales" (321); "Lèvres voilées"
     (326); "Quand naissent les dieux" (332).

     A critique of masculine discourse for its having
     ignored the voice of women's desire. Takes Nietzsche, in
     only the most indirect way, as representative of the
     traditional language that has erected exclusionary
     oppositions, "burying" the maternal and the feminine.
     Assumes the voices of male-identified mythological
     "heroines" to show how they all derive from the "death"
     of the feminine. Uses "water" as an elemental--and
     feminine--image (as well as word play with "mer/mère")
     for the rediscovery of the long repressed "mother." The
     title suggests that recovered "marine lover/woman."

309 ———. <u>Ce Sexe qui n'en est pas un</u>. Paris: Les
     Editions de Minuit, 1977.

     "Le miroir de l'autre côté" (329); "Ce sexe qui n'en
     est pas un" (316); "Retour sur la théorie psychanaly-
     tique" (334); "Pourvoir du discours, subordination du
     féminin" (341); "Cosi fan tutti" (318); "La mécanique
     des fluides" (328); "Questions" (342); "Le marché des
     femmes" (327); "Des marchandises entre elles" (320);
     "'Françaises,' ne faites plus un effort" (325); "Quand
     nos lèvres se parlent" (333).

     A collection of eleven texts, ten previously published,
     including a philosophical tale, interviews, and critical
     essays. Provides an invaluable albeit somewhat repeti-
     tive overview of Irigaray's contributions to feminist

theory. Often difficult for the pieces presuppose
familiarity with both philosophy and psychoanalytical
theory and, at the same time, they embody the Derridean
refusal to employ logical discursive language. (See 263,
265, 345, 346, 347, 459).

310   _____. Le corps-à-corps avec la mère. Ottawa: Eds. de
la Pleine Lune, 1981.

"Le corps-à-corps avec la mère" (317); "Nietzsche,
Freud et les femmes" (340); "Les femmes-mères: ce
sous-sol muet de l'ordre social" (338).

Contains an essay that is a critique of psychoanalytic
theory and a call for women's reclaiming their own
understanding of their sexuality; and two interviews with
Luce Irigaray that address her interest in the
"maternal"/"feminine" and in a female discourse.

311   _____. Et l'une ne bouge pas sans l'autre. Paris:
Minuit, 1979.

In a lyrical and richly imaged monologue, "I" directly
addresses her mother and expresses her painful (psychological) status as daughter and as woman. First, evokes
the "imprisonment" and "weightiness" of the infant
daughter who is "in a dream which must not have been
(her) own." Uses images of stillness and pure sensation
to suggest the highly intense pre-verbal stage of
dependency on the mother. Also suggests the role of
mirrors in the formation of the girl child's identity—
one that will reproduce the mother's—as mother and
daughter eternally exchange and fuse identities. Shows
the girl's turning to the father in an acting out of the
Oedipal drama, the entry into "normal" female socialization as defined in masculine terms. Then, uses images of
the daughter's and mother's "nothingness" and "blindness"
to present the absence that is the "feminine" in culture
and in traditional psychoanalytic theory: "everywhere is
empty of you." Poses, as a moving and angry refrain, the
questions, "Where are you? Who am I? Where am I?" which
evoke the nullity of female personhood. Also, presents
mothering as woman's sole ascribed function in our
culture, a generation-to-generation legacy of both "milk"
and "ice," of life and of death. Ends with a tender wish
that mother and daughter, woman and woman, "speak" to
each other, "move together," "remain alive" together as

whole individuals in what would be a new symbolic order.
A beautiful piece. (See 269).

311a   Trans. as "And the One Doesn't Stir without the
        Other" in Signs 7, No. 1 (Autumn 1981), 60-7.

312   ————. Le Langage des déments. The Hague/Paris:
        Mouton, 1973.

0. Introduction; I. Hypothèses de recherche et description des épreuves; II. Description de la population
étudiée; III. Analyse des consignes; IV. Réactions
comportementales à la consigne; V. Epreuves de répéti-
tions; VI. Epreuves des séries; VII. Epreuve de paradigmes
de conjugaison; VIII. Epreuve de dépendances intra-
verbales; IX. Epreuve de réitérations redondantes de
marques; X. Epreuves de transformations; XI. Epreuves de
sélection lexicale; XII. Dépendances intraproposition-
nelles; XIII. Dépendances interpropositionnelles; XIV.
Epreuve de production de phrases; XV. Etude du langage
spontané et/ou semi-induit; XVI. Etude d'un groupe de
contrôle de déments séniles; Conclusions.

A lengthy and technical study of the impact of senile
dementia on the ability to understand and manipulate
language. Concludes that the senile are no longer
"speaking subjects" able to initiate speech acts, but
rather respond passively to their examiners or repeat
stereotyped structures from their past. The bibliography
lists other papers on language disorders in schizophrenics
and aphasics. Indicative of Irigaray's interest in
non-normative language.

313   ————. Passions élémentaires. Paris: Editions de
        Minuit, 1982.

Irigaray's major themes weave a piece that is both
poetic and didactic. Describes the male psycho-sexual
economy and criticizes its destructive consequences for
women and men. Man appropriates the organic, primal
power of the "earth-mother" to ensure his own existence.
Her life forces ("blood and milk, air and water and
light") thus circumscribed and congealed, woman is the
invisible prisoner of the phallocentric imperative.
Proposes alternatives that will reconcile the sexes: man
should make peace with the elemental physical universe
from which he came instead of fearing and repressing this
"homeland"; man should also acknowledge the autonomy of

woman, her sexual specificity, for only when difference
is perceived can a sexual economy of reciprocity and
exchange exist. Borrows Derrida's "copula" to evoke a
"jouissance" born of proximity, movement, and irreducibility. Reminiscent of Leclerc's Parole de femme (469)
both in its themes and its style. Often suggestive and
compelling.

314   ———. Speculum de l'autre femme. Paris: Les Editions
        de Minuit, 1974.

La Tache aveugle d'un vieux rêve de symétrie:
L'inconnue de la science; La petite fille (n')est (qu')
un petit garçon; Au commencement s'arrêterait son
histoire; Une "cause" encore: la castration; "L'envie du
pénis"; Une pénible évolution vers "la féminité"; Une
sexualité bien noire?; Le pénis=l'enfant du père; L'après
"coup" de la castration; Une indispensable "poussée de
passivité"; L'hom(m)osexualité féminine; Un rapport
sexuel impraticable; "La femelle est femelle en fonction
d'un certain manque de qualités" (336). Speculum: Toute
théorie du "sujet" aura toujours été appropriée au
"masculin"; χόρη: jeune vierge pupille de l'oeil; Comment
concevoir une fille?; Une mère de glace; ...si, prenant
l'oeil d'un homme fraîchement mort,...; La mystérique; Un
a priori paradoxal; ...l'éternelle ironie de la communau-
té...; L'incontournable volume (335). L'ὑστέρα de
Platon: Le praticable de la scène; Les dialogues; Le
détournement de l'hystérie (masculine); La "sortie" de la
caverne; Le temps d'accommoder, d'approprier, l'optique;
La vision du père: un engendrement sans histoires; Une
forme toujours la même; Le parachèvement de la παιδεία;
La vie en philosophie; La connaissance divine; Un entre-
deux inarticulé: la schize entre sensible et intelligible;
Le retour au nom du père; La jouissance de "la femme"
(315).

Three complementary essays that constitute an "exploration of the masculine imaginary." Irigaray's first major
contribution to feminist theory prompted her expulsion
from the Lacanian Ecole freudienne. Speculum studies
Western psychoanalytic and philosophical theories (in
particular Freud and Plato) to demonstrate the circular
reasoning and specular economy in which they are
grounded. One of the earliest feminist critiques to
apply a Derridean perspective to the representation of
woman, the feminine. An historically important text.

Long and often arduous. (See 345, 213, 459, 263, 271, 347.)

ESSAYS AND ARTICLES

315   ⸺. "L'ὑστέρα de Platon." Speculum de l'autre femme.
       Paris: Editions de Minuit, 1974, 301-457.

Explicates Plato's allegory of the cave to show how it
reflects and legitimizes phallogocentrism. Develops at
length the view presented in "Speculum" (335) that
Western philosophy, based on the primacy of ideal forms
whose consistency is guaranteed by a divine Being, has
estranged human beings from their origin in the material/
maternal. The prisoners' movement from the shadowy
depths of the cave into the light and toward the sun/
Truth/father represents an "ideal" rebirth, a passage to
adulthood predicated upon renouncing and forgetting the
earth/mother. Analyzes spatial and perceptual metaphors
to reveal the monolithic nature of the Platonic model,
assured by a complex mirroring of the unitary (male)
first cause. Subjects, identified with the male
divinity, create the physical world as a hall of
mirrors. Matter, represented as female, is formless,
"pure mimetism," reflecting only the sameness of the
(male) subject. Comments through the essay on how
language shares and perpetuates this specular mediation
of men and matter. Argues also that the discourse of
Reason and Truth remains blind to its own circular
self-generation, to its domestication of Otherness, and
to the fear that keeps in place its specular machinery.
Addresses briefly the need to return to the material
origin and the difficulties this would entail. A dense
and reiterative analysis.

316   ⸺. "Ce Sexe qui n'en est pas un." Les Cahiers du
       GRIF No. 5, (1975).

Attacks the phallocentrism of the Freudian model of
feminine sexuality, which assigns to woman the role of
"prop in the acting out of man's fantasies." Affirms
that feminine sexuality is significantly different--plural
not singular--and bases her argument on the morphology of
the genitals ("made up of two lips that kiss continuously.
Thus, within herself she is already two--but not
divisible into ones that touch each other") and the
greater number of erogenous zones ("She experiences

sexual pleasure pretty much everywhere.") Woman's
irreducible multiplicity makes possible a relation to
otherness not centered on differentiation and appropriation. Feminine sexuality and feminine language are
homologous: "in what she says also--at least when she
dares to--woman touches herself all the time." Concludes
by stating that liberating women's desire will require
the reevaluation of a cultural system founded on the
exchange of women. Advocates change and cautions against
simply reversing the existing order. A core text,
concise and generally accessible.

316a   Reprinted in (309).

316b   Trans. as "This Sex Which Is Not One" in (19).

317   ———. "Le corps-à-corps avec la mère." Le corps-à-
        corps avec la mère. Ottawa: Eds. de la Pleine Lune,
        1981, 11-33.

The text of a lecture delivered at a Quebecois
colloquium on "Women and Madness," 1980. Opens with a
critique of the male psychoanalytic establishment for not
"listening" to women and claims the absence of women's
"word" is one cause of their madness. Develops the
concept of female madness as grounded in the mother-child
relationship, in the desire of and for the mother that
masculine culture has repressed in order to maintain
order. Argues patriarchal culture is founded on an
original "matricide" that is ignored in mythology, whose
focus is the Father (e.g., the myths of Clytemnestra and
Oedipus). Examines in particular the Oedipal theory,
central to psychoanalysis, saying the "pre-Oedipal"
maternal bond has traditionally been viewed retro-
spectively--and distorted and forbidden--i.e., through
the lens of the Oedipal stage. Goes on to completely
reinterpret the relation to the mother from a feminist
perspective, valorizing the umbilical rather than the
phallic connection and maintaining that this perspective
does not privilege one sex over the other. Then,
advocates several measures for women to reclaim their own
sexuality: (1) reject the conventional maternal role as
it is defined through male needs; (2) reaffirm the full
sense of woman's "maternity," i.e., as "creator"; (3)
revive the sacrificed "mother" by asserting her desire,
her "jouissance"; (4) invent the "mother tongue," that
which speaks the "body-to-body"; (5) refuse normative

heterosexuality, in the sense of the culturally imposed
renunciation of the mother for the father and the
extremely limited phallic model of female sexuality.

318 ————. "Cosi fan tutti." Vel No. 2 (August 1975).

A strong critique of psychoanalysis focusing on Lacan's
formulation of the relationship of woman to language.
Claims that by positing logical coherent language as an
Absolute, Lacan becomes himself the prisoner of his
"projective encircling logic ('encerclante machinerie
projective')." Within this monosexual model woman is
entirely objectified and dispossessed. She can neither
experience nor name her sexual pleasure. This
"jouissance" is configured only as that otherness
("faille," "béance") which guarantees the oneness of the
phallic order. Requires familiarity with Lacanian theory.

318a   Reprinted in (309).

319 ————. "La Croyance même." Les Fins de l'homme. Paris:
        Editions Galilée, 1981, 367-93.

A "child's story" or "theoretical fiction" presented at
the 1980 Colloque de Cerisy, whose stated purpose is to
create "associations" about sexual difference. Begins
with the story of a female patient (in analysis), a story
it claims cannot be understood in traditional psychoanalytic structures. First, makes this tale into an
allegory of the destruction of the feminine that
underlies Christian theological discourse—one can have
"faith" or "belief" only in what is not true, in this
case, the unitary/paternal myth underlying religion.
Then, connects this leap of faith and the suppression of
the feminine it implies to Derrida's "La carte postale,"
his reading of Freud's account of the child, Ernst.
Elaborates on the child's "spool game," his attempt to
"master presence-absence" by throwing and retrieving the
threaded spool. Translates this game into the psycho-
sexual dynamics of the son/mother relationship, in which
the boy, through male mediation, also comes to believe
precisely what is not true: that he can master presence-
absence and rejoin (appropriate) the mother. Evokes
language as the vehicle for this "belief" system, the
masculine discourse that destroys difference by making
the "other" into the "same." Itself uses the interpenetration of theological and psychological lexicons (e.g.,

the "child-king"="God") to show the parallels in their
representation of the feminine. Ends with an evocation
of the true "poet's" discourse that "calls to the other,"
that breaks from "the circle of ownership/the proper"
("le cercle du propre"), and calls this "abandoning of
all calculation" the only possible future "divineness."
Frustratingly unreadable.

Followed by a brief discussion that seeks to elucidate
certain points about sexual difference, as evoked in
Irgaray's account of the early mother/son relationship
and that joins this account to her analysis of the
acquisition of language and of women's place in discourse.

319a   Reprinted without the discussion as La Croyance
même. Paris: Editions Galilée, 1983.

320   ———. "Des marchandises entre elles." La Quinzaine
littéraire 215 (August 1975).

Asserts that socio-cultural exchange occurs exclusively
among men and therefore is grounded in well-concealed
homosexuality. Within this phallocentric economy,
however, literal male homosexuality is subversive and
forbidden because it exposes the true functioning of
society, and also shortcircuits the commerce of women
that assures the abstraction of desire. Feminine
homosexuality, even more foreign and threatening, is
misunderstood in the Freudian model for it is cast
entirely in terms of a virility complex.

320a   Reprinted in (309).

320b   Trans. as "When the Goods Get Together" in (19).

321   ———. "Dire d'eaux immémoriales." Amante marine de
Friedrich Nietzsche. Paris: Minuit, 1980, 7-80.

Speaks in the words of the male-defined mythological
heroine, Ariadne, whose own voice has been silenced and
who has only echoed alien masculine discourse. Addresses
a male interlocutor, expressing her triumphant "return"
and blaming masculine language and culture for institut-
ing death, darkness, appropriation, absence, mastery, and
exclusionary sameness. Evokes her universe as outside of
these masculine principles. Uses a vocabulary of sensa-
tions and primal elements, especially "la mer" ("the sea"
and a pun on "the mother"), to suggest the recovered

maternal force of life, light, sharing and corporal
pleasure--that which is most threatening to and has been
"killed" by patriarchy. Contrasts masculine and feminine
desire, saying the former, destructive of the earth and
humanity, is in its twilight. Warns the masculine
"listener" that he must abandon that to which he clings
in order to be truly "reborn." Employs an epic tone in
its critique of the tragic myths that support our
culture. A long incantation that must be entered into.

322   ————. "Elle appelle toujours la nuit." Sorcières 18
         (1979), 26-7.

Refers to Marguerite Duras's film, Navire night, in a
difficult and elliptical text. Evokes woman's alienation
by using images of darkness ("It is at night that she
appears") and of the "Father, the all-powerful day" that
illuminates her.

323   ————. "Expression et signe." Etudes psychopatho-
         logiques 1 (February 1971), 17-28.

Looks at the language used by schizophrenics--one that
does not reveal the institutionalized dichotomies of
"normal" language--in order to find the "economy"
involved in this "singular" verbal production. Explains
how schizophrenic discourse is insubordinatable to the
standard linguistic binary notion of language and is,
specifically, an avatar of the un-coded, un-socialized
maternal "word." Also shows the inapplicability to
schizophrenic language of certain analytic categories of
generative grammar, though sees grammar's focus on the
initial formulation of language--on its primary elements--
as more pertinent here than the linguistic analysis of a
whole, constraining discourse. Puts into question the
sufficiency of Saussurian sign theory (comprising the
signified and the signifier) for the schizophrenic, again
on grounds relating to the maternal language's insubordi-
natability to traditional concepts of meaning. Evokes
schizophrenic enunciations as multiple and heterogeneous
breaks or spaces in linear meaning. This interrogation
of accepted linguistic dichotomies, though not directly
concerned with women, prefigures Irigaray's critique of
cultural dualisms that affect women and her elaboration
of a contestatory feminine language.

323a   Reprinted as "Le schizophrène et la question du
         signe" in Semiotexte 2, No. 1 (Spring 1975), 31-42.

324 ———. "La Femme n'est rien et c'est là sa puissance."
Histoire d'elles 21, (March 1980), 3.

Reviews Baudrillard's book, De la séduction, and refutes
strongly the latter's thesis, "Woman is nothing and
therein lies her strength." Says the book refuses to
distinguish "a seductive woman's body" from "a mascarade
of seductive femininity," thereby completely misreading
female desire.

325 ———. "'Françaises,' ne faites plus un effort..." La
Quinzaine littéraire 238 (August 1976).

A brief analysis of pornography as a total appropriation
of women's bodies and pleasure, the purpose of which is
to demonstrate male power. The rituals created by and
for men reveal a sexual economy built upon cruelty,
repetition, loss and death. Calls on women to leave the
pornographic scene and explore new dreams and desires.

325a   Reprinted in (309).

326 ———. "Lèvres voilées." Amante marine de Friedrich
Nietzsche. Paris: Minuit, 1980, 81-127.

Contrasts "femininity" as traditionally defined--an
"otherness" that maintains the masculine order--and
"woman" as she really is--the "truth" that culture has
"masked." Cites Nietzsche to show our culture's self-
protective designation of women as "liars," "hysterics,"
and "actresses," and reinterprets those terms ironically
for women's real experience in male society. Also
distinguishes masculine "castration" from feminine
"neutering," the two having been assimilated to the male
model in psychoanalytic discourse. Says the only female
experience of "castration" is genital mutilation.
Explains how women's lives are incommensurable with
masculine concepts and discourse. Examines the role of
traditional female deities (e.g., Athena) as idealized
"saviors" and mediators for men. Shows the destruction
of the "mother" in mythology and the complicity of
male-conceived "heroines" in this masculine vision.
Recovers Persephone, she who transgressed and returned to
the "depths" of original maternal power, and the
unsubjugated woman's voice of Ariadne.

327 ————. "Le Marché des femmes." Sessualità e politica.
    Ed. Armando Verdiglione. Feltrinelli, 1976.

An analysis of the sexual exploitation of women that
combines Marxist and psychoanalytic perspectives. First
presents Lévi-Strauss's anthropological model, based on
the exchange of women, as an example of the profoundly
phallocentric mental structures governing culture ("le
règne de l'hom(m)o-sexualité masculine"). Then applies
Marx's analysis of value to a study of the status of
women. Women, like the merchandise exchanged in Marx's
model, have both a utilitarian role and a purely social
or metaphysical one. Value is abstract and relational,
not intrinsic. Woman's value derives from her function
as reflection of man's desire. Elaborates on women's
social roles (mother, virgin, prostitute) and problems
(frigidity, separation from other women and from their
own sexual specificity) in the light of this exchange
model. Concludes by inquiring how this economy would
change if women entered it as active participants who
"socialize differently the relation to nature, matter,
the body, language, desire." A valuable effort to
articulate materialism and psychoanalysis, two often
warring approaches, within a feminist framework.

327a   Reprinted as "Noli me tangere ou de la valeur des
       marchandises" in Sexualité et politique. Ed.
       Armando Verdiglione. Paris: UGE, 10/18, 1977,
       217-37.

327b   Also reprinted with minor changes in (309).

328 ————. "La 'Mécanique' des fluides." L'Arc 58 (1974),
    49-55.

Irigaray's contribution to the issue on Lacan. Criticizes Lacan for ascribing primacy to form and solidity in
his theory and thereby relegating the feminine (nonspecu-
lar and fluid) to the subordinate role of Other. Contends
that despite this phallocentric focus Lacan includes
fluidity in his model, appropriating it via the (male)
libido and the death instinct. However, in so doing, he
misunderstands and misrepresents the properties of fluids.
Dense and probing. Very useful for readers well versed
in Lacan. (See 267 and 345).

328a   Reprinted in (309).

329 ——————. "Le miroir, de l'autre côté." _Critique_ No. 309
          (February 1973), 179-88.

      Develops the story of Les Arpenteurs (The Surveyors), a
      film by Michel Soutter, into an allegory of the Derridean
      feminists' dilemma: the difficulty/necessity of crossing
      through the mirror of representation to another (feminine)
      dimension where the identity of the Subject and the
      discursive logic of narrative have disappeared. Lucien-
      Léon, although tempted to step through the mirror and
      leave the scene of representation, is immobilized by his
      attachment to logical ordering, differentiation, and the
      law. Alice-Ann moves restlessly back and forth from
      "Wonderland" to the (male) world that paralyzes her.
      Both fiction and manifesto, this philosophical tale
      distills Irigaray's essential themes, including reflec-
      tions on literature.

329a   Reprinted in (309).

330 ——————. "Misère de la psychanalyse: De quelques
          considérations trop actuelles." _Critique_ 365 (October
          1977), 879-903.

      A scathing review of Eugénie Lemoine-Luccioni's Partage
      des femmes (479) and Moustapha Safouan's La sexualité
      féminine dans la doctrine freudienne, in the form of an
      "open letter" to the male (i.e., male-identified)
      psychoanalytic establishment. Criticizes traditional
      analysts (such as Lemoine-Luccioni) for separating
      politics, philosophy and history from the unconscious and
      for being unaware of psychoanalysis's own foreclosing
      presuppositions about the analytic subject. Contends
      analysts defend the existing order by considering the
      unconscious only as repository of the past, rather than
      reserve for the future--a prejudgment for which Irigaray
      attacks Lemoine-Luccioni. Rejects "universal" a priori
      psychoanalytic models that prevent new "singular" and
      open-ended "listenings." Is hostile to Lacan but more to
      his unquestioning disciples (such as Lemoine-Luccioni)
      who deny sexual difference and the body and who ignore
      their own investment in the analytic process. Gives
      examples of confusion in both books between facts and the
      analysts' normative "phantasies." Also criticizes
      traditional representations of women that arise from the
      discourse of the male sex only and that repress feminine
      desire and language. Vitriolic but compelling.

331 ———. "Psychanalyse et sexualité féminine." Les
       Cahiers du GRIF 3 (June 1974), 51-65.

   Analyzes views of·female sexuality in traditional
   psychoanalytic theory and the inaccuracies and
   insufficiencies of those views. Criticizes, first,
   Freud's ideas about women for positing male sexual
   development and the penis as the norm, thus condemning
   women to necessary passivity, masochism, neurosis, envy,
   frigidity, or pathology. Freud, calling female sexuality
   the "dark continent of psychoanalysis," never progressed
   in his study beyond the "prehistory of woman" since he
   did not consider socio-economic or cultural determina-
   tions in women's sexual development. Then, outlines the
   principal contributions and limitations of Freud's
   critics (Horney, Klein, Jones), and discusses at length
   the importance of Lacan's concept of the "phallus," the
   "symbol of masculine desire," the "guarantee of the
   continued functioning" of the traditional order in all
   spheres (the "real," "imaginary," and "symbolic" systems
   under which we live). After a nod to Françoise Dolto for
   insisting on the multiplicity of women's erogenous zones,
   concludes with a list of probing questions arising from
   the premises underlying traditional psychoanalytic theory:
   Why must the parameters of women's erogenous zones be
   limited? Why must women's libidinal structuring be seen
   as determined before puberty, thus ignoring, for example,
   the importance of maternity? Why must women's maternal
   function be viewed as more important than their erotic
   function? Why is female homosexuality interpreted
   according to the model of male homosexuality? Why is
   masculine/feminine difference still seen as the opposition
   active/passive? Says we must study historical determinants to undo the hold of the "phallus" on "discourse, on
   truth, on desire." A straightforward, informative piece.

332 ———. "Quand naissent les dieux." Amante marine de
       Friedrich Nietzsche. Paris: Minuit, 1980, 129-204.

   Evokes desire, through mythological and Christian
   metaphors, as it has been understood in our culture:
   finite, stagnant, "dead." Suggests this notion of desire
   arises from the original "murder" of the mother, for
   which reason masculine desire tries continually to
   recreate that lost love. Uses the figures of Apollo,
   Dionysus and Artemis in recounting the establishment of
   the patriarchal order. Describes women's desire as in a

state of "exile," of "wandering in the destiny of the
man-god." Asks, through polarized images such as dawn/
sunset, sky/sea, if such destructive oppositions are
insurmountable. Explains the genesis of the "eternal
feminine" within a sexuality based on the "phallic cult"
and the destruction of maternal power. Also takes the
story of Christ, traditionally viewed as glorifying the
Word of the Father at the expense of the subjugated
mother, and reinterprets it as an echo of the original
"crucifixion" of the virgin mother--thus demonstrating
how the maternal/feminine is the support of all Christian
culture. Sees another meaning in the Christ story, that
of a different relationship between flesh and word, of a
reinsertion of the body in culture. Asks many provocative questions to point up the arbitrariness of traditional interpretations of Western myths.

333 ———. "Quand nos lèvres se parlent." Les Cahiers du
GRIF 12 (June 1976), 23-8.

An imaginary dialogue of love with and for other women
that calls on them to cease using the "same language"/the
"language of sameness" ("parler le même") that is univocal
and self-reflective masculine discourse. Evokes the
"economy" of that discourse, one based on masculine
desire (opposition, exchange, appropriation, self/other,
death). Advocates instead the language of the different
feminine economy, a language of life, light, love,
non-exclusion, limitlessness, multiplicity. Uses
pronouns and puns effectively to suggest this perturbed
and pluralized discourse. Also uses the "lips" of the
title as referring to women's mouths and to their sexual
("speaking") organs that "touch one another." Insists
women's sexual identity predates and is independent of
masculine definitions, definitions that "imprison" and
"exile" women. Says, "We will manage to speak ourselves
("nous dire") some day." Incantatory. (See 269).

333a   Reprinted in (309).

333b   Trans. as "When Our Lips Speak Together," in Signs
       6, No. 1 (Autumn 1980), 69-79.

334 ———. "Retour sur la théorie psychanalytique."
Encyclopédie médico-chirugicale, gynécologie 3 (1973),
167 A-10.

"La Théorie freudienne": Summarizes Freud's theory of the development of feminine sexuality, stressing the primacy of the male paradigm.

"L'Opposition d'analystes femmes à l'optique freudienne": Sketches the contributions of Karen Horney and Melanie Klein.

"Une tentative de conciliation: Ernest Jones": Discusses Jones's attempts to reconcile Freud's formulations with modifications by analysts such as Horney and Klein.

"Compléments à la théorie freudienne": Reviews the contributions of adherents Helena Deutsch and Marie Bonaparte.

"L'Ordre symbolique: Jacques Lacan": Summarizes the pivotal role of the castration complex in the Lacanian model. The castration complex assures the child's passage from the imaginary to the symbolic order, of which the father is guarantor: "the father introduces them [mother and child] or reintroduces them, to the demands of symbolization of desire through language, that is, to the necessity of its passage through request."

"'L'Image du corps': Françoise Dolto": Mentions her research on the development of body images and her focus on the plurality of erogenous zones.

"Questions sur les prémisses de la théorie psychanalytique": Concludes this primarily descriptive article by calling for a reevaluation of psychoanalytic theory that will acknowledge and elucidate the influence of the cultural system of which it is a part. Proposes specific issues for consideration.

334a   Reprinted in (309).

335   ———. "Speculum." Speculum de l'autre femme. Paris: Editions de Minuit, 1974, 165-298.

An interrogation of the masculine theory of the subject elaborated by Western philosophy and incorporated into psychoanalysis. Asserts that philosophers have created a transcendental (male) subject whose existence depends upon appropriating and denaturing the sensible (feminine). Focuses on Neoplatonist philosopher Plotinus to evoke this representation of the feminine: matter-woman is without form, impassible, unchanging, sterile, a concave mirror that reflects real (ideal) forms. Examines Descartes's "cogito" to demonstrate the male subject's break with its beginnings in sensation, its self-generation, and its perpetuation of self-as-center. (This specularizing economy is described at greater length in 315.) Then uses the story of Antigone to illustrate the constitution of the subject and the underpinnings of phallocentric culture. The separation of Antigone and her brother Polyneices represents the schism between conscious and unconscious, between the law of the father and living exchange between the sexes. Antigone's burial alive, which assures the moral order of the community, is exemplary of the fate of woman: "Powerless on earth, she remains the ground in which the manifest spirit has its obscure roots and draws its force." Criticizes the pretentiousness and circular reasoning of male theorists whose fear of otherness has led to disempowering blindness. Combines her description and criticism of the traditional representation of woman with a positive re-evaluation of the feminine (see especially the section entitled "la mystérique"). Asserts the necessity of acknowledging sexual difference and thereby creating an economy of reciprocity, not domination. Briefly raises certain problems inherent in such a project and suggests possible ways of beginning this "nocturnal vagabondage." A very provocative piece. Often a dense, sinuous, theoretical-lyrical style makes the text extremely difficult.

336 ⎯⎯⎯⎯. "La Tache aveugle d'un vieux rêve de symétrie." Speculum de l'autre femme. Paris: Editions de Minuit, 1974, 7-161.

A dialogue with Freud's essay "Femininity." Uses his famous last text on women as the warp and woof on which to weave her own explications, interrogations, and associations. Creates a sometimes intricate pattern of alternating voices. Maintains that Freud subordinates all aspects of femininity to a male paradigm of desire (penis envy, maternity as its substitute in the adult woman, feminine homosexuality as a virility complex, among other examples): "'Sexual difference' is dependent upon a problematics of the same." This appropriation of the representation of the feminine, this reduction of woman to a mirror of the male subject continues a long-standing false symmetry. Thus, it denies woman any access to her self, any relation to the mother unmediated by phallocentric theory. Points out the unasked and unanswered questions as well as the contradictions that are the traces of Freud's blind spot, his own unconscious desire. Comments repeatedly, for example, on the

inadequate attention paid to the socio-historical
determinants of sexuality. The most accessible of the
three essays in Speculum (314).

INTERVIEWS WITH

337 ———— and Catherine Clément. "La femme, son sexe, et le
     langage." La Nouvelle critique No. 82 (March 1975),
     36-9.

     Capsulizes the main themes of Irigaray's re-evaluation
     of women's sexuality and relation to language. Focuses
     first on the three texts that comprise Speculum de
     l'autre femme (314). "La Tache aveugle d'un vieux rêve
     de symétrie" (336) and "La Caverne de Platon" (315) both
     critique the same phallic ontology: for Freud the primacy
     of the penis, for Plato the primacy of the idea.
     "Speculum" (335) examines the history of philosophy to
     uncover how idealist philosophers such as Plato,
     Aristotle, Descartes, Kant, and Hegel founded their
     systems upon the exclusion of the feminine. Irigaray
     comments briefly on hysteria, the pathology of silenced
     groups, in particular women, who, barred from language,
     must express themselves through their bodies. Moving to
     a discussion of Marx, affirms that his philosophy is
     equally incompatible with the feminine. Responds to
     Clément's orthodox Marxist analysis of class struggle by
     asserting the specificity of the exploitation of women.
     Comments on the problematic nature of the relation of
     politics and women and calls for women to simultaneously
     seek equality and avoid absorption into the male system.
     Concise and informative.

338 Dumouchel, Thérèse and Marie-Madeleine Raoult. "Les
     femmes-mères: ce sous-sol muet de l'ordre social."
     Luce Irigaray. Le corps-à-corps avec la mère. Ottawa:
     Eds. de la Pleine Lune, 1981, 75-89.

     After an introduction by Dumouchel that praises
     Irigaray for exposing the dangers for women of
     traditional psychoanalysis and for "leaving" the dominant
     language to "write the body," discusses women as the
     "foundation" of the patriarchal edifice: says "Man-God-
     the Father" "killed" the mother to take power. Explains
     the "maternal" in our culture as defined by male
     "phantasies" and calls for a complete rethinking of the
     mother-daughter relation. Attacks the dominant discourse
     for "renouncing" desire, joy, life and advocates that

"mothers" be "women"--by expressing their never-heard
desire.

339   Gauthier, Xavière, et al.   "L'Autre de la nature."
        Sorcières 20 (1980), 14-25.

    Brings up various aspects of the relationship between
women and nature and looks at that relationship from
different perspectives.   Contains several central themes:
the concept of "nature" and the traditional association
of women with nature in patriarchal definitions;
"bisexuality" as a potentially suspect and easily coopted
codeword for monolithic androgyny; the question of
"difference" between women and men and the implications
of sexual "equality" for the difference of the sexes;
women's relationship to production and to reproduction;
and strategies for discovering, inventing and instilling
the feminine as a positive and present social value.   The
participants introduce different vocabularies and
approaches to these questions: de Vilaine looks to
anthropological inquiry; Gauthier, to sociological and
ecological; Irigaray, to psychoanalytic and mythological/
archetypal.   All agree that the destruction of nature by
masculine culture is inextricable from the destruction of
the feminine and that other, life-giving values must be
found and elaborated.   Irigaray's analysis of the issues
is particularly subtle and it regards suggested solutions
to problems with caution: the call for "bisexuality,"
very much in vogue, is suspect since it tends to reinforce the current masculine assimilation of difference
into sameness and neutralizes women's oppression and
their sexuality into a single prescriptive model.
Irigaray urges the assertion of sexual difference not to
show quantifiable "advantages" or "lacks" for either sex,
but to allow "otherness" ("altérité") to exist and
express itself.   Irigaray also sees as dangerous calls
for equality between the sexes, since they imply making
women into men, into "the incarnation of the will of the
Father."   Using the figure of Athena as a symbol of the
traditional definition of femininity--a masculine creation
established by destroying the mother in favor of the
father--Irigaray discusses the historical separation of
women from the act of producing (creating, imagining) and
their assimilation to re-production (a "re-doubling" of
masculine creation).   Ends with a call to women to go
beyond the stage of merely criticizing patriarchal
culture and to produce "our desires, our pleasures, our
'works.'"   An informative, nicely woven discussion.

340   Lamy, Suzanne and André Roy. "Nietzsche, Freud et les
      femmes." Luce Irigaray. Le corps-à-corps avec la
      mère. Ottawa: Eds. de la Pleine Lune, 1981, 35-72.

      Begins with an introduction by Lamy that cautions
      against "fixing" Irigaray's ideas but that nonetheless
      acknowledges feminism's debt to Irigaray's interrogation
      of psychoanalysis and philosophy. The interview discus-
      ses Irigaray's Amante marine de Friedrich Nietzsche
      (308), which it calls a "questioning of the discourse of
      traditional philosophy." Refuses the classifications of
      "theory" and "fiction" as part of a necessary destruc-
      tion by women of all categories. Evokes women's speaking
      ("parler-femme") as continuous, subversive, expressive of
      their "jouissance." Speaks of the critical rejection of
      Irigaray's "incomprehensible" and "scandalous" writing
      and of her break with the psychoanalytic establishment.
      Describes a psychoanalysis conceived and "thought" by
      women as one in which the unconscious would not be an
      object, castration would not be a central issue, and
      analysis and political activism would not be incompatible.
      Elaborates on the importance of the mother-daughter rela-
      tionship for Irigaray, what she calls the "most obscure"
      part of our culture. Also talks about the male response
      to the female demand for autonomous sexual identity.

340a   Extracts published in Spirale No. 12 (October
        1980), 3.

341   "Pouvoir du discours/subordination du féminin: entre-
      tien." Dialectiques No. 8 (Spring 1975), 31-41.

      Provides an excellent overview of Irigaray's principal
      theories, as well as a sense of the interconnection and
      internal evolution among those theories. Referring to
      Irigaray's book, Speculum (314), explains, first, why a
      critique of Freud is the foundation of her analysis:
      Freud defined women's sexuality in relation to men's, as
      absence and lack, and so there aren't two full sexes in
      his ideas. Freud's "sexual indifference," far from
      exploratory scientific theory, is a restatement of
      established fact, an uncritical reaffirmation of the
      patriarchal ideology under which he lived. This critique
      of Freud's neglect of feminine sexual specificity and of
      the limitations of his work can then open psychoanalysis
      to new and fruitful inquiry, specifically into "sexual
      difference and what that difference might effect in the
      unconscious impact on language." Irigaray argues that

discourse is "sexuated" and must be examined as such: the
dominant masculine discourse prizes linearity,
systematicity, logic, opposition, economy, and therefore
restricts the philosophical possibilities of such figures
as the "subject," "substance," and the "idea." She
suggests strategies for women's dismantling of phallocentric language: initially, mimetism or imitating the
discourse in place to undo it from within; then, "distur-
bance, excess, simultaneity, fluidity," all means to
explode phallocentric forms and figures. Finally, the
interview connects Irigaray's strategies for linguistic
revolution with struggle in the political arena: in ways
analogous to their subverting of discourse, women should
"revolt against the forms and nature of politics themselves," but not within the masculine framework of
dichotomized and hierarchized power struggles. It is
imperative that women recognize their sex-specific
exploitation in order to operate a political critique
"from their position at once within (as objects of
exchange) and without (as outside of laws) the system."
Both critiques, of discourse and politics, together will
alter women's symbolic and real place in society.
Becomes increasingly difficult to read, but remains
strong, convincing and original. Also prefigures the
title of Irigaray's subsequent book, Ce Sexe qui n'en est
pas un (309), in describing women's position in current
discourse as the "unimaginable" other sex ("un autre
sexe, d'un[e] autre femme").

341a   Reprinted in (309).

342 "Questions." Ce sexe qui n'en est pas un. Paris: Les
     Editions de Minuit, 1977, 117-63.

   A selection from various unpublished exchanges with
students and colleagues in which Irigaray elucidates and
develops the work begun in Speculum de l'autre femme
(314). The major questions addressed are: how to speak
of feminine sexuality as other; how to find or invent its
language; how to articulate for women their sexual and
social exploitation; how women can situate themselves in
relation to political structures; how they can liberate
themselves from patriarchal culture; what questions women
should ask male language, theory, and science; how to ask
these questions without being censured and repressed yet
again; how to modify psychoanalytic practice to include
the feminine. The entire piece illustrates the difficulty faced by those theorists of the feminine who reject

certainty and authority and seek to evoke that which is
incompatible with the conventions of male discourse.
Irigaray must repeatedly sabotage her criticisms and
explanations by introducing irreducibility and interrogation. The result is a rich, complex, and often elusive
text.

* Raoult, Marie-Madeleine and Thérèse Dumouchel. "Les
  femmes-mères: ce sous-sol muet de l'ordre social."
  Luce Irigaray. Le corps-à-corps avec la mère. Ottawa:
  Eds. de la Pleine Lune, 1981, 75-89.

  (See 338).

* Roy, André and Suzanne Lamy. "Nietzsche, Freud et les
  femmes." Luce Irigaray. Le corps-à-corps avec la
  mère. Ottawa: Eds. de la Pleine Lune, 1981, 35-72.

  (See 340).

343 "Women's Exile." Ideology and Consciousness 1 (1977),
    57 76.

An excellent, concise overview of Irigaray's work: a
reexamination of how the masculine imaginary has silenced
women and a search for "a possible space for the feminine
imaginary." Criticizes the assumptions of universality
that have guided and blinded theoretical giants (stresses
Freud, Lacan, and Marx here) and their followers.
Demonstrates that the same phallocentric paradigm--in
which woman is the negative complement of man, the
absence that assures masculine presence--informs
psychoanalysis, linguistics, and politics. Proposes that
the sexual differences she uncovered studying schizo-
phrenia (men schizophrenics have a greater ability to
articulate their madness than do women) are symptoms of
the general economy that exiles women from language, from
themselves, and from other women. Discusses how a focus
on the female sexual morphology--two lips that are
contiguous but cannot be distinguished from each other--
would confound the concepts of unified subject and proper
meaning and undercut the foundations of the patriarchal
social and cultural order which remains in place. Calls
for women to unite around specific issues, but cautions
that social equality is not enough, that women must also
invent "new forms of organization, new forms of struggle."
Preceded by a short, informative introduction.

343a   Trans. and reprinted from Seles Samtaler om
         Psykiatri (Six Talks on Psychiatry). Ed. Fredrik
         Engelstad. Oslo: Pax, 1976.

ESSAYS AND ARTICLES ABOUT

*   Berg, Elizabeth L. "The Third Woman." Diacritics 12
    (Summer 1982), 11-20.

    (See 371).

344 Burke, Carolyn. "Introduction to Luce Irigaray's 'When
    Our Lips Speak Together.'" Signs 6, No. 1 (Autumn
    1980), 66-8.

    Presents Irigaray's text as a "love poem" for all
    women. Says it enacts the "disconcerting of language"
    essential to the author's interrogation of linguistic
    "meaning." Sees "When Our Lips Speak Together" as one
    attempt by Irigaray to "speak female," as a disruption
    and rejection of masculine logical argument. Calls the
    essay an "exploration of plurality" of all kinds--
    syntactic, grammatical, psychological, semantic, and
    corporal. (See 333).

345 ————. "Irigaray Through the Looking Glass."
    Feminist Studies 7, No. 2 (Summer 1981), 288-306.

    Presents Luce Irigaray's general enterprise as
    philosopher and psychoanalyst--that of exploring
    analogies between female sexuality and a women's
    language--through an examination of her writing in
    context: describes Le langage des déments (312) as an
    early study of language and sexual difference in
    schizophrenics; summarizes the purpose of Speculum de
    l'autre femme (314) as understanding "why female
    sexuality could not be articulated within Western
    theoretical discourse"; says the necessary "disconcert-
    ing" of inadequate masculine language and logic occurs in
    the form and substance of Ce sexe qui n'en est pas un
    (309); claims women's sensual/emotional experiences,
    absent in the dominant discourse, are expressed in Ce
    sexe and, more poetically, in the subsequent Et l'une ne
    bouge pas sans l'autre (311); and refers to the recent
    Amante marine (308) as a critique of Nietzsche's
    typically masculine kind of thought. Traces Irigaray's
    trajectory from her starting point as a dissident
    Lacanian (and Freudian) psychoanalyst, summarizing the

theoretical disagreements between Lacan and Irigaray and
the latter's attempt to "rename herself" outside of the
"Name-of-the-Father." Also indicates the vital
connections between Derridean deconstructive philosophy
and Irigaray's thought, in particular their comparable
articulations of "fables" about sexuality, fables that
have temporary, non-absolute authority. Then, looks at
the shift in Irigaray's writing from a theoretical to a
"fluid" language, stressing the "intertextual" resonances
in Ce sexe. Evokes the new ideological "place" from
which this text arises and the concomitant difficulties
for the text's reader. Explains the "insidious"
references and strategies used in selected essays from Ce
sexe (see 329, 318, 328, and 333). Expands on Irigaray's
search for an "other side"--a conceptual realm beyond and
outside of masculine phallogocentrism--and the ways the
reader of Irigaray participates in that search. Ends
with queries about the applicability and usefulness of
Irigaray's work for other critics, saying her "non-
directive" deconstructive strategies, if not translatable
into action, are eminently suitable intellectual
approaches for feminists. Defends Irigaray's "dream"
against various critiques of her ideas. An essential
entry into the work of this major figure.

* Féral, Josette. "Du texte au sujet." Revue de
  l'Université d'Ottawa/University of Ottawa Quarterly
  50, No. 1 (January-March 1980), 39-46.

(See 217).

346 Marini, Marcelle. "Scandaleusement autre..." Critique
    373-374 (June-July 1978), 603-21.

Defends the work of Luce Irigaray against the criticisms of the Lacanian Ecole freudienne, as exemplified by
the article "Le langage-femme existe-t-il?" by Marie-
Christine Hamon (292). Stresses Irigaray's originality
and courage, her divergence from Lacanian orthodoxy, and
the far-reaching socio-political implications of the
formulations. Refers to Speculum de l'autre femme (314)
and, more particularly, Ce sexe qui n'en est pas un
(309). Situates Irigaray as a feminist thinker who
bridges the gap between psychoanalytic and Marxian
perspectives. A trenchant and polemical piece that
presents much of its praise of Irigaray's provocative
approach in the guise of self-righteous attacks by a
frightened male psychoanalytic establishment.

347 Plaza, Monique. "Pouvoir 'phallomorphique' et psychologie
     de 'la Femme'." Questions féministes 1 (November 1977),
     91-119.

     A materialist feminist critique of psychoanalyst Luce
     Irigaray's examination of femininity and affirmation of
     sexual specificity. Contends that by taking sexuality as
     the focus of her analysis, rather than the socio-economic
     order that mediates all experience of the body, Irigaray
     chooses an illogical an incomplete perspective. Differ-
     ence must be deconstructed not upheld. Warns that
     Irigaray's Neo-Freudianism, in which woman does not yet
     exist, offers no account of the psycho-social reality of
     women and hinders the feminist struggle against oppres-
     sion. Although Irigaray does acknowledge the influence
     of the social on the development of the psyche, she fails
     to provide an in-depth study of the articulation of
     social and sexual and thus remains within the traditional,
     essentialist model. She does not distinguish between
     phallomorphism and phallocentrism: "The discourse of men
     is not motivated by the shape of their sex organ but
     obeys patriarchal organization." Asks probing questions.
     An important piece that illustrates the often bitter
     polemics between materialist feminists and theorists of
     the feminine who work with psychoanalytic and philosoph-
     ical paradigms.

     347a Trans. and reprinted as "'Phallomorphic' Power and
           the Psychology of 'Woman'" in Ideology and Conscious-
           ness 4 (1978), 4-36.

348 Wenzel, Hélène Vivienne. "Introduction to Luce
     Irigaray's And the One Doesn't Stir without the
     Other." Signs 7, No. 1 (Autumn 1981), 56-9.

     Presents Irigaray's brief book by saying it "gives
     lyrical if anguished voice to the silenced daughter of
     the mother-daughter relationship." Situates the text
     within Irigaray's rereading of all psychoanalytic theory
     "regarding the female subject." Calls the book a
     "daughter's retrospection," addressed to her mother, and
     analyzes its three-part lyrical movement. (See 311).

349 Kamuf, Peggy. "Abraham's Wake." Diacritics (March
     1979), 32-43.

A review of some of the works and ideas of the
psychoanalyst Nicolas Abraham. Discusses his rereading
of Freud's "Wolf Man" case. Also refers to Abraham's
importance for Derridean thought. Of interest for
feminist inquiry into women and language is Abraham's
"phantom theory," his analysis of "an initial dual unity
(mother-child) and its gradual re-organization within the
symbolic order." Connects the child's coming to language
with "the repression of the mother's unconscious." Also
examines Abraham's "radical" reading of the Oedipus
Complex, one that focuses on sexual prohibition as
imposed on the mother, rather than the child, and thus
opens to a questioning of the "social and moral order."
Sees as the essential goal of Abraham's psychoanalytic
theory the "modifying" of the structure of "the great
abominable Truth--postulated but inexistent--which
nevertheless rules the Universe in constantly revised
forms." Difficult.

Kofman, Sarah:

BOOKS AND COLLECTIONS OF ESSAYS

350 ———. Camera obscura de l'idéologie. Paris: Galilée,
    1973.

1. "Marx--Magie noire": Le monde renversé; La table
tournante; La chambre close; La chambre claire; 2.
"Freud--L'appareil photographique": L'antichambre du
photographe; Le stéréotype; Le développement du négatif;
3. "Neitzsche--La chambre des peintres": Le trou de la
serrure; Les chambres de Léonard; Le confessionnal de
Rousseau; Décence, indécence; L'éblouissement; 4. "L'oeil
du boeuf--Descartes et l'après-coup idéologique":
Document--Usage de la chambre obscure (de Gravesande).

Uses the central image of the camera obscura to examine
Marx's, Nietzsche's and Freud's critiques of false views
of the place of the individual in the world. Says that,
for classical philosophers and artists, camera obscura
was a machine that transparently "imitated nature" and
functioned like a "divine eye" that had no "point of
view." Then shows how Marx, Nietzsche and Freud inverted
this classical view: the Marxian ideology of revolt, the
Nietzschean philosophy of "perspectivism," and the
Freudian revelation of the unconscious all gave lie to
the notion of human autonomy and harmony with the world.
Employs visual metaphors in a psychoanalytic framework to

evoke real and illusory ways of perceiving human knowledge. Difficult but suggestive.

*   ————, Lucette Finas, et al. <u>Ecarts: Quatre essais à
   propos de Jacques Derrida</u>. Paris: Fayard, 1973.

(See 220).

351   ————. <u>L'enfance de l'art: Une interprétation de
   l'esthétique freudienne</u>. Paris: Payot, 1970.

La double lecture; La fascination par l'art: L'art
comme modèle de connaissance des processus psychiques; La
méthode de lecture de Freud: L'oeuvre d'art comme texte à
déchiffrer; L'art dans l'économie de la vie: Le point de
vue métapsychologique; De la création artistique à la
procréation: Les limites d'une psychanalyse de l'art.

An interpretation of Freud's aesthetics and his
attitude toward the artist that proceeds by a "symptomal"
reading of his works on the subject. Says such a reading
of "symptoms" uncovers "more or other" things in the
texts than their strictly literal message. Implies an
interesting parallel between Freud's "symptomal" reading
of artistic texts (which he saw as analogous to dreams)
and Kofman's own symptomal reading of Freud's texts.
Talks about the contradiction at the heart of Freud's
aesthetic theories: sees his discovery of the universal
similarities between different "psychic (artistic)
productions" and his unmasking of the narcissistic
illusion of artistic heroism as demystifying the
traditional metaphysical view of the artist; but says his
ideas and his own position as author, at the same time,
reinforce this traditional "theological and ideological"
conception of the artist. Situates this portion of
Freud's thought in the period when he saw works of art as
a means of entry into the unconscious and analyzed the
artist in the framework of child/father psychic dynamics.
Insists on Freud's belief in the inseparability of affect
(the effect of art on the spectator/reader, as well as
the affect of the artist) from the symbolic representation
or text that transforms it. Calls this relation between
affect and representation a form of "economy." Elaborates
Freud's ideas on the link between art and narcissism and
between art and death. Ends with a discussion of Freud's
understanding of the limits of psychoanalysis's ability
to explain "creation" and "the enigma of art."

352 ───────. L'énigme de la femme: La femme dans les textes
de Freud. Paris: Galilée, 1980.

Part One: "L'énigme et le voile"--1. "La guerre des
sexes" (359); 2. "Spéculation, observation" (368); 3.
"Les retards de Freud" (366); 4. "L'autre" (355); 5. "Une
énigme excitante" (370). Part Two: "Freud mène
l'enquête"--1. "L'intérêt pour l'énigme de la femme"
(361); 2. "La certitude immédiate de la différence"
(357); 3. "L'indécision et l'aporie introduites par la
science anatomique" (360); 4. "La psychologie: sa
stérilité, son impuissance" (365); 5. "La psychanalyse:
le devenir-femme de l'enfant" (364).

Examines Freud's entire corpus to illuminate the
complexity of his ideas on female sexuality. Highlights
the points of his discomfort, confusion, delay, and
speculation regarding "the woman's enigma." Also
analyzes Freud's "pseudo-solutions" to the questions
about women his works raise, "explanations" (e.g., "penis
envy" and "hysteria") in fact designed to control
frightening and "criminal" female and maternal sexuality.
Takes a dual viewpoint--that of Freud as both fascinated
and panicked by women--to "deconstruct" the ambiguous and
often contradictory strategies he uses. Part One is a
general critique of Freudian theory on women; Part Two is
a close reading of Freud's texts, one that frequently
evokes Luce Irigaray's reading of those same texts (see
314). Though the chapters flow from one to another,
several can be read separately. A dense and rich
exploration of one of the key figures for French feminist
inquiry.

353 ───────. Nietzsche et la scène philosophique. Paris:
10/18, 1979.

Avant-propos; Le complot contre la philosophie; Le
masque de la sérénité; Le mauvais oeil; Les présupposés
de la logique; La comédie du stoïcisme; Figures du
sauveur; Descartes piégé; Baubô, Perversion théologique
et fétichisme; Tartuferies des philosophes; Kant ou "Le
Médecin malgré lui"; Appendice.

Situates this study within the recent abundance of
books on Nietzsche, stating its purpose to be "the
precise reading of certain texts" by the philosopher.

Says her project is the "polemical" rehabilitation of an
author too often criticized for being insufficiently
"serious" or "linear" in his thought. Praises Nietzsche's
"comic" unmasking of the "puerilities" of his predeces-
sors, his critique of their "hypocritical" and "tyranni-
cal" imposition of a false and reassuring image of the
world. Because he saw the truly "tragic," pre-Socratic
face of philosophy, Nietzsche represents for Kofman its
potential greatness: its ability to address the ambiguities and uncertainties of life. Takes as underlying
premise that Nietzschian theory has an affinity with
classical tragic theater. An example of one influence on
feminist thought, the debunking of the myth of human
autonomy and certainty.

354 Kofman, Sarah. Le respect des femmes: Kant et Rousseau.
     Paris: Galilée, 1982.

     "Tenir les femmes en respect"; "L'économie du respect:
     Kant"; "L'ombre de la clôture: Rousseau."

     Studies the concept of men's "respect" for women in
     terms of the masculine psychological needs it fulfills,
     the needs of the masculine "sexual economy." Claims this
     respect is the flip side of the degradation of women
     (c.f., the virgin/whore dualism) and is an act of social
     and sexual control masquerading as moral elevation. Says
     the idealization of women allows men to keep themselves
     at a distance, thus preventing their being "fascinated"
     and "castrated" by female sexuality. Argues this
     respectful distance also permits men to avoid degrading
     "the mother." Discusses the correlative role of the
     prostitute: she prevents the general "prostitution" of
     all women, thus making male respect for women possible.
     Takes as examples (1) the theories of Kant on moral
     respect--apparently to be felt for both women and men but
     addressed to women because of their sex only; and (2) the
     ideas of Rousseau, for whom general morality depended on
     the virtue of women. Draws similarities between the two
     authors to show that their cases are not isolated, but
     part of a general "complicity" to control women through
     "respect."

ESSAYS AND ARTICLES

355 ———. "L'autre." L'énigme de la femme: La femme dans
     les textes de Freud. Paris: Galilée, 1980, 39-42.

Gives, in addition to his fear of woman's autonomous
sexuality, a further reason for Freud's delaying publication of his work on the pre-Oedipal maternal phase: his
fear that the "radical alterity" of woman he discovered
would challenge psychoanalysis itself. Claims that, in
response, Freud maintained the Oedipal moment as the
principal one in development.

356 ———. "Ça cloche." Les Fins de l'homme. Paris:
Editions Galilée, 1981, 89-116.

A paper presented at the Colloque de Cerisy, 1980, on
Derrida. Takes as point of departure Derrida's critique
of "humanism" or traditional "metaphysics"--that the true
purpose of its universalizing of "mankind's ends" is to
"master" sexual difference, to reconfirm phallocratic
supremacy--and uses it as framework for critiquing other
"pseudo-scientific discourses." Focuses primarily on
Freud as an example of how pure speculation--in Freud's
case, about female sexuality--is transformed into
"natural," "observed fact," in a way that "camouflages"
his real "phallocentric ends." Analyzes in detail
Freud's theory of "penis envy," his elaboration of the
active/passive-masculine/feminine dualism, and his ideas
about fetishism as specific cases where feminine
sexuality is subordinated to masculine sexuality. Then,
examines Derrida's reading of Freud and, from that, his
text, Glas, to show how Derrida reintroduces the
"unbearable" ambiguities and "oscillations" that Freud
and all Western metaphysics have sought to fix and
master. Ends with a discussion of the multiplicity, the
"ungraspability" of the Derridean text, which Kofman says
characterizes sex as well: states this Derridean sex/text
parallel, "The question of sexuality as an undecidable
oscillation repeats, is the same as that of the text."
Concludes that Derrida's text undoes the polarized
structures that are at the base of Western ideology by
being "heterogeneous," that is, neither monolithic nor
oppositional, but "interwoven," "entwined," "irreducible."
Increasingly specialized and difficult.
Followed by a brief debate where Kofman pursues her
discussion of fetishism as elaborated by Freud (and read
by Derrida) and elucidates Freud's contradictory attitude
toward femininity and the implications of his "penis
envy" theory.

357 ———. "La Certitude immédiate de la différence."
     L'énigme de la femme: La femme dans les textes de
     Freud. Paris: Galilée, 1980, 125-7.

     Exposes Freud's contradictory stance on sexual
     difference, in which he says that the masculine/feminine
     "opposition" is both "primary" (the product of anatomy)
     and cultural (the product of social habit).

358 ———. "Graphématique et Psychanalyse." Ecarts: Quatre
     essais à propos de Jacques Derrida. Ed. Lucette Finas,
     Sarah Kofman, et al. Paris: Fayard, 1973, 149-204.

     Posits that while there is no "genealogy" of influence
     behind Derrida's texts, the works of certain earlier
     thinkers cannot be "avoided": those of the pre-Socratics,
     Mallarmé, Bataille, Heidegger, Hegel, Nietzsche and
     Freud. Examines in particular Derrida's continued return
     to Freud, the "displacements" and transformations of
     psychoanalysis he makes. Also sees resemblances between
     the two thinkers, especially the disturbing "strangeness"
     of their positions. Draws parallels between Freud's
     unconscious and Derrida's "différance," in regard to
     "writing" ("traces" in psychic and graphic writing),
     maintaining nonetheless that Derrida's rereading of Freud
     is a critical "simulacrum" of influence. Discusses
     Derrida's opening of literature to psychoanalysis and
     vice-versa.

359 ———. "La guerre des sexes." L'énigme de la femme:
     La femme dans les textes de Freud. Paris: Galilée,
     1980, 11-15.

     Situates feminist claims within psychoanalytic inquiry
     in the context of Freud's absolutist position on the
     unquestionable truth of his findings. Explains the
     "concessions" Freud made--in particular his acknowledg-
     ment that "pure" masculinity and femininity are
     theoretical constructs and his thesis about human
     bisexuality--as designed to appease feminists of the
     time and to prevent a "war of the sexes." Concludes
     that his theory of universal bisexuality, never applied
     to his own femininity, served really to silence
     "virile" women.

360 ———. "L'indécision et l'aporie introduites par la
science anatomique." L'énigme de la femme: La femme
dans les textes de Freud. Paris: Galilée, 1980, 129-33.

Discusses Freud's views on bisexuality as being, rather
than the egalitarian ones he claimed they were, in fact
detrimental to women: they focus on woman's bisexuality
only, the necessary result of her relation to the
masculine norm.

361 ———. "L'intérêt pour l'énigme de la femme." L'énigme
de la femme: La femme dans les textes de Freud. Paris:
Galilée, 1980, 119-24.

Argues Freud's method of addressing the "woman's enigma"
in his New Lectures on Femininity evinces his continued
"double strategy" of declaring one thing—in this case,
the limits of psychoanalysis and the usefulness of
"poetry"—and textually doing another—criticizing
poetry's "deceptiveness." Also criticizes his duplici-
tous appeal for the attention of women analysts.

362 ———. "L'opération de la greffe." Ecarts: Quatre
essais à propos de Jacques Derrida. Ed. Lucette Finas,
Sarah Kofman, et al. Paris: Fayard, 1973, 112-20.

Evokes Jacques Derrida's concept of "writing" and the
"text," calling it "strange" and "disturbing"—whence his
critics' charges of his "unreadability." States Derrida
opposes the traditional notions of Book and Author,
notions grounded in Western metaphysics's idea of a
single and authoritative consciousness. Says for Derrida
the text is a "heterogeneous," "limit-less," and
uncategorizable composite of "grafts" (versus a unified
"corpus") that are always rewriting themselves and other
texts. Difficult.

363 ———. "Philosophie terminée, philosophie interminable."
Qui a peur de la philosophie? Collected papers of the
Groupe de recherches sur l'enseignement philosophique.
Paris: Flammarion, 1977, 15-37.

Reflects on how philosophers have conceived the
relationship of philosophy to life and to politics.
Describes classical philosophers as associating the

learning of philosophy with intellectual maturity, thus
separating the "pure" mind from the body and implying
that acquiring philosophy is antithetical to living
life. Sees Nietzsche as having reversed this view of a
necessary "maturity," since he believed philosophy was
inseparable from life, from "the body and its desires."
Elaborates further on these two attitudes toward
philosophy by tracing ancient philosophical thought from
Callicles, to Socrates, to Plato. Raises issues of
importance to intellectual feminism: 1) Nietzsche's anti-
maturity stance contests the classical "metaphysical"
conception of history as linear and "evolutionist," since
philosophy for him is not independent of the changing
flow of human desires and he does not assume aging is a
"virile" movement toward understanding and wisdom; 2)
Classical philosophy associated philosophical reasoning
with doubt and critical rebellion and promulgated a
"return to order" after this "cathartic" reflection;
thus, classical philosophy, contrary to Nietzschian
thought, helped maintain the political status quo. Looks
at the consequences of these views about intellectual
maturity for the teaching of philosophy to adolescents.

364 ————. "La psychanalyse: le devenir-femme de l'enfant."
L'énigme de la femme: La femme dans les textes de
Freud. Paris: Galilée, 1980, 145-272.

A long and systematic critique of Freud's ideas on
female development. Takes as focus within his theories
of sexual differentiation how the female sex evolves from
the original bisexuality of children. Individual
sections within the essay are:
   "La bisexualité originaire"--Discusses Freud's
positivist approach to studying woman as product of
differentiation and the various paths of female
development: "normal," "hysterical," and "masculine
overcompensation." Develops his concept of "hysteria" as
an "accident" on the road from bisexuality to femininity.
Presents the Freudian view of homosexuality and heterosexuality, saying for him neither alone is the psychic
"norm," but rather both.
   "Le développement de la sexualité--différence entre
filles et garçons"--Elaborates on the evolution of the
young girl toward "normal femininity," a maturation
process Freud thought far more complicated than that of
the young boy.

"L'identité des deux sexes aux premiers stades de la
libido"--Describes the similarities between girls and
boys in the early stages of libidinal development and
Freud's shift from an insistence on symmetrical
bisexuality to a stress on the male developmental model.
Says the penis, through Freud's theory of the "phallic
stage," becomes the norm against which female organs--
specifically the clitoris--are compared.

"La puberté--les deux tâches supplémentaires de la
fille"--Explains the two supplementary tasks a girl must
accomplish to arrive at "normal femininity": she must
repress her initial masculinity (move from clitoral to
vaginal erogenous identification); and she must change
love object from mother to father. Says these female
tasks, not necessary for boys, are for Freud based on
"socio-biological" imperatives. Goes on to examine
Freud's complex and contradictory attitude toward the
female/passive and male/active association, saying he
both rejects and espouses it. Also presents Freud's
views of the mother-daughter relationship as transformed
from positive to negative and the decisive elements
involved in that shift in the girl's "penis envy" to
"castration."

"Le désir du père et l'instauration de la féminité"--
Describes the girl's desire for the father--for Freud her
attempt to satisfy her "penis envy"--as an essential step
toward "normal femininity." But shows how Freud adds yet
another condition for women to fulfill: they must replace
the desire for the penis with the desire for a child.
Demonstrates the ambiguities in Freud's apparent identification of the feminine with the maternal.

"Le complexe d'Oedipe de la fille"--Summarizes Freud's
problematic idea of the female Oedipal experience--a
presumably happy stage of "repair" and healing that she
will nonetheless have to surmount later on. Also
discusses Freud's distinction between female and male
superego formation, whose troubling moral consequences
for women he both propounded and sidestepped.

"Le complexe de masculinité de la fille"--Explains
Freud's late treatment of woman's "masculinity complex"
(her refusal to recognize her "castration"), for him a
defiant "abnormal" form of development. Calls this area
of theory his most speculative and recuperative.

"Les conséquences de la bisexualité"--Sees in Freud's
view of woman's original "bisexuality" the cause of her
ongoing "instability" and "ungraspability"--that is, "the
woman's enigma." Claims Freud calls upon "natural"
explanations to shore up his speculative ideas.

"Supplément rhapsodique"--Describes Freud's final
thoughts on women, "peculiarities" of mature women he
observed in psychoanalysis. Argues these thoughts served
to reinforce his earlier theories and are, ultimately,
extremely damaging to women.

365 ――――. "La psychologie: sa stérilité, son impuissance."
     L'énigme de la femme: La femme dans les textes de Freud.
     Paris: Galilée, 1980, 135-44.

Explains Freud's transformation of previous positivist
"psychological" conventions into new "psychoanalytic"
concepts, e.g., active/passive associations with men and
women. Says this reformulation is another example of his
blurring of sexual differences to avoid really confronting
them.

366 ――――. "Les retards de Freud." L'énigme de la femme:
     La femme dans les textes de Freud. Paris: Galilée,
     1980, 23-37.

Posits that Freud was quick to write about women to
forestall having to really deal with women's sexuality.
Says the Freudian texts in which the pre-Oedipal mother-
daughter relationship is discussed are late ones, the
delay being the result of his fear of women's sexuality
and the "death" it brought. Gives other examples of
Freud's deferring publication out of his "anguish of
death," the effect of his repression of his own
"shameful" incestuous desire for his mother.

367 ――――. "Le simulacre." Ecarts: Quatre essais à propos
     de Jacques Derrida. Ed. Lucette Finas, Sarah Kofman,
     et al. Paris: Fayard, 1973, 133-48.

Asserts that Derrida's ideas on writing, not just
negations of traditional metaphysical beliefs, are
positive affirmations of "play" and "différance." Argues
Derrida's "deconstruction" proceeds by a "double gesture"
of (1) inverting traditional hierarchies, then (2)
presenting new ideas ("simulacra") incommensurable with
old ideologies and that produce "effects of meaning"--but
not meaning. Says Derridean texts are "games" that are
not anarchic but that "open and close" on their own
rules. Claims his texts call upon other texts in a
process of "dissemination" or "grafting." Continually
undoes and refines its own affirmations.

368 ———. "Spéculation, observation." L'énigme de la
femme: La femme dans les textes de Freud. Paris:
Galilée, 1980, 17-21.

Argues that Freud's continued distinction between works
based on philosophical "speculation" and those using
scientific "observation" were a defense against accusations that he himself was guilty of speculation or bias.

369 ———. "Un philosophe inoui." Ecarts: Quatre essais à
propos de Jacques Derrida. Ed. Lucette Finas, Sarah
Kofman, et al. Paris: Fayard, 1973, 123-32.

Uses a series of metaphors that link sound with meaning
to define Derrida's destruction of the foundations of
Western metaphysics: logocentrism, presence, and the
privileging of the "voice" ("logophonocentrism") or the
authority of a unified self. Joins the myth of a
coherent and appropriative voice with the "Law of the
Father" and explains Derrida's preference for "writing"
as a form of disruption comparable to the "feminine."
Says Derridean philosophy favors "sight" over voice,
daring to "look at woman." Remains aware of the
impossibility of finding a "meaning" or a single
Derridean "philosophy," since his texts work to destroy
the concept of fixed meaning. Says Derrida's "grafted"
texts can only be heard with a "third ear."

370 ———. "Une énigme excitante." L'énigme de la femme:
La femme dans les textes de Freud. Paris: Galilée,
1980, 43-116.

A long essay with many subdivisions, some of which are
full discussions in themselves. Treats the underlying
reasons for Freud's consistently raising the "enigma of
woman": the problem was sure to arouse polemical
responses and thus remain unresolved. Says for Freud,
woman is "enigmatic" because of her sexuality--which
sexuality was his "idée fixe" and privileged object of
study. Subheadings are as follows:
"Le privilège de l'homme"--Offers one methodological
reason why woman was an "enigma" for Freud: he observed
only that which he knew best, himself (and a man). Sees
this as the origin of his normative masculine model and
his obscuring of female sexuality.

"L'inaccessibilité de la femme"--Describes a further
cause for delay in Freud's addressing women's experience:
his belief that, for various psychological and social
reasons, it "resisted" clinical observation.

"La langue suspendue"--Speaks of Freud's efforts to
break the "silence" of "resisting" women patients, whom
he believed deceptively withheld their "secrets." Claims
his approach was that of becoming "accomplice of the
hysteric," lying in kind and forcing her to espouse his
point of view.

"La pudeur"--Says the self-sufficiency of the silent
and "enigmatic" woman was intolerable for Freud, for
which reason he developed the theory that women "veil"
their sexuality to "hide" their "natural deficiencies."
Adds "penis envy" as another cause for women's presumed
physical vanity and modesty.

"La femme narcissique"--Sees Freud's essay, "On
Narcissism: An Introduction," as breaking with his
traditional treatment of women as "veiled enigmas" and as
opening a new path of inquiry on women. Says "On
Narcissism," rather than positing in woman some innate
lack, instead affirms her "self-sufficiency," the
positive narcissism or love of self she develops.
Elucidates Freud's distinction between this female type
of narcissism and the male "object-love" or narcissism
that transfers valuation from self to the loved object.
Clarifies Freud's suggestion that, contrary to female
envy of the penis, what is operative here is male envy of
female indifference and of her retention of original
libidinal wholeness. Says this envy is really a
fascination in men for their own "double," their own lost
self and original narcissism. Traces parallels to this
male attraction to female narcissism in the ideas of
Nietzsche, suggesting philosophy anticipated psychoanalysis. Discusses how Freud "backtracks" in this essay
from this rich but frightening line of thought about
women by bringing moral considerations to bear on these
male and female forms of love. Sees Freud as reasserting
the virtue of the masculine model in a way that absorbs
and neutralizes the positive female narcissism he had
previously delineated. Ends with a critique of René
Girard's misreading of the essay--his belief that Freud
himself was victim of the female "coquettish" strategies
that for Girard constitute the "enigma" of woman.
Concludes that interpretations like Girard's reduce the
stress on sexual difference that makes Freud's essay so
important.

"Criminelle ou hystérique"--Asks why Freud abandoned
his potentially positive view of women's narcissism in
favor of drawing "criminal" consequences from their
self-sufficient form of love. Says Freud was afraid of
his own discoveries.

"Sexe fort ou sexe faible?"--Demonstrates the central
role of myth in the masculine and seemingly "rational"
discipline of psychoanalysis by showing how Freud's
theory of "penis envy" is a "reaction to panic," a
"fiction" that transforms too-fascinating woman into a
"hysteric" and manipulable patient.

"La relève des mères"--Describes the "double gesture"
characteristic of all Freudian thought on women: on the
one hand, a recognition of the "phantasmic omnipotence"
of enigmatic woman (of the mother), on the other, the
attempt to master or turn aside woman's power in favor of
men. Evokes the masculine anxiety aroused by female
"otherness" and the cultural taboos established to
control female power. Also explains the theory of "penis
envy" as a maneuver to deprive woman of power--to
"castrate woman"--by giving her an "immature sexuality"
and the vengeful desire to castrate men in return.
Discusses Freud's Oedipal "solution" to the problem of
women's power, a solution that accomplishes the "death"
of the omnipotent mother (though this power and death are
in fact "phantasmatic"). Makes parallels between the
passage from the original sensory knowledge the child
acquires from the mother to the knowledge of the father's
socialized law and logic and the passage from myth and
dream to the science of psychoanalysis. Calls this
passage a "compensation" or "sublimation" of female power
that restores to "civilized" man his "full sexual power."

"L'envieuse de pénis, la putain, l'homosexuel, le
fétichiste"--Joins Freud's notion of woman's presumed
"penis envy" with his "theory-fiction" about the
prostitute: both, by destroying woman's power and
objectifying her, multiply man's power. Says both are
two socially distinguished sides of the same male coin:
forbidden incest.

"Le trône et l'autel sont en danger"--Takes Leonardo da
Vinci as example of Freudian Oedipal "hero" who triumphed
over his father, thus freeing himself to accomplish great
works.

"Le roc"--Uses the term to describe the "insurmountable
biological fact" Freud assumed a woman's "rejection of
femininity" to be. Says he saw such a rejection--
impervious to psychoanalysis--as woman's abomination of

woman. Also uses "rock" to mean female sexuality, the
limit Freud kept hitting against, his real unexplored
"enigma."

370a   "La pudeur" and "La femme narcissique: Freud et
         Girard." Revue française de psychanalyse 44, No. 1
         (January-February 1980), 195-210.

370b   "La pudeur" and "La femme narcissique" trans. as
         "The Narcissistic Woman: Freud and Girard" in
         Diacritics 10, No. 3 (Fall 1980), 36-45.

370c   "Sexe fort ou sexe faible" and "La relève des
         mères" trans. as "Ex: The Woman's Enigma" in
         Enclitic 4, No. 2 (Fall 1980), 17-28.

ESSAYS AND ARTICLES ABOUT

371   Berg, Elizabeth L. "The Third Woman." Diacritics 12
      (Summer, 1982), 11-20.

      Compares the theories of the feminine formulated by
Sarah Kofman in L'Enigme de la femme (352) and by Luce
Irigaray in Speculum de l'autre femme (314) and l'Amante
marine (308). Contends that Kofman's more deconstructive
model has greater power to make possible "the penetration
of women into the masculine world and the order of the
symbolic" and to reconcile those feminists who demand
equality and those who stress sexual difference.
Summarizes Kofman's reading of Freud and explains that it
distinguishes three avenues for feminine sexuality:
hysteria--woman alienated from her truth, narcissism--
woman as self-sufficient but mute possessor of truth, and
bisexuality--the woman who affirms the contradictory
co-existence of opposites. Develops the positive
potential of this "third woman" for feminist theory.
Proposes that although Irigaray is sensitive to the
danger of a theoretical double bind--that woman, be she
represented or unrepresentable, serves as a mirror for
man's projections--and attempts to focus on "the blank
spaces of masculine representation," she increasingly
evokes the feminine as Origin, thus regressing to a
metaphysics of presence and remaining "entrapped by the
second woman." Finds that Kofman, like other readers,
does not acknowledge fully Irigaray's contributions, but
instead uses her as a means of engaging with great men.
Very insightful and clearly written.

Kristeva, Julia:

BOOKS AND COLLECTIONS OF ESSAYS

372 ————. Des Chinoises. Paris: des femmes, 1974.

A personal notebook of information and analysis
inspired by Kristeva's trip to China in 1974 and her
desire to compare the situations of women in Chinese and
Western cultures. Is representative of the period of
Kristeva's enthusiasm for Chinese communism. Argues for
a fundamental relativity of perspective, for a respect
for China's "otherness," an otherness our Western
monotheistic and capitalist bias cannot perceive and
which destroys falsely "universal" notions of Man and
History. Taking the status of women as its central
framework for observing China, claims the role of women
and the function of the family there have a "specificity"
unknown to Western culture. Sees the "new" forces
visible in China's progress--women, young people,
artists, poets--as precisely those elements capitalist
monotheism has repressed. Describes woman in Western
societies as "beyond the threshold ot expression," as
"voice-less," "negative," a "mute body," and emblematic
of all "stranger(s) to social cohesion"--in other words,
"women, (they) don't exist." Then, in a series of essays
on Western women, discusses the following theoretical
issues: (1) sexual difference: traces the biblical/
historical origins of the rift between the sexes, a split
specifically in relation to religion and political law
(man possesses and is the law, the Word, and power,
whereas woman, excluded from power and knowledge, is
defined solely by her social function of reproduction).
Urges that the solution to this rift not be one that
adopts "phallic" or monolithic and "totalitarian" notions
of sexual identity (absorption of one sex by the other),
but rather one that dismantles and redefines relations
between the sexes; (2) women's relation to the "symbolic,"
to the Word: says Christianity gave women the choice
between "virginity" or "martyrdom," thus denying their
corporality and excluding them from the "Verb." The
repressed maternal body has been allowed to emerge only
as it is defined for patriarchal needs. Evokes this
maternal/paternal drama in psychoanalytic terms, joining
psychic and linguistic structures; (3) women's relation
to time: argues the "words" women have repressed in
themselves, in the name of the masculine symbolic and

familial order and its linear chronology, have the
potential to "explode the whole edifice." Locates that
repressed feminine language in the unconscious, which is
itself a-temporal, and suggests there is another
temporality in female "jouissance" and pregnancy--both of
which are breaks in the established chronological order;
(4) women and suicide: positing the traditional
psychological drama in which the young girl comes to
identify with the father (the law, the superego),
therefore making any identification with the mother a
form of "death," "sacrifice," or "suicide"; suggests this
latter gesture can be viewed as a profoundly radical
questioning of the symbolic order. In the second part of
the book, studies Chinese women through an examination of
the following areas: (1) the structure of the Chinese
family--hypothesizes a matrilineal and matrilocal family
heritage, dating from ancient China, along with a second
"agnatic" or patrilineal model. Cites historical
documents as it traces family configurations in detail.
Discusses the regression of women's status under
Confucian doctrine. Also connects family structures to
linguistic ones as it analyzes Chinese spoken and written
language; (2) socialism and feminism--claims early 20th
century Chinese political movements against feudalism are
inseparable from feminist movements advocating changes in
family and moral structures. Elaborates on the role
Chinese women played in the political activity of this
century; (3) the evolution of the Chinese communist
party's attitude toward women's issues (1920's-present),
including Mao's efforts for women's emancipation and the
reform of the Marriage Law (1950) in favor of equality
and responsibility for women; (4) "glimpses" ("entrevues")
of Chinese women's bodies and voices and of individual
women viewed in their roles as mother, worker, artist,
intellectual and lover ("In China there are no women's
and men's professions"); (5) concluding thoughts about
possible similarities between women of the two cultures
(e.g., the necessity for women to identify with masculine
values to achieve recognition) and possible differences
(e.g., the apparent Chinese "censorship of sexual
difference," minimizing the distinctions between women
and men), though Kristeva hesitates before her own
Western conceptual prism. An affectionately positive
presentation of China and an unusually personal text.
(See 269 and 27).

372a   Trans. as <u>About Chinese Women</u>. New York: Urizen
        Books, 1977.

372b   Partially trans. as "On the Women of China," Signs
        1, No. 1 (Autumn 1975), 57-81.

373   ———. Desire in Language: A Semiotic Approach to
        Literature and Art. Ed. Leon S. Roudiez. New York:
        Columbia University Press, 1980.

        Preface; Editor's Introduction (465); "The Ethics of
        Linguistics" (402); "The Bounded Text" (440); "Word,
        Dialogue and Novel" (418); "How Does One Speak to
        Literature?" (388); "From One Identity to an Other"
        (397); "The Father, Love, and Banishment" (421); "The
        Novel as Polylogue" (424); "Giotto's Joy" (413);
        "Motherhood According to Giovanni Bellini" (416); "Place
        Names" (419).

        A collection of translations of Kristeva's essays
        dating from 1970-1980. Kristeva's preface describes her
        purpose and method throughout these essays: to discover
        "the determinative role of language in all human
        sciences," by means of "semanalysis," or a description of
        "signifying phenomena, while analyzing, criticizing, and
        dissolving 'phenomenon,' 'meaning,' and 'signifier.'"
        Calls the two "instrumentalities" or theoretical foci of
        her work the "speaking subject" (the "agent" engaged in a
        process of "enunciation") and the "specific object"
        (literary and artistic texts or realizations of linguistic
        enunciations). Says the concern in each essay is "to
        subvert the very theoretical, philosophical or semiologi-
        cal apparatus" with which it is engaged. Also indicates
        as sources of her theory (1) her work as a psychoanalyst,
        in constant contact with the individual's "double"
        relationship to language: "If the overly constraining and
        reductive meaning of a language made up of universals
        causes us to suffer, the call of the unnamable, on the
        contrary, issuing from those borders where signification
        vanishes, hurls us into the void of a psychosis that
        appears henceforth as the solitary reverse of our
        universe"; and (2) her being a woman and therefore able
        to question to its limits "the signifying venture of
        men." (See 465).

374   ———. Polylogue. Paris: Seuil, 1977.

        "Politique et littérature" (436); "Comment parler à la
        littérature" (388); "Le sujet en procès" (437);
        "L'expérience et la pratique" (404); "Le père, l'amour,

l'exil" (421); "D'une identité l'autre" (397); "Polylogue"
(424); "Objet ou complément" (420); "Matière, sens,
dialectique" (417); "Du sujet en linguistique" (398); "La
fonction prédicative et le sujet parlant" (407);
"L'éthique de la linguistique" (402); "Ellipse sur la
frayeur et la séduction spéculaire" (399); "La joie de
Giotto" (413); "Maternité selon Giovanni Bellini" (416);
"Contraintes rythmiques et langage poétique" (389); "Noms
de lieu" (419); "D'Ithaca à New York" (395); "La Femme,
ce n'est jamais ça" (479); "Les Chinoises à 'contre-
courant'" (406).

A collection of Kristeva's previously published essays
that analyzes "various processes of symbolization"--from
the earliest (spoken) languages of children to literature
and painting, and up to technical discourses (linguistics,
semiotics, epistemology, psychoanalysis)--taking as its
central focus the speaking "subject" or self. Calls each
process studied a "logos" or a signifying system, whence
the book's title "polylogue," a "pluralization of
rationality." Traces, for the important historical eras
(Middle Ages, Renaissance, and 20th century), the
emergence each time of a new "positivity of meaning,"
after the destruction of previous codes ("negativity" or
the "dissolution of meaning"). Sees modern psychoanalysis as perhaps the ultimate signifying discourse,
since it "opens onto an abyss" in which biology joins
psychology, the body joins meaning, and psychosis
threatens to engulf rationality completely. Says that
if, in past eras, each crisis of meaning was expressed
through the "universal" languages of religion, philosophy,
literature and the arts, the modern crisis of Western
reason, having demystified the "individual" and the
"community," must give rise to new responses, with new
configurations of individual and collective relationships.
Hypothesizes that these individual/collective responses
will be "multiple"--the "multiplication of languages, of
logics, of powers" on a new register--and not perpetu-
ations of the traditional univocal, rational discourse.
Sees as the most important "singular" or individual new
response the emergence of sexual difference: the
feminine, heretofore exiled from discourse and meaning,
will introduce new "tensions" into all symbolizing
processes, new "passages" ("traversées") between body and
thought. The entire book is rich, varied, and essential
for an understanding of Kristeva's particular view of the
relation of the "feminine" to language. There is much

internal repetition among the essays and some of the
pieces are far less accessible than others. (See 459 and
269).

375 ————. Pouvoirs de l'horreur: Essai sur l'abjection.
      Paris: Seuil, 1980.

"Approche de l'abjection" (383); "De quoi avoir peur"
(393); "De la saleté à la souillure" (391); "Sémiotique
de l'abomination biblique" (433); "...Qui tollis peccata
mundi" (431); "Céline: ni comédien ni martyr" (386);
"Douleur/horreur" (396); "Ces femelles qui nous gâchent
l'infini..." (387); "'Juivre ou mourir'" (414); "Au
commencement et sans fin..." (385); "Pouvoirs de
l'horreur"(426).

A collection of essays representative of Kristeva's
more recent concerns with the problems of "horror" and
"abjection" in literature, including their relation to
analytic theory, the history of religion, and the works
of particular authors (especially Céline). Each essay in
some way elucidates a theory and then "dissolves" it
through insistence on its ambiguities. Each essay
prepares for the next. The entire book reveals moments
of personal intervention by Kristeva as she self-
consciously views her own project.

375a   Trans. as Powers of Horror: An Essay in Abjec-
       tion. New York: Columbia University Press, 1982.

376 ————. La Révolution du langage poétique: l'avant-garde
      à la fin du XIXe siècle: Lautréamont et Mallarmé.
      Paris: Seuil, 1974.

Part I--Préliminaires théoriques: I. Sémiotique et
symbolique; II. La négativité: le rejet; III. L'hétéro-
gène; IV. La pratique; Part II--Le dispositif sémiotique
du texte: I. Rythmes phoniques et sémantiques; II.
Syntaxe et composition; III. Instances du discours et
altération du sujet; IV. Le contexte présupposé.
Part III--L'état et le mystère: I. Le texte à l'intérieur
d'une formation économique et sociale; II. Maintien et
limitation du pouvoir et de la conscience de classe; III.
L'anarchisme politique ou autre; IV. Le mariage et la
fonction paternelle; V. Le mystère--Doublure du code
social; VI. L'instance du pouvoir à sujet absent; VII. La

traversée des frontières; VIII. A la recherche d'une
souveraineté: le héros, le théâtre, le chant.   Furieux
d'intelligence.   Bibliographie.

A massive study about experiments in poetic language of
the late 19th century, experiments exemplifying cultural
"ruptures" that can give rise to major social and
political change.   States at the outset that literary
activism, or practices that "destroy" and "rebuild"
traditional discourse, does for the individual "subject"
what political revolution does for society as a whole.
Establishes immediately Kristeva's belief in fundamental
parallels between the linguistic production of meaning
and economic and political systems of production.   First,
sets forth its theoretical framework and its basic
epistemological concepts in tremendous detail, while
acknowledging its affinities with the works of Marx,
Hegel, Freud, Lacan, Derrida, and others: (1) Claims
sciences such as semiotics, as they are currently
practiced in Western (capitalist) societies, partake of
and perpetuate the repression of the "subject" (the "I")
and of the body that characterizes those social systems
in general; therefore, sets as its goal the introduction
of a truly "materialist" grounding of the "subject," that
is, its dynamic linguistic, corporal and social
situation; (2) explains Kristeva's idea of the "process"
or "production of meaning" ("procès de signifiance")
through the definition of such key concepts as the
"semiotic 'chora'" (pre-verbal psychic/biological
"pulsions" that generate an infinite number of
signifiers); the "thetic" or the "symbolic" (a domain of
meaning, of elaboration that "identifies" the subject;
the "mirror stage" (the psychoanalytic term Kristeva uses
for the constantly traversed threshold between the
semiotic and the symbolic; "jouissance" (the subversive
pleasure characteristic of the semiotic domain that
always threatens to "explode" into language even as
language tries to repress it); "geno-text" and "pheno-
text"; and a host of other specialized terms from
linguistic theory; (3) elaborates on the notion of
"negativity," at once the "cause" and the "organizational
principle" of the whole process of meaning, and its
characteristic of "expenditure," or the "casting out"
("rejet") brought on by a subject seeking and surpassing
"unity"; (4) explains "heterogeneity," or the basis for
Kristeva's redefinition of "materialism"; (5) and
discusses the idea of a "signifying practice," the

textual formation of a system of representation that has
social implications (using the example of Lautréamont's
poems). Then, characterizes in minute detail the various
qualities of the "pheno-text" or the semiotic system, in
their "morpho-phonemic, syntactic, pronominal and
contextual" manifestations (using Mallarmé's and
Lautréamont's texts as examples). In the section that
follows, shows the contributions and the limitations of
Marx's analysis of history through a retracing of
communism in France. Presents as well a chapter crucial
for understanding Kristeva's subsequent ideas about
women: in "Marriage and the Paternal Function," uses
marital-familial structures metaphorically both to
analyze "symbolic paternity" and the repression of the
"maternal" that characterize bourgeois Western culture
and to show how authors such as Mallarmé and Lautréamont
react to those sexual constraints and imperatives. Cites
Mallarmé as associating poetic "mystery" (Kristeva's
musical and rhythmic semiotic "chora") with the feminine,
though Kristeva finds this designation too "fetishistic,"
too close to the real social "idolizing" of women of that
era. Develops the notion of a "phallic mother," one who
possesses a power unlike that of the "phallus" or the
"father"--a power that has compelled poets and yet has
never been articulated by them (in the same way society,
Kristeva claims, has "socialized" or neutralized
eroticism). Presents, in early form, some of Kristeva's
ideas about sexual differentiation and the production of
language. Finally, develops, in ontological, historical,
and economic terms, Kristeva's theory about the
capitalistic nation-state, a social grouping that served
certain ideological needs and that has been severely
questioned in this century. The book's conclusion,
"Furieux d'intelligence," is a very good summary of the
entire book. Over all, a fresh and fascinating attempt
to connect these 19th-century poets with their concrete
world, to join poetic production with its social and
economic context. Much of this immense work is
accessible only to the specialist. (See 456 and 463).

377   ———. Sémeiôtiké: Recherches pour une sémanalyse.
           Paris: Seuil, 1969.

           "Le texte et sa science" (441); "La sémiotique, science
           critique et/ou critique de la science" (434); "L'expan-
           sion de la sémiotique" (403); "Le sens et la mode" (436);
           "Le geste, pratique ou communication?" (409); "Le texte
           clos" (440); "Le mot, le dialogue et le roman" (418);

"Pour une sémiologie des paragrammes" (425); "La productivité dite texte" (428); "Poésie et négativité" (423); "L'engendrement de la formule" (400).

A collection of essays representative of Kristeva's early connection with and distance from structuralist literary analysis. Demonstrates her method of "semanalysis" or study of the determinative role of language in all human "sciences," including literature and semiotics. The first essay, "Le texte et sa science" (441), introduces the book's intention to provide a theoretical framework for a scientific and "material" analysis of texts. (See 457).

378 ————. Le Texte du roman: Approche sémiologique d'une structure discursive transformationnelle. The Hague/ Paris: Mouton, 1970.

0. Introduction; 1. "Du symbole au signe"; 2. "La méthode transformationnelle et son application sémiotique"; 3. "La transformation actantielle"; 4. "La génération des complexes narratifs"; 5. "L'intertextualité"; 6. "La cosmogonie romanesque"; 7. Conclusion.

Representative of Kristeva's earliest work on semiotics and its use as a method for analyzing narrative structures—specifically, the novel. The "Introduction" defines "text" and "novel" in specialized terms and specifies the corpus Kristeva will study, the works of the 14th century author, Antoine de la Sale. Succeeding chapters summarize linguistic theory and clarify the concepts of "sign" and "symbol," transformational grammar (American and French approaches), and intertextuality. Explains in various ways the narrative generation of de la Sale's prose texts. Of interest for Kristeva's subsequent work on the feminine is the section on courtly poetry (in "L'intertextualité") and the ambiguous valorization of woman visible in de la Sale's works. Describes the cult of "Identity," "Identification" and "One-ness" in literature of the era. Elaborates on woman as "other different from the Same (man)," as inconceivable "difference" who is therefore erased from literary discourse. Connects this ambivalence—valorization and occultation—of the feminine to social structures of the time and to cultural practices (e.g., carnivals and theater) that reflect similar dual attitudes. Ends with

a discussion of time and space in the novel. For the
specialist only.

BOOKS EDITED

379 ————. Essays in Semiotics/Essais de sémiotique. The
     Hague/Paris: Mouton, 1971.

A large collection of essays, in French and English, by
various semioticians and linguists. The forty three
essays are grouped into the following categories: general
problems; linguistics; discourse analysis; anthropology;
semiotics of art; kinesics; zoosemiotics; meetings;
bibliographies. Kristeva's introduction, "Le lieu
sémiotique," traces the history of semiological inquiry
and defines its current enterprise: "seizing signifying
practices...while taking into account the different and
multiple systems that bring meaning into play." Says
semiotics should be the "scientific theory" of our era,
the modern theoretical replacement for unseated classical
philosophy. Kristeva's essay, "L'expansion de la
sémiotique" (See 403), describes the expanding critical
"space" of current semiotics in which the discourses of
both classical philosophy and linguistics itself come
into question. Advocates "polyvalent" studies of the
various "particularities" of signifying systems that are
outside of the language of simple communication. In
calling semiotics an active and generative "social
practice," and not just a reflection or description of
objects, prefigures Kristeva's later concern with
language and cultural change. The volume, very
specialized, does not touch on women's issues but is
typical of Kristeva's earliest work.

380 ———— and Jean-Michel Ribette. Folle vérité: Vérité et
     vraisemblance du texte psychotique. Paris: Seuil, 1979.

"A vrai dire" (Preface); Julia Kristeva, "Le vréel"
(444); Silla Consoli, "Le récit du psychotique"; Pierre
Marie, Jean-Marie Prieur, "Freudaineries (Lisette,
Michèle et les autres)"; Béatrice Polattini, Niké
d'Astorg, "Du dessin à la lettre: le signe, vérité du
corps"; Jean-Michel Ribette, "Le phalsus (Vrai/semblant/
vraisemblance du texte obsessionnel)"; Antoine Compagnon,
"Psychose et sophistique"; Julia Kristeva, "Le démon
littéraire" (392); Gislhaine Meffre, "L'invraisemblable
fascisme de Céline"; Jean Petitot-Cocorda, "Sur ce qui

revient à la psychose"; Michel de Certeau, "Folie du nom et mystique du sujet: Surin."

A collection of essays from a seminar in psychiatry Kristeva conducted in 1977-78, on the topic of "mad truth" or delirium. Kristeva's preface states that the words of the mentally ill expose the basic "malaise" of all language, that of oscillation (for the speaker and listener) between shared communication and distance or "alterity." Explains how psychosis, through its unbridled manifestation of desire, throws the sciences of psychoanalysis and semiotics into question.

381   ——— et al. La Traversée des signes. Paris: Seuil, 1975.

Julia Kristeva, "Pratique signifiante et mode de production" (427); Julia Kristeva, "Remarques sur le 'mode de production asiatique'" (432); François Cheng, "Le 'langage poétique' chinois"; Michelle Loi, "Poésie et politique en Chine"; Discussion; Madeleine Biardeau, "Théories du langage en Inde"; Discussion; Pierre-Sylvain Filliozat, "La poétique sanskrite"; Discussion; Pierre-Sylvain Filliozat, "La grammaire sanskrite de Panini"; Discussion; Eva de Vitray-Meyerovitch, "La 'poétique' de l'Islam"; Discussion; Julia Kristeva, "A propos du 'discours biblique'" (384); Daniel Sibony, "D'un sciage de la lettre (Kafka I)."

A collection of essays on language and literature (produced during a seminar led by Kristeva in 1973-74) whose stated intention is to break free of the "prison" of Occidental rationality and "modes of production" that constrain all research done in the West. Seeks to "open" its intellectual enterprise by exploring the language and literature produced by civilizations with a different "temporality" and "historicity": China, India, Islam, and Judaism. Says such cultures can contribute to the general change in the conception of the "subject" and "meaning" that marks current literary and scientific research. Aims not for an "impossible" synthesis of understanding, but for a "plurality" of attitudes.

ESSAYS AND ARTICLES:

382   ———. "Actualité de Céline." Tel Quel 71/73 (Fall 1977), 45-52.

Bases the current relevance of Céline on the forms his
subversion of rationality took--fascism and anti-
Semitism--both of which, Kristeva claims, are symptomatic
of this century's crisis of truth. Says Céline manifests
the "decentering" of identity characteristic of modern
"psychosis" or the crumbling of traditional socio-
political values. Sees as other signs of crisis the
women's movement, pornography, drugs, and violence, all
of which have left the social margins to become accepted
parts of the "system." Elucidates the relationship
between the Western crisis of identity (since Freud and
Saussure) and "poetic language" (fiction and poetry)
while explaining how Céline extended the limits of the
"signifiable."

383 ————. "Approche de l'abjection." Pouvoirs de
     l'horreur: Essai sur l'abjection. Paris: Seuil, 1980,
     7-39.

An arcane introduction to Kristeva's concept of
"abjection," in its psychoanalytic, philosophical, and
linguistic implications. Describes it as a "violent,
dark revolt of being" involving the "subject" in a
particular relation to the abject "object" that "disturbs
identity, system, order." Calls literature the "signifier" of the "abjection of self"--an experience in which
the body, the unconscious, and "jouissance" come into
play. Goes on to examine the "terrain" of the abject in
representative modern literature (Dostoevski, Proust,
Joyce, Borges, Artaud). Opaque.

384 ————. "A propos du 'discours biblique.'" La Traversée
     des signes. Ed. Julia Kristeva et al. Paris: Seuil,
     1975, 223-7.

An introduction to a paper on biblical discourse that
points out how the Bible formulated, for the first time
ever, "the conditions necessary for the enunciation of a
truth": by isolating and glorifying the "paternal
function" as the basis for all social, linguistic and
historical unity (the "Word" of the "Father" that brought
order and community), the Bible set in place a discourse
that even now constitutes us and our culture and that
inevitably speaks "through us." Says this discourse is
the logical and moral support of Western culture and is
precisely what all modern social, artistic and political

movements, including those of women, contest. Gives a
brief geographic history of the "symbolic contract" with
monotheism that the Bible represents and recounts. A
provocative historical look at the instauration of "the
One, the Father, the truth made law in discourse," at the
expense of "the mother it represses."

385 ————. "Au commencement et sans fin..." Pouvoirs de
l'horreur: Essai sur l'abjection. Paris: Seuil, 1980,
221-42.

"Listens" to Céline's texts as "struggles" with the
"mother tongue," as renderings of "the unnamable truth of
emotion" hidden inside him. Says Céline's style "resur-
rects" the "emotional, maternal abyss" in which "emotion
turns into sound." Further explores the principal
characteristics of Célinian language--sentence segmenta-
tion and syntactic ellipsis--in several of his works.

386 ————. "Céline: ni comédien ni martyr." Pouvoirs de
l'horreur: Essai sur l'abjection. Paris: Seuil, 1980,
155-62.

Treats the works of Céline as literature, as "a
reassumption, through style, of what lies hidden by
God"--"abjection and piercing laughter." Says "the true
'miracle' of Céline resides in the very experience of
one's reading," in which one is thrown into a "strange
state" by the text's "nakedness," a state like that of
"defilement" and "sin." Investigates the wellsprings of
Céline's anti-Semitism and the "disgust" that marks his
universe.

387 ————. "Ces femelles qui nous gâchent l'infini..."
Pouvoirs de l'horreur: Essai sur l'abjection. Paris:
Seuil, 1980, 183-201.

Examines the place of the "mother" or the feminine in
Céline's fiction. Says she is "split in two," into the
"ideal" "focus of the artist's gaze" and the "repulsive
and fascinating" image of "suffering, illness, sacrifice,
and downfall." Follows this split into Céline's ambiva-
lent ideas on love and sexual desire. Traces the
representation of women (and, by implication, men) in
some of his works, as far back as his doctoral disserta-
tion.

388 ———. "Comment parler à la littérature?" Tel Quel 47
     (Fall 1971), 27–49.

Analyzes avant-garde literature as the only discourse
that has survived and can survive other forms of social
repression and as the "laboratory" which will bring forth
true political and social change. Uses the works of
Roland Barthes as example of and prism for its analysis
of current "discursive/ideological" mutation. Locates in
Barthes's ideas precursors of such important Kristevan
concepts as "negativity," "desire," and "heterogeneity."

388a   Reprinted in (374).

388b   Trans. in (373).

389 ———. "Contraintes rythmiques et langage poétique."
     Analyse du discours, Colloque de Toronto. Ed. P. Léon
     and F. Miterrand. Montreal, 1976, 215–38.

Examines "pre-grammatical" linguistic processes (the
"semiotic") which, it claims, modern linguistics has
ignored in favor of studies of language as synthetic and
"meaningful" (the "symbolic"). Describes this pre-logical
discourse, acquired earlier in linguistic development, as
"emotional," "connotative," and "rhythmic." Goes on to
characterize, quite technically, the semiotic language
and to demonstrate its appearance in literature.

389a   Reprinted in (374).

390 ———. "De la généralité sémiotique." Etudes litté-
     raires 10, No. 3 (December 1977), 337–46.

Discusses the debate in semiotic theory over a
hermeneutics of "generalizability" versus one of
"particularity." Expresses Kristeva's belief that
semiotics should use a polyvalent, multiple approach
addressing the various specific situations of the
"speaking subject." Also talks about different semiotic
methods of textual reading and the "position" of the
researching subject. Raises the question of the
psychoanalytic dynamics of textual interpretation.

391 ———. "De la saleté à la souillure." <u>Pouvoir de</u>
<u>l'horreur: Essai sur l'abjection</u>. Paris: Seuil, 1980,
<u>69-105</u>.

Uses a psychoanalytic and anthropological framework to
examine notions of the "sacred" and "defilement,"
specifically in regard to taboos and to "dread, incest
and the mother." Explores the "feminine," which for
Kristeva is not any sort of essence, but rather "an
'other' without a name, which subjective experience
confronts when it does not stop at the appearance of its
identity." Says the confrontation with the "feminine," a
state of "ecstasy," appears in the works of a few rare
authors--e.g., Céline. Looks at rituals of "pollution"
and "purification" in various cultures in their relation
to "fear of the archaic mother...fear of her generative
power."

392 ———. "Le démon littéraire." <u>Folle vérité: Vérité et</u>
<u>vraisemblance du texte psychotique</u>. Ed. Julia Kristeva
and Jean-Michel Ribette. Paris: Seuil, 1979, 203-06.

Restates Kristeva's belief that "literature" is not an
application of normative discourse but a specific
"linguistic economy" that expresses "boundary experiences" ("expériences limites"). Calls this phenomenon of
the rendering of a "mad truth" the effect of the "literary
demon" which operates in the "vréel" (see 444). Takes as
articulations of this theory chapter 8 of the Gospel of
Saint Luke, Dostoevski's <u>The Possessed</u>, and the works of
Céline, this last author evincing the meeting of words
and "psychosis."

393 ———. "De quoi avoir peur." <u>Pouvoirs de l'horreur:</u>
<u>Essai sur l'abjection</u>. Paris: Seuil, 1980, 41-67.

Explores the psychoanalytic phenomenon of the "object"-
-the object of desire in Freudian and Lacanian terms--and
its role in the constitution of the "subject." Uses the
maternal body as metaphor for the site of this constitution. Describes the state of "fear" the child experiences
during this sexual and sexuating process, and the related
states of "phobia," "want," "aggressivity," and "narcissism." Connects linguistic development to these infantile
experiences and designates "abjection"--"the crossroads
of phobia, obsession and perversion"--as a state

"eminently productive of culture" by its symptom, "the
rejection and reconstruction of languages."

394 ———. "Des Chinoises à Manhattan." Tel Quel 69
(Spring 1977), 11-16.

The epilogue to the American edition of Des Chinoises
(372). Reflects, two years later, on Kristeva's trip to
China and on subsequent events, including Mao's death--
all of which for Kristeva point up the profound
differences between the American, European and Chinese
concepts of time. Describes American temporality as at
once "universal" and "specific," as immeasurably long and
instantaneously brief. Says Europe, an older civilization, is experiencing a crisis in its sense of time. And
claims China challenges all Western concepts of chronology, though it is becoming more westernized in the wake
of Mao's death. Discusses the situation of women in
China in light of current social changes there, pointing
to the retrogressive campaign against a "conspiring"
Chiang Ching (Madam Mao). Inquires with sadness about
the fate of the strong and outspoken Chinese women she
had met, in view of that country's present need for order
and conformity.

395 ———. "D'Ithaca à New York." Promesse Nos. 36-37
(Spring 1974).

A travelogue about the United States that associates
the continuous departure, arrival, rupture, renewal of
travelling with the feminine, versus the false mastering,
fixing and "knowledge" of a place associated with
traditional (masculine) modes of travelling. Joins the
fragmented travelling subject ("I") with fragmented
discourse. Makes judgments about American and European
economic systems, political events, and academic institutions from Kristeva's Marxian perspective. Assesses
American women's movements as naive, yet visible, audible,
and active. A refreshing and spontaneous piece.

395a   Reprinted in (374).

396 ———. "Douleur/horreur." Pouvoirs de l'horreur: Essai
sur l'abjection. Paris: Seuil, 1980, 163-82.

Presents Céline's works as "narratives of suffering and
horror," both by theme and by narrative stance ("con-

trolled by the necessity of suffering"). Locates this
"suffering" or "abjection" as "the place of the (speaking)
subject," that of the limit between "inside and outside,
ego and other, desires and prohibitions." Evokes the
effect of abjection in literature as the fact that the
speaking subject no longer narrates, but "cries out" with
"maximal stylistic intensity." Considers several of
Céline's works for thematic and narrative evidence of
"suffering/horror."

397   ———. "D'une identité l'autre." Tel Quel 62 (Summer
       1975), 10-27.

       Demonstrates epistemologically how "any theory of
language is a tributary of the conception of the subject
that it posits," either explicitly or implicitly.
Examines three "moments" in the history of linguistic
theory to point out the "place" they designate for the
speaking subject. Shows how all theories of meaning are
part of and put forth an ideology. Examines the
signifying process Kristeva calls "poetic language"--
using Céline--as a questioning of the stability and the
unicity attributed to the concepts of "meaning" and
"subject" in place in our culture.

397a   Reprinted in (374).

397b   Trans. in (373).

398   ———. "Du sujet en linguistique." Langages 24
       (December 1971), 107-26.

       Examines critically traditional linguistic theory since
Saussure, in terms of its presuppositions about the
speaking subject. Borrows from mathematical terminology
to define the concept of "theory," then revises the ideas
of Saussure and Chomsky. Finds parallels between the
evolution of psychoanalysis and that of linguistic theory.

398a   Reprinted in (374).

399   ———. "Ellipse sur la frayeur et la séduction spécu-
       laire." Communications 23 (1975), 73-8.

       Elaborates on "seeing" and identity, on cultural myths
about the (visible and illusory) body and the preserva-
tion of social order. Suggests there is another
"phantasmic" way of seeing, somewhere between "the view

of a real object" and "hallucination," a mode that is
called upon when we watch a film. Says this other
"specular" mode, like other "semiotic" discourses, bears
traces of pre-socialized, pre-verbal corporal "pulsions."
Extremely difficult.

399a   Reprinted in (374).

400   ———. "L'engendrement de la formule." Sémeiótiké:
       Recherches pour une sémanalyse. Paris: Seuil, 1969,
       278-371.

An extremely long synthesis of Kristeva's assumptions
about and approaches to literary analysis. First,
defines the key terms ("text," "semanalysis") in her
study of textual engendering or production, of signifying
process rather than static objects. Also clarifies the
Kristevan concepts of "geno-text" and "pheno-text."
Elaborates on Kristeva's view of the position of the
"theorizing" or speaking subject—traditionally a
transcendent "authority," a stance Kristeva rejects—
through an analysis of Philippe Sollers's Nombres, a text
which is itself about the theory of discourse. The
examination of linguistic processes in Nombres, with its
references to Mallarmé, Artaud, and other "anti-normative"
writers, is extremely technical.

401   ———. "Les Epistémologies de la linguistique."
       Langages 24 (December 1971), 3-13.

Examines the question of what an epistemology of
linguistics can be by first tracing the history and
methods of various modern philosophies of science, then
assessing the current status of linguistics. Purports
that any epistemology of linguistics must, like that of
all human sciences, both embrace a "theory of the
(speaking) subject" and examine its own internal
workings, not just describe a static external "object" of
study. Technical.

402   ———. "L'éthique de la linguistique." Critique 322
       (March 1974), 206-16.

Reevaluates the ethics of modern linguistic discourse
and takes as premise that late 19th century general
transformations in society and discourse (Marx, Freud,
Nietzsche) of necessity made for breaks in prevailing

definitions of the "social contract" and therefore of the
ethical. But maintains that early 20th century linguistics held on to an outdated notion of its "object" of
study and thus remained out of sync with changing ethical
definitions.

402a   Reprinted in (374).

402b   Trans. in (373).

403   ————. "L'expansion de la sémiotique." Séméiótiké:
       Recherches pour une sémanalyse. Paris: Seuil, 1969,
       43-59.

       Describes the expanding purview of semiotic research
       and its accompanying critique of both classical
       philosophy and of its own precepts. Summarizes the
       limitations of previous linguistic approaches. Says
       semiotics is now oriented away from the norms of
       utilitarian communication and toward "magic" or "sacred"
       and poetic texts. Sees the tools of expanded semiotic
       inquiry as coming from the study of distant cultures,
       from mathematics, and from a newly incorporated Marxist
       perspective on language and social structures. Advocates
       an active role for the semiotician as writer or "maker,"
       and not just "describer."

404   ————. "L'expérience et la pratique." Bataille. Paris:
       UGE, 10/18, 1973, 267-301.

       Demonstrates the contemporary "dissolution" of
       bourgeois and Christian ideology and the simultaneous
       dissolution of language, as represented by the works of
       Georges Bataille. Says Bataille introduces "laughter"
       and eroticism as techniques of subversion.

404a   Reprinted in (374).

405   ————. "Femme/mère/pensée." Art Press International 5
       (March 1977), 6-8.

       Places the women's movement in the context of general
       20th century "crises" in which both the notion of a fixed
       human identity and rationality itself have been put into
       question. Describes the various attacks on Western
       monotheism that have occurred--including feminism--
       disruptions that mark the surfacing of forces "repressed"

by socialization. Says women's creation can be subversive if it calls upon the "maternal" or pre-verbal,
pre-linguistic forms of knowledge. Links the written or
spoken text with the body and advocates a feminist
literature that breaks with traditional reason to
communicate "symbolic experiences." Says women, by their
double attachment to both socialized language ("culture")
and pre-social biological forces ("nature"), are
particularly well-suited to finding a discourse that puts
conventional concepts of subjectivity into question.
Claims maternity is the explicit manifestation of this
dual tie to culture and nature. Ends with a critique of
the feminist call for "equality," saying equality is a
"myth" that denies sexual specificity. Good general
presentation of Kristevan ideas on women.

406   ———. "Femmes chinoises." La Quinzaine littéraire
No. 192 (August 1974), 19-20.

Compares Western and Chinese women in terms of their
social status. Sees the current situation in the two
cultures as almost opposite, in that what Western culture
has repressed—eroticism and the female body—has been
visible and operative in modern Chinese social progress.
Offers China as a model, though imperfect, of a culture
that is questioning its oppressive traditions and in
which sexual equality itself sparks social change.

406a   Reprinted as "Les Chinoises à 'contre-courant'" in
Tel Quel 59 (Fall 1974), 26-29 and in (374).

406b   Partially trans. as "Chinese Women Against the
Tide" in (19).

407   ———. "La fonction prédicative et le sujet parlant."
Langue, Discours, Société: Pour Emile Benveniste. Ed.
Julia Kristeva et al. Paris: Seuil, 1975, 229-59.

Describes the importance of the work of Emile
Benveniste, a forerunner of the current "revolution" in
the Western conception of language, by virtue of its
analyzing the "speaking subject" in the context of its
particular social institutions. Says Benveniste opened
other disciplines to the study of language.

407a   Reprinted in (374).

408 ———. "Four types of Signifying Practice." <u>Semiotexte</u>
     1 (Winter 1974), 65-74.

     Develops Kristeva's ideas on the process of signifi-
     cation through a discussion of the "speaking subject,"
     for Kristeva a divided subject operating at once in two
     levels of articulation: the conscious, socialized, or
     "symbolic" level ("pheno-text") and the pre-linguistic,
     pre-Oedipal, instinctual or "semiotic" level ("geno-
     text"). Posits the inextricable link for Kristeva
     between the subject's linguistic and psychic processes or
     "movements." Examines this double process (semiotic and
     symbolic) underlying all signification by tracing four
     types of "signifying practices" that are, to different
     degrees, "coded" by social laws and communicative
     exigencies: the practices of "narration," "metalanguage,"
     "contemplation (theory)," and "text." Evokes for each
     one the phonic, rhythmic, syntactic, and psychosexual
     configurations that characterize it at various points in
     the traversal between semiotic and symbolic. Technical
     but informative.

409 ———. "Le geste, pratique ou communication?"
     <u>Sémeiôtiké: Recherches pour une sémanalyse</u>. Paris:
     Seuil, 1969, 90-112.

     Reflects on the importance the language of gesture has
     had for "anti-normative" thinkers and on its complemen-
     tary relation to logocentric "communicative" discourse.
     Contrasts systems of thought that valorize verbal (vocal
     or sound) discourse with those that focus on non-phonetic
     codes. Calls for the expansion of semiotics to include
     study of gestural languages, a study it goes on to
     elaborate. Refers to American work in the area of
     kinesics.

410 ———. "Héréthique de l'amour." <u>Tel Quel</u> 74 (Winter
     1977), 30-49.

     Explores the centrality of maternity as a feminist
     issue, in its complex and paradoxical aspects. Distin-
     guishes "woman" from "mother," in an effort to illuminate
     the psychological dynamics in our culture that absorb
     femininity into maternity. Traces at length the story/
     myth of the Virgin Mary to point up the "heterogeneous"--
     and not just repressive and monolithic--importance of

this figure: views the Virgin Mother as source of both
humanity and non-humanity, agent of socialization and
a-socialization, triumph of the "symbolic" (the Paternal,
de-sexualized order) and repository of the "semiotic"
(non-verbal and sexualized). Establishes definitions of
love that both form and are formed by Mary's roles as
mother, daughter and bride of Christ. Also, examines why
so many women choose motherhood, a constraint in our
culture, even while many feminists reject it and its subversive potential. Ends with a call for a new ethic—a
"heretical" ethic or "héréthique"—based not on traditional morality, which is destructive for women, but, on
the contrary, on the feminine components of "body, language and 'jouissance.'" Is accompanied by a running
marginal text that is a first-person poetic transcription
of the theories developed in the essay. Rough going.

411   ———. "Idéologie du discours sur la littérature." La
         Nouvelle critique 70 (Colloque de Cluny, April 1970),
         122-7.

Posits that the discourse about literature that our
culture uses "is, by definition, ideological," in the
sense that it serves the needs of the dominant and
dominated social groups. Illustrates this point with
several examples, including Hegel's philosophical
"recuperation" of literature and formalism's subordination of literature to linguistics. Aligns the kind of
textual analysis it advocates—equally ideological—with
"revolutionary avant-garde" literature, in that both
"deconstruct" the fundamental presuppositions (about
rationality, about language) of our culture.

412   ———. "Il n'y a pas de maître à langage." Nouvelle
         revue de psychanalyse 20 (Fall 1979), 119-40.

An extremely difficult but sometimes lyrical exposition
of how linguistics and psychoanalysis together can
provide a comprehension of the "discourse of the
unconscious." Begins with allegorical representations of
various "speaking subjects" whose different "enunciations"
are expressed during the psychoanalytic process. To show
how a "listening" of the particular subject's language—
for Kristeva the "ethical" purpose of psychoanalysis
itself—is possible in a Freudian context, summarizes,
first, Lacan's contribution to the combining of linguistics with psychoanalysis. Explains Lacanian theory on
the interpenetration of linguistic and psychic structures,

and also his utilization of the concepts of "metaphor"
and "metonymy." Then, elaborates on the disruptive
phenomena--e.g., "psychosis," "women"--that necessitate a
reformulation of linguistic and psychoanalytic theory.
Says such elements introduce "heterogeneity" into
previously monolithic semiotic and analytic models,
models that posited a desired mastery of language and
thus foreclosed a whole range of linguistic "enunciations." Contends women's recent wish to give voice to
sexual difference has caused an "insurrection" in
language. But warns against the refusal by women to
participate in the "phallic" symbolic or logical order--
and their opting solely for the "phantasmic" "maternal"
domain of pulsionistic discourse--as a neo-essentialist
"reduction" of their full linguistic subjectivity.
Argues that the "feminine" must "think" and "write
itself" for both sexes, thus giving expression to a new
"melancholy," a "painful embrace with the dark continent
of the maternal." For the initiated only.

413   ———. "La joie de Giotto." Peinture Nos. 2-3 (January
       1972).

Attempts to cross the boundary between the observing/
reading subject of a painting and the painting itself, a
site of "meaning-plus, space-plus color." Wishes to undo
the traditional objectification of a painting, its
separation from the seeing subject, by recovering "the
thread of speech" that joins them and by articulating a
theory of the "practice of painting" (a dynamic process
of "translation" of "pulsions" on a colored surface).

413a   Reprinted in (374).

413b   Trans. in (373).

414   ———. "'Juivre ou mourir.'" Pouvoirs de l'horreur:
       Essai sur l'abjection. Paris: Seuil, 1980, 203-19.

Studies Céline's polemical pamphlets (anti-Semitic and
anti-communist) as extensions of the same literary
concerns that characterize his fiction. Points up the
internal contradictions in these "raving" tracts. Puts
at the center of Céline's fascistic attacks a "rage
against the Symbolic" and the attempt to "substitute
another Law" for it. Probes in detail the psycho-
familial dynamics of his anti-Semitism.

415 ———. "Lire la Bible." Esprit 69 (September 1982),
     143-52.

   Proposes reading the Bible as an elaboration of psychic
conflicts, a reading attentive to parallels between Old
Testament processes and acts and the pre-Oedipal psychic
dynamics of identity formation. Says such a focus on the
"subject" uncovers a similar rejection of the "mother/
object" in both Biblical codes and childhood psychic
dramas. Sees a common "fascination/repulsion" ambivalence
(toward the maternal) operative in the emergence of both
Biblical Law and subjective identity (the "Law of the
Father"). Also discusses the nature of divine love as
"unnamable" and "invisible," qualities comparable to
infantile "phantasmic" and forbidden desires. Puts the
reader/interpreter of the Bible in the same position as
the psychoanalyst/interpreter of the psychological
"text": both confront the "sacred," or polyvalent and
dislocating symbolizations. Suggestive.

416 ———. "Maternité selon Giovanni Bellini." Peinture
     Nos. 10-11 (December 1975).

   Compares the artist with woman in terms of reproduction.
Sees the maternal body as the site of the subjugated,
socialized "feminine" and yet also of the un-socialized,
"pulsionistic" and "psychotic" female subject—that is,
as a kind of juncture of the paternal symbolic drama of
male domination with the maternal/semiotic displacement
toward female power. Says the artist's symbolic practice
of painting, like childbirth, is his/her entry into
civilization and social order, and yet whose painting is
inscribed with the unconscious, with the "jouissance" of
its presocialized existence. Examines several of
Bellini's works. An opaque essay.

416a Reprinted in (374).

416b Trans. in (373).

417 ———. "Matière, sens, dialectique." Tel Quel 44
     (Winter 1971), 17-34.

   Reconsiders Hegel's dialectical materialism as a
"logic" or dynamic practice, rather than objectified

historical fact. Uses a linguistic and psychoanalytic framework, rather than a purely philosophical one.

417a   Reprinted in (374).

418   ———. "Le mot, le dialogue et le roman." Sémeiôtiké: Recherches pour une sémanalyse. Paris: Seuil, 1969, 143-73.

Supports the construction of a semiotic model of poetic production and effect that would "cross" the different textual "surfaces" of cultural context, the individual writer, and the addressed reader. Develops these different interactive "texts" whose configuration it calls "carnivalesque," in highly technical linguistic terms.

418a   Trans. in (373).

419   ———. "Noms de lieu." Tel Quel 68 (Winter 1976), 40-56.

Explores the ways Western culture, at moments of crisis in its rational/logical foundations, has turned to childhood as refuge from (discursive) death and as guaranty of (reproductive) life. Gives as examples Rousseau's and Freud's investigations of child-adult relationships. Distinguishes between "infantile" and "child's" language, the former defined as the potential language of the adult that is in the child, the latter simply as the language a child possesses. Presents, in psychoanalytic terms, the drama that is maternity (and the child itself) for a woman, her instauration as "object" in relation to the Father and the child. Also discusses "infantile space" and its relation to linguistic development. Extremely obscure piece.

419a   Reprinted in (374).

419b   Trans. in (373).

420   ———. "Objet, complément, dialectique." Critique 285 (February 1971), 99-131.

Assesses the "science of language." Outlines the important moments in the history of semiotics and, for each, its understanding of the conscious subject or self.

420a   Reprinted as "Objet ou complément" in (374).

421   ———. "Le Père, l'amour, l'exil." Samuel Beckett.
       Ed. Tom Bishop and Raymond Federman. Paris: Edition de
       l'Herne, 1976, 246-52.

Studies the power of two of Beckett's works (Premier
amour and Pas moi). Looks at their undoing of the
"sacred" (God, the Father) and the new form of love that
results from that undoing ("love-exile" and the liberation of the "feminine").

421a   Reprinted in (374).

421b   Trans. in (373).

422   ———. "Phonetics, Phonology and Impulsional Bases."
       Diacritics 4, No. 3 (Fall 1974), 33-7.

Elaborates on Kristeva's idea of the "semiotic process"
or the dynamics and qualities of the "pre-production" of
texts, through a discussion of Mallarmé's poems. Analyzes, specifically, the "rhythmic constraint" in such
poetry, or the "repetition and redistribution of the
phonic and semantic potentialities proper to the language
[that] produce new structures of signification." Describes the simultaneous processes that move between the
semiotic and the symbolic, or between the "articulating
body" (the "semiotic chora" or "drives," "pulsions") and
the text (semantic "condensations" or "displacements").
The "text" is the "threshold of language" or the "trans-
linguistic" space between the semiotic and the symbolic,
the space where "signification is pluralized at the same
time that it is dissolved." Says poetic language such as
Mallarmé's restores to language its repressed "passions"
by putting into question "the unity of the national-
maternal language." Difficult and highly specialized
vocabulary, but points toward later extensions of the
revolutionary potential of language.

423   ———. "Poésie et négativité." Séméiôtiké: Recherches
       pour une sémanalyse. Paris: Seuil, 1969, 246-77.

Treats one type of signifying practice, poetic
language, while focusing on the particular aspect of
"negativity"--that is, the presence in poetic writing of

unassimilated difference or opposition. Says such
oppositions are otherwise always absorbed into the
univocal logic of the dominant discourse. Compares
poetic and non-poetic "texts" or significations to
contrast the place of the "signifying subject" in each,
which place for poetic writing permits "negation."
Selects various poets (Baudelaire, Lautréamont, Mallarmé)
to illustrate the transgressions of rationalism in their
texts. Increasingly technical. Prepares the way for
later work on the avant-garde.

424 ———. "Polylogue." Tel Quel 57 (Spring 1974), 19-55.

Discusses the multiple disconcerting effects on
Kristeva of Philippe Sollers's book H, in the context of
the political upheavals of this century. Recounts, as a
sort of digression, Kristeva's own ongoing experience of
the "dissolution" of her self, of her "je," as emblematic
of the modern crisis of the "subject." This autobiogra-
phical passage is written in a fragmented and complicated
language that reflects Kristeva's "listen[ing] to the
black heterogeneous territory (of her) body/text."
Identifies as determinant for her "journey" or the
movement her self is experiencing "sexual difference":
claims that, as subject, women generally experience both
a loss of identity in "jouissance" (the feminine position)
along with a "crossing over" to the phallic position of
the construction of identity--a double experience of self
that avant-garde writers also undergo. Puts forth as the
only possible solution "to what we now call women's
problem" the "abolition" of the constantly resurging and
dominating phallic mode of discourse, through women's
disruptive activism against sexual, familial and discursive constraints. After this meditation, analyzes the
style of H as a musical "polylogue" and as a linguistic
disruption of the "family" or of masculine psychic/sexual
structures. Also examines other "polylogues" or literary
breaks in the history of signifying processes. An
essential, yet almost impenetrable essay on women.

424a Reprinted in (374).

424b Trans. as "Polylogue ('H')" in Contemporary Litera-
      ture 19 (1978), 336-50.

424c Also trans. in (373).

425 ———. "Pour une sémiologie des paragrammes."
Sémeiôtiké: Recherches pour une sémanalyse. Paris:
Seuil, 1969, 174-207.

Posits the shortcomings for literary analysis of
structuralism's a-historicity and its immobility before
advocating a "paragrammatic" or multi-leveled, multi-
gestural view of poetic discourse. Defines "text" as the
juncture of several codes or contexts. Explains in very
specialized terms the qualities of poetic language
arising from the complex levels of paragrammatic
structures.

426 ———. "Pouvoirs de l'horreur." Pouvoirs de l'horreur:
Essai sur l'abjection. Paris: Seuil, 1980, 243-48.

A concluding piece to the collection (375) that
summarizes the way "horror" functions in literature--
Kristeva says: "All literature is probably a version of
the apocalypse that seems to me rooted...on the fragile
border where identities do not exist." Sees Céline as
the ultimate example, after many others, of an author
fascinated by the power of abjection. Justifies her
study of the horror of being as part of the general questioning of repressive codes, especially Judeo-Christian
monotheism, codes upon which the "sleep" of individuals
and societies rests.

427 ———. "Pratique signifiante et mode de production."
Tel Quel 60 (Winter 1974), 21-33.

Investigates the "signifying practice" or the dynamic
process that is at once the "constitution and the crossing
over ('traversée')" of systems of representation. Posits
as the site of this process the "speaking subject" or the
self that moves toward unity and a stable identity even
while it constantly unravels or breaks with that unity.
Also states that this practice of the production of signs
belongs to a particular socio-economic system of
production and correlates with other practices of that
system, e.g., family relations and religion. Says there
is a "complicity" among capitalism, Christianity, and the
patriarchal family to reinforce one another and to retain
dominance. Claims the relations within all these systems
of Western culture give preference to unity, homogeneity,
and coherence, at the expense of "madness," "poetry,"
heterogeneity, desire and the feminine. In this light,

and using Hegelian theory, sees art as evidence of
subversion, of the rising up of repressed desires and
pulsions, though art has also, paradoxically, been a
necessary "safety valve" for the dominant system.
Expands on the relation between Christian monotheism and
the repression of sexuality, the feminine, and sexual
difference. Locates the beginning of a rupture of the
Western order in the late 19th century, particularly
visible in the "revolution" of poetic language, but also
in political and social movements. Reiterates the
essential Kristevan concepts of the "symbolic" and the
"semiotic"--or the logical, pre-given, static function of
language versus the pre-verbal, pulsionistic processes of
production in the unconscious--since these linguistic
functions of stasis and contestation are inherent to all
other social systems (the state, the family, religion) as
well and provide, says Kristeva, strategies for change.
Describes how the structures of language produce and
reflect the ideology of sexual dominance, in that the
linguistic/poetic subject or self is the site of sexual
differentiation (between the "phallic" or symbolic
function and the "feminine/maternal" or semiotic process).
Explains in detail the production of "meaning," the
process of naming and identifying that characterizes and
is "sacred" to Western thinking but that is not
necessarily shared by other civilizations. An essential
but difficult essay.

427a   Reprinted in (381).

428 ———. "La productivité dite texte." Sémeiótiké:
     Recherches pour une sémanalyse. Paris: Seuil, 1969,
     208-45.

     Reveals our culture's blindness about writing as a
process or production and its attachment to consumable
"objects" or written works instead. Sees as one result
of this our predilection for representation or "verisimilitude" in literature, a preference supported by
established literary criticism. Contends this penchant
for "realism" reaffirms a certain ideology. Argues for a
demystification of the ideal of verisimilitude. Proceeds
with a description of semantic and syntactic verisimilitude or "meaning" as a mirror reflection and a discussion
of Raymond Roussel's works as ones that disrupt realism
and discursive projection.

429 ———. "Psychoanalysis and the Polis." Critical
Inquiry 9, No. 1 (September 1982), 77-92.

A paper prepared for a collection of essays on the
politics of interpretation. Critiques the general
American intellectual response to radical "moments of
thought"--in this case, psychoanalysis--as one of
resistance, rejection, or neutralization. Examines the
reasons why psychoanalysis's "decentering of the speaking
subject" threatens the foundations of Western knowledge:
it puts into question the illusion of neutral, a-political
interpretation; and it cannot arrive at one absolute
meaning--the strongest desire in our culture--but instead
continually "dissolves meaning." Also shows how the
quest for certainty and meaning can have enormous
political implications by looking at fascism and
Stalinism. Proceeds by summarizing, first, the psychic
dynamics of the hermeneutic enterprise, comparing the
processes of analytic and psychoanalytic interpretation.
Then, looks at several forms of interpretation, including
political thought and the literary text (using the works
of Céline as example of "political delirium in avant-garde
writing"). Concludes that the necessary search ought not
be for an interpretive system of truths, but for the
lucid recognition of a culture in crisis.

430 ———. "Quelques problèmes de sémiotique littéraire à
propos d'un texte de Mallarmé: Un coup de dés." Essais
de sémiotique poétique. Ed. A. J. Greimas et al.
Paris: Larousse, 1972, 208-34.

Discusses and analyzes Mallarmé's text, Un coup de dés,
in the framework of Kristeva's redefinition of semiotic
methods and of the literary text. First, criticizes
traditional linguistic approaches for not acknowledging
their own "ideological" implications (their unquestioned
belief in the existence of a fixed or idealized "object"
of study and a studying "subject"). Takes instead as its
purpose the self-conscious analysis of its own presuppositions and methods, through the study of a "text." Then,
specifies and elaborates on its use of the terms:
"semanalysis" (Kristeva's method, which examines the
production of meaning as a process, an "engendering," and
not as a static description); "text" (a "production"--
literary, historical or political--that breaks with
classical discursive systems); "genotext" and "phenotext"
(two "states" of and within the generation of meaning and

of the text); and other highly specialized vocabulary.
Refers to, as its model for the "decentering" or
"disrupting" of the traditional communicative system
studied in linguistics, Freud's study of dreams: the
"site" of the production and transformation of "meaning"
("signifiance") in dreams is similar to the "scene" upon
and in which certain texts operate "displacements" and
"transgressions " of meaning. Sees also a similar
destabilization of the "subject" in both dreams and
literary texts. Finally, reads Mallarmé's poem--an
example of such avant-garde transgressive texts--as a
"theater" whose mode and operation Kristeva theorizes and
characterizes in complex detail. Presupposes a specialized knowledge of linguistic and semiotic concepts and
history. Not directly concerned with women, but gives an
idea of Kristeva's earlier elaboration on writing that
has social as well as literary implications.

431   ———. "...Qui tollis peccata mundi." Pouvoirs de
       l'horreur: Essai sur l'abjection. Paris: Seuil, 1980,
       133-54.

Analyzes the New Testament and the message of Christ as
a "wholly different system of meaning" from that of the
Old Testament. Bases that difference on the concept of a
"wholly different (Christian) speaking subject" for whom
"abjection is no longer exterior (as in the Old Testament)
[but] is permanent and comes from within"--resulting in a
"speaking being who is innerly divided." Discusses also
the different relationship to the mother in the Christic
story, as well as the latter's development of the notion
of "sin" and woman's role in it.

432   ———. "Remarques sur le 'mode de production
       asiatique.'" La Traversée des signes. Ed. Julia
       Kristeva et al. Paris: Seuil, 1975, 11-30.

In line with Kristeva's stated goal of a "pluralistic"
exploration of non-Western systems of production--
artistic and socio-economic--examines the general
outlines of "Asiatic" sexual, class and cultural
structures. Uses Marx's study of "Asiatic" communities
as starting point for a discussion that focuses,
principally, on Chinese economic and family configurations. Claims Chinese women, "excluded from relationships of production and therefore from political power,
represent...reproduction and the elements of negativity
and pleasure that function within it." Finally, describes

some of the semiotic particularities of the Chinese language.

433 ———. "Sémiotique de l'abomination biblique." Pouvoirs de l'horreur: Essai sur l'abjection. Paris: Seuil, 1980, 107-31.

Investigates the role of "impurity" in biblical thought through both an historical (the history of religions) and a psychoanalytic (the structuration of the subject's identity) approach. Situates the issue of impurity in the general context of the subordination of maternal power to symbolic order (the "Law"). Cites references to defilement, taboos, and abominations from the Old Testament.

434 ———. "La sémiotique, science critique et/ou critique de la science." Séméiótiké: Recherches pour une sémanalyse. Paris: Seuil, 1969, 27-42.

Places semiotics in relation to primary linguistic models of signifying practices, in order to identify the epistemological and ideological particularities of the semiotic science. Specifies the object and methods of semiotic study, which it views as potentially subversive of scientific thought. Connects semiotics to Marxist economic and materialist concepts. Defines literature, in semiotic terms, as not an entity in itself, but a particular linguistic practice or production.

435 ———. "Le sens et la mode." Séméiótiké: Recherches pour une sémanalyse. Paris: Seuil, 1969, 60-89.

Takes stock of the status of traditional linguistics (the study of "signs") as having reached its apogee and the point of a necessary "demystification" of itself. Presents Roland Barthes's "Système de la mode" as an example of perturbation of the ensconced "subject-sign," univocal signifying model. Traces back to the linguistic presuppositions Barthes subverts, including "representation," "communication," and "rationalism." Favors analysis of "texts" or textual surfaces over words in a chain of "meaning."

436 ———. "Sujet dans le langage et pratique politique." Tel Quel 58 (Summer 1974), 22-7.

Discusses the inextricable link between politics and
literature, between political revolution and linguistic
disruption. Reiterates the critical Kristevan concepts
of the symbolic/semiotic and linguistic "practice," in
order to re-articulate the ways language adheres to
political systems and social change.

436a   Reprinted as "Politique et littérature" in (374).

437   ———. "Le sujet en procès." Tel Quel 52 (Winter
       1972), 12-30.

Inquires into the "subject" ("self") as a generator of
theory, using Artaud as a case of a thinker whose
"strange" ideas, too threatening to our culture, were
naturalized as "art." Takes as its bases the following:
the Lacanian psychoanalytic concept of a "divided"
subject, which for Kristeva functions in the domains of
the semiotic and the symbolic; redefined Marxist "materialism" in which dynamic process (versus reification) of
the subject is reinstated; an extended notion of Hegelian
"negativity," for Kristeva the "logic" of the process by
which the signifying subject functions; psychic "pulsions"
and corresponding notions of "rejection" ("rejet") and
"pleasure" ("jouissance") as visible in works such as
Artaud's.

437a   Reprinted in Artaud. Paris: UGE, 10/18, 1973,
       197-207, and in (374).

438   ———. "The System and the Speaking Subject." Times
       Literary Supplement (October 12, 1973), 1249-52.

Discusses the single generalizable "discovery" of
semiotics, which is that all sign systems (ideologies,
social codes, literatures and arts) function like
languages—that is, they manifest the same presuppositions about meaning and the "signifying subject" as any
other social practice. Says semiotics's use of the
linguistic model automatically embeds all its research in
"sociality" or aspects that reinforce the "social
contract" of communication and utility. Claims that
model limits the purview of semiotics, as the latter
cannot tackle non-utilitarian, "transgressive" expressive
practices. Says semiotics, to open its possibilities,
must clarify and critique its own assumptions, in
particular its theory of the speaking subject as a

unified "transcendental ego." Advocates instead exploration of the speaking subject as "divided subject," since
such an inquiry would be able to address other a-social,
poetic languages. Explains how, paradoxically, semiotics
could never encompass such transgressions—it being a
homogeneous "metalanguage" itself—but could show what
"lies outside" its own scope. Calls this act of semiotic
analysis a "moral gesture" with broad social implications.

438a   Reprinted in The Tell-Tale Sign: A Survey of
        Semiotics. Ed. Thomas A. Sebeok. Lisse,
        Netherlands: Peter de Ridder Press, 1975, 47-55.

439   ———. "Le Temps des femmes." 34/44: Cahiers de
        recherche de sciences des textes et documents No. 5
        (Winter 1979), 5-19.

In what Alice Jardine calls "Kristeva's most extensive
and direct analysis of feminism as an intellectual
movement in the 1970's," interrogates our ways of
thinking about history and historical time. Says
traditional historicisation is based on the "paternal
function" or the systems of inherited thought that have
been destructive for women and, yet, of which women are
also a part. Situates the break from the "chimeras" of
"historical tradition," "linguistic unity," and geographical nationalism in the 1920's-1930's economic crash and
rise of national socialism, at which point new suprana-
tional "human groupings" or "socio-cultural ensembles"
based on "symbolic denominations" emerged. The problematic of women situates itself within this time change
toward a trans-European and worldwide scope, in three
"attitudes" or movements: (1) the early women's movement,
which "aspired to gain a place in linear time"; (2) the
post-1968 refusal of linear temporality and of conventional modes of political change, in a search for "the
specificity of female psychology" or for sexual difference; and (3) the mixture of 1 and 2, that is, the
combination of "insertion into history" and "refusal of
the subjective limitations imposed by this history's
time." Asks what women can do if they do not wish to be
excluded from language and symbolic systems and yet do
not wish to perpetuate current systems. Elaborates
several responses and approaches, including women's
subversion of the symbolic order, the making of a female
"countersociety," the refusal of motherhood, and literary
creation. The essay asks more questions than it answers

and offers few strategic suggestions, except Kristeva's
own cryptic preference for an "interrogation of the
founding separation of the socio-symbolic contract," or a
"bringing out of the singularity of each person." An
obscure text. (See 460)

439a   Trans. as "Women's Time" in Signs 7, No. 1 (Autumn
       1981), 13-35.

440   ————. "Le texte clos." Sémeiótiké: Recherches pour
      une sémanalyse. Paris: Seuil, 1969, 113-42.

Demonstrates convincingly how the structures of language
produce and impose the ideologies of dominance of our
culture. Begins by defining "text" as the material
"slice" of signification to which ideology adheres and
"intertextuality" as the convergence of linguistic,
social and historical factors in a text. Traces
historically the significance of "symbolization" and the
related signifying practice that is the novel, specifically, Antoine de la Sale's Jehan de Saintré. While
elaborating on the evolving characteristics of the novel,
evokes the period in which courtly love was prominent.
Illuminates the importance of the seeming valorization of
woman as in fact an affirmation of the (superior) male
term ("sameness") that absorbed woman, the "other" term.
Says courtly love's pseudo centering of woman--in effect
a negation of the feminine--erased sexual difference and
mirrored women's exclusion from economic and social participation. Sees the same structures of hierarchy and
domination in literature and society. This brief discussion within the longer essay is critical to Kristevan
thought on language and sexism.

440a   Trans. in (373).

441   ————. "Le texte et sa science." Sémeiótiké:
      Recherches pour une sémanalyse. Paris: Seuil, 1969,
      7-26.

Puts forth Kristeva's purpose in this whole collection
of essays: to study language as it operates in literature, literature being for Kristeva an instance of
language engaged in a transformative act. Explains the
ideological "recuperation" of texts by traditional
literary criticism, a distortion that a semiotic analysis
of a text's signifying practices can reduce. Questions

standard concepts of "meaning," "subject," "history," and
"text." Takes as its enterprise the construction of a
"discourse" that would illuminate textual functioning--a
discourse arising from semiotics that would also be
critical of its own methods.

442 ———. "Le théâtre moderne n'a pas lieu." 34/44
     (Winter 1977-78), 13-16.

States that modern theater does not exist--does not
"take (a) place" outside of the text. Bases that
contention on the absence in the modern era of a communal
"sacred locus" or "place" of theater, the consequence of
which is the relegation of all previous theatrical
"sacredness" to the realm of language. Claims this is
the result of "a new subject and a new society" that
render archaic the old ideological constructs of
theatrical "verisimilitude." Says the only options left
for performed theater are either non-verbal forms (sound,
gesture) or ironical and stereotyped "verisimilitude"
(e.g., Beckett, Ionesco). Also claims theater is now
inseparable from cinema, since both reconstruct the
modern "subjective space" that includes the visual, the
acoustic and the gestural.

442a Trans. as "Modern Theater Does Not Take (A) Place."
      Sub-Stance 18/19 (1977), 131-4.

443 ———. "Un nouveau type d'intellectuel: le dissident."
     Tel Quel 74 (Winter 1977), 3-8.

Calls for a reevaluation and reforging of the relation
between the individual and the collectivity, between the
intellectual and the "masses," in light of the current
reduction of the role of the intellectual in Western
societies. Says this new relation, necessary for the
future of Western culture, will dismantle the "fascistic"
homogenization of discourse and will recombine "singular"
voices, desires, and "unconsciouses" with communal
expression and political values. Views the modern
"explosion" of all rational systems--the Family, the
State, the Party--of which intellectual dissidents have
been the agents, as portents of these new individual/
social arrangements. Distinguishes as types of dissidents
political rebels, psychoanalysts, avant-garde writers,
and women--this last group, women, being by definition
"exiled" in relation to the dominant political and

symbolic powers. Says woman is eternal "singularity"
(exiled from the monolithic and univocal Law in place).
Designates reproduction as the most problematic issue for
women, in that it maintains the stability of the dominant
culture, yet also introduces into culture powerful
a-social passions, contradictions, and psychological/
biological forces. Makes the central Kristevan claim
that "truly feminist innovation" will not be possible
until "maternity, feminine creation, and the relation
between the two" are illuminated. Ends with Kristeva's
presentation of herself as "exiled," as a dissident who
must work to dismantle all institutions (conceptual,
linguistic, sexual) through "permanent analysis"--disso-
lution, multiplication--of them. An interesting and
controversial piece.

444   ———. "Le vréel." Folle vérité: Vérité et vraisem-
       blance du texte psychotique. Ed. Julia Kristeva and
       Jean-Michel Ribette. Paris: Seuil, 1979, 11-35.

       Describes the shift in the designation of "truth"--from
the classical to the modern eras--as from Cartesian
truth-as-logical "being" (a belief that exiled madness
from the expressible) to 20th century truth-as-"real"
(the Lacanian term that embraces madness, poetry, and
mysticism). Calls this enlarged domain of desired
expressibility the "vréel," which it says "exceeds"
socialized discourse and still cannot be signified by
it. Claims, as in previous Kristevan studies, that this
"vréel" is the realm of the "archaic," pre-Oedipal
mother, the place where she surfaces into and disrupts
paternal discourse. Uses this notion of the "vréel" to
consider psychotic "texts" and what they tell about the
limits of discourse and the speaking subject. Goes on to
elucidate in detail (1) the historical evolution of the
conception of truth; (2) the Freudian idea of truth; (3)
the situation of the hysteric; (4) linguistic parallels
to psychoanalytic conceptions of truth; and (5) examples
of texts that evince a crisis of truth. Includes a
discussion among seminar members. Technical.

INTERVIEWS WITH

445   Boucquey, Eliane. "Unes femmes." Les Cahiers du Grif 7
       (1975), 22-7.

       An illuminating discussion in which Kristeva's ideas on
female identity, both social and linguistic, and on

feminine "creation" are articulated. Begins with
Kristeva's distinguishing between the female identity
that can and should operate to transform socio-economic
structures (the domain of the "conscious") and the one
that functions as a "symbolic effect" in regard to
structures of power and language. Further refines this
second "symbolic" aspect--the one Kristeva is principally
interested in--into two phenomena: (1) the "woman's
effect," that of woman as a "mute support" for all the
systems in place. From this marginal position, woman can
choose either to contest the dominant powers or to
identify with and seek to obtain the very same position
of power. Kristeva advocates the first choice, women's
permanent critique of prevailing structures. Delineates
two dangers arising from women's subordinate position,
their simply reproducing "phallic" powers or their
regressing into a "pre-Oedipal," "phantasmic" refusal of
logic, intellectuality, and reality. Kristeva supports a
mediating solution: that women "make what is repressed
(in our culture) speak by means of 'aesthetic' or
'intellectual' sublimations"; and, connected to this
first phenomenon, (2) the "maternal function," that
element in psychoanalytic theory that concerns the
pre-Oedipal relation of the subject (the "self," the
"agent") to the mother. Elsewhere calls this domain the
"semiotic" (characterized by the desires and rhythms of
the unconscious), in contrast with the "symbolic" (the
conscious domain of logic and aesthetic realization).
Kristeva favors a reevaluation of the maternal function
that would emphasize its role as source of expressive
innovation (in literature, art, politics), that would
have it articulate itself in a conscious "symbolic"
realization--resulting in new discourses. Views women's
and men's differing experiences of psychic socialization
(their opposing experiences of the Oedipal drama) as the
root of their differing relations to the maternal
function and to its aesthetic expression--which is more
problematic for women. Finally, cautions against
"sexualizing" and generalizing cultural productions as
"masculine" or "feminine." Advises instead that women be
given the "economic and libidinal" means to express
themselves as individuals, in order that a multiplicity
of specific, "singular" discursive responses emerge.

446 "De la généralité sémiotique." Etudes littéraires 10,
     No. 3 (December 1977), 337-46.

     Discusses the debate in semiotic theory over a herme-

neutics of "generalizability" versus one of "particularity." Expresses Kristeva's belief that semiotics should
use a polyvalent, multiple approach addressing the
various specific situations of the "speaking subject."
Also talks about different semiotic methods of textual
reading and the "position" of the researching subject.
Raises the question of the psychoanalytic dynamics of
textual interpretation.

447 Delaunay, Jacqueline. "L'Autre du sexe." Sorcières 10
     (1978), 37-40.

    Discusses briefly the relationship of sexuality to
artistic expression from a psychoanalytic and semiotic
point of view. After stating that both male and female
artists, when they paint or write, undergo a "de-centering" or "distancing" from their identity (as artist) and
from their sexuality ("the relationship of an aesthetic
work to sex"), Kristeva admits there are some differences
between women and men: for women, this sexual "confrontation" when producing a work of art is more "violent."
Kristeva explains, in psychoanalytic terms, the relationship between women's identity and the creation of new
languages; the relationship between women's appropriating
language and their producing plastic arts; and finally,
the relationship between maternity and artistic
production.

448 Enthoven, Jean-Paul. "Julia Kristeva: A quoi servent les
     intellectuels?" Le Nouvel observateur (June 20, 1977),
     98-134.

    Inquires, first, into Kristeva's choice to be part of a
highly "elite" intellectual elite, to which she responds
by both defending the intellectual's vital function ("he/
she affirms and propagates difference" or alternative
"discourses," which is socially perceived as dissidence)
and questioning the necessity of the intellectual's
political "engagement" (a notion, Kristeva says, based on
an outdated conception of the "individual-and-society"
relationship). Locates Kristeva's view of the relation
of the individual to community in her own experience as a
Bulgarian-trained intellectual who emigrated to Paris and
joined the avant-garde intelligentsia of the 1960's.
Discusses her political and intellectual trajectory
regarding questions of "subjectivity" and language.
Defines Kristeva's relation to feminism as that of an
intellectual: conditional and critical when necessary

(e.g., about certain feminist rejections of individual
experience or of motherhood). Examines Kristeva's work
on particular authors (Céline, Mallarmé, Beckett) whose
texts offer rich insights into questions about language,
ideology, rationality, and identity. Elaborates on the
importance of semiotics for understanding discursive
manifestations of the modern "crisis of the individual"
and of "rationality." Refines the meaning of
"dissidence" for Eastern and Western countries, the
latter bearing such manifestations of disruption as
psychoanalysis, sexual contestation, and avant-garde
art. Ends with an evaluation of the intellectual's
relation to politics in France, one that Kristeva says
must refuse comfort and the status quo and remain
questioning and critical.

449   "La Femme, ce n'est jamais ça." Tel Quel 59 (Autumn
      1974), 19-25.

A discussion with women of the "psychanalyse et
politique" feminist group that raises crucial questions
about the nature and purpose of Kristeva's work and its
relation to feminism. After explaining her work on the
literary avant-garde as an effort to understand disruption
of linguistic communication and as a means of breaking
and reconstructing social constraints, Kristeva designates
women as "that which is not" in our culture. She
advocates works and acts by women that are "negative" (a
contestation of what "is"). Sees her own work as
exploring texts that "dissolve" traditional sexual
identities and as recovering the heretofore censored
"feminine." Discusses Kristeva's experiences in China,
for her the scene of great sexual and political emancipation, including her realization of the profound
differences between the problems Chinese and Western
women face. Finally, distinguishes "rationalized" or
coopted feminism (e.g., the creation of the French
Secretariat for Women's Condition) from true social
transformations based on fundamental changes in language
and the "speaking subject." Cautions against a feminism
that merely extends and identifies with the concept of
power in place. Sees the "solution" to women's problem
as "infinite," as the unknown multiple result of the
freeing of all that is repressed in our culture. This
freeing will automatically involve all oppressed classes
and races, whose struggle, Kristeva claims, is the same.

449a   Reprinted in (374).

449b   Trans. as "Woman can Never be Defined" in (19).

450   Féral, Josette.   "China, Women and the Symbolic: An
       Interview with Julia Kristeva."   Sub-Stance 13 (1976),
       9-18.

       Raises general questions, mostly historical, about
       women in China. Kristeva, who sees in ancient China "a
       highly developed matrilinear and matrilocal society"
       against which Confucian doctrine exerted a patriarchal
       counter-influence, traces the modern Chinese struggle for
       sexual equality, including Mao's efforts to liberate
       women and the Communist Party's current subordination of
       purely feminist demands. Argues for a necessary cultural
       relativity in which the situation of Chinese women, "who
       come from Confucianism and feudalism," is not viewed in
       the same terms as that of Western women, "products of
       capitalism and monotheism." Also raises the question of
       the effect of the specifically Chinese family structure
       on Chinese symbolic forms, to which Kristeva replies that
       "there is something maternal" in those forms, though
       Chinese discourse is generally "not capable of speaking
       about sexual problems." Finally, discusses women's
       artistic creation in the context of Kristeva's "semiotic"
       and "symbolic" stages: women's identification with the
       mother in the pre-Oedipal or semiotic stage, different
       from men's, propels them away from "socialist realism"
       art and toward the limits of expression. Kristeva
       advocates women's embracing all avant-garde breaks with
       traditional expressive discourses as a way to advance
       their cause. Translation is very uneven.

451   Forrester, Viviane.   "Quand Julia Kristeva invite à
       'traverser les signes.'"   La Quinzaine littéraire
       (January 1-15, 1976), 21-2.

       Discusses la Traversée des signes, the collected papers
       from a seminar which Kristeva conducted in 1973-74, and
       the linguistic issues that seminar explored: the ways an
       analysis of Third-World discourses (e.g., Chinese, Indian,
       Moslem, Judaic) can illuminate and free Western "re-
       pressed," monotheistic and capitalistic ones; the need
       for a psychoanalytic "listening" of all languages that
       will "hear" the power of their processes of production;

and the general "crisis of rationalism" taking place in
Western culture, which, Kristeva says, is in part a
problem of discourse: the constraining concepts of a
singular, absolute subject (ego) and of univocal meaning
are crumbling, like those of any "totalitarian" system.
Brief but dense.

452   Gauthier, Xavière.   "Oscillation du 'pouvoir' au 'refus.'"
      Tel Quel 58 (Summer 1974), 99-100.

Expresses briefly Kristeva's thoughts on two inextricable questions: what, for Kristeva, is the "writing
subject" and what, if anything, is a "feminine writing."
Answers, to the first, that a writing subject or a writer
of literature makes "modifications in the linguistic
fabric" by disrupting the "phallic" master's discourse
that rules our culture. Says this subject, in introducing presocialized or transgressive "pulsions"
("jouissance") into the meaningful dominant language,
"traverses" a "process of sexual differentiation." Calls
this a "bisexuality" which allows for the renewal and
multiplication of the resources of meaning. Characterizes women's perspective on the dominant language as a
view "from a foreign country," making them "strangers to
the language" who "suffer" when they speak. Says women
who write experience sexual differentiation or the
passage between the pulsionistic and the phallic. But
they must, according to Kristeva, maintain a "negative
function" in their writing, i.e., "reject all that is
finite, definite, structured, meaning-ful" in prevailing
linguistic codes, and not just cross over to reproducing
and identifying with the powers in place. Claims that,
in all experiences, social and symbolic, being a woman in
this culture automatically makes one "a subject in
process."

      452a   Trans. as "Oscillation Between Power and Denial"
             in (19).

453   Glucksman, Christine and Jean Peytard.   "Littérature,
      sémiotique, marxisme." La Nouvelle critique No. 38
      (November 1970), 28-35.

Reveals Kristeva's theory of culture--her study of all
systems of representation--as one incorporating Marxist
dialectical materialism, that is, a theory analyzing the
links between ideology and "sign systems." Elucidates
"semanalysis," Kristeva's method of analyzing a cultural

"text" (literature, art, film) that also examines the
"place" of the text's "speaking subject." Says this
method utilizes linguistics, psychoanalysis and
historical materialism, while constantly engaging in
dialectical criticism of these sciences. Traces definitions of "literature" and connection to the values of
particular social and economic systems, with the late
19th century representing a break in Western idealist and
positivist beliefs. Describes Kristeva's idea of "limit
texts," ones that contest and renew "our relation to
language, sex and meaning." Delves into highly technical
areas of linguistic and semiotic theory.

* Peytard, Jean and Christine Glucksman. "Littérature,
   sémiotique, marxisme." La Nouvelle critique No. 38
   (November 1970), 28-35.

   (See 453).

454 Rossum-Guyon, Françoise van. "Questions à Julia Kristeva
   à partir de Polylogue." Revue des sciences humaines
   No. 168 (October-December 1977), 495-501.

   An exchange of correspondence that raises general
   questions about Kristeva's work and her own coming to an
   exploration of women, femininity, and feminism. Asks,
   first, if the question of a specific women's writing is
   relevant to her call for a subversion of all codes, to
   which Kristeva responds, "Writing is ignorant of sex."
   Kristeva is more interested in a radical challenge to the
   notions of "meaning" and the signifying "subject" and is
   suspicious of assigning a diluted sexual identity to this
   challenge. But she does acknowledge the existence of
   certain thematic and stylistic particularities in women's
   texts, including, respectively, love, sensation, dissat-
   isfaction, and deneutralization, ellipsis. Then, asks
   how Kristeva's personal awareness of women's issues
   informs her work, to which Kristeva gives a double
   response: first, her support of individual, versus
   collective approaches for women, in the sense of each
   woman's coming to her own truth about her "femininity";
   and, second, her preoccupation in her theory with the
   "ethical" or with a critique of all theoretical models
   that invalidate other and different human experiences,
   such as women's. Kristeva is interested in the "feminine
   problematic" to the extent that it coincides with and is
   emblematic of "the (larger) fundamental challenge to the
   concepts of identities and laws that we are now

experiencing." She criticizes the rejection by some
women of masculine logic and analysis as a form of
"totalitarianism." A good overview of Kristeva's concept
of and position in regard to feminism.

ESSAYS AND ARTICLES ABOUT

455 Andermatt, Verena. "Julia Kristeva and the Traversal of
     Modern Poetic Space." Enclitic 1, No. 2 (Fall 1977),
     65-77.

     Evaluates Kristeva's whole critical enterprise while
     focusing specifically on her treatment of the "plastic
     space"--the text or the canvas--in literature, art and
     film. Criticizes Kristeva's "inattention" to this spatial
     surface on the grounds it "reveals an inappropriately
     theological stance and academic seizure of critical
     authority" ("theological" here refers to Kristeva's
     assuming the ability to determine limits). Considers the
     visible dimension as it is "denegated," in favor of an
     insistence on abstract "traversal," in several of
     Kristeva's studies. Says that, rather than an area of
     "praxis," Kristeva wishes space to be a poetic "pulsive
     field of absence"--a constrictive view her own theory
     frequently contradicts. Sees progress toward recognition
     of the presence of poetic space in Kristeva's post-1974
     work. The prose of this article is nearly impenetrable.

456 Beaujour, Michel. "A Propos de l'écart dans La Révolution
     du langage poétique de Julia Kristeva." The Romanic
     Review 66 (1975), 214-33.

     While not directly concerned with the issue of women,
     summarizes and responds to some of Kristeva's basic
     theories--as presented in La Révolution du language
     poétique (376)--from which her ideas about "the feminine"
     subsequently arise. Limits its discussion and critique
     to Kristeva's ideas on the "text" and on poetic language,
     situating her analysis in a long tradition of theories of
     the poetic and the avant-garde and claiming it is not the
     "revolutionary" study it takes itself to be. Locates the
     source of this paradoxical "conservatism" in Kristeva's
     own use of established "thetic" or logical discourse to
     present her "poetic" or avant-garde ideas--that is, in
     the contradiction between her stylistic and intellectual
     strategies. Also claims Kristeva's central thesis is
     quite simple and hardly new: that poetic language (and
     the "text" in which it operates) broke, in the late 19th

century, from normative and referential discourse. Says
Kristeva articulates the "economic, political and sexual"
imperatives behind that rupture in her chosen terms of
analysis: the "semiotic," the "symbolic," and "negativity." The "poetic," closely allied with the "semiotic,"
is the disruptive "emergence of pulsions, of the
corporeal" that destroys "syntax and signification,"
mechanisms of the symbolic. Says it is only implied by
Kristeva that the reader must pierce the "veil" or the
superficial appearance (meaning) of a text to get to the
"truth" or the "real," which is a material "thickness"
("épaisseur") that "acts" upon the (reading) subject"--
again, claims Beaujour, an old idea. Also judges
Kristeva's theories in relation to Jakobsonian linguis-
tics--saying she breaks with the idea of the communicative function of language--and to reader theory--
criticizing her for not addressing the status of the
reader. Finally, criticizes Kristeva's general manner of
assertion in her book, in that each statement, too dense
and "fleeting," entails too much reference that cannot
immediately be verified or pursued. Concludes,
nonetheless, with strong praise for the excitement and
provocativeness generated by Kristeva's study. An
illuminating and useful partial entry into a massive and
difficult work.

457 Caws, Mary Ann. "Tel Quel: Text and Revolution."
      Diacritics 3, No. 1 (Spring 1973), 2-8.

An early presentation of the work of the journal Tel
Quel that discusses three of its members' publications--
Julia Kristeva's Sémiótiké (377), Marcelin Pleynet's
L'Enseignement de la peinture, and Philippe Sollers's
Logiques--in the context of that collective's work.
Describes Tel Quel's central focus on "the practice of
the text, on the methods of its production, and on the
multiplicity of its possible meanings" in the "transgressive" works of "revolutionary" authors such as Sade,
Lautréamont, Mallarmé, Artaud and Bataille. Claims such
subversive texts point up how writing and political
revolution are necessarily "homologous acts" against the
"suppressive/repressive habits and methods of bourgeois
society, expressed in its grammatical, literary, and
social laws." Says Tel Quel's cooperative or "interdis-
cursive" approach, producing a body of texts which act on
one another, is a counter to proprietary authorship and
"individualistic intellectualism." Locates the journal's
roots in Derridean, Maoist and post-Freudian thought

about writing as a material, transgressive and sexual
act. Describes Kristeva's early study, Sémiótiké, as a
study of "the ways in which the text produces itself,"
using her method of "semanalysis," or "the analysis of
signs to reveal their emptiness." Useful for understanding the history of Kristeva's intellectual enterprise and
of the important Tel Quel "movement" of the early 1970's.

458 Conley, Verena. "Kristeva's China." Diacritics (Winter
     1975), 25-30.

     Reviews Kristeva's Des Chinoises (372), which it
regards essentially as a "differently committed criticism"
that in effect seeks to "deconstruct" the "Anglo-Saxon,
generally male critical stance" by being "inconclusive."
Sees Kristeva's purpose in Des Chinoises as searching for
"the other"--a culture of heterogeneity and of "cohesion
of both sexes" which Western culture lacks. Takes as its
own central frame of analysis Kristeva's "poetization of
the body and space," that is, Kristeva's presentation of
women as an "interlac[ing] of affirmation and negation,"
of "presence and absence" in space and time. Sees as the
new contribution of this book its "deconstruction" of
Western "axioms of family and childbearing," through its
analysis of how Chinese child development, different from
ours, manifests itself in language (for Kristeva, written
and spoken Chinese connects "biological pulsions" with
"the body of language," thereby incorporating the
"feminine"). Refers frequently--perhaps excessively--to
parallels between Kristeva's work and that of her
husband, Philippe Sollers. Has nearly unreadable,
impossibly long sentences, but is often provocative.

459 Féral, Josette. "'Antigone' or the Irony of the Tribe."
     Diacritics 8, No. 3 (Fall 1978), 2-14.

     An interpretive essay about Julia Kristeva's Polylogue
(374) and Luce Irigaray's Speculum de l'autre femme (314)
and Ce sexe qui n'en est pas un (309). Using the myth of
Antigone as emblematic, tries to articulate a feminist
perspective on women and the symbolic while claiming that
traditional psychoanalytic theory is "inadequate" for
such an interpretation. Says Freudian psychoanalysis,
which is based on belief in the structuring of the
"subject" or ego, perceives woman "through the grid of
masculine sexuality." Sees instead Lacanian psychoanalysis and, from it, Kristevan theory of the subject, along
with Irigaray's search for a feminine specificity, as

ways to get at the position of woman--her "difference" in
relation to the symbolic. Traces, first, Freudian theory
of sexual difference as based on the Oedipal complex (a
refusal of the mother), a theory which results in a
negative definition of woman. Woman is the "other," the
void, the silent one. This view, by denying the existence
of autonomous female sexual pleasure in the name of
reproduction, also absorbs femininity into maternity--for
which reason Kristeva advocates woman's "safeguarding"
her pleasure ("jouissance"). Says this desire and the
discourse that arises from it are not commensurate with
masculine definitions, are not singular, not univocal
(Irigaray). Claims that, in relation to masculine
definitions, woman is left "fragmented," "wandering,"
without the certainty enjoyed by the male ego and its
origins ("speculum" is the image for the "spiral" or
"coil" that is woman's unresolvable place). Says
Kristeva's proposed solution involves "giving a place and
a function to (woman's) difference within the constitution
of the subject," in a process that attempts to "subvert
the symbolic" (Oedipal, phallic, repressive) from the
interior, "by struggling against the repression of the
maternal body, by permitting it to reemerge in order to
break, to shatter all the structuring forms of law."
Devotes much more attention to Kristeva than Irigaray,
but finds in both the "same...necessity of a return to
the origin" (the repressed maternal body) and the same
need for woman to constitute a language of her own. This
essay is a good effort to explicate these highly obscure
texts, but it is one which itself borders on the
impenetrable.

460 Jardine, Alice. "Introduction to Julia Kristeva's
     'Women's Time.'" Signs 7, No. 1 (Autumn 1981), 5-12.

     Prefaces Kristeva's essay by terming her writing
modality a "future perfect" that disconcertingly inter-
weaves different temporal spaces. Defines Kristeva's
special use of the word "history" as referring to the
recent period of the French reevaluation of philosophy.
Says this reevaluation and Kristeva's approach to history
posit a crumbling of the pillars of Western culture:
"anthropomorphism, humanism and truth." Sees Kristeva's
view of the "feminine"--and woman herself--as that which
has always "threatened" Western history and as concepts
which in themselves are immensely complex. Also situates
Kristeva's own feminism in relation to French and American
struggles and describes it as a consistent rejection of

"any thought that desexualizes the structures forming us
and our thought." Describes Kristeva's goal as changing
the entire way the "speaking subject" is "thought," an
effort to which she believes "poetic texts" have contributed. A good introduction to Kristeva's work in general.
(See 439).

461 ————. "Pre-Texts for the Trans-Atlantic Feminist."
Yale French Studies No. 62 (1981), 220-36.

Addresses the question of the "feminine"--in modern
Western culture in general and in France and America in
particular--"both as concept and identity." Situates the
point of rupture with such beliefs as "Truth," "Subject,"
"God," "Man," in the late 19th century, a time when
"woman" and "the feminine" were dislocated in Western
thought from passive, negative concepts to central,
problematic ones. Shows the discrepancies between
American and French feminist strategies, based on
different "epistemological legacies," while arguing
against the need to choose one of these "camps" over the
other. Insists women must "remain active in and
attentive to the signifying practices of our times" as
they treat the issues of feminist fiction (writing) and
feminist reading (critical strategies). Offers Julia
Kristeva's work as a uniquely promising "space for
dialogue between American and French feminism(s)," one
attentive to both literature and culture, to conceptual
languages and social/political realities. Traces
Kristeva's general ideas about the "semiotic" and "symbolic" processes and women's particular relation to
them--one of exile, often characterized in their writing
by "a decentering of the subject," silence, and multiplicity. Finally, uses Woolf's The Waves and Wittig's Les
Guérillères as examples of texts that reflect
women writers' ongoing "war"--the first, implicit, the
second, explicit--with the "laws" in place. Makes
observations about the "thematics" and "figurations" in
the two works, in regard to such issues as language,
technique, voice, time, imagery, and syntax. Definitely
not for the lexically or conceptually uninitiated.

462 ————. "Theories of the Feminine: Kristeva." Enclitic
4, No. 2 (Fall 1980), 5-15.

Posits that "woman," "the feminine," are central to
contemporary French thinking about language in general
and poses the questions central to that thinking,

including questions about the implications of using
"woman" as a metaphor for reading, the intention behind
that use, and the sex of the person using the metaphor.
These issues, treated differently in France and America,
are summarized as the conflict between "woman as process
and woman as sexual identity," between inquiry into
symbolic or psychic dialectics versus "natural reality"
or representation, between woman as "absent" object of
contemplation versus agent of prescribed action. Argues,
rather, for a rapprochement of the two critical stances,
which necessitates, first, an understanding of the French
critics' "metaphorization" of woman, then, a new
conjunction of American "ethical discourse" with French
"negativity," to arrive at a new theory of the "speaking
subject," or women's and men's relation to discourse--
specifically, the theory articulated by Julia Kristeva.
Summarizes concisely Kristeva's ideas on conceptual and
epistemological issues, specifically the "semiotic" and
the "symbolic," in her "neo-Marxist-Freudian framework."
Also, situates Kristeva in relation to the question of
"l'écriture féminine"--a concept with which she disagrees,
except insofar as for women, like others on the margins
of our culture, the production of meaning may involve a
different process, leading to "limit-texts." Kristeva
refuses to isolate a specific sexual identity, but,
rather, investigates "sexual differentiation" in a text.
An excellent introduction to Kristeva and to French
feminist inquiry in general.

463 Lewis, Philip E. "Revolutionary Semiotics." Diacritics
     4 (Fall 1974), 28-32.

     A review essay on Julia Kristeva's La Révolution du
     langage poétique (376) that also prepares for the essay
     that follows in the journal, "Phonetics, Phonology and
     Impulsional Bases" (422). Outlines the basic issues
     Kristeva addresses in La Révolution: the textual work of
     the poetic avant-garde and "the status of the critical
     text in relation to the literary text"; the intellectual
     roots of her study; and the implications of her reevalua-
     tion of the field of semiotics. Describes, admiringly,
     the "superdisciplinary" breadth of the book, saying this
     breadth resists brief assessment. Situates La Révolution
     in relation to Kristeva's earlier works, to the ideologi-
     cally self-aware theories of Barthes, Derrida and Lacan
     and to Marx's ideas on work, all of which informed her
     thinking about language. Explains Kristeva's reorienta-
     tion of semiotics away from the conventional study of

communication and toward both the philosophical question
of the "semiotic process" ("the generation of signifiers
on a ground of psychic instincts") and the conceptual
problem of the "text" (as process, germination, or
"engendering"). Discusses how this elaboration of a new
theory of the text also involves a reevaluation of the
"subject," the "I" that is engendered by and engenders
the text. In describing the Kristevan "doubled subject"
(engenders and is engendered), clarifies her redefinition
of the terms "semiotic" and "symbolic" and joins that
dislocated subject to the work of the avant-garde author:
he/she "attempt(s) to overcome the repressive structure
of subject unity, to disrupt the status of the subject,
and consequently of the individual, in the bourgeois
system." Claims Kristeva argues that such authors,
though necessarily marginal, perform the most fundamental
and, in the long run, effective act of subversion. An
extremely helpful entry into Kristeva's long and complex
book.

464 Quaghebeur, Marc. "Julia Kristeva, une philosophie de
      l'avant-garde." Les Lettres romanes 26 (1972), 360-88.

Articulates Kristeva's "vision of the world" in an
extremely opaque "explanation" and critique of her ideas.
First, defines the three terms central to her vision--
"process" ("procès"), "experience," and "practice"--all
of which center on "permanent movement," dislocate the
traditional notion of the "subject," and mark literary
texts. Defines these terms outside of their conventional
Western, dichotomized, "idealized" false meanings. Says
"process" is a "topologization of movement, a spatial
dynamic" characteristic of all realities whose "logic" is
"negativity": "experience" is an "attitude" or "gesture"
of the "subject" in constant disruption (a "subject"
freed of repression and stagnation and whose experience
is "jouissance" or pleasure); "practice" is a dynamic
that connects various "subjects," eventually engendering
social action. Then, elaborates on the Kristevan
"subject" along the lines of Hegelian, Marxist (Maoist)
and Freudian (Lacanian) thought, using psychoanalytic
imagery to evoke it--specifically, the Orestian archetype
connects the Orestian orientation toward death, madness,
and desire with the primacy of the feminine in this new
concept of the subject. Explains Kristeva's break with
the Marxist notion of history and her construction of a
different "idea of materiality." Finally, discusses the
Kristevan view of the role of the literary avant-garde--

to disrupt language in order to bring disruption of the
concrete world--even while criticizing the schism between
text and objective reality and between inaccessible texts
and the mass of readers. Makes the important general
criticism that, while Kristeva's position is doubtless
closer to the "truth" of the universe around us, "the art
she advocates does not escape from socio-economic conditioning and its negativity runs the risk of remaining a
'dead-letter' ('lettre morte')"--that is, privileged and
marginal. Also judges her ideas on the transition from
language to reality to be "satisfying solutions for the
imagination but not sufficiently articulated in terms of
reality." A valuable piece once deciphered--but very
rough going.

465   Roudiez, Leon S. "Introduction" to Julia Kristeva's
      Desire in Language: A Semiotic Approach to Literature
      and Art. Ed. Leon S. Roudiez. New York: Columbia
      University Press, 1980, 1-20.

      Provides, first, a personal, political and intellectual
biography of Kristeva and summaries of her published
works, all of which involve a "dialectical relationship"
between practice and theory. Presents as her major
influences and analytic tools, structuralism, linguistics
and semiotics, and, especially, Lacanian psychoanalysis.
Explains, for purposes of understanding Kristeva's
essays, her central concept of the "speaking subject," or
the subject "divided between unconscious and conscious
motivations, that is, between physiological processes and
social constraints." Also defines the two "signifying
processes" Kristeva posits, the "semiotic" and the
"symbolic," which account for the split in the speaking
subject. Evokes Kristeva's view of the position of the
intellectual, that of an "exiled" dissenter "challenging
all orthodoxies," whether of the government or the
opposition, the Left or the Right. Describes Kristeva's
feminist position as unorthodox, quoting her defense of
an only "conditional" backing of feminism and of childbearing as consistent with cultural activity. Ends with
notes on the translation of and terminology in Kristeva's
works, calling her writing "expository prose," but prose
written from a viewpoint that is "off-centered" in relation to all established doctrine--whence her special use
of particular vocabularies. Gives a glossary of important
problematic terms. An excellent introduction to this
major theoretician. (See 373).

466   **Lafontaine, Dominique** and Geneviève Lorent.   "Si
      l'écriture des femmes."   Les Cahiers du GRIF 23-24
      (December 1978), 153-6.

      Examines the notion of a "woman's writing" for its
      importance and its dangers.   Traces the issue from its
      tentative beginnings to the later belief in a specifi-
      cally feminine writing linked to women's "restored" or
      "dis-alienated" bodies (Cixous, Irigaray).   Locates the
      roots of the question in the 1960's Parisian avant-garde
      critical movement denouncing "logocentric ideology"
      (Derrida, Barthes, Kristeva) and shows that movement's
      contradictory "deconstructing"/"reconstructing" practices.
      Raises the contradiction inherent in describing what
      "feminine writing" is and the resulting danger of
      establishing a "recipe" or normative model.   Says the
      intellectual stance that identified "women" with what is
      repressed and "un-said" in masculine discourse evolved to
      calling this the "feminine," a language therefore
      accessible to men as well.   Refutes this linguistic
      "equality" by pointing to cultural and historical condi-
      tions that give lie to it.   Argues instead that women's
      writing (the "symbolic laws" in all of us) is anchored in
      history.   Asks, "What can (women) say?" if their choice
      is between adopting the restrictive, so-called new
      "feminine" writing or perpetuating the old masculine
      restrictive discourse.   Answers that, rather than search
      for a "feminine writing," we should acknowledge and
      explore a different (women's) writing "practice" grounded
      in historical context.   A fairly good general overview of
      the problem.

467   **Lamy, Suzanne.**   "Voyage autour d'une écriture."   Revue de
      l'Université d'Ottawa/University of Ottawa Quarterly 50,
      No. 1 (January-March 1980), 34-8.

      Alludes joyfully to the "deliverance" brought by the
      recent surge of feminine writing even while acknowledging
      the impossibility of defining this writing.   Evokes its
      "markings": resistant to labels, combining theory with
      fiction, broken, unfixable, open.   Contrasts such writing
      with traditional "psychological" or "sociological" women's
      stories which, it claims, have "documentary" rather than
      literary value.   Locates some of the origins of recent
      feminine writing: its literary foremothers, the current
      general crisis of our civilization, existentialism,
      surrealism, and psychoanalysis.   Insists in particular on

the importance of psychoanalysis for opening to the unconscious.

* **Lanctôt, Mireille** and Madeleine Gagnon. "Femmes du Québec, un mouvement et des écritures." <u>Magazine littéraire</u> No. 134 (March 1978), 97-9.

(See 255).

Leclerc, Annie:

BOOKS AND COLLECTIONS OF ESSAYS

468 ———. <u>Epousailles</u>. Paris: Grasset, 1976.

Ecrire, encore; Percevoir; Corps de ma mère et modestement de l'amour; Alexandre et Marie: l'histoire est un tricot; De la mort, soudain; Descartes: la gourmandise de perfection; En ces jardins, la vie; Trains.

A very personal affirmation of humanity's capacity to love, nurture, and experience pleasure ("la jouissance") and of women's special relationship to these life forces ("la puissance"). Recreates and probes a series of privileged moments to develop a philosophy grounded in the fusion of mind and body. A powerful example of "women's writing" in which discursive social criticism and lyrical fervor are inextricably intertwined.

"Ecrire encore": Establishes the opposition "pouvoir"-- that which negates life--"puissance"--that which promotes it and whose source is the body. Because women have been systematically denied access to power they have not been "corrupted" and turned away from the body. Women must speak and write for it is through them that the life forces will find expression. However, women should not categorically reject men or the past. Feminism must be rooted in a desire to join together ("épousailles") not to separate.

"Percevoir": Opposes the normative view of perception, its role in understanding and appropriating the world, with her own: "to perceive is to enjoy ("percevoir est jouir")."

"Corps de ma mère et modestement de l'amour": Recounts how, as a child, her mother's body sparked the experience of love as the transcendent union of self with "the entire earth, time, humanity." This "indecent," subversive love is never culturally acknowledged and is mutilated to fit within the limits of the family and the couple.

"Alexandre et Marie: l'histoire est un tricot." Relates another privileged moment from her childhood, when, at the home of dearly loved neighbors, she learns to knit. The pleasure of creation and of the effortless passage from not knowing to knowing leads to several insights. Watching Marie embroider in silence, as usual, she realizes that this woman, like all women, is a "weaver of humanity." Marie "weaves the place that perpetuates our destiny and our union with the earth." Leclerc feels she is part of an historical continuum and resolves to carry on women's handiwork ("ouvrage") through writing.

"De la mort soudain": The death of Leclerc's mother reveals a paradoxical truth: death, like pleasure, creates life, opens the self. Violent grief jolts the mourners into an awareness of their community, of the love they share.

"Descartes: la gourmandise de perfection": Answers the question "What is philosophy good for?" "It creates pleasure, and pleasure permits birth...it opens my life forces, makes me big, wide, tall, I mean outside myself, joined to and diluted in others..." But only on one condition--if the reader goes beyond the text as source of truth and instrument of control. Emphatically refutes the separation of body and mind, redefining thought ("la pensée") to reflect her holistic vision: "the desire to rouse, to waken, to increase the body's life forces... Thought seeks something more in the nature of happiness than knowledge." Contends that theory and order, though always made to serve the oppressor, are necessary and invaluable: "To the earth, to the life forms that inhabit it forms are essential, and it is useless and ultimately suicidal to confuse them with power."

"En ces jardins, la vie": Further develops her preceding point using the example of the royal gardens at Versailles. A symbol of despotism as well as classical order and perfection these gardens are nonetheless the source of exquisite joy. This is not because "puissance" and "pouvoir" are linked in a "terrible dialectical pact" but because power has always appropriated reason, order, language, science, the arts. Yet, to reject all that structures life on the grounds that it is corrupt is to fall into the worst scepticism and impotence. One must not "confuse the human life forces with male power."

"Trains": A compelling evocation of trains as a
metaphor of human life forces. Concludes by repeating
her belief that love is "the path of radical subversion."

469 ───────. Parole de femme. Paris: Grasset, 1974.

Analyzes the oppression of women, characterizing it as
essentially psychological, not material, and distinguishing it from that exercised against other exploited
groups. Includes a version of the myth of the origins of
inequality: man's vengeance against his mother for having
denied him the capacity to create life. Critiques at
length male values--action, appropriation, control,
force--and establishes a Manichaean opposition: man=death,
woman=life. Explains that this value system is rooted in
a problematical sexual identity, that is, it represents
man's attempts to maintain the sense of self experienced
during erection.
Calls upon women to invent alternatives to the male
world and to reinvent themselves. The first step toward
revolution is to break the silence surrounding all that
is specifically female and has been stolen and disdained
by men. Women must express their difference and
celebrate their sexuality. Leclerc begins this process
by recounting her own experience of menstruation, intercourse, and childbirth. Women's language ("une parole de
femme") is identified with a feminine thematics. Leclerc
does not discuss style per se, nor does she address the
issue of women's relation to the Symbolic.

*   ───────, Hélène Cixous, and Madeleine Gagnon. La venue à
      l'écriture. Paris: UGE, 10/18, 1977.

(See 87).

ESSAYS AND ARTICLES

470 ───────. "Communication." Liberté Nos. 106-107 (July-
October 1976), 15-19.

Paper from the "Rencontre québécoise internationale des
écrivains." Insists on the importance of "pleasure"
("jouissance") as the source of women's writing and
speaking. Calls the feminine in writing "the emergence
from silence," the expression by women of all the secrets
kept within their bodies.

471 ———. "Je vais te manger." <u>Sorcières</u> 1 (January 1976),
        28-30.

Exalts all woman's bodily functions by playing with the
words "(se) nourrir" (to feed one's appetite) and "manger"
(to eat). Both words are metaphors for "living with
one's body open and eager" and for the organic relationship between the body and nature.

472 ———. "La Lettre d'amour." Hélène Cixous, Madeleine
        Gagnon and Annie Leclerc. <u>La Venue à l'écriture</u>.
        Paris: UGE, 10/18, 1977, 117-52.

Compares writing to an act of love, in a text, itself a
"love letter," that calls on women to write their unwritten stories. Makes fluid and multiple use of two central
images to describe women's relationship to writing, past
and future: (1) the "woman-servant" ("femme servante"),
who has been forced to serve the cultural masters and
whose own words have remained silenced within the prison
of her body: and (2) the "mother," who, as an act of
love, gives birth to a new self that will break with
women's past silence. Evokes the ambiguity and mystery
of Vermeer's paintings as the perfect visual correlative
of women's at once subordinate and yet potentially
powerful status. Argues that women must find and unite
with the "woman-servant" locked within them and, through
such intimate knowledge of themselves, uncover the
unspoken language of their bodies that their writing can
inscribe. Contrasts the destructiveness of the
traditional meaning of love--possession, obligation,
limitation, abnegation of women--with "revolutionary"
love that is new, open, pleasurable, creative, and
therefore frightening to the established order. Ends
with a lyrical utopian vision of a new order built on
such love, to which women's writing--the expression of
their authentic desire--will contribute. Moves from
being difficult and somewhat confusing to being incantatory and moving.

472a   Partially trans. in (19).

473 ———. "Mon Ecriture d'amour." <u>Les Nouvelles litté-
        raires</u> No. 2534. (May 26, 1976), 19.

Comments briefly on the nature of feminine writing--
above all "an extension ("un prolongement") and a quest

for pleasure ("jouissance")--and on the subversive
socio-political impact of texts that say "yes" to life.

474   ────. "Postface." Marie Cardinal. Autrement dit.
       Paris: Grasset, 1977, 207-20.

Using Autrement dit (74) as an example, reflects on
"speaking" ("la parole") and "writing" ("l'écriture") as
two different physical acts of exchange, the first a
"vague," the second an "ordered" form of expression.
Admires the spontaneity and openness of Cardinal's text
as qualities that solicit a responsive word from the
listener/reader; also, in a powerfully imagistic passage,
praises Cardinal for transcending her woman-writer's fear
of external judges (les "maîtres"). Ends with an exhortation to women to "speak...ramble, dare the vague,
...wander" so as never again to flee (writing) out of
fear.

ESSAYS AND ARTICLES ABOUT

475   Andersen, Margret. "La Jouissance--Principe d'écriture."
       L'Esprit créateur 19, No. 2 (Summer 1979), 3-12.

In an admiring, even affectionate, overview of
Leclerc's important post-1968 texts, Parole de femme
(469), Epousailles (468), and "la Lettre d'amour" (472),
encapsulates the basic premises of Leclerc's theories
about women's language and writing. Posits, first,
Leclerc's critique of the mind/body split in Western
thought, a split whose consequence has been the joyless,
lifeless and possession-centered male "anti-language"
that prevails. Leclerc exhorts women to express the
"feminine and feminist" language of love that has lain
dormant in their bodies. Then, summarizes Leclerc's
theoretical biography, contrasting her earlier 1960's
texts with her subsequent radical calls for the invention
of a women's language ("une parole de femme"). Finally,
tries to define this women's language as Leclerc sees it:
the "marvellous subversion" of the dominant language
(through humor and ridicule, not through male-identified
destruction and conquest) and the affirmation of human
"pleasure" ("jouissance"), of "birth...deliverance...
life." Though somewhat internally repetitive and more
heavily reliant on quotation than interpretation (the
author acknowledges and justifies this as a refusal to
"enclose" so vital a corpus), this essay has two principal
strengths: it places Leclerc's works in the context of

her philosophical background and training; and it
personalizes Leclerc's ideas by connecting them to the
writing of this essay itself.

* Cesbron, Georges. "Ecritures au féminin. Propositions
de lecture pour quatre livres de femmes." Degré second
4 (July 1980), 95-119.

(See 4).

476 Delphy, Christine. "Proto-féminisme et anti-féminisme."
Les Temps modernes 346 (May 1975), 1469-500.

A materialist feminist reading of Annie Leclerc's
Parole de femme (469). Criticizes Leclerc for situating
her reflections at the level of individual revolt (proto-
feminism) rather than collective political struggle.
Asserts that her argumentation "is exactly sexist
ideology seen in a mirror, reversed but identical": it
is essentialist--claiming a first principle, life: it is
biologist--maintaining that sexuality, the experience of
the body unmediated by social influences, created and
sustain human values; it is "ideological"--positing that
these values determine social organization and not vice
versa. Develops a lengthy analysis of women's work to
show the inaccuracy of Leclerc's psychological approach
to oppression: Leclerc accepts the traditional sexual
division of labor as natural. She contends that if
women's work is demeaned it is because of the ascendancy
of male values. Delphy contends that the sexual division
of labor is a social phenomenon. Women's work is devalued
because of women's relation to production: they perform
unpaid work for men. This material exploitation is the
only basis for a viable theory of oppression. Allows
that aspects of Parole de femme are useful: its attacks
on devaluing myths and the attention paid to creating a
positive female body image. Claims, however, that the
absence of reflection on the role of socio-economic
factors undermines these contributions so seriously that
the book (and others like it), a-historical and thus
reactionary, does a disservice to feminism. Acerbic. An
important piece illustrating the factionalism that has
characterized much feminist debate.

477 Gauthier, Xavière. "Lettre à Annie Leclerc." Les Nouvelles littéraires No. 2560 (November 25, 1976), 11.

Reacts to Epousailles (468), approving Leclerc's

condemnation of power ("le pouvoir") and her desire to
write from the body. Criticizes her simplistic tendency
to propose love as an answer to all problems and to
ignore the implications of history and the unconscious.

478   Lejeune, Claire. "L'écriture et l'arbre du milieu."
      Les Cahiers du GRIF 7 (June 1975), 35-41.

      Reflects on the act of writing as a liberating "subver-
      sion," as a "coming to oneself" that is constantly moving
      and renewing itself. Sees writing as an "androgynous
      place" with the potential for destroying patriarchy and
      its foundation, "positivism" (logical, univocal). Says
      "poetic" writing can "destructure" the positivist
      tradition that has enslaved the "feminine" and recreate
      original freedom of meaning. Traces the "psychic
      itinerary" toward the liberating of the feminine through
      writing that "transgresses," that "de-appropriates," that
      "relates" with others.

479   Lemoine-Luccioni, Eugénie. Partage des femmes. Paris:
      Seuil, 1976.

      Introduction; La fable du sang; Grossesse et féminité;
      De la partition à la castration symbolique; Le frère et
      la soeur; L'hermaphrodite; Beauté; Conclusion.

      A Lacanian clinical study based on the testimonies of
      pregnant women undergoing psychoanalysis with Lemoine-
      Luccioni. Posits that woman is intrinsically and
      irremediably "divided" by her being at once "creator" and
      "creature" (a created being herself), whereas man, since
      creation is external to him, is naturally "unified." Says
      woman suffers as a result of this inherent partition and
      seeks a kind of unity in love, but one that only rein-
      forces her "otherness." Claims the division within woman
      and between men and women is unchangeable. Makes rigid
      dichotomies between man's ability to compensate for his
      "lack" through possession of woman and of knowledge and
      woman's inability to so compensate in any but an
      "imaginary" way. Accepts Freudian theory and defines
      "woman" in the Lacanian sense of that which does not in
      itself exist but upon which man--and language (the
      "symbolic")--depend, and therefore that which must
      "disappear" for the social order to change. Takes a
      problematic political stance: "It is indeed true that
      woman finds herself caught in virile paradigms and

systems of representation. But I do not conclude from
that that she ought not to be caught in them. I don't
know anything about it." Chapters, together, constitute
a full analysis of women's psychological relation to the
masculine systems of representation under which they
live:

"La fable du sang"--First, defines her use of "fable"
as a purely self-referential, a-historical story
recounted during the psychoanalytic process. Then,
presents the "fable" of a particular patient who makes
frequent reference to blood and who becomes pregnant
during the course of her analysis. Also interprets
specific elements of this patient's story. Summarizes
this woman's decision to have a child as a way both to
flee from her homosexuality and to affirm herself as a
woman without the need of a man. Takes this case as a
paradigm of the use of a child to reconfirm, albeit
falsely, the sexual identity of the parents and thus
revalidate the cultural order.

"Grossesse et féminité"--Using the case of the patient
described above, elaborates on the theoretical issues it
illuminates: "pregnancy as a narcissistic crisis," or the
idea that, because pregnancy interferes with woman's
aspiring to ideal beauty (her way of denying her
"animality"), a regressive and dangerous narcissism takes
the place of that "cult" of beauty. Says that in this
narcissism, the developing child becomes an "imaginary
object" that fulfills the mother's desires; "the specular
image and pregnancy," or the idea that in pregnancy,
woman abandons the primitive "mirror stage" in which she
is held because the child fulfills the role of the
idealized self-image; "from two to three," or the
"doubling" of the pregnant woman's body (into hers and
the child's, and also hers and her mother's) in which she
regains what she has lost; "the change of sex," or
childbirth as providing woman with the illusion of
possessing a penis, an illusion soon dispelled; "woman as
a speaking being," or women's and men's contrasting
relation to the symbolic, based on the phallus as symbol
of participation in language. Puts forth the Lacanian
theory about sexual difference, that of "the impossibility of the sexual relation as a relation; an
impossibility which is the very condition of man's and
woman's language." Says that when women speak, they
"steal the word from man and castrate him." This section
is important but extremely difficult; "the imaginary
partition," or the abandonment woman experiences through
separation from her child, her mother, her father.

Claims love makes it possible for woman to "seize the
real" and to come to speech.

"De la partition à la castration symbolique"--Examines
the question of women's madness, beginning with the case
of a particular "delirious" patient, and then tracing the
issues of: woman's innate partition and reparatory
narcissism; the "scopic pulsions" or the "specular image"
that govern the feminine libido; and female "hysteria"
and woman's "slave" relationship to man. Takes as central
thesis that "woman passes from imaginary partition to
symbolic castration" through identification with an
Other, through "a meeting and a response (with and from
the Other) that give her pleasure" and provide her with
"her status as a (speaking) subject." Considers in
detail the example of Saint Theresa as woman.

"Le frère et la soeur"--Discusses the model of
brother-sister love, which it calls the only "spoken
love," by citing literary examples, especially Goethe.
Says brother-sister epitomizes fundamental sexual
difference, from which language arises.

"L'hermaphrodite"--Sees hermaphrodism as evidence of
the human search for unity: an individual, having understood the failure at the core of the male/female sexual
relation, is led to "satisfy himself/herself all alone."
Uses literary examples (e.g., Tournier).

"Beauté"--States, "A woman is defined in our language
and in our society by her beauty, and not by her sexual
ability." Says this "love of (mere) form" constitutes a
negation of woman as a "desiring subject," rendering her
an object that "offers itself to be seen" but that does
not see. Connects this difficulty in seeing with the
difficulty in representing artistically, taking an
example of a woman painter. Concludes that, since the
masculine organ (and the corresponding ability to see) is
in fact not "real" but a "lack," women have no reason to
envy or covet it. Rather, views as the appropriate
feminist project the strengthening of sexual difference.
Requires knowledge of Lacanian theory. (See 271 and 330).

480 ──────. Le rêve du cosmonaute. Paris: Seuil, 1980.

Prologue; Le cri; La jouissance comme limite; L'identification, fabrique du continu; L'écrit; Le lien social;
Epilogue.

Takes "cosmonaut" as central metaphor for man's impossible desire to "leave this world" and enter "into
another/an Other," a desire that is the consequence of

his continued "fall" from original unity. Uses Lacanian
theory to locate the individual's initial "break" with
unity (with union with the Mother) at birth (the birth
"cry"), a break that will repeat itself and that gives
rise to "pulsions" or desires, and therefore to the
founding of exchange, of language, of the symbolic. Says
the "body," from this initial cry or "call" to the Other,
continues to "speak" as it continues to desire (e.g.,
during "jouissance" and at death). Presents as principal
dilemma the hypothesis that, were the divided subject to
find unity (the Mother) again, it would lose language in
the process. Explains how the establishment of society--
the edification of the "law of the Father"--is built on
the exclusion of "jouissance," of the Mother, though this
maternal body keeps erupting into culture, especially
when women bring continuity and flow into the discontinuity of the social order. Chapters in this exposition of
the human "tragedy" of division are as follows:

  "Le cri"--Discusses the initial birth cry and the
child's "fall" into "anguish," an experience that will be
repeated throughout life. Describes the forms and
consequences of this repetition. Compares individuals to
"cosmonauts," who seek out another space, only to find it
is the same, original one. Gives examples of authors
writing out of and in response to this ongoing "anguish"
(e.g., Artaud).

  "La jouissance comme limite"--Speaks about literary
accounts of love as "delayed" transcriptions of a
discourse comparable to that uttered by analysands. Expands on Bataille's ideas on "pleasure"/"orgasm" ("jouissance"), in which "the body proper loses its limits."
Talks about woman's experience of "jouissance," more than
man's, as revealing to her the "impossibility of the
real" (of real sexual union, of a real male/female
relation). Using the Lacanian psychological "registers,"
describes women's and men's differing relationship to the
symbolic and to creating.

  "L'identification, fabrique du continu"--Defines the
human act of "identification" as "recognizing oneself in
the other." Elaborates on the process of sexual identification for women and men and one of its consequences,
narcissism.

  "L'écrit"--Explores the passage from the original "cry"
to writing, which it qualifies as a "desperate effort, at
the limits of sacrifice and at the limits of possibility." Posits Freud's argument that creating is a turning
away from reality toward one's "phantasmatic life," then

extends it to say that the great artist returns to
reality by creating and introducing "a new category of
real things." Discusses Joyce and Mallarmé through the
grid of Lacanian theory on writing.

"Le lien social"--Prolongs the previous chapter by
looking at how the writer's reinsertion and modification
of reality affect all "men's (sic) understanding of
reality." Wonders why women, if they could, would want
to partake of the masculine creative dynamic, which
excludes "the Mother." Analyzes how feminine and
masculine sexual dynamics are inscribed in social
institutions. Argues for an affirmation of sexual
difference--but not based on the repression of one
sex--as necessary for "desire of the Other."

"Epilogue"--Talks about the 1980 dissolution by Lacan
of the Freudian School of Paris, which it calls, in
psychoanalytic terms, a "rupture." Highly specialized.

481   ———. "Ecrire." Sorcières 7 (1977), 13-14.

Describes woman's psycho-sexual dynamics when moving to
the "neuter" position of writer. Contrasts the experience of a "doubling" of identity for a woman and a man
when they write, his being "de-structuring," hers being
multiplying and more "violent." Says his writing is one
of comforting reaffirmation of systems, hers is
subversion.

482 **Levallois-Colot, Anne.** "'Voyez comme l'on danse.'"
     L'Arc 58 (1974), 21-4.

Addresses the problematic relation of the woman psychoanalyst to Lacan as "master," saying she can either "play
the master" ("faire le maître") and join the men's side
or "play the hysteric" ("faire l'hystérique") and join
the women's side. Says Lacan paid his "debt" toward
women--the one incurred by his inevitable possession and
transmission of knowledge--by being aware of and
"displacing" his untenable position in relation to all
disciples, including women.

 *   **Lorent, Geneviève** and Dominique Lafontaine. "Si l'écri-
     ture des femmes." Les Cahiers du GRIF 23-24 (December
     1978), 153-6.

     (See 466).

483 "**Luttes de femmes.**" Tel Quel 58 (Summer 1974), 93-103.

Takes stock of the "women's problem," which it says has
become a large-scale public issue and which it calls the
springboard for "interesting reflections" on women's role
in society and on ideology, as it relates to Freudian and
Marxist thought. Evaluates the practical and theoretical
results of different feminist movements in regard to the
existent "social contract" and the dominant rational
discourse. Situates the women's movement within the
general upheaval in the capitalist system of production
and reproduction. Warns against a new "fetishization" of
women, or the "narcissistic" isolation of their concerns
from other social changes. Regrets the paucity of
feminist journals in France. Introduces the short pieces
about women's writing that follow by revealing they had
been rejected by Le Monde des livres as "incomprehensible"--a judgment Tel Quel describes as serving the male
order, as reactionary "servitude." Reaffirms the strategic importance for women's progress of current changes in
"signifying practices." Sections that follow are:
Xavière Gauthier, "Existe-t-il une écriture de femmes?"
(284); Xavière Gauthier, "Il y a comme des cris, mais
silencieux," an interview with Marguerite Duras (194);
Xavière Gauthier, "Oscillation du 'pouvoir' 'au refus,'"
an interview with Julia Kristeva (452); and "Nouvelles
éditions 'des femmes' au MLF," a brief presentation of
the theoretical issues explored by the feminist group
"politique et psychanalyse" and the goals behind its
founding of the publishing house, "éditions des femmes."

484 **Magli, Ida.** "Pouvoir de la parole et silence de la
     femme." Les Cahiers du GRIF 12 (June 1976), 37-43.

A sample "inventory" of the various ways women are kept
from language in our culture. Cites, first, Lévi-Strauss
on the exchange of women--the objectification of women
into a cultural "sign" in the earliest societies--as the
basis of women's exclusion from the active, central
communicative group (the power that "gives and takes").
Says "woman" is the primary "sign" (and not an active
signifier), the signifying value that supports the
masculine system. Claims this is the reason conquerors
always seized the women of the vanquished enemy--to
dispossess them of their "exchange currency." Goes on to
explore the tradition of "word as act" in Judeo-Christian
thought, a tradition which again excluded women from

language (divine Law) and which was perpetuated in the
liturgy. Says fear of women's too-great power was behind
this verbal deprivation. Gives examples of present-day
exclusions of women from the "contractual power" that is
language.

485 **Mannoni, Maud.** "Le malentendu." L'Arc 58 (1974), 56-61.

Addresses the relationship between Lacanian theory and
practice, saying psychiatric treatment has been little
affected by his ideas and that Lacan himself wrote almost
nothing about his practice. The "misunderstanding" of
the title is that of the public towards Lacan, and also
that of the traditional analyst towards her/his "crazy"
patient. Explains Lacan's critique of the traditional
analyst's participation in her/his patient's illness, a
critique he elaborated through his theory of the "real,"
"imaginary," and "symbolic" registers. Develops the
implications of Lacan's message for profound social and
ethical change.

486 **Marini, Marcelle.** "Les femmes et les pratiques d'écriture. Quelques réflexions." Pénélope No. 3 (Fall
1980), 58-68.

Reflects on how women's reevaluation of language is
part of an upheaval in the entire "socialized imagination" or the "symbolic system that determines
inter-subjective relations"--relations between text and
writer, reader and subject. Views women's writing as
their affirmation of their individual and collective
participation in the elaboration of culture. Says that
while some women opt for either silence or a return to
traditional discourse, others "crack" the dominant
language that has objectified them. Sees all these
changes in symbolic production as "inscribing themselves"
in the history of language, in the way social changes
mark daily life. Cautions that changes in language must
have a concrete dimension as well and must not be
normative. Gives a good short bibliography. Lucid and
informative.

* **Marks, Elaine** and George Stambolian, eds. Homosexualities and French Literature. Ithaca: Cornell University
Press, 1979.

(See 532).

487 ———. "Lesbian Intertextuality." <u>Homosexualities and</u>
    <u>French Literature</u>. Ed. George Stambolian and Elaine
    Marks. Ithaca: Cornell University Press, 1979, 353-77.

   Traces the representation of Sapphic sexuality in
   women's texts, finding a shift from portrayals of
   limited, restrained relationships between women (e.g.,
   Colette's lesbianism as a "sentimental retreat") to
   limitless, revolutionary expressions of passion between
   women (e.g., Wittig's lesbians as autonomous and mobile
   women). Sees increasing self-consciousness among recent
   lesbian writers and offers Wittig's centering of her
   writing on the lesbian body itself as the strongest
   instance of this change. Also follows formal and
   stylistic shifts in Sapphic texts, in particular the
   change in the chronological framework of lesbian love
   from Colette's "exotic" past, to Leduc's "anguished"
   present, to Wittig's "apocalyptic" and boundless future.
   Concludes that, until recently, the lesbian has been
   portrayed in literature through phallocentric stereotypes
   and that only now are these images being shattered.

488 **Martel, Cosette.** "Le e muet d'Ariane." <u>Sorcières</u> 7
    (1977), 41-2.

   Looks at the "mute" or "feminine e" as it has been used
   in French poetry and poetic theater, as a kind of metaphor for the feminine in writing. Says this so-called
   "silent e" in fact speaks, marks, and is heard in a
   different way.

489 **Mathieu, Nicole-Claude.** "Masculinité/féminité."
    <u>Questions féministes</u> 1 (November 1977), 51-67.

   Shows how the idea of the "masculine," as conveyed in
   language, connotes something "more," whereas "feminine"
   carries the value of "less." Says "sexual grammars" that
   designate presumed "masculine" or "feminine" comportments
   are totally arbitrary and distinguishes between biological
   "sex" and psycho-social "gender," the latter being determined by social conditioning and varying in different
   cultures. Views all social processes in Western culture
   as reinforcing the sexual dichotomy (and therefore banning
   homosexuality) and hierarchy (and therefore fearing "uni-
   sex") to keep social order and current power structures.
   Describes how those who fear "sexual non-distinction" use
   women's childbearing role as their most potent argument.

490 **Moi, Toril.** "The Missing Mother: the Oedipal Rivalries
     of René Girard." <u>Diacritics</u> 12, No. 2 (Summer 1982),
     21-31.

     Criticizes Girard's work (<u>Mensonge romantique et vérité
     romanesque</u>, <u>La Violence et le sacré</u>, <u>Des choses cachées
     depuis la fondation du monde</u>) for its pretentions to
     universal validity, its faulty reasoning, and its unwit-
     ting sexism. Argues that Girard's theory of triangular
     or mimetic desire is incapable of accounting for feminine
     desire because it excludes the mother from the Oedipal
     triangle and posits heterosexuality as instinctive.
     Focuses on Girard's readings of Freud to show the defi-
     ciencies of his thinking.

Montrelay, Michèle:

BOOKS AND COLLECTIONS OF ESSAYS

491 ———. <u>L'ombre et le nom: Sur la féminité</u>. Paris:
     Minuit, 1977.

     "Sur <u>Le ravissement de Lol V. Stein</u>" (205); "Parole de
     femme. Sur le transfert de l'hystérique" (497); "A
     propos du narcissisme et de sa mise en scène dans la
     postface aux <u>Lois de l'hospitalité</u>" (492); "Recherches
     sur la féminité" (500); "Pulsions I: A propos du plaisir
     d'organe" (498); "Pulsions II: Le saut du loup" (501);
     "Pulsions III: Le rejeton de la pulsion" (499); "Histoire
     de Louise I: Une phobie" (495); "Histoire de Louise II:
     L'ombre" (494); "Fragment sur <u>Nathalie Granger</u>"; "Textes
     à l'infini" (502); "La dernière femme?" (493).

     A collection of essays, each of which addresses in some
     way Montrelay's concept of "the shadow" ("l'ombre") or
     the realm of femininity, the "realm of nothing" that
     marks the unconscious and, in analogous ways, symbolic
     representation or language. Is completely within the
     Lacanian theoretical framework. Essays vary from sugges-
     tive but difficult to incomprehensible.

ESSAYS AND ARTICLES

492 ———. "A propos du narcissisme et de sa mise en scène
     dans la postface aux <u>Lois de l'hospitalité</u>." <u>L'ombre
     et le nom: Sur la féminité</u>. Paris: Minuit, 1977, 41-54.

     A composite of fragments from her previous studies on

narcissism. First, traces the concept of narcissism from
its initial Freudian sense of libidinal investment of
sexual energy in the self, rather than an external object.
Sees a single source for both investments of sexual
energy (in self and external object): "Eros," the force
in each individual that coexists with and opposes the
instinct for death ("Thanatos"). Pushes the question of
Eros further to examine its "structure," its dynamic
connection to Thanatos, by introducing Lacanian theory of
the "mirror stage," or the childhood experience of a
false image of "wholeness" that underlies the "imaginary
mastery" called the "ego." Says this coherent "ego" or
eroticized image of the self--Eros--is in constant danger
of being "crumbled" and destroyed by the opposing forces
of Thanatos. Joins the desire for "fusion" or wholeness
with the production of language, the symbolic materiali-
zation of a bond. In the second part, analyzes Pierre
Klossovski's book, Les lois de l'hospitalité, as example
of a text that clearly evinces the relation between
language and narcissism. Very rough going.

493   ———. "La dernière femme." L'ombre et le nom: Sur la
       féminité. Paris: Minuit, 1977, 161-4.

       Evokes the writing in recent texts by women who have
       "let language come to them," with all its words and
       sounds, as well as its "holes" and "refuse." Cautions
       about the "strange" effect these texts have on men: they
       feel robbed of their "femininity" by these women's
       affirmation of theirs, and in this way suffer the same
       "trauma" inflicted on young girls by the father. Ends
       with an ambiguous message about the usefulness of
       reaffirming sexual opposition in this way.

494   ———. "Histoire de Louise II: L'ombre." L'ombre et le
       nom: Sur la féminité. Paris: Minuit, 1977, 133-46.

       Describes the "launching" of the human being (beginning
       with the birth cry) out of its "shadowy," primordial,
       unknowable structure, into the "Other" order, the order
       of "condensation" and "objectification" where representa-
       tion takes place. Evokes the psychic and physio-erotic
       consequences of birth for the mother, as well as the
       child (especially "jouissance," which Montrelay associ-
       ates with "the Shadow," "the feminine"). Then, examines
       the symptoms of a woman in analysis with Montrelay and
       explores their psycho-familial causes--in this case, the

trauma of a paternal "perversion." Presumes knowledge of Lacanian theory.

495 ──────. "Histoire de Louise I: Une phobie." L'ombre et le nom: Sur la féminité. Paris: Minuit, 1977, 119-31.

Text of a talk given at a 1976 conference in Strasbourg. Uses the case of a woman painter in analysis with Montrelay to get at the psychological source of the patient's "anguish" and, ultimately, the source of female sexual "anguish" in general. Finds at that source a "hole," an absence, the site of the "maternal castration" that also makes it impossible now for the child/patient to express her suffering. Claims this "hole" in the symbolic fabric was opened by a "phobia" and links phobia with the maternal body, and then with the problematic status of feminine desire in general. Extends the literal images--drawings, paintings and voice pictures--that shaped this patient's development to the level of the abstract "imagery" that is part of the Lacanian developmental model. Potentially fascinating but increasingly hard to follow.

496 ──────. "L'Imaginaire au féminin." Le Récit et sa représentation. Proceedings from the Colloques de Saint Hubert, May 1977. Paris: Payot, 1978, 165-174.

Starting from parallels between poetry and the discourse of the psyche, purports to use a poem by Francis Ponge, "Rough Sketch of a Fish" ("Ebauche d'un poisson") to gain access to "psychic mechanisms" underlying the "complexity of life." Uses Winnicott's object relations theory in conjunction with portions of the poem to evoke the dynamics of psychic "space," the site, first, of the relation with the mother ("the feminine"), then of language and representation. Also brings in semiotic concepts of the sign/signifier/signified to suggest problems that arise when symbolic space stops "circulating" (e.g., hallucination, phobia). Shows the affinities between the objects of phobic responses and objects as they are presented in Ponge's work. Refers to Montrelay's idea of the "shadow" ("l'ombre"), the name she gives to "the space opened by feminine pleasure" ("jouissance"), the "holes" in the symbolic fabric (see 491). Concludes, "The place that he (Ponge) opens is...the feminine imagination." Impenetrable for those unfamiliar with psychoanalytic theory.

497 ⎯⎯⎯⎯. "Parole de femme. Sur le transfert de l'hystérique." L'ombre et le nom: Sur la féminité. Paris:
Minuit, 1977, 25-39.

   The text of a speech given for the Freudian School in
Paris in 1967. Considers the discourse of patients in
psychoanalysis and hypothesizes that the circular
"rhythms," the periodic "ebbs and flows" of that
discourse result from the fluctuating relation of words
to meaning, the oscillating link between signifier and
signified. Calls these rhythms "feminine discourse" and
sees them as arising from the unconscious, the space of
the "Other." Puts this "feminine discourse" of the
unconscious in the psychoanalytical context of the
process of transference, examining how it explodes
linguistic oppositional categories to engage in
"nonsense" as well as "sense," to engage both "body" and
language. Terms this "magical" "body-word" of the
analysand a manifestation of "jouissance." Is rooted in
Lacanian theory and terminology and is extremely specialized.

498 ⎯⎯⎯⎯. "Pulsions I: A propos du plaisir d'organe."
L'ombre et le nom: Sur la féminité. Paris: Minuit,
1977, 83-96.

   The text of a talk given at the conference of the
Freudian School in 1972. Establishes Lacan's reinterpretation of Freud's conception of Eros: Freud's view of
Eros as the force underlying all unity and cohesiveness
in the world was subverted by Lacan's belief that erotic
manifestations are really fragmented ("morcelés") and
diverse in nature. Goes on to analyze and interrogate
Freud's theory of "pleasure" from the point of view of
"the body in its relation to the unconscious," or the way
biological organs work to maintain and "organize" sexual
energy. Calls this "organization" a form of "homeostasis"
and says it emerges in various activities, e.g., speaking.
Claims these manifestations of organized energy are always
"open," "limitless" "surfaces," "heterogeneous" texts
that resist meaning because of the infinite number of
"repressed" elements that lie in the "holes" of their
fabric. Describes the moments--"traumatic" events--when
these repressed elements severely threaten to break
psychic/biological homeostasis (e.g., psychic or hysterical episodes). Resists comprehension.

499 ───────. "Pulsions III: Le rejeton de la pulsion."
          L'ombre et le nom: Sur la féminité. Paris: Minuit,
          1977, 111-18.

      Evokes the unconscious in Lacanian terms, as having a
      knowledge that is known only to itself and that escapes
      the grasp of the individual subject, for which reason the
      discourse of the unconscious is "unthinkable" and
      "unrepresentable." Says the mechanisms of the unconscious
      can be perceived only through analogy with those of
      language, since both the unconscious and language
      manifest "pulsions" or movements in and out of meaning,
      pulsions Lacan calls "jouissance." Elaborates on the
      mechanism of these pulsions, using Lacanian concepts and
      highly technical diagrams. Almost unreadable.

500 ───────. "Recherches sur la féminité." Critique 278
          (July 1970), 654-74.

      Takes stock of psychoanalytic theories of femininity,
      beginning with the "contradictory conceptions" of Jones
      and Freud. Summarizes Freud's view of femininity as one
      based on a single male-defined libido ("phallocentrism"),
      Jones's on a specifically feminine, internal "libidinal
      organization" ("concentricity"). Then, reviews a 1964
      collective study of femininity, Recherches psychanaly-
      tiques nouvelles sur la sexualité féminine. Says the
      book succeeds in going beyond the Freud/Jones alternative
      because it validates both, through its direct transcrip-
      tion of the contradictory discourses of patients in
      analysis. But criticizes the study for not formulating
      explicitly how Fruedian and Jonesian thought do in fact
      coexist and does so itself: says these contradictory
      views of female sexuality are incompatible and that "this
      incompatibility (itself) is specific to the feminine
      unconscious." Analyzes in detail the two "modes" in
      which "phallocentrism" and "concentricity" confront one
      another in the feminine unconscious: anguish and sublima-
      tion. Elaborates on what is now standard Lacanian theory
      on language or conscious and unconscious "representation,"
      including the idea that "femininity" (unrepressed "pul-
      sions") is outside of and constantly threatens the systems
      of representation in place. Discusses female pleasure
      and "jouissance" in terms of their "function in the
      (libidinal) economy." Gives examples of expressions of

feminine sexuality in literature, including Duras.   Clear.
(See 268).

500a   Reprinted in (491).

501   ————.   "Le saut du loup."   L'Arc 58 (1974), 25-30.

Applying Lacanian theory to Freud's "Wolf Man" case,
unearths the "strange beings" in the unconscious that
inhabit the "interstices" between words, that is, the
"feminine." Does so by uncovering the gaps in Freud's
analysis of the case. Reconstructs, in a Lacanian
framework, this child's traumatic experience with his
parents. Difficult.

501a   Reprinted, with some changes and additions, in
        (491).

502   ————.   "Textes à l'infini."   L'ombre et le nom:Sur la
       féminité.   Paris: Minuit, 1977, 149-59.

Distinguishes women's and men's relationship to
language, using a Lacanian framework: says men are
separated from language (by the penis, that object that
"obliterates meaning"), whereas for women, language is an
"extension of themselves." Articulates the options for
women that result from this connection to words: either
they can "pretend" to be separated from language and
imitate men's writing, or they can "let the words do as
they please." But sees recent avant-garde writing by
women (Chawaf, Hyvrard) as transcending these alternatives: "Everything is there" in these "textes-jouissance."
Describes these texts as full of "violence" and "hate,"
as manifesting the "wild theater" that is in the feminine
imagination; also applauds their "exploding" of words,
their movement, their "rhythm of imperceptible births."
Evokes the centrality of the mother-daughter relation for
these works. Talks about why these texts are disconcerting, particularly their expressing a "femininity" that is
different from the male psychic experience and definition
of femininity: "Women's texts do not stop setting fire to
the Name (of the Father, the Law)." Suggestive but hard.

INTERVIEWS WITH

*   ————, Françoise Collin, et al. "Débats." Le Récit et
     sa représentation. Proceedings from the Colloques de
     Saint-Hubert, May 1977. Paris: Payot, 1978, 133-9.

(See 180).

503 **Olivier, Christiane.** Les enfants de Jocaste: L'empreinte
de la mère. Paris: Denoël/Gonthier, 1980.

Avant-Propos; Discours imaginaire: 1. La conspiration
du silence; 2. Au commencement était Freud; 3. Continent
noir ou plage blanche? 4. Le différent oedipien, origine
de tous les différends; 5. Anatomie ou destin? 6. Souvenir
d'enfance (qui n'est pas de Léonard de Vinci); 7. Le
désert blanc; 8. La toile d'araignée; 9. L'impossible
rencontre; 10. Words ou War; 11. Voyageuse sans bagages;
12. Famille: théâtre moderne pour pièce antique;
Commencements.

A psychoanalytic study of the mother-child relationship
and its consequences for feminine and masculine sexuality.
Sees the care and education of children as a "monosexual"
activity, i.e., the province of women only (c.f., Jocasta,
the mother of Oedipus), and explains how this imbalance
of present mother/absent father causes and perpetuates
misogyny. Begins with a description and critique of
Freud's omission of Jocasta (feminine desire)--the "black
continent"--from his male-centered Oedipal theory and
goes on to write "the other (feminine) psychoanalysis."
Reexamines in detail the asymmetrical experiences of
little girls and boys in which the latter's desire for
the mother is recognized and halted by the incest taboo,
whereas the former's relationship with the mother is
"desexualized"; contends the mother's nonrecognition of
the little girl as a sexualized being leads the girl
later to seek validation of her sexual identity in the
"look," the desire of men. Sees as prime consequence of
this developmental difference the continued refusal and
resentment, on the part of man, of his original desire
for the mother, a resentment that fuels his misogyny.
Claims this reflects the fundamental paradox of misogyny:
it is caused and perpetuated by generation after generation of women mothering in a patriarchal society of
absent fathers. Contains Olivier's personal account of
her childhood ignorance of her sexuality, due to her
body's lack of reference points. Elucidates the precise
stages of female and male adult development, including
men's and women's differing expectations of love: says
woman seeks "unity" in love, the joining of her "subject"
and "object" selves that constitutes her wholeness as a
person. Argues that all women and men must transcend the

vestiges of the original relationship with the mother
that are in them, to achieve a truly successful male/
female sexual relation. Chapter on language locates the
origin of speech at the moment of the birth separation
from the mother and attributes the sexism of language to
its being the possession and product of men (and masculine
fears) only. Says the existing language "annihilates"
women and, for that reason, many feminists are calling
for an authentic, non-alienating, un-censored "feminine
language." Offers as means to combat women's real social
oppression: 1. men's full participation, in the family
and in society, in all the tasks of the "Mother" and
their putting aside their continued "sublimation," thus
giving women, too, access to both regression and sublimation; 2. the "de-idolization" of the Mother and the
establishment of a parental equilibrium, to assure that
"sexualization" does not turn into "sexism." Expresses
the wish to speak for both the woman and the analyst, in
order to maintain "emotion and thought" in its presentation.

504 **Ouvrard, Hélène.** "La littérature féminine québécoise--
une double libération." Culture française No. 4
(Winter 1977), 11-24.

Gives an overview of some of the many female writers
who have emerged from the closed and repressive culture
of Quebec and situates these authors in the "familial"
context of French Canadian society. Sees these women as
"double" victims of both their feminine and Quebecois
conditions. Goes on to examine the works of the most
important post-World War II writers: Gabrielle Roy
(fascinated with geographical "vastness"); Germaine
Guèvremont (novels of the "elsewhere" ['l'ailleurs']);
Anne Hébert (expresses her sense of "being dispossessed);
Marie-Claire Blais (shows a nostalgia for childhood);
Claire Martin and Michèle Mailhot (concerned with women's
experience of love); Monique Bosco and Françoise Loranger
(deal with women's search for identity); Andrée Maillet
(an opening toward other places and cultures); and
political and avant-garde writers such as Loranger and
Louky Bersianik (concerned with "féminitude"). Useful.

505 **Pelzer, Birgit.** "'Ma seule défense est...'" Les Cahiers
du GRIF 7 (June 1975), 28-34.

Hypothesizes about what women's creativity would be
after first looking at the meaning of "creativity" itself:

sees the latter as essentially relational, as dependent
on the individual's relation to the ever-ungraspable yet
present world or reality. Says creativity is a reaction
to and perception of this problematic relation. Opposes
it to "reason," in the sense of "rigorous knowledge,"
and, in sociological terms, to the depersonalizing and
narrowing forces at work in society. Identifies women as
without identity or place in this culture except the ones
assigned to them. Raises possible objections to that
idea, then designates as one aspect of women's creation
the "absence of fixity, of objectivity, of continuous-
ness," the "fluid porousness" most appropriate for
rendering the ambiguity of reality.

506 **Perrein, Michèle.** "Ainsi parle une telle qui écrit."
     Magazine littéraire No. 180 (January 1982), 18-19.

     Gives this novelist's opinion on the existence of a
     "feminine literature": says it has existed since the
     first women writers but that it cannot be defined or
     systematized. Evokes it as a "voice that escapes us" but
     refuses all labels and "ghettos," saying they "kill"
     literature and the freedom it provides.

507 **Philippe, Anne.** "Communication." Liberté Nos. 106-107
     (July-October 1976), 239-43.

     Paper from the "Rencontre québécoise internationale des
     écrivains." Claims it is impossible to separate a
     woman's social and political situation from her function
     as a writer. Writing is "the same as an act of love,"
     though the meaning of that act will vary in each culture.

  * **Porte, Michelle** and Marguerite Duras. Les Lieux de
     Marguerite Duras. Paris: Editions de Minuit, 1977.

     (See 191).

508 **Rabant, Christiane.** "A l'écoute du signifiant 'femme.'"
     Ornicar? 11 (1977), 51-8.

     Discusses Montrelay's ideas about "listening" to the
     discourse of the feminine unconscious or of feminine
     pleasure ("jouissance") (491), saying this "listening"
     takes place in a "space," a "hole," the absence of the
     "verb." Claims Montrelay's writing itself is a manifesta-
     tion of such a discourse. Uses Lacanian theory to compare
     this listening to the metaphorical process that is writ-

ing, both being based on a "substitution" or "metonymy."
Evokes women's writing in psychoanalytic terms of parent-
child dynamics, specifically using Duras's texts as
examples of "passages of the woman to the mother," of
expressions of the "primary" or "feminine" imagination.
Almost unreadable.

509 ―――. "C'ex: temporalités de l'imaginaire." Sorcières
12 (1978), 24-9.

Tries to elucidate the "silence" that is the "impossible description" of women's "jouissance"--that is, a
positive but difficult imaginative expression of the
feminine. Says "femininity" cannot be represented by
existing forms and images, since it is instead the
"rending," the "holes" or openings in the phallic symbolic
fabric. Using Derridean and Lacanian precepts, associates
feminine "jouissance" with "orifices" and "pulsions" and
with a different notion of space and time. Almost
unreadable.

510 Ragland-Sullivan, Ellie. "Jacques Lacan: Feminism and
the Problem of Gender Identity." Sub-Stance 11, No. 36
(1982), 6-20.

Argues forcefully that Lacan's psychoanalytic model is
not phallocentric and, in fact, provides the best
epistemology for feminists wishing to demystify "the
basic causes and differences of sexual personality."
Reviews major elements of the Lacanian paradigm (Desire,
Law, the mirror-stage process, the Phallus, the Real, the
Imaginary, the Symbolic Order...) to demonstrate that
sexual identity "is learned through the dynamics of
identification and language. Contends that by reading
Lacan ideologically and literally Irigaray and other
feminist critics are unable to see in his theory a
blueprint for change based on "informed comprehension of
structural cause and effect." A particularly well-written
piece.

511 Ravelli, Catherine. "De l'intérêt de la féminitude pour
le féminisme." La Revue d'en face 4 (November 1978),
18-23.

Argues persuasively against theories of any "positive"
feminine specificity--in language or in writing--by
saying "féminitude" is a purely negative, externally-
imposed condition. There is, for women (versus other

groups) no pre-oppression community, culture or language
to which they can seek to return. Also rejects the idea
of a "feminine being," of anything described as "of women"
or "as women," since it reintroduces a female "essence"
of which all women become the symbol. Explicitly refutes
Cixous's and Gauthier's theories of a marked "feminine
text" saying such belief in feminine specificity (1)
ghettoizes, (2) generalizes to the point of dogmatism,
and (3) steers away from questioning women's social behavior by merely positing their alienation. Each woman
must make "an examination of the self," of her own "separation from herself."

* **Ribette, Jean-Michel** and Julia Kristeva. <u>Folle vérité:</u>
   <u>Vérité et vraisemblance du texte psychotique.</u> Paris:
   Seuil, 1979

   (See 380).

512 **Richman, Michèle.** "Eroticism in the Patriarchal Order."
   <u>Diacritics</u> (Spring 1976), 46-53.

   An appraisal of George Bataille's contributions to an
   understanding of eroticism and the role of women in
   society. Explains Bataille's debt to Mauss's "essay on
   the gift," and describes his notion of eroticism as gift
   ("dépense"), loss of self, and violence, a mechanism
   through which society discharges its need for disruption
   and excess. Illustrates this thesis through references
   to his novels, in particular, the mother/son relationship
   in "Ma mère." Makes comparisons with Lévi-Strauss, who
   is criticized for an overly economic and insufficiently
   ideological approach.

513 **Righini, Mariella.** <u>Ecoute ma différence.</u> Paris: Grasset,
   1978.

   Préface; "Appelez-moi Lilith"; "L'autre que je suis";
   "Le sempiternel féminin"; "A la manière d'eux"; "Ce mal
   étrange venu d'ailleurs"; J'écris ton nom: identité"; "Le
   premier sexe"; "Elle était une fois"; "Culture baroque";
   "Parfum de femme"; "Toutes en lèvres."

   Strongly defends sexual physiological and psychological
   difference and argues against such feminist ideas as
   "androgyny" or "equality": "I have never had the slight-
   est doubt about my difference. It is manifest, visible,
   tangible...incontestable." Says "equality" is merely the

giving up of one's female self in order to identify with
and appropriate masculine culture; calls equality only a
step on the way to fully asserting "féminitude" and
claiming feminine identity. Blames masculine culture for
"killing" women's true selves and for punishing noncon-
formist women as "hysterics" and "witches." Espouses a
highly individualist affirmation of self as woman, con-
signing feminist group contestation to the past. Exalts
maternity as women's triumph. Decries the "monosexism"
of language, history and culture in which the masculine
is the norm and calls for a more "feminine" humanity.
Ends with a discussion of women's polarized relation to
the dominant discourse: either they adopt it or they
remain silent. Applauds the explosion of the "feminine
word" in France and sides with the belief in a "feminine
writing" of the body. Rather oversimplified.

514 **Rivière, Anne** and Xavière Gauthier. "Des femmes et leurs
     oeuvres." _Magazine littéraire_ No. 180 (January 1982),
     36-41.

     A list of important books by French women that appeared
     from 1972 to 1982. Gives brief commentaries provided by
     some of the authors listed. Useful.

515 ————. "Il y a de l'extérieur." _Sorcières_ 12 (1978),
     10-13.

     Rejects the dichotomy for women between accepting mascu-
     line standards of research and refusing them in favor of
     "feminine" kinds of work and calls for an alternative: an
     other (woman's) theory. Says women must free themselves
     of their stance of denial toward knowledge--a stance that
     reinforces traditional masculine definitions of Truth--and
     take upon themselves the authority to elaborate the struc-
     tures of their work. Obscure.

Rochefort, Christiane:

BOOKS AND COLLECTIONS OF ESSAYS

516 ————. _C'est bizarre l'écriture: Récit._ Paris:
     Grasset, 1970.

     Seeks to demystify the process of writing a book by
     telling the "real facts," from start to finish, of the
     experience that became her novel _Une rose pour Morrison_
     (1964). In a personal, funny and associational account

that criticizes the profusion of "obscure" and "discursive" literary commentaries (which she calls "masturba-
tion"), follows her journal record of her daily work.
Traces the internal sources of her book, its character
development, her self-criticism, and her rewriting. The
question of writing as act, not thought, and the concomitant problem of language, which she, an "over-literate,"
has received as a borrowed whole, are central for
Rochefort: "To really write is to un-write," that is to
"write oneself." "Writing is an act of love."

ESSAYS AND ARTICLES

517   ———. "Are Women Writers Still Monsters?" New French
        Feminisms: An Anthology. Ed. Elaine Marks and Isabelle
        de Courtivron. Amherst: University of Massachusetts
        Press, 1980, 183-6.

        Portion of a speech given at the University of Wiscon-
        sin in 1975. Decries the over-determination of women
        authors, who are inevitably viewed first and essentially
        as women. Explains her own response to such a personal
        kind of criticism: says she "blinded" herself to her
        femaleness and thought of herself as an individual. Also
        speaks of the traditional male disdain for and suppression
        of women's writing. Claims literature has no sex but
        that women, because of their particular experience,
        history and ways of thinking, have a different relation-
        ship to writing.

518   ———. "Communication." Liberté Nos. 106-107 (July-
        October 1976), 113-22.

        Paper from the "Rencontre québécoise internationale des
        écrivains." Uses Rochefort's experience and that of
        other women writers in history to argue that writing is
        inseparable from oppression. Calls for a refusal and
        destruction of the "dominant ideology," which is the only
        language we have. Wanders a bit.

INTERVIEWS WITH

519   Arsène, Cécile. "The Privilege of Consciousness."
        Homosexualities and French Literature. Ed. George
        Stambolian and Elaine Marks. Ithaca: Cornell
        University Press, 1979, 101-13.

        Situates sexuality in writing in the context of the

writer-reader relationship, advocating "intimacy" and
communication, rather than the "sadistic" relationship
with a "dominating" author that characterizes "formalist,"
"intellectual" texts. Rejects social labels and roles,
specifically those imposed on homosexuals, and encourages
the transcending of social oppression. Says it is
important to draw inspiration from one's experience of
oppression and to use that creativity to break social
barriers. Cites Wittig as an example of a writer who
refuses feminine roles and who exalts female sexuality in
her revolt.

520   Crochet, Monique. "Entretien avec Christiane Roche-
       fort." The French Review 54, No. 3 (February 1981),
       428-35.

       Rejects the idea of a "feminine style," saying it
       perpetuates women's role as the "colonized," and opts for
       literary revolt on the level of social morality. Calls
       for social protest against bourgeois morality, which for
       Rochefort includes freeing herself from the constraints
       of traditional literary conventions.

  *   Green, Mary Jean, et al. "An Interview with Christiane
       Rochefort."

       (See 521).

  *   Higgins, Lynn, et al. "An Interview with Christiane
       Rochefort."

       (See 521).

521   Hirsch, Marianne, Mary Jean Green, and Lynn Higgins. "An
       Interview with Christiane Rochefort." L'Espirt créateur
       19, No. 2 (Summer 1979), 107-20.

       Talks about language and writing as social instruments
       that have affected the lives of women and all oppressed
       groups. Speaks of the personal consequences of her own
       decision to write and to challenge the "good writing" of
       the "master." Insists on the importance of creating new
       symbolic universes that contest existing structures of
       desire and power. Gives concrete examples of the
       devastation wrought by social exploitation, calling upon
       writers to confront those issues and to communicate with
       their readers.

522 **Rollin, Marie-Simone.** "L'être ou l'anéantie." <u>Sorcières</u>
     12 (1978), 14-16.

     Describes the excitement and difficulty of her encounter
     with Hegelian theory in its full vitality, rather than
     its simplified explicated form. Says women can theorize
     "from themselves" to change an "intolerable world."
     Opaque.

523 **Rubin, Gabrielle.** <u>Les Sources inconscientes de la
     misogynie</u>. Paris: Robert Laffont, 1977.

     Préface; Introduction; La prématuration; Le Désir de
     retour; L'Interdit fondateur; Le premier objet d'amour;
     Naissance de la Loi; La place du père; La Phantasmère; La
     Grande Déesse; Le société et l'amour; L'acquisition de la
     maîtrise; Le phallus et le pouvoir; Le prototype maternel;
     La méconnaissance de la Loi; Psychanalyse et science-
     fiction; Les dents et le sang; La femme dans le roman
     policier; Conclusion.

     A psychological and anthropological inquiry into the
     source of universal sexual asymmetry and inequality that
     privileges the differing male/female relationship to the
     mother. Focuses on the child's earliest months when both
     girl and boy are attached to the "all-powerful" mother,
     which it calls the "Phantasmère." Says this primordial
     mother is "repressed' and that misogynistic attitudes are
     reflective of ongoing unconscious hate of the original
     mother. Sections of this unified study are as follows:
        "Introduction"--Posits that misogyny, in the form of
     both denigration and idealization of woman, served a
     specific psychological purpose in the past. Stating that
     misogyny is "a fact of culture and not a fact of nature,"
     gives many examples from anthropology of the universal
     absence of female power. Contrasts woman's real, lived
     inferiorization with the "phantasmic" power she possesses
     in the human unconscious, calling this "cleavage" the
     "symptom" of a profound "trauma" that our ancestors
     resolved by subjugating women.
        "La prématuration"--Situates the origin of misogyny at
     the "birth of Man," when the incest taboo was instated.
     Points to the fact that the newborn human, female and
     male, is totally incapable of caring for itself, whence
     its powerful attachment to its mother. Calls this bond
     "the principal source of misogyny."

"Le désir de retour"--Contrasts the human evolution
toward physiological independence with the ongoing
psychological need for maternal protection, with the
latter dominating. Says the latter has made for our
positive creative spirit, but also our mastering and
destructive intellect. Describes the conflict between
the desire to return to the womb and the wish to dominate
the maternal and sees the incest taboo as a way to
counterbalance primordial maternal power.

"L'interdit fondateur"--Asserts that society's way of
preventing the desired "return to the mother" (and
dependency on her) is the incest taboo and that this
taboo is "the foundation of civilization." Looks into
whether this taboo is a "fact of nature" or a "fact of
culture" and determines it is at the juncture of the two.

"Le premier objet d'amour"--Says that the existence of
a law against incest presupposes a desire for incest and
that both the prohibition and the desire exist on the
level of "phantasies." Traces the differing experiences
of girls and boys in relation to this wish for "fusion"
with the mother.

"Naissance de la Loi"--Looks at the beginnings of
humankind to find the moment when the incest taboo began
and speculates it was the time man understood his role in
procreation.

"La place du père"--Claims that the realization that
men participated in procreation caused a reaction against
the preceding order, that of the "Great Goddess." Says
individual desires to "kill" the Mother coalesced into a
real group debasement of woman and the elevation of the
Father.

"La Phantasmère"--Gives examples of the unconscious
need to debase woman, a need in which the "phantasmatic
Mother" is confused with real women. Calls this
confusion the "heart" of misogyny. Describes the
"Phantasmère" as the "Great Goddess" into which the real
mother is transformed in every child's psyche and
outlines this transformation process in Freudian terms.

"La Grande Déesse"--Repeats the importance of the
primitive "Great Goddess" and her earthly counterpart,
the "all-powerful Mother." Cites anthropological
evidence of mother/goddess worship. Interprets circum-
cision of Jewish boys as symbol of a break with the
mother and alliance with the father. Sees the Christian
dichotomy between virgin and whore as reinforcing the
incest taboo.

"La société et l'amour"--Explains how the incest taboo,
by closing off the "primitive" channel for sexual energy,

led to the diverse expressions of that energy in
civilization, thus making culture dependent on sexual
repression and the renunciation of the Mother. As a
result, the "incestuous fixation" lodges itself in the
unconscious and sexuality and love remain repressed.

"L'acquisition de la maîtrise"--Summarizes the
evolution from birth to adulthood, from dependency to
independence, or from the "status of object" to that of a
"subject." Uses Freudian and Lacanian framework.

"Le phallus et le pouvoir"--Posits that "the fear of
losing the phallus" obliges the child to renounce the
first love object, the Mother. Distinguishes "phallus"
from "penis" in order to distinguish female from male
Oedipal dynamics. Refuses the Freudian monolithic model
of development based on the penis, saying the "penis
envy" theory is based on the inferiorization of woman.

"Le prototype maternel"--Reinterprets the male and
female Oedipal processes in a way that makes them fully
parallel and ascribes more autonomy to the girl. Discusses the confusion of the adult love object with the
Mother. Sees a possible cure for misogyny in separating
the "Phantasmère" from real women.

"La méconnaissance de la Loi"--Shows what happens when
the incest taboo is not respected: child psychosis occurs
(e.g., autism).

"Psychanalyse et science-fiction"--Illustrates the real
confusion that exists between the "phantasmère" and women
through mythological and literary examples, especially
from science fiction. Makes the claim that science
fiction has a particularly strong tie to the unconscious.

"Les dents et le sang"--Finds in cultural customs, as
in science fiction, the same mixture of inferiorization
and overevaluation of woman. Takes the image of the
"vagin denté" ("toothed vagina") and the myths about
menstruation as examples of the fear of maternal power
that persists.

"La femme dans le roman policier"--Sees detective
novels as reflecting "the myths of our time" and thus as
a repository of modern folklore regarding women. Finds
the same evil/virtuous feminine imagery.

"Conclusion"--Describes the consequence of the woman/
mother confusion for love: individuals search in love to
regain their original unity, but often they seek an
impossible "absolute" or "crazy" love. Offers as a
beginning of a solution for misogyny the equal recognition
of responsibility by women and men for the creation of
the negative image of the "Phantasmère; and the definitive
renunciation of the "Phantasmère" through truly adult

love relationships. Says adult love implies the full
development of both partners. Much internal repetition
but informative.

524 **Salomé, Lou Andréas.** "La Femme du ressentiment." La
     Barre du jour No. 50 (Winter 1975), 65-77.

Claims, in an apostrophe to Salomé's lesbian lover, to
be writing done in the author's "own name" and in "all
[her] bisexuality."

525 **Santos, Emma.** Ecris et tais-toi. Paris: Stock, 1978.

Evokes in harsh, disconnected, telegraphic style the
author's past descent towards psychological destruction
and hospitalization and her subsequent ascent towards
life and writing. Claims, "They have forced us [women]
to write--writing is feminine, speech is feminine," since
women have always, until now, been deprived of the means
to express their sex. Ends with the defiant challenge
that she will listen to no one's advice:..." she now has
"only her sex," and "that [my sex] I will never sell to
them by using men's words and language."

526 **Savary, Claire.** "Quand Lacan manque la femme ou du
     manque de l'écriture féminine chez Lacan." Chroniques
     1, Nos. 6-7 (June-July 1975), 90-6.

Criticizes Lacan's phallocentric approach--his failure
to "work as much from the feminine to the masculine as
from the masculine to the feminine"--and gives various
examples. Affirms that women, like men, are subjects.
They can participate in the Symbolic, experience Desire,
and write, without becoming men. Both poetic and
discursive.

527 **Schiff, Dominique.** "Sciences exactes." Sorcières 12
     (1978), 31-2.

Traces women's traditional relationship to theory as
formed by social ideals of female conformity, submission
and imitation, rather than autonomy. Says women therefore do not express their "desire" to know.

528 **Schneider, Monique.** Freud et le plaisir. Paris: Denoël,
     1980.

Part I--Sous le signe de la faute: 1. "La nocivité

sexuelle"; 2. Le père coupable; 3. Lieux et contours de
la séductrice; 4. Le procès de la sorcière et le recours
à Oedipe; Part II--La nécessité théorique ou le plaisir
maîtrisé: 1. Le plaisir comme menace; 2. L'excitation
maîtrisée; 3. Le sadisme comme paradigme; 4. La faille du
plaisir; Part III--"J'ai succombé au charme..."; 1. Le
paradoxe du plaisir sexuel; 2. Entre les mains d'un
créateur; 3. Au-delà: L'excitation sacrilège

   Using Freud's texts and correspondence, analyzes how
his discussion of "pleasure" is always double: his
defense of the liberation of repressed pleasure is
accompanied by an "accusation," a prohibition against
transgression of the "Law"; in other words, sexual
pleasure as therapeutic "solution" is always linked to
pleasure as the "etiology of neuroses." Goes on in the
first part to trace Freud's ideas on these dual aspects
of pleasure, the beneficial and the dangerous: the
introduction of the Father in Freud's elaboration of the
sexual "drama" as "protector" against a "fall into the
void," as well as seducer/agent of trauma and neurosis.
Discusses Freud's abandoning of the question of seduction
(paternal or maternal) to elaborate his Oedipal theory,
in which the active mother-seductress is rendered an
object ("This [maternal] figure is indissolubly threat of
punishment and threat of pleasure," force of life and
force of death). Sees Freud's "erection" of a "vertical
and superhuman" paternal figure as the "killing" of the
Mother. In the second part, examines how the "maternal"
continued to haunt Freud's research, as evident in his
ongoing "assault" on it through "theoretical conquest."
Says "knowledge" confronts its adversary, "pleasure," and
pleasure (the maternal) is no longer presented as inert,
but as an increasingly active and "pulsionistic" force to
be mastered. Discusses the diads of sadistic/masochistic
impulses and voyeurism/exhibitionism in light of this
conflictual model. Contends the "abandoning of the
archaic mother" is the defeat of the dangerous "woman,"
the figure responsible for pleasure and "perdition" in
Freud's moralizing system. In the third part, compares
particular texts of Freud to show how they reveal, in
style and theme, his paradoxical attitude toward pleasure
and how they represent the ways both theoretical mastery
and empirical recognition of pleasure coexist in his
works. Says this "cleavage" between feminine and
masculine principles (passivity and mastery, respectively) is somewhat attenuated in his work on aesthetics,
where the artist navigates and mediates between the two

domains. Examines the psycho-sexual dynamics of the
Freudian conception of the artist and identifies his
"tragic" depiction of Leonardo's destiny as artist with
Freud's own necessarily "tragic" acknowledgment of the
inevitability of pleasure. Clear but somewhat
specialized.

529 ─────. La Parole et l'inceste: de l'enclos linguistique
à la liturgie psychanalytique. Paris: Aubier Montaigne,
1980.

Introduction: La parole désenvoûtée ou l'utopie d'un
métalangage; Le langage, le sacré et le matricide
fondateur; La défense linguistique contre la matrice
émotionnelle; L'espace de la parole. Un nouvel horizon
linguistique; L'interprétation et la parole souillée;
L'inceste et la parole.

A highly specialized study that combines linguistic and
psychoanalytic precepts in order to "demystify" the
belief that language "informs" or conveys truth. The
introduction traces the modern, post-Saussurian understanding of language as relational, as dynamic process
rather than the enunciation of static objects. Puts into
question the research process and the traditional belief
in the researcher's role as external observer, as well as
the idea that his/her observations can be rendered in
"neutral" or scientific language. Says this myth of a
"superior," informed, theoretical discourse depends on
the existence of a "benighted," unprocessed, "mythic"
language, like that of witchcraft. Goes on to evoke this
non-theoretical discourse as the expression of the
"maternal." Suggests the only linguistic truth is not
the mastery of science over myth, but the ongoing
confrontation between the two discourses, one that is
particularly evident in the privileged situation of the
psychoanalytic session. Sections are as follows:
Le langage, le sacré et le matricide fondateur—joins
Saussure's destruction of the transparency of meaning
(his linguistic revolution) with Freud's ideas about the
"wounds" inflicted by knowledge (the psychoanalytic
revolution). Examines the Freudian separation between
and theory of evolution from the "affective narcissism"
associated with the mother to the "knowledge" associated
with the father, along with the "matricide" the latter
performs on the former. Evokes this "violent passage"
from the mother to the father through mythological,
biblical and literary representations. Sees the scien-

tific discourse of psychoanalysis also as trying to
diagnose or "master" the magical language of the unconscious (the maternal). Looks at the Oedipal story in
light of the destruction of original maternal power it
represents.

La défense linguistique contre la matrice émotionnelle--
interrogates methodologically the theory of the maternal-
paternal passage toward language, saying it presupposes
the existence of a "pure" language or knowledge and of a
"neutral" point of observation. Likens this method and
the process it describes to a sacred "purification" in
which a "sacrifice" (of the maternal) is performed.
Investigates more closely linguistic theory (specifically,
Jakobson's model) on the acquisition of language as the
crossing of a "threshold" at a "decisive moment."

L'espace et la parole--Studies Wittgenstein's ideas
about the "multiple movements of structuration or
signification," that is, his dynamic model of language
formation that resists "enclosing" the process. Discusses
the various kinds of languages, verbal and "body," and
the relegation of "marginal" or rejected forms to the
domain of art and artistic expression.

L'interprétation et la parole souillée--Elaborates
Lacan's "ironic" or internally double hypothesis about
"ascension" to language or the symbolic, including his
reinterpretation of the Oedipal myth and his privileging
of the paternal figure, at the expense of the maternal
one. Talks about the Oedipal "paradox," or Oedipus's
representing at once the prohibition of and the desire
for incest.

L'inceste et la parole--Posits that "jumping" into and
examining the psychoanalytic session as if it were an
isolated, "virgin" situation is a myth. Opts instead for
reading the psychoanalytic "text" that is enunciated
there in combination with the analyst's interpretive text
(e.g., reading Freud's work on dreams). Describes the
relation of the "word" articulated in analysis to
subjectivity, metaphorization, and transgression, and
claims the patient's word is inevitably made "guilty" by
its existing in reference to the analyst's word, the
"law." But sees the maternal dimension as present in the
effect of remembering the patient experiences--the sense
of prior recognition--in hearing the analyst's word.
Ends with an examination of Freud and his patient, Dora,
that focuses on the "language act" or the dramatic action
that occurs between the two during their psychoanalytic/
interpretive encounter. Difficult.

530 **Schor, Naomi.** "Female Paranoia: The Case for Psycho-
     analytic Feminist Criticism." <u>Yale French Studies</u>
     No. 62 (1981), 204-19.

Posits that there is little feminist literary criticism
that uses a feminist psychoanalytic perspective and goes
on to "outline a new (psychoanalytic) feminist thematics
grounded in (psychoanalytic) feminist hermeneutics."
Proceeds, first, by analyzing one of Freud's minor essays
on femininity to explore at once correlations between
"theory" and "paranoia" and presumed differences between
male and female theory building--female theorizing being
associated with madness and deviance. Takes from Freud
the basing of paranoia/theory in woman's body and uses
that grounding to claim that female theory "is, by
definition, a materialism riveted to the body." Then,
considers another element of Freud's text, his focus on
the role of the "clitoris" in woman's paranoia, and
elaborates on the "clitoral" function (versus "vaginal
function") in female theory. Sees recent French feminist
theory on women's writing as "vaginal" in focus. In
contrast, declares that "the clitoris is coextensive with
detail" or a "clitoral" analysis with a detailed reading
of what has "generally been ignored by male critics."
Concludes by illustrating this approach through a reading
of Poe's tale, <u>The Mystery of Marie Roget</u>. Bold and
suggestive.

531 ————. "Le Sourire du spinx: Zola et l'image de la
     féminité." <u>Romantisme</u> Nos. 13-14 (1976), 183-95.

Applies Freud's theory of female sexuality and Barthes's
hermeneutic code to a study of the enigma of femininity
in Zola's work. Postulates that "the femininity of a
character creates from the start an enigma whose solution
will not necessarily coincide with the ending of the
text." A comparison of <u>Nana</u> and <u>Une Page d'amour</u> reveals
woman as both "médusante" (the unknown of desire that
traps men) and "médusée" (ignorant of or estranged from
her own sexuality). Affirms that applying the hieratic
code to gyneco-centric nineteenth century fiction brings
out the prevalent mytho-pathology expressed in the semantic network of woman, writing, and marble. Corroborates
her thesis by sketching the narrative structures of
Balzac's <u>Peau de chagrin</u>. Concludes with an appeal for a
risk-taking reading ("une lecture non-sécurisante") of
Zola, for the recognition of the importance of the
unknown and the unknowable in his works.

* **Sève, Lucien,** Catherine Clément, and Pierre Bruno.
  <u>Pour une critique marxiste de la théorie psychana-</u>
  <u>lytique</u>. Paris: Editions Sociales, 1973.

  (See 141).

* **Soquet, Jeanne** and Suzanne Horer. <u>La création étouffee</u>.
  Paris: Pierre Horay, 1973.

  (See 302)

532 **Stambolian, George** and Elaine Marks, eds. <u>Homosexuali-</u>
     <u>ties and French Literature</u>. Ithaca: Cornell University
     <u>Press</u>, 1979.

  Preface: "Considerations of a Transfuge," Richard
  Howard; "Introduction," George Stambolian and Elaine
  Marks; Cultural Contexts: "Sexual and Literary," Robert
  Champigny; "Sexuality: A Fact of Discourse," interview
  with Serge Leclaire; "A Liberation of Desire," interview
  with Félix Guattari; "Rethinking Differences," interview
  with Hélène Cixous (117); "What Interests Me Is Eroti-
  cism," interview with Alain Robbe-Grillet; "The Privilege
  of Consciousness," interview with Christiane Rochefort
  (519); "Paradigm," Monique Wittig (547); "We are in
  History," interview with Eric Bentley; "Triumphs and
  Tribulations of the Homosexual Discourse," Jean-Paul Aron
  and Roger Kempf; Critical Texts: "Homosexuality and the
  French Enlightenment," Jacob Stockinger; "The Homosexual
  Paradigm in Balzac, Gide, and Genet," Gerald H. Storzer;
  "Weak Men and Fatal Women: The Sand Image," Isabelle de
  Courtivron; "Visions of Violence: Rimbaud and Verlaine,"
  Paul Schmidt; "Sexuality in Gide's Self-Portrait,"
  Wallace Fowlie; "The Myth and Science of Homosexuality in
  "A la recherche du temps perdu," J. E. Rivers; "Cocteau's
  Sexual Equation," René Galand; "The Religious Metaphors
  of a Married Homosexual: Marcel Jouhandeau's <u>Chronique</u>
  <u>d'une passion</u>," Frank Paul Bowman; "Sartre's <u>Homo/</u>
  Textuality: Eating/The Other," George H. Bauer; "Sartre's
  <u>La nausée</u>: Fragment of an Analytic Reading," Serge
  Doubrovsky; "Toward a Literature of Utopia," Stephen
  Smith; "Lesbian Intertextuality," Elaine Marks (487).

  A collection of interviews and essays that explores
  homosexuality--as a textual tradition and as a multifaceted instrument for the re-evaluation of cultural
  assumptions about language, literature, sexuality, and

their articulation. Several texts illustrate aspects of
recent feminist inquiry.

Théoret, France:

ESSAYS AND ARTICLES

533 ————. "Au retour du refoulé, la fiction." Chroniques
1, Nos. 6-7 (June-July 1975), 109-12.

A series of reflections on language and writing that
includes several comments on the specificity of women.
Explores at greatest length whether fiction can be an
agent of change and if so in what ways.

534 ————. "Cochonnerie." La Barre du jour Nos. 56-57 (May-
August 1977), 12-19.

In a series of spontaneous, pulsionistic fragments,
rejects the writing and language of the "already-in-place,
the already-read, the already-said." Reclaims the
silenced "hysteric," or the dangerous language of the
repressed imagination, of desire, that must express
itself. Disconnected but suggestive.

535 ————. "Communication." Liberté Nos. 106-107 (July-
October 1976), 122-25.

Paper from the "Rencontre québécoise internationale des
écrivains." Distinguishes between "non-feminist" and
"feminist" women writers in this discussion of women's
fictional texts: the former write with "the same preoccupations as men," the latter write from "reflection on
their situation as women." Claims "women's writing will
be one of intervention and lucidity, or else it will work
against women themselves." Ardently espouses "texts of
struggle," those of women "living in their novels."

536 ————. "Dépendances." La Barre du jour No. 50 (Winter
1975), 28-30.

Outlines a two-step strategy for women to come to writing and, ultimately, to transform it: first, "decenter
knowledge" by introducing women as subjects into life and
history. This stage requires perfectly clear language and
not "poetic confusion." Second, once women are individually and collectively rooted in history, write fiction.

* ———— and Nicole Brossard. "Préface." La Nef des
  sorcières. Montreal: Quinze, 1976, 7-13.

  (See 55).

* ————, Nicole Brossard, Madeleine Gagnon, et al.
  "Tables rondes." Revue de l'Université d'Ottawa/
  University of Ottawa Quarterly 50, No. 1 (January-March
  1980), 9-29.

  (See 59).

537 ————. "Une Voix pour Odile." La Barre du jour No. 50
  (Winter 1975), 30-6.

  Demonstrates, in stream-of-consciousness style, a
  "fiction" whose source is "where [Théoret] has come from"
  and "where [she] is" now. Honors Odile, a maternal
  reference both to Théoret's own mother and to all her
  Quebecois foremothers, "progenitors of living-dead" whose
  history is "silence and death." Difficult to read.

* **Thomas, Ann,** Viviane Forrester, and Monique Wittig.
  "Virginia Woolf, précurseur du mouvement de libération
  des femmes." Viviane Forrester. Virginia Woolf.
  Paris: O.R.T.F. et La Quinzaine littéraire, 1973, 51-64.

  (See 239).

538 **Turkle, Sherry.** Psychoanalytic Politics: Freud's French
  Revolution. New York: Basic Books, 1978.

  Introduction: "Freud's French Revolution"; Part One:
  The French Freud: 1. The Social Roots of Psychoanalytic
  Culture; 2. "Reinventing" Freud in France; 3. May 1968
  and Psychoanalytic Ideology; Part Two: Politics in
  Psychoanalysis: 4. For or Against Lacan; 5. Psychoana-
  lytic Societies and Psychoanalytic Science; Part Three:
  Psychoanalysis in Politics: 6. Psychoanalysis as Schizo-
  analysis: Antipsychiatry; 7. Psychoanalysis as Science:
  The University; Part Four: Psychoanalysis in Popular
  Culture: 8. Psychoanalysis as Popular Culture: The Perils
  of Popularity; 9. "Saving French Freud"; Conclusion:
  "From May 1968 to the New Philosophy"; Epilogue: "Lacan
  in America: Poetry and Science."

An extremely informative and useful entry into the
current relationship of psychoanalysis to French culture,
a relationship described as shifting in May 1968 from
resistance to "infatuation." Contrasts the initial
American and French receptions of Freud and the very
different directions psychoanalytic interpretation and
practice have taken in the two countries: American
"therapy" is optimistic and centered on personal change
and "cure," whereas French psychoanalysis is a theoretical
"science" concerned with understanding and "listening,"
rather than curing. Explains the post-1968 appeal of
psychoanalysis in France for political and social
activists—including feminists—by focusing on Lacan, the
figure who "reinvented" Freud and who introduced "new
forms of social criticism" that adapted well to French
radical politics. Describes the profound ideological
conflicts within the French psychoanalytic community.
Raises questions about the fundamentally contradictory
nature of analysis in France: it is "resolutely anti-
institutional" and subversive, yet it is based on the
institutionalized structure of teacher/disciple, analyst/
analysand. Highly recommended.

539 **Tytell, Pamela.** "Lacune aux U.S.A." L'Arc 58 (1974),
     79-82.

Identifies the causes of the "ideological resistance"
among American psychoanalysts to Lacanian thought: the
difficulty of his writings; the problem of terminology
and translation; and the differing conceptions of the
unconscious in the two cultures, stemming from their
different intellectual traditions. Says certain American
universities are opening the door to Lacan, especially
departments of literature and philosophy, though cautions
that the American literary discourse on Lacan may in fact
be contrary to his aims. Argues for the importance of
Lacanian thought for feminism: it offers a thorough
analysis of sexual oppression—material, ideological,
linguistic—that goes far beyond simple "biologizing"
arguments.

540 **Vaillancourt, Marie-Claire.** "Les agissements en rupture
     d'une écriture continue: sans discernement." La
     Nouvelle barre du jour Nos. 90-91 (May 1980), 139-43.

Evokes women's writing as "resisting" conformist thought
and as participating in a continuous "disordering" and

"decentering." Uses Derridean terms to describe women's
writing as a "departure" from this world and as the
creation of another universe.

541 **"Variations sur des thèmes communs."** <u>Questions féministes</u>
     1 (November 1977), 3-19.

Announces publication of this "theoretical" journal and
introduces the themes and problems it will address.
First, defines the "theory" it will practice as an
"analysis" of women's oppression" that will take varied
forms and will be comprehensible to all. Advocates a
"feminist science" that will examine women's "real"
material oppression and question the traditional discourse
of the "human sciences." Then, identifies its political
perspective as "radical," one that refuses all "natural-
ist" or "essentialist" definitions of women (including
what it calls "neo-feminine" claims of sexual difference)
and looks to social context. Also rejects the idea that
thought or language are "masculine," saying rather that
they are "based on power relationships" and hierarchy,
not biological agency. Denies the notion of "principal"
and "secondary" political struggles within traditional
political frameworks. Further, examines in detail the
different "tactical positions" within the feminist movement: (1) Marxist, which, it says, does not sufficiently
analyze women's oppression and looks basically at class
struggle only; (2) neo-essentialist, by which it refers
to currents seeking a specific "women's language," a "language of the body," or definitions of sexual difference--
all of which it deems dangerous for being "a-social,"
"a-historical," and a-conceptual. Says they all reinforce
masculine myths of women. Criticizes the re-valorization
of women as "witches" as reaffirming Church doctrine; and
(3) "egalitarian," which seeks "equality" with men--
impossible, it argues, in a culture in which men are
oppressors. Calls instead for "the destruction of the
"patriarchal system." Afterwards, considers the three
"moments" in the evolution of women's struggle: "femininity," or the stage of acceptance; "feminitude," or recognition of a collective cultural identity as women; and
"feminism," or the movement to attack the social roots of
oppression. Finally, elucidates the relation between the
political and the biological, as it has deterined women's
condition and as it now justifies a separate women's
struggle. Persuasive.

541a   Trans. as "Variations on Some Common Themes" in
        Feminist Issues No. 1 (Summer 1980), 3-21.

541b   Partially trans. in (19).

542 Vilaine, Anne-Marie de. "Le corps de la théorie."
     Magazine littéraire No. 180 (January 1982), 25-8.

     Calls recent "theoretical" texts by women, in Barthes's
     words, at once "the movement of a break (with the past)
     and the movement of a new beginning." Situates Kristeva's
     "negative" texts in the first group (see 376) and psycho-
     analytic texts on the relation of the unconscious to the
     feminine in the second (e.g., Irigaray's Speculum (314)
     and Ce sexe qui n'en est pas un (309); Schneider's De
     l'exorcisme à la psychanalyse). Summarizes the main ideas
     of these and other theoreticians (Montrelay, L'ombre et le
     nom (491); Lemoine-Luccioni, Partage de femmes (480);
     Leclerc, Parole de femme (469) and Epousailles (468);
     Cixous, La jeune née (138)). Refers to books that deal
     with female identity and the place of the woman writer
     (Garcia, Promenade femmilière (272); Herrmann, Les
     voleuses de langue (293); Didier, L'écriture-femme (6),
     and also points to the number of "texts/dialogues" written
     by two women bouncing their thoughts off one another
     (e.g., Clément and Cixous, La jeune née (138); Duras and
     Gauthier, Les parleuses (192). Concludes by saying that
     this diverse research into the feminine has led to the
     emergence of new values. Useful general introduction to
     some major authors.

543 Villemaire, Yolande. "Pour une parthénogenèse de la
     parole 'hystérique' (matrice vierge)." La Barre du
     jour No. 50 (Winter 1975), 37-44.

     Uses the central image of "hysteria" to evoke both the
     psychic dynamics that produce women's writing ("a nervous
     pregnancy") and the form of that writing ("unreadable
     ravings" combined with a collage of visual images). Is
     itself an example of such a "pre-text" that is incompat-
     ible with the patriarchal model. Succeeds in being
     unreadable.

544 Weksler, Malka and Evelyne Guedj. Quand les femmes se
     disent. Paris: Seuil, 1975.

     Tries to follow in the spirit of Duras's and Gauthier's
     les Parleuses (192) by having women "just speak as women,

because they are women." In personal and popularized
language, traces each author's individual path towards
leftist, then feminist politics. Also includes interviews
with American women in the Socialist Worker's Party.

Wittig, Monique:

ESSAYS AND ARTICLES

545 ───────. "The Category of Sex." Feminist Issues 2, No. 2
        (Fall 1982), 63-8.

A brief but compelling and well-paced development of an
argument about sexual dominance: its nature, sources, and
consequences. Takes us step-by-step from Wittig's
premise--"It is oppression that creates sex and not the
contrary"--to the effects of sex as a category on women.
Vehemently rejects any notion of a "natural" sexual
difference that could "explain" women's oppression,
saying such a notion instead emanates from the "dominant
thought" that justifies existing social structures of
"slavery." Claims that since dominance is a social, not
natural phenomenon, the category of sex does not exist a
priori, before society. Characterizes the systems of
dominance that posit an a priori sexual difference and
that affect all women as metaphysical/ontological,
scientific, and Marxist/economic. Also explains how the
category of sex "founds society as ("naturally")
heterosexual," thus imposing on women the compulsory
reproduction of the species. Sees as a further consequence of the category of sex the assimilation of women
only to that category: they cannot ever be "outside of"
their identities as sexual beings. Concludes, "The
category of sex is a totalitarian one"--whence its
complete political, legal, mental and physical grip on
women's lives--and must therefore be abolished. Builds
up and weaves a difficult but subtle line of reasoning.

546 ───────. "On ne naît pas femme." Questions féministes 8
        (May 1980), 75-84.

Argues, as outlined in the English synopsis at the end,
for a "materialist feminism," which "aims at conquering
the status of subject" as traditionally defined by
culture. Sees lesbianism as a way of "acting out" this
materialist feminism. Takes issue with current "cultural
feminist" and "neo-Darwinian" views that look either to
biology or to the "sex-class division of labor" for the

cause of women's oppression. Both these views, Wittig
claims, are ineffectual and dangerous: the first is
limited, for it "implies that society is founded on
heterosexuality"; the second "stands in the way of...anal-
ysis" by "naturalizing" the situation of the oppressed.
Claims, "We must destroy the political categories of
'women' and 'men.'"

546a   Trans. as "One is not Born a Woman" in Feminist
        Issues No. 2 (1980).

547   _____. "Paradigm." Homosexualities and French Litera-
        ture. Ed. George Stambolian and Elaine Marks. Ithaca:
        Cornell University Press, 1979, 114-21.

Calls for a new conception of female sexuality based
upon pleasure, not reproduction and the heterosexual
enslavement of women. Argues that lesbianism is the
mechanism by which this new conception will be realized,
since "lesbian," unlike "woman," is a positive term
signifying a healthy, unoppressed sexual identity. Says
lesbianism not only destroys categories of material
enslavement ("woman" as an oppressed group like the
"proletariat"), it also gives women the semantic power to
"name" and to redefine themselves.

548   _____. "La Pensée straight." Questions féministes 7
        (December 1979), 45-53.

Criticizes current "intellectual constructs"--in particular, structuralist analyses of language and of the
unconscious--from a "lesbian point of view," claiming
such "a-historical" theories cloud the "material causes
of oppression." Says the result of such specialized
ideas and categories (which Wittig calls "straight
thought") is twofold: first, only specialists can
"decipher" and "find" the very symbols they themselves
have put in place; second, and more important, these
theories are all based on and perpetuate heterosexual
presuppositions and structures only (e.g., "women,"
"men," "difference"). Thus, claims homosexuals and
lesbians cannot continue to speak of "men" and "women,"
examples of "universalizing" categories which must
disappear from all spheres of life: "Lesbians are not
women."

548a   Trans. as "The Straight Mind" in Feminist Issues 1
        (Summer 1980), 103-11.

549   ———. "Un jour mon prince viendra." Questions
       féministes 2 (February 1978), 31-9.

       A short story, in the science fiction mode, in which
       theory is embedded. Evokes, with suggestive imagery and
       mythic tone, an apparently paradisical garden in which
       there are also traces of violence. In this imagined
       order, male "bodies" are enslaved by ruling "beings" who
       both feed and caress them, but also abuse and ridicule
       them. Blurs gender references in a strong critique of
       women's status as kept objects. Expresses powerfully the
       true imprisonment caused by passivity: calling for revolt,
       says, "Isn't it written that in risking it (death), you
       will cease being a slave?"

INTERVIEWS WITH

*   ———, Viviane Forrester, and Ann Thomas. "Virginia
       Woolf, précurseur du mouvement de libération des
       femmes." Viviane Forrester. Virginia Wolfe. Paris:
       O.R.T.F. et La Quinzaine littéraire, 1973, 51-64.

       (See 239).

ESSAYS AND ARTICLES ABOUT

550   Shaktini, Namascar. "Displacing the Phallic Subject:
       Wittig's Lesbian Writing." Signs 8, No. 1 (1982),
       29-44.

       Examines Wittig's textual strategies, focusing on Le
       Corps lesbien. Stresses the notion that Wittig "over-
       writes," "displaces" phallogocentric metaphor and myth.
       Begins by defining phallogocentrism and lesbian language.
       Moves to recount Hesiod's transformation of a prepatriar-
       chal Pandora to an object of gift-exchange and the role
       of Athena as mediator between Zeus (phallic subject) and
       the young woman (feminine object). Then explains that
       Wittig's transformation of Osiris into a lesbian subject
       "operates a reversal in the signifying system and a
       displacement of subjectivity." Continues with a series
       of brief interpretations of other myths and metaphors—
       embarcation, the moon, Christ, Orpheus and Eurydice.

551   Wenzel, Hélène Vivienne. "The Text as Body/Politics: An
       Appreciation of Monique Wittig's Writings in Context."
       Feminist Studies 7, No. 2 (Summer 1981), 264-87.

A presentation of the "oeuvre" of Wittig that takes as
its framework the general French feminist concern with
women and language. Sees Wittig as in the vanguard of
the current critique of patriarchy and language, but also
as resolutely against subsequent propoundings of an
"écriture féminine" grounded in female sexuality (see
102 and 469). First, examines "écriture féminine" and
critiques it on the basis of its dangerous "essentialism"
or biological determinism, thus its regressive perpetuation of traditional ideology about women. Discusses in
particular Cixous's explorations of writing and sexual
difference, of women's expressing their libidinal drives,
in the context of what it sees as Cixous's problematic
political stands on lesbianism and feminism. Summarizes
the theoretical opposition to "écriture féminine," opposition that favors analyses of women's real, material
oppression (see 541 and 291). Then, outlines Wittig's
challenge to the concept of a unique feminine writing
through an analysis of her works--all of which evince an
evolving radical feminist viewpoint that, ultimately,
redefines woman. Says Wittig's totally woman-identified
universe renders sex differences and categories "irrele-
vant"; also shows how her later work argues against the
coercive heterosexual ideology underlying all cultural
concepts (see 548 and 546). Explains Wittig's belief in
the need for a new feminist discourse combined with concrete activism. Cogent and useful.

552 **Yaguello, Marina.** <u>Les mots et les femmes: Essai</u>
     <u>d'approche socio-linguistique de la condition féminine.</u>
     Paris: Payot, 1979.

Introduction; "Langue des hommes, langue des femmes"
(554); "L'image des femmes dans la langue" (553).

A study of women and unspoken language whose perspec-
tive--unusual for French feminist inquiry on this issue--
is socio-linguistic. The "Introduction" posits that "the
individual's relationship to language passes through her/
his relationship to society," thus accounting for linguistic variations according to class, race and sex status.
Calls language a "cultural mirror" that both reflects and
sustains traditional symbolic representations of women.
Says differences in linguistic behavior are cultural, not
natural in source.

553   ———. "L'image des femmes dans la langue." Les mots
et les femmes: Essai d'approche socio-linguistique de
la condition féminine. Paris: Payot, 1979, 89-195.

Looks at the image of women that is transmitted by
various elements of language and suggests strategies for
bringing about linguistic and, from it, social change.
Subheadings are as follows:
"Genre et sexe: la métaphore sexuelle"--Explores the
relationships between gender in language and sex roles,
saying grammatical gender is "useless" and dangerous.
Claims the origin of linguistic gender is not important,
but the ideology and symbolism it conveys are.
"Masculin/féminin: dissymétries grammaticales"--Shows
how a gendered language such as French functions, in
particular in its dissymmetries between masculine and
feminine agents and in the absorption of the feminine by
the masculine.
"Masculin/féminin: dissymétries sémantiques"--Presents
the glaring semantic dissymmetries between masculine and
feminine, the feminine almost always carrying pejorative
connotations.
"La langue du mépris"--Points out the ways women's
bodies have systematically been denigrated in the
language of insult and obscenity. Posits that the power
to insult is a prerogative of the dominant group.
"Faut-il brûler les dictionnaires?"--Reveals the
"hidden" sexism in dictionaries, which are presumed to be
purely denotative and neutral. Says dictionaires,
ideological creations, introduce conservative views
through the examples and associations they give.
"La femme sans nom, la femme sans voix"--Looks at the
linguistic indicators that reflect women's social status,
e.g., the lack of professional titles for women, their
change of name in marriage.
"L'action volontariste sur la langue, ou: Peut-on
infléchir l'évolution naturelle des langues?"--Urges that
voluntary action be performed on language in order to
exploit and undermine, respectively, the possibilities of
both freedom and domination language contains. Calls for
conscious contestation and violation of language, with
the goal of eventual deeper change in mentalities.

554   ———. "Langue des hommes, langue des femmes." Les mots
et les femmes: Essai d'approche socio-linguistique de
la condition féminine. Paris: Payot, 1979, 13-87.

A discussion of the linguistic comportment of women in
its social context. Subheadings are as follows:
   "L'héritage des anthropologues"--Traces the early anthropological studies of language and sex in "primitive"
societies, giving examples of linguistic segregation
based on taboos and exogamy. Also lists linguistic
differences in these studies by category: phonetic,
morphological, syntactic, and lexical.
   "Du descriptivisme ethno-folklorique à la socio-linguistique"--Moves from "primitive" to modern societies to
show the persistence, in new guises, of traditional
constraints on women's language. Gives examples of
differences between men's and women's linguistic "registers" but stresses that the interpretation of these
differences is what is crucial.
   "Les éléments de l'interaction verbale"--Insists on the
centrality of context or verbal interaction for understanding differential linguistic comportments among women
and men. Discusses the factors involved in verbal
exchange: power, initiative, credibility, stereotypes.
   "A la recherche d'une identité culturelle"--The most
pertinent chapter: refers to the current effort by many
women to free themselves of the linguistic constraints
upon them. Also describes the refusal by some women to
adopt the masculine language in place, in favor of the
search for a specifically feminine language. Declines to
take a position on "l'écriture féminine" and turns its
attention to oral, not written communications.
   "Le discours féministe et anti-féministe"--Examines
feminist discourse from the point of view of both the
feminist "in-group" and the "out-group" of the dominant
ideology.

555 **Yvon, Josée.** "La Poche des autres." La Barre du jour
     No. 50 (Winter 1975), 78-104.

     Seeks to "explode" language as it is by various means
that express anger and disorder. Uses quotes, shocking
photos, and pieces of sensational stories as an analogue
to women's ongoing self-mutilation and psychological
scarring. Claims writing, like the words and images in
this piece, must "touch the essential/the tragic problem
of living and the comic aspect of living." Leans toward
a Marxist orientation in calling for the "destruction of
all taboos" by "ordinary people." Highly polemical but
effective.

SPECIAL ISSUES APPENDIX

L'Arc. "Jacques Derrida." 54 (1973).

Clément, Catherine. "Le sauvage"
Derrida, Jacques. "Glas"
Clément, Catherine. "A l'écoute de Derrida" (144)
Buci-Glucksmann, Christine. "Déconstruction et critique
  marxiste de la philosophie
Levinas, Emmanuel. "Tout autrement"
Laruelle, François. "Le texte quatrième"
Cixous, Hélène. "L'essort de Plusje" (93)
Ollier, Claude. "Pulsion"
Jabès, Edmond. "Sur la question du livre"
Laporte, Roger. "Bief"
Lotringer, Sylvère. "Le dernier mot de Saussure"
Giovannangeli, Daniel. "La question de la littérature"

L'Arc. "Lacan." 58 (1974).

Clément, Catherine. "Un numéro" (169)
Lacan, Jacques. "'Aimée'"
Rabant, Christiane. "La bête chanteuse" (206)
Levallois-Colot, Anne. "'Voyez comme l'on danse'" (482)
Montrelay, Michèle. "Le saut du loup" (501)
Rousseau-Dujardin, Jacqueline. "Du temps, qu'entends-je?"
Felman, Soshana. "La méprise et sa chance" (211)
Irigaray, Luce. "La 'mécanique' des fluides" (328)
Mannoni, Maud. "Le malentendu" (485)
Roudinesco, Elisabeth. "Cogito et science du réel"
Ronat, Mitsou. "'Grammaire' de l'inconscient"
Tytell, Pamela. "Lacune aux U.S.A." (541)
Lowe, Catherine. "Salammbô"

L'Arc. "Simone de Beauvoir et la lutte des femmes." 61
 (1975).

Clément, C., Pingaud, B. "Une femme pour d'autres"
Simone de Beauvoir interroge Jean-Paul Sartre
Clément, Catherine. "Enclave esclave" (150)
Des femmes en lutte
Michel, Andrée. "Naissance d'une conscience féministe"
Cixous, Hélène. "Le rire de la Méduse" (102)
Le Bon, Sylvie. "Le deuxième sexe: l'esprit et la lettre"
D., C. (Delphy, Christine). "Pour un féminisme
  matérialiste" (186)
Roudy, Yvette. "La seconde révolution des Américaines"
Reed, Evelyn. "La biologie et le destin de la femme"

La Barre du jour. "Le corps, les mots, l'imaginaire." Nos.
 56-57 (May-August 1977).

Brossard, Nicole. "Introduction"
Théoret, France. "Cochonnerie" (534)
Amyot, Geneviève. "Dites-le avec des fleurs"
Gagné, Sylvie. "Mots d'elle" (246)
Charbonneau-Tissot, Claudette. "L'Inimagination"
Bouchard, Louise. "Dis quelque chose"
Beaulieu, Germaine. "Energie"
Bosco, Monique. "Corps-Mort"
Brossard, Nicole. "La Tête qu'elle fait" (60)
Cloutier, Cécile. "Utinam!"
Villemaire, Yolande. "Mon coeur battait comme un bolo"
Gagnon, Madeleine. "Des mots plein la bouche" (251)
Bersianik, Louky. "Noli mi tangere"
Lanctôt, Mireille. "La Cocotte d'argile"
Lévesque, M.-Andrée. "L'Hystérie: L'écriture"
Théoret, France. "Fragment d'une lettre"
Savard, Marie, fille de Germaine. "L'Ile était une fois"
Bédard, Nicole. "Peintre (du) féminin"
Massé, Carole. "L'Inimaginaire"
Denis, Johanne and Savardy, Claire. "Le Discours des
  interventres"

La Barre du jour. "Femme et langage." No. 50 (Winter 1975).

Brossard, Nicole. "Préliminaires" (56)
Brossard, Nicole. "E muet mutant" (50)
Théoret, France. "Dépendances" (536)
Théoret, France. "Une Voix pour Odile" (537)
Villemaire, Yolande. "Pour une parthénogenèse de la
  parole 'hystérique' (matrice vierge)" (543)

Gagnon, Madeleine. "La Femme et le langage: sa fonction
  comme parole en son manque" (254)
Guilbault, Luce. "Sans titre"
Gagnon, Odette. "Sans titre" (260)
Salomé, Lou Andréas. "La Femme du ressentiment" (524)
Yvon, Josée. "La Poche des autres" (555)
Bédard, Nicole. "L'Oscillé(e)" (40)

Bulletin de Recherches et d'Etudes Francophones Féministes
  (BREFF).

   An indispensable research tool for students and scholars
of French women's studies. Published by the Department of
French and Italian, University of Wisconsin-Madison.
Provides up-to-date information about conferences,
publications, research and other events involving French and
Francophone feminism, women's literature, and feminist
theory. Summarizes the relevant contents of important
journals and magazines. Appears three or four times a year.

Les Cahiers du GRIF. "Dé/pro/ré/créer." 7 (June 1975).

   Editorial
   Le Grif, "Création, Langage, Culture" (290)
   Boucquey, Eliane. "Choisir ou créer" (43)
   Kristeva, Julia. "Unes femmes" (445)
   Pelzer, Brigit. "'Ma seule défense est...'" (505)
   Lejeune, Claire. "L'Ecriture et l'Arbre du Milieu" (478)
   "Lettre ouverte sur la condition des femmes chercheurs au
     CNRS"
   "Les Femmes et le cinéma: Documents et témoignages"

Les Cahiers du GRIF. "Elles consonnent." 13 (October 1976).

   Editorial
   Cixous, Hélène. "Le sexe ou la tête?" (103)
   Collin, Françoise. "Quelques questions à Hélène Cixous"
     (112)
   Denis, Marie. "Pour parler je ne crains personne" (187)
   "Le langage pauvre" (discussion) (179)
   Huston, Nancy. "Conjurations" (305)
   Panier, Christine. "Les dactylos n'ont pas de langue"
   Gouat, Marie-Claire. "Société de culotte cousue"
   Varda, Agnès. "Je t'écris, te parle cinéma"
   Maillet, Antonine. (Interview)
   Dallier, Aline. "Annette Messager: un langage de
     plasticienne"
   Pelzer, Birgit. "Dada danse et ombres"

Dubois, Margareta. "Dans la famille internationale"
Storti, Martine; Le Garrec, Evelyne; Odile, Marie. "Femmes
   et journalisme"
"Lire ensemble" (discussion)
Denis, Marie. "Des militants cramponnés"

Les Cahiers du GRIF. "Parlez-vous française?" 12 (June
   1976).

   Collin, Françoise. "Polyglo(u)ssons" (177)
   D., Alice. "D'une folle à l'autre"
   Aubenas, Jacqueline. "Abécédaire quotidien et tout en
      désordre" (33)
   Huston, Nancy. "S'en prendre à la lettre" (307)
   Vercheval, Jeanne. "Dire Brouillon"
   Lou. "Lettre à Francis"
   Irigaray, Luce. "Quand nos lèvres se parlent" (333)
   Bensmaine, Mimi. "Des mots pour 'me' dire"
   P., Birgit. "Je n'ai jamais su parler"
   Aubenas, Jacqueline. "Pas de langue, cent langages"
   Panier, Christine. "Dialogue corps-pensée à la danse"
   Tennstedt, Martine; Minet, Margriet. "Immigrées"
   Magli, Ida. "Pouvoir de la parole et silence de la femme"
      (484)
   Maillet, Antonine. (interview)
   Dallier, Aline. "Les travaux d'aiguille"
   "Le GRIF interroge M. A. Macchiocchi sur le fascisme"

Cahiers Renaud-Barrault. "Marguerite Duras." 89 (1975).

   Benmussa, Simone. "Présentation"
   Barrault, Jean-Louis. "Silence et solitude"
   Foucault, Michel; Cixous, Hélène. "A propos de Marguerite
      Duras" (201)
   Gauthier, Xavière. "La danse, le désir" (202)
   Regnault, François. "Comme"
         Texts
   Sarraute, Nathalie. "C'est beau"
   Sarraute, Nathalie. "Le gant retourné"
   Régy, Claude. "'C'est beau,' théâtre de la violence"
   Cixous, Hélène. "Le Livre des Mortes"
   Cixous, Hélène. "Le Paradire"

Critical Inquiry. "Writing and Sexual Difference." 8, No. 2
   (Winter 1981).

   Showalter, Elaine. "Feminist Criticism in the Wilderness"
      (25)

Jacobus, Mary. "The Question of Language: Men of Maxims and
The Mill on the Floss"

Homans, Margaret. "Eliot, Wordsworth, and the Scenes of the
Sisters' Instruction"

Gubar, Susan. "The Blank Page" and the Issues of Female
Creativity

Vickers, Nancy J. "Diana Described: Scattered Woman and
Scattered Rhyme"

Auerbach, Nina. "Magi and Maidens: The Romance of the
Victorian Freud"

Zeitlin, Froma I. "Travesties of Gender and Genre in
Aristophanes' Thesmophoriazousae"

Kolodny, Annette. "Turning the Lens of 'The Panther
Captivity': A Feminist Exercise in Practical Criticism"

Gardiner, Judith Kegan. "On Female Identity and Writing by
Women"

Stimpson, Catharine R. "Zero Degree Deviancy": The Lesbian
Novel in English"

Spivak, Gayatri Chakravorty. "'Draupadi' by Mahasveta Devi"

Diacritics. "Cherchez la femme." 12, No. 2, (Summer 1982).

Review Articles

Johnson, Barbara. "My Monster/My Self"

Berg, Elizabeth L. "The Third Woman" (371)

Moi, Toril. "The Missing Mother: the Oedipal Rivalries of
René Girard" (490)

Kahn, Coppelia. "Excavating 'Those Dim Minoan Regions,'
Maternal Subtexts in Patriarchal Literature"

Dialogue

Kamuf, Peggy. "Replacing Feminist Criticism" (13)

Miller, Nancy K. "The Text's Heroine: A Feminist Critic and
Her Fictions" (23)

Texts/Contexts

Jardine, Alice. "Gynesis" (11)

Interview

Derrida, Jacques; McDonald, Christie V. "Choreographies"

Diacritics. "Textual Politics, Feminist Criticism." 5, No. 4
(Winter 1975).

Review Articles

Felman, Shoshana. "Women and Madness: The Critical
Phallacy" (213)

Schor, Naomi. "Mother's Day: Zola's Women"

Gallop, Jane. "The Ghost of Lacan, the Trace of Language"
(264)

Conley, Verena. "Kristeva's China" (458)

Foley, Helen P.   "Sex and State in Ancient Greece"
Miller, Nancy K.   "The Exquisite Cadavers: Women in
   Eighteenth-Century Fiction"
McConnell-Ginet, Sally.   "Our Father Tongue: Essays in
   Linguistic Politics"
                    Texts/Contexts
Kamuf de Magnin, Peggy.   "Rousseau's Politics of Visibility"
                    Motion Pictures
Greenberg, Caren.   "'Carnal Knowledge': A Woman is Missing"

Dialectiques. "Femmes." No. 8 (Spring 1975).

Marx-Aveling, Eleanor and Edward.   "La Question féminine"
Marx, Eleanor.   "Comment devons-nous nous organiser?"
Kautsky, Louise.   "Un Salut d'Angleterre"
Lafargue, Laura.   "Un Salut de France"
Irigaray, Luce.   "Pouvoir du discours/subordination du
   féminin: entretien" (341)

Enclitic. "Special Feminist Issue." 4, No. 2 (Fall 1980).

Jardine, Alice A.   "Theories of the Feminine: Kristeva"
   (462)
Kofman, Sarah.   "Ex: The Woman's Enigma" (370c)
George, Diana Hume.   "The Myth of Mythlessness and the New
   Mythology of Love: Feminist Theory on Rape and Pornography"
Cixous, Hélène.   "Arrive le chapitre-qui-vient"
Gallop, Jane.   "Sade, Mothers, and Other Women"
Bartkowski, Frances.   "Feminism and Deconstruction: "a
   union forever deferred" (35)
Schwichtenberg, Cathy.   "'Near The Big Chakra'": Vulvar
   Conspiracy and Protean Film Text"
Lieberman, Jo-Anne.   "'My Hidden Enemy': Mothering and
   Narrative in 'Wuthering Heights'"

Esprit. 6 (June 1976).

                    "La Part des femmes"
Thibaud, Paul.   "Introduction"
Quere, France.   "Pour un féminisme total"
Giard, Luce; Meyer, Philippe; Wuilleumier, M.-C.   "Note
   conjointe sur l'éminente relativité du concept de femme"
Bisilliat, Jeanne.   "Femme tue"
Cottin, Jean.   "Ouvrières 'aux pièces'"
Colanis, Alice.   "Les insignifiantes"
Giard, Luce.   "La fabrique des filles"
Fogarty, Patricia.   "Aux antipodes"
Corpet, Véronique.   "Petite géographie des luttes"

SOS-Femme (extrait de lettres)
Schulmann, Fernande. "Et pourtant ça bouge..."

L'Esprit créateur. "Contemporary Women Writers in France."
19, No. 2 (Summer 1979).

Andersen, Margret. "La Jouissance--Principe d'écriture"
   (475)
Cothran, Ann. "Narrative Structure as Expression of the Self
   in Sarrazin's 'L'Astragale'"
de Courtivron, Isabelle. "'Le Repos du guerrier': New
   Perspectives on Rochefort's Warrior"
Farrell, C. Frederick Jr. and Edith R. "Marguerite
   Yourcenar: The Art of Re-Writing"
Gelfand, Elissa D. "Albertine Sarrazin: The Confined
   Imagination"
Kreiter, Janine Anseaume. "Perception et Métaphorisation
   dans "Le Planétarium': Ebauche d'une Analyse Lexicologique"
Lamont, Rosette C. "Charlotte Delbo's Frozen Friezes"
Murphy, Carol J. "Thematic and Textual Violence in Duras'
   'Dix heures et demie du soir en été'"
Robinson, Jean Hardy. "Poetic and Philosophic
   Counterpoint in Gennari's 'La Fugue irlandaise'"
de Courtivron, Isabelle. "Violette Leduc's 'L'Affamée': The
   Courage to Displease"
Interview. An Interview with Christiane Rochefort by
   Marianne Hirsch, Mary Jean Green and Lynn Higgins (521)

Feminist Studies. 7, No. 2 (Summer 1981).

          "The French Connection."
Jones, Ann Rosalind. "Writing the Body: Toward an
   Understanding of 'L'Ecriture Féminine'" (12)
Wenzel, Hélène Vivienne. "The Text as Body/Politics: An
   Appreciation of Monique Wittig's Writings in Context" (551)
Burke, Carolyn. "Irigaray Through the Looking Glass" (345)

Feminist Studies. 6, No. 2 (Summer 1980).

          "Simone de Beauvoir."
Preface
Felstiner, Mary Lowenthal. "Seeing 'The Second Sex' Through
   The Second Wave"
Le Doeuff, Michèle. "Simone de Beauvoir and Existentialism"
Dijkstra, Sandra. "Simone de Beauvoir and Betty Friedan: The
   Politics of Omission"
Fuchs, Jo-Ann P. "Female Eroticism in 'The Second Sex'"

Liberté. "La Femme et l'écriture." Nos. 106-107 (July-
October 1976).

                    First Session
Brossard, Nicole. "Allocution d'ouverture" (46)
Papers: Navarre, Yves
        Leclerc, Annie (470)
        Barreno, Maria Isabel
Debate (183)
                    Second Session
Lejeune, Claire. "Allocution d'ouverture"
Papers: Desanti, Dominique
        Bosco, Monique
        Ouellette, Madeleine
        Linhartova, Véra
Debate
                    Third Session
Papers: Rochefort, Christiane (518)
        Théoret, France (535)
        Chatelet, Noelle
        Karp, Lila
Debate
                    Fourth Session
Desanti, Dominique. "Allocution d'ouverture"
Papers: Beaudet, André
        Perrein, Michèle
        Paradis, Suzanne
        Delay, Florence
Debate
                    Fifth Session
Papers: Gold, Herbert
        Stefanova, Nevena
        Philippe, Anne
        Lamb, Myrna
        Gagnon, Madeleine (250)
Debate
Paper: Sarduy, Severo

Magazine littéraire. No. 180 (January 1982).

                "Femmes: Une autre écriture?"
Gauthier, Xavière. "Autre écriture?" (283)
Perrein, Michèle. "Ainsi parle une telle qui écrit" (506)
Clédat, Françoise. "L'écriture du corps" (135)
Cortanze, Gérard de. "L'infini plaisir des sens"
Sebbar, Leïla. "Témoigner"
Vilaine, Anne-Marie de. "Le corps de la théorie" (542)
Huston, Nancy. "Mouvements et journaux de femmes" (306)

Pujebet, Dominique and Ruth Stegassy. "Les collectionneuses"
Ajame, Pierre et al. "La parole est aux hommes"
Rivière, Anne and Xavière Gauthier. "Des femmes et leurs
    oeuvres" (514)

Magazine littéraire. No. 158 (March 1980).

                    "Marguerite Duras."
Weizzaenpflen, Catherine. "Un itineraire de raréfaction"
Forrester, Viviane. "Voir. Etre vue" (200)
Tytell, Pamela. "Lacan, Freud et Duras" (207)
Gauthier, Xavière. "Marguerite Duras et la lutte des
    femmes" (203)
Farges, Joel. "Tourner le désastre du film"

Les Nouveaux cahiers. "Femmes, voix d'elles Juives." 46
(Autumn 1976).

                    Etude
Bogler, Colette; Bogler, Denise; Garson, Catherine;
    Gdalia, Janine; Okonowski, Martine; Stora-Sandor, Judith.
    "Le Statut de la Femme dans la Bible"
                    Histoire
Scherr, Lilly. "La Femme juive à travers les Siècles"
          Littérature: le Regard des autres
Sudaka, Jacqueline. "Sara l'inverse"
Fennetaux-Lasry, Jacqueline; Sudaka, Jacqueline. "Myriam, le
    don sans corps"
Spire, Marie-Brunette. "Les Reporters de l'Enfer hébraïque"
Fennetaux-Lasry, Jacqueline; Spire, Marie-Brunette. "Sarah
    l'exclue"
Cottenet-Hage, Madeleine. "La juive comme autre"
                    Essais
Atlan, Liliane. "Le Rêve des Animaux rongeurs"
"Elle dit"
de Fontenay, Elisabeth. "Divisées à l'infini"
Malraux, Clara. "Une certaine Femme juive"
Moati, Nine. "Scènes"
Sudaka, Jacqueline. "Traces"
                    Entretiens
Avec Simone Benmussa
Avec Hélène Cixous (119)

La Nouvelle critique. Dossier Femmes. 82 (March 1975).

"Une réelle égalité"
"Des personnes communistes de sexe féminin"
"Présentation du project de loi-cadre du P. C. F."

Gilles, Christiane. "La C. G. T., les femmes"
"Femmes, le changement," Débat entre Christiane Collange,
    Ménie Grégoire et Gisèle Moreau
Dumont, Yvonne. "L'année internationale des femmes"
"La Femme, son sexe et le langage," Entretien entre
    Catherine Clément et Luce Irigaray (337)
Clément, Catherine. "La Femme dans l'idéologie" (152)
Cixous, Hélène. "La noire vole" (inédit)

Nouvelle revue de psychanalyse. "Bisexualité et différence des
sexes." No. 7 (Spring 1973).

Ovide. "Salmacis et Hermaphrodite. Cénis et Cénée"
Pontalis, J.-B. "L'insaisissable entre-deux"
Brisson, Luc. "Bisexualité et médiation en Grèce ancienne"
Pouchelle, Marie-Christine. "L'hybride"
Cachin, Françoise. "Monsieur Vénus et l'ange de Sodome"
Gillibert, Jean. "L'acteur, médian sexuel"
Aron, Claude. "Les facteurs neuro-hormonaux de la sexualité
    chez les mammifères"
Kreisler, Léon. "L'enfant et l'adolescent de sexe ambigu ou
    l'envers du mythe"
Stoller, Robert. "Faits et hypothèses: un examen du concept
    freudien de bisexualité"
Fédida, Pierre. "D'une essentielle dissymétrie dans la
    psychanalyse"
Fliess, Wilhelm. "Masculin et féminin"
Anzieu, Didier. "La bisexualité dans l'auto-analyse de
    Freud"
Groddeck, Georg. "Le double sexe de l'être humain"
Lewinter, Roger. "(Anti) judaisme et bisexualité"
Nunberg, Herman. "Tentatives de rejet de la circoncision"
David, Christian. "Les belles différences"
Green, André. "Le genre neutre"
McDougall, Joyce. "L'idéal hermaphrodite et ses avatars"
Boehm, Félix. "Le complexe de féminité chez l'homme"
Winnicott, D. W. "Clivage des éléments masculins et féminins
    chez l'homme et chez la femme"
Khan, M., Masud R. "Orgasme du moi et amour bisexuel"
Alby, Jean-Marc. "L'identité sexuelle: pour quoi faire?"
Cixous, Hélène. "Partie"

Les Nouvelles littéraires. "Des Femmes en écriture." No.
2534, (May 26, 1976).

A dossier brought together by Hélène Cixous. Responds to
the questions: Can one speak about feminine writing? Does
it exist? Includes brief pieces by Hélène Cixous (95),

Chantal Chawaf (78), and Madeleine Gagnon, (249) an
interview with Annie Leclerc (473), as well as conversations
and poetry of a number of other women.

<u>Partisans</u>. "Libération des femmes, année zéro." Nos. 54-55
(July-October 1970).

Présentations
Le Mouvement de libération des femmes en France
Le Mouvement de libération des femmes aux Etats-Unis
      <u>Part One</u>: American Texts (translated)
      <u>Part Two</u>: French Texts
Durand, Emmanuèle. "Le viol"
Un groupe de femmes. "La femme en morceaux"
Kohen, Anne. "Une lutte de femmes à propos de la maternité:
  réflexion et mise en pratique"
Quelques militantes. "L'interdiction de l'avortement:
  exploitation économique"
Rochefort, Christiane. "Le mythe de la frigidité féminine"
Aline. "La culture, le génie et les femmes"
Quelques militantes. "Nous proposons..."
K., J. "Les militantes"
Nelcya. "Quelques réflexions"
Nadia. "Toutes ces femmes...Une caricature: la prison"
Dupont, Christine. "L'ennemi principal" (184)
      <u>Part Three</u>
Anne et Jacqueline. "D'un groupe à l'autre (la révolution
  sexuelle aux Etats-Unis, en Suède et en Scandinavie,
  l'U.R.S.S., le Mouvement de mai, les féministes)"
      <u>Part Four</u>
Larguia, Isabel. "Contre le travail invisible"
Anne. "La révolution dans la révolution à Cuba"
Godchau, Jean-François. "Lutte de sexes ou lutte de classes"
Fanny. "De cela je reconnais la société coupable"
Godchau, Jean-François. "Bibliographie"

<u>Pénélope</u>. "Les femmes et la création." No. 3 (Fall 1980).

Bonnet, Marie-Joe. "Introduction"
Braidotti, Rosy. "Qui sait calculer les effets des idées?"
  (2)
Dupont-Viau, Gaëlle. "Pour une histoire de mot"
Louis, Michèle. "Les femmes troubadours"
Gaborit, Lydia. "La création orale"
Lapidus, Jacqueline. "Travail collectif et création
  individuelle: L'expérience d'un groupe de femmes poètes"
Labrot, Monique; Eude, Jeanne; Fournier, Martine; Nevroltis,
  Noëlle; Devret, Annick. "A corps et à cris"

Krakovitch, Odile. "Les femmes dramaturges et la création au
théâtre"
Vincent, Geneviève. "Femmes de scène: les Danseuses (XIX-XX
siècle)"
Poindron-Karnaouch, Denise. "Des créatrices: Les femmes
russes (1880-1914)"
Gauthier, Marie-Véronique. "Le discours traditionnel sur la
Créatrice (Germaine Tailleferre)"
Bloch, Michelle. "La Femme et la Création" (41)
Pasquier, Marie-Claire. "Gertrude Stein, écrivain"
Marini, Marcelle. "Les femmes et les pratiques d'écriture.
Quelques réflexions" (486)
de Torne, Brigitte Carsonnac. "L'étrange identité de la
poésie féminine"
Beghadid, Dominique. "A propos des femmes cinéastes"
Rosner, Mirela. "Une Utopie: La montagne sacrée ou les
plaisirs cachés"
Dallier, Aline. "Activités et réalisations de femmes dans
l'art contemporain (les oeuvres dérivées des techniques
textiles traditionnelles)"
Calmis, Charlotte. "Entre ombre et lumière. Histoire d'un
portrait peint...ou pari sur un regard..."
Aide-mémoire imparfait des principaux groupes féministes
ayant privilégié la création
Bibliographie

Questions féministes. 1 (November 1977).

"Variations sur des thèmes communs" (541)
Delphy, Christine. "Nos amis et nous. Les fondements cachés
de quelques discours pseudo-féministes"
Mathieu, Nicole-Claude. "Masculinité/féminité" (489)
Hanmer, Jalna. "Violence et contrôle social des femmes"
Plaza, Monique. "Pouvoir 'phallomorphique' et psychologie de
'la Femme'" (347)

La Quinzaine littéraire. "Les Femmes existent." 192 (August
1-31, 1974).

Watté, Pierre. "Eve contre Oedipe"
Borie, Jean. "Les femmes du célibataire"
Fabre-Luce, Anne. "Sexualité féminine et réussite sociale"
Pierre, José. "Les reines de la main gauche"
Meillon, Jacqueline. "'Les hommes protégés'" (Robert Merle)
Bourgeois, Michel. "'La vie comme elle vient'" (Flora Dosen)
Chesneaux, Jean. "Numéro spécial des 'Temps modernes'"
Turlan, Catherine. "Jeunes filles, jeunes femmes"
(Collection Ariane)

Mariancie, Ritta. "Les femmes américaines revendiquent"
Descamps, Christian. "'L'âge des femmes'" (Juliet Mitchell)
Kogan, Emile. "'Une semaine comme une autre'" (Baranskaïa)
Kristeva, Julia. "Femmes chinoises" (406)
Mannoni, Maud. '"La Moitié du ciel'" (Claudie Broyelle)
"'La Femme et ses images'" (Pascal Lainé)
"Une maison d'édition par et pour les femmes"
Herrmann, Claudine. "Le sexe du langage" (299)
"Questions à des écrivains"
Fonfreide, Marcelle. "Les femmes et le cinéma"

Revue de l'Université d'Ottawa/University of Ottawa Quarterly.
"Conférence des femmes-écrivains en Amérique." 50, No. 1
(January–March 1980).

Smart, Patricia; Yanacopoulo, Andrée. "Présentation"
Brossard, Nicole. "Séance inaugurale" (57)
Brossard, Nicole; Théoret, France; Saint-Denis, Janou; Bosco,
    Monique; Boucher, Denise; Paradis, Suzanne; Bersianik,
    Louky; Gagnon, Madeleine. "Tables rondes" (59)
Cotnoir, Louise. "Contribution des femmes écrivains du
    continent américain à la littérature"
Lamy, Suzanne. "Voyage autour d'une écriture" (467)
Féral, Josette. "Du texte au sujet" (217)
Makward, Christiane. "Nouveau regard sur la critique
    féministe en France" (17)
Pascal, Gabrielle. "La femme dans l'oeuvre de Gabrielle Roy"
Smart, Patricia. "La Poésie d'Anne Hébert: une perspective
    féminine"
Paterson, Janet M. "L'écriture de la jouissance dans
    l'oeuvre romanesque d'Anne Hébert"
Couillard-Goodenough, Marie. "La Femme et le sacré dans
    quelques romans québécois contemporains"
Bayard, Caroline. "Nicole Brossard et l'utopie du
    langage" (67)
Dupré, Louise. "L'écriture féminine dans Les herbes rouges"
Cloutier, Cécile. "'L'Euguélionne': texte et significations"
Barrett, Caroline; des Rivières, Marie-José. "La femme dans
    la littérature populaire québécoise (1945–1966)"
    Proceedings of Conférences Vanier 1979
Girou-Swiderski, Marie-Laure. "Présentation"
Lacelle, Elisabeth J. "Hommage à Annie Jaubert"
Jaubert, A. "La symbolique des femmes dans les traditions
    religieuses: une reconsidération de l'Evangile de Jean"
Davis, Natalie Zemon. "Gender and Genre: Women as
    Historical Writers, 1400–1820"
Steffens, Caryll. "A Brief Look at Dorothy Dinnerstein's
    'The Mermaid and the Minotaur'"

Lafon, Dominique. "L'image de la femme dans le théâtre
québécois"

La Revue des Sciences Humaines. "Ecriture, Féminité,
féminisme." No. 168, (1977).

Cixous, Hélène. "Entretien avec Françoise van Rossum-Guyon"
(118)
Kristeva, Julia. "Questions à partir de Polylogue" (454)
Allen, Suzanne. "Plus-Oultre" (31)
Varga, A. Kibédi. "Romans d'amour, romans de femmes, à
l'époque classique"
Duchet, Michèle. "Du sexe des livres, à propos de l'essai
'Sur les femmes' de Diderot"
Desvignes, Lucette. "Le théâtre de Voltaire et la femme
victime"
Mozet, Nicole. "Féminité et pouvoir après 1830: le cas
étrange de Félicité des Touches (Béatrix)"
Didier, Béatrice. "Femme/Identité/Ecriture, à propos de
'l'Histoire de ma vie' de George Sand"
Brahimi, Denise. "Réflexions sur trois romans de George
Sand"
Schaettel, Marcel. "Quelques images de la femme dans la
poésie de Charles Cros"
de Palacio, Jean. "La féminité dévorante. Sur quelques
images de la manducation dans la littérature décadente"
Makward, Christiane Perrin. "La critique féministe; éléments
d'une problématique" (15)
van Rossum-Guyon, Françoise. "Sélection bibliographique"

Romantisme. "Mythes et représentations de la femme." Nos.
13-14 (1976).

        Les deux natures
Hoffmann, Paul. "L'héritage des Lumières: mythes et modèles
de la féminité au XVIIIe siècle"
Michaud, Stéphane. "Science, droit, religion: trois contes
sur les deux natures"
Knibiehler, Yvonne. "Le discours sur la femme: constantes et
ruptures"
Wajeman, Gérard. "Psyché de la femme: note sur l'hystérique
au XIXe siècle"
Léon, Monique. "'Le Dictionnaire de la Femme' ou anthologie
de la femme-signe"
        Parole ouvrière et discours politique
Devance, Louis. "Femme, famille, travail et morale
sexuelle dans l'idéologie de 1848"

Perrot, Michelle. "L'éloge de la ménagère dans le discours
  des ouvriers français au XIXe siècle"
Auclert, Hubertine. "Rapport du troisième Congrès national
  ouvrier (Marseille, 20-31 octobre 1879)"
Rebérious, Madeleine; Dufrancatel, Christiane; Slama,
  Béatrice. "Hubertine Auclert et la question des femmes à
  'l'immortel congrès':
Agulhon, Maurice. "Un usage de la femme au XIXe siécle:
  l'allégorie de la République"
          Fantasmes du corps féminin
Didier, Béatrice. "Sexe, société et création: 'Consuelo' et
  'La Comtesse de Rudolstadt'"
Pich, Edgard. "Littérature et codes sociaux:
  l'anti-féminisme sous le Second Empire"
Schor, Naomi. "Le sourire du sphinx: Zola et l'enigme de la
  féminité" (531)
          Victoriennes et "femmes libres"
Basch, Françoise. "Mythes de la femme dans le roman
  victorien"
Blin, Michèle. "Une pédagogie pour jeunes filles pauvres:
  de'Claudine à l'école' à 'Mes apprentissages'"
Debouzy, Jacques et Marianne. "Sentiment et société dans le
  roman américain à la fin du XIXe siècle: Stephen Crane,
  Theodore Dreiser"

Signs. "French Feminist Theory." 7, No. 1 (Autumn 1981).

Jardine, Alice. "Introduction to Julia Kristeva's 'Women's
  Time'" (460)
Kristeva, Julia. "Women's Time" (439a)
Kuhn, Annette. "Introduction to Hélène Cixous's
  'Castration or Decapitation?'" (129)
Cixous, Hélène. "Castration or Decapitation?" (103a)
Wenzel, Hélène Vivienne. "Introduction to Luce Irigaray's
  'And the One Doesn't Stir without the Other'" (348)
Irigaray, Luce. "And the One Doesn't Stir without the Other"
  (311a)
Robinson, Lillian S. "Introduction to Christine Fauré's
  'Absent from History' and 'The Twilight of the Goddesses,
  or The Intellectual Crisis of French Feminism'"
Fauré, Christine. "Absent from History"
Fauré, Christine. "The Twilight of the Goddesses, or The
  Intellectual Crisis of French Feminism" (210a)

Sorcières. "Ecritures." 7 (1977).

Sorcières, "...nos traversées" (287)
Dumonastier, Marie. "Ecriture d'identité"

Lemoine-Luccioni, Eugénie. "Ecrire" (481)
Plusieurs femmes. "A la croisée de nos écritures"
Blasquez, Adélaide. "Pavane pour un Je défunt"
Méhadji, Nadjia. "Traits du corps"
Igrecque. "La galerie des glaces à perpétuité"
Champroux, Huguette. "La nuit transfigurée"
Rollin, Marie-Simone. "Initiales"
Laïk, Madeleine; Schuller, Josée. "Ecritures de vive voix"
Herrmann, Claudine. "Les difficultés du langage écrit"
    (296)
Rivière, Anne. "Rubrique"
Champroux, Huguette. "L. L."
Martel, Cosette. "Le e muet d'Ariane" (488)
Sultan, Peggy Inès. "La récompense"
Brossard, Nicole. "Si je jouis" (58)
Boukobza-Hajlblum, Claude. "Retrait" (44)
Thérame, Victoria. "Mississipi-ventre"
Sorcières. "...faire une revue"

Sorcières. "Théorie." 12 (1978).

Gauthier, Xavière. "Je te croyais indomptable"
        Theory
Cassin, Barbara. "Code code code codé" (76)
Rivière, Anne. "Il y a de l'extérieur" (515)
Rollin, Marie-Simone. "L'être et l'anéantie" (522)
Daguenet-Teissier, Maryvonne. "Le concret c'est de
    l'abstrait rendu familier par l'usage" (182)
Huston, Nancy. "Le cercle de lumière" (304)
Rabant, Christiane. "C'ex: temporalités de l'imaginaire"
    (509)
Schiff, Dominique. "Sciences exactes" (527)
Canto, Monique. "La théorie immobile" (73)
Echard, Nicole. "Anecdote interdite"
Alémonière, Patricia. "Proposition pour une submersion de
    la théorie économique par les fluides"
Alphant, Marianne. "Ranger, déranger" (32)
        Books
Clédat, Françoise T. 'Le soleil et la terre' and
    'Rougeâtre' (Chantal Chawaf)
G., X. 'Portrait d'Unica Sürn' (Françoise Buisson)
Stacke, Agnès; Gauthier, Xavière. 'Les Cahiers du GRIF:
    mères, femmes'
Buisson, Françoise. 'Mémoires de Louise Michel'
S., A. 'Notre corps, nous-mêmes' (Boston Collective)
Huston, Nancy. 'Prisonnières' (Catherine Erhel and Catherine
    Leguay)

Fabre, Sylvie. 'Territoires du féminin avec M. Duras'
(Marcelle Marini)

Sub-Stance. "$\frac{VERSION}{FEMINISMS}$: A Stance of One's Own." No. 32, (1981).

Lydon, Mary. "Myself and M/others"
Skoller, Eleanor Honig. "Threads in Three Sections: A
Reading of 'The Notebooks of Malte Laurids Brigge'"
Schwichtenberg, Cathy. "Erotica: The Semey Side of
Semiotics"
Duren, Brian. "Cixous's Exorbitant Texts" (124)
Féral, Josette. "Towards a Theory of Displacement" (218)
Chambers, Ross. "Histoire d'Oeuf: Secrets and Secrecy in a
La Fontaine Fable"

Tel Quel. 58 (Summer 1974).

                         "Lutte de femmes"
(Introduction)
Gauthier, Xavière. "Avertissement" (483)
Gauthier, Xavière. "Existe-t-il une écriture de femmes?"
(284)
Duras, Marguerite; Gauthier, Xavière. "Il y a comme des
cris, mais silencieux" (194)
Kristeva, Julia; Gauthier, Xavière. "Oscillation du
'pouvoir' au 'refus'" (452)
Gauthier, Xavière. "A travers les thèmes" (483)
des femmes. "Nouvelles éditions 'des femmes' au MLF"

Tel Quel. "Recherches féminines." No. 74, (Winter 1977).

Kristeva, Julia. "Un nouveau type d'intellectuel: le
dissident" (443)
Mattelart, Michèle. "Les femmes et l'ordre de la crise"
Leibovici, Martine. "La position féminine dans la Bible"
Kristeva, Julia. "Héréthique de l'amour" (410)
Risset, Jacqueline. "Sept passages de la vie d'une femme"
Thomas, Chantal. "Juliette, ô Juliette"
Forrester, Viviane. "Féminin pluriel" (241)
Podolski, Sophie. "Inédits"
Houdebine, Anne-Marie. "Les femmes et la langue" (303)
Maurice, Christine. "Des femmes dans le savoir: la revue
'Signs'"
Rasy, Elisabeth. "Notes du Mouvement des femmes en Italie"

Les Temps modernes. "Les Femmes s'entêtent...perturbation ma
soeur." Nos. 333-34 (April-May 1974). Reprinted as Les
Femmes s'entêtent. Paris: Gallimard, 1975.

de Beauvoir, Simone. "Présentation." Trans. in (19)
        I. Encerclement
Bruneton, Ariane. "La chambre et les champs"
Bernheim, Nicole-Lise. "Les pommes de terre"
Enjeu, Claude; Savé, Joana. "Structures urbaines et
    réclusion des femmes"
"Ça commence comme ça la mort..."
Francève, "Le travail des femmes dans un hypermarché"
Un groupe de femmes. "La caserne des femmes"
"Je suis dans la rue avec une femme..."
Le Garrec, Evelyne. "Les camarades et la grève des
    femmes"
Claudine. "La parole des femmes dans la presse féminine"
"Une femme un être..."
Liliane. "L'école des femmes et le discours des sciences
    de l'homme"
D., C. "Mariage et divorce: l'impasse à double face"
"Je suis tout en haut d'une ville corse"
"L'enfant posthume"
        De l'un à l'autre (1)
Danièle. "Un accouchement, un avortement"
Bernheim, Nicole-Lise. "Le sang"
        II. Rupture du cercle
"Lettre de Sara H: la phénomère"
Mano, Claude, Christine. "La maternité, fonction sociale"
"J'entre, avec une femme qui me semble être ma mère..."
"Je n'ai rêvé qu'une fois à mon père"
Françoise. "Qui t'a fait père?"
"Depuis toujours qu'il s'habite lui-même..."
Mai. "Un viol si ordinaire, un impérialisme si quotidien"
"Nous sommes sur le quai d'un métro..."
C., Annie. "Les révolutionnaires, Thionville et nous"
Erika. "Journal d'une femme-alibi"
Denis, Marie. "Hors la loi"
"Nous femmes..."
Annie et Anne. "Lutte des femmes et révolution"
"Rêve féministe"
Marxie-Jo. "Qu'est-ce que l'humanisme?"
"Un cauchemar que je faisais de manière répétitive"
        De l'un à l'autre (2)
Cathy. "L'autre bout de la chandelle"
"La phénomère"
Dominique, Josiane. "La rue"
"Peur de soi"

III. Désirs-délires
"Je voudrais un enfant"
Claude. "Questions d'un moi en mouvement à un mouvement
   Sur-moi"
"Les groupes de conscience vus par mon inconsciente"
Un groupe de femmes. "Variations sur le désir d'enfant
   et le rôle maternel"
"Mère-ma-mort"
Vicky. "Harmonie, ou si l'homosexualité m'était contée"
"La quadrature du sexe"
Anne. "La difficile frontière entre homosexualité et
   hétérosexualité"
"J'entre dans un réfectoire"
Evelyne. "Les belles histoires de la Ghena Goudou"
"La marge attire..."
Barreno, Maria Isabel. "Quatrième fable..."
Anne. "Il n'y a pas de deuxième sexe"
"Rue Nationale"
Catherine. "De quelques identifications"
"Ni l'un ni l'autre"
Cathy. "Il nous manque une tête politique"
Claudine. "On dit 'femme'"
"Ni fleurs ni couronnes"
"Sexes"
"En guise de postface"

Women and Literature. "French Issue." 7, No. 1 (Winter 1979).

        Articles
Makward, Christiane. "Quebec Women Writers"
Knapp, Bettina L. "Louise Labé: Renaissance Woman
   (1522-1566)"
Fink, Béatrice C. "Ambivalence in the Gynogram: Sade's
   Utopian Woman"
Andermatt, Verena. "Hélène Cixous and the Uncovery of a
   Feminine Language" (120)
        Notes
Maclean, I. W. F. "Women and Literature in Seventeenth
   Century France"
Miller, Nancy K. "Women and Literature in the Eighteenth
   Century"
Gallop, Jane. "Psychoanalysis in France" (270)

<u>Yale French Studies</u>. "Feminist Readings: French Texts/
American Contexts." 62 (1981).

Introduction (10)
        Literary and Sexual Difference:
            Practical Criticism/Practical Critique
Felman, Shoshana. "Rereading Femininity" (212)
Sivert, Eileen. "'Lélia' and Feminism"
Hirsch, Marianne. "A Mother's Discourse: Incorporation
    and Repetition in "La Princesse de Clèves'"
Scharfman, Ronnie. "Mirroring and Mothering in Simone
    Schwarz-Bart's 'Pluie et vent sur Télumée Miracle' and
    Jean Rhys' 'Wide Sargasso Sea'"
            Rethinking Literary History
Stanton, Domna. "The Fiction of 'Préciosité' and the Fear
    of Women"
Jones, Ann Rosalind. "Assimilation with a Difference:
    Renaissance Women Poets and Literary Influence"
            The Politics of Theory, The Theory of Politics:
                The Transdisciplinary Questioning
Spivak, Gayatri Chakravorty. "French Feminism in an
    International Frame" (27)
Gelfand, Elissa. "Imprisoned Women: Toward a Socio-
    Literary Feminist Analysis"
Schor, Naomi. "Female Paranoia: The Case for
    Psychoanalytic Feminist Criticism" (530)
Jardine, Alice. "Pre-Texts for the Transatlantic
    Feminist" (461)

"La Femme n'est rien et c'est là sa puissance" (324)

"La femme, son sexe, et le langage" (337)

"Femmes chinoises" (406)

"Femmes du Québec, un mouvement et des écritures" (255)

"Les Femmes et la langue" (303)

"Les Femmes et l'écriture" (24)

"Les femmes et les pratiques d'écriture. Quelques
réflexions" (486)

"Les femmes, le langage et 'l'écriture'" (9)

"Les femmes-mères: ce sous-sol muet de l'ordre social" (338)

"La fiction et ses fantômes, Une lecture de l'Unheimliche de
Freud" (94)

"La Fiction vive: Entretien avec Nicole Brossard sur sa
prose" (66)

"Figures d'histrion" (236)

Les Fils de Freud sont fatigués (137)

"La fin d'une parade misogyne: La psychanalyse lacanienne" (34)

Folle vérité: Vérité et vraisemblance du texte psychotique.
(380)

"La fonction prédicative et le sujet parlant" (407)

"Four types of Signifying Practice" (408)

"'Françaises,' ne faites plus un effort..." (325)

"French Feminism in an International Frame" (27)

"Freud et Lacan, Symbolique et production idéologique" (153)

Freud et le plaisir (528)

The Future of Difference (7)

"Le geste, pratique ou communication?" (409)

"The Ghost of Lacan, the Trace of Language" (264)

"Grâce à la différence" (95)

"Graphématique et Psychanalyse" (358)

"La guerre des sexes" (359)

"Gynesis" (11)

"Hélène Cixous and the Uncovery of a Feminine Language" (120)

"Les hérésistances du sujet" (96)

"Héréthique de l'amour" (410)

"Histoire de Louise I: Une phobie" (495)

"Histoire de Louise II: L'ombre" (494)

"Histoire d'un sourire" (168a)

"Hommage fait à Marguerite Duras, du ravissement de Lol V.
Stein" (204)

Homosexualities and French Literature (532)

"Hors corps" (224)

"Idéologie du discours sur la littérature" (411)

"Il n'y a pas de maître à langage" (412)

"Il y a comme des cris, mais silencieux" (194)

"Il y a de l'extérieur" (515)

"L'image des femmes dans la langue" (553)
"L'Imaginaire au féminin" (496)
"L'imaginaire féministe" (289)
"Impertinent Questions: Irigaray, Sade, Lacan" (265)
"L'impossible réel, ou le leurre en vente" (154)
"Imprisoned Women: Toward a Socio-Literary Feminist
    Analysis" (288)
"L'incarnation fantasmatique" (155)
"Inconscient et langage dans la psychanalyse" (156)
"L'indécision et l'aporie introduites par la science
    anatomique" (360)
"L'infini plaisir des sens" (84)
"L'intérêt pour l'énigme de la femme" (361)
"Interview avec Chantal Chawaf" (81)
"Interview with Hélène Cixous" (114)
"Interview with Simone de Beauvoir" (36)
"Interview with Simone de Beauvoir" (39)
"Introduction I: Discourses of Anti-Feminism and Feminism."
    New French Feminisms (20)
"Introduction III: Contexts of the New French Feminisms."
    New French Feminisms (21)
"Introduction" (278)
"Introduction." La Poétique du mâle (181)
"Introduction: Miroirs du sujet" (157)
"Introduction to Hélène Cixous's 'Castration or
    Decapitation?'" (129)
"Introduction" to Julia Kristeva's Desire in Language: A
    Semiotic Approach to Literature and Art (465)
"Introduction to Julia Kristeva's 'Women's Time'" (460)
"Introduction to Luce Irigaray's And the One Doesn't Stir
    without the Other" (348)
"Introduction to Luce Irigaray's 'When Our Lips Speak
    Together'" (344)
"Introduction." Yale French Studies (10)
"Irigaray Through the Looking Glass" (345)
"L'Iris d'Horus" (225)
"Jacques Lacan: Feminism and the Problem of Gender Identity"
    (510)
"J'écris" (71)
"Je suis l'amour même" (242)
"Je vais te manger" (471)
La jeune née (138)
"La joie de Giotto" (413)
"La Jouissance--Principe d'écriture" (475)
"'Juivre ou mourir'" (414)
"Julia Kristeva and the Traversal of Modern Poetic Space" (455)